YOUTH · UNIVERSITYand CANADIAN SOCIETY

ESSAYS IN THE SOCIAL HISTORY OF HIGHER EDUCATION

EDITED BY
PAUL AXELROD ■ JOHN G. REID

McGill-Queen's University Press
KINGSTON, MONTREAL, LONDON

© McGill-Queen's University Press 1989
ISBN 0-7735-0685-3 (cloth)
ISBN 0-7735-0709-4 (paper)

Legal deposit second quarter 1989
Bibliothèque nationale du Québec

Printed in Canada on acid-free paper

Canadian Cataloguing in Publication Data

Main entry under title:
Youth, university, and Canadian society
Includes index.
Bibliography: p.
ISBN 0-7735-0685-3 (bound) –
ISBN 0-7735-0709-4 (Pbk.)
1. Education, Higher – Canada – History. 2. Universities
and colleges – Social aspects – Canada – History.
3. College students – Social conditions – Canada.
4. Canada – Intellectual life.
I. Axelrod, Paul Douglas II. Reid, John G.
(John Graham), 1948–   .
LA417.Y68 1989   378.71   C88-090468-2

The editors are grateful to University of Ottawa Press for
permission to reprint, in English translation, the article by
Michael Behiels first published as "Le Père Georges-Henri
Lévesque et l'établissement des sciences sociales à Laval,
1938–1955," in *Revue de l'Université d'Ottawa* 52, no. 3
(1982): 355–76.

This book has been published with the help of a grant from
the Social Science Federation of Canada, using funds
provided by the Social Sciences and Humanities Research
Council of Canada.

Contents

Contributors

Paul Axelrod is an associate professor of Social Science and History at York University and the author of *Scholars and Dollars: Politics, Economics, and the Universities of Ontario, 1945–1980* (1982).

Michael Behiels, professor of History at the University of Ottawa, is the author of *Prelude to Quebec's Quiet Revolution: Liberalism vs Neo-nationalism* (1985).

Judith Fingard, professor of History at Dalhousie University, is the author of *Jack in Port: Sailortowns of Eastern Canada* (1982), and *The Anglican Design in Loyalist Nova Scotia* (1972).

Chad Gaffield is professor of History at the University of Ottawa and the author of *Language, Schooling and Cultural Conflict: The Origins of the French Language Controversy in Ontario* (1987).

Yves Gingras is professeur-attaché de recherche in the Department of Sociology, Université du Québec à Montréal, co-author of *Histoire des sciences au Québec* (1987), and co-editor of *Sciences et médecine au Québec: perspectives sociohistoriques* (1987).

Patricia Jasen holds a Canada Research Fellowship at Lakehead University in Thunder Bay. Her PhD thesis from the University of Manitoba was entitled "The English Canadian Liberal Arts Curriculum: An Intellectual History, 1800–1950."

Nancy Kiefer received her MA in History from the Ontario Institute for Studies in Education and works as a consultant with the Ontario Heritage Foundation.

Susan Laskin holds an MA in Geography from the University of Toronto and works as an editorial associate with the *Historical Atlas of Canada*.

Malcolm MacLeod is an associate professor of History at Memorial University. His publications include *Peace of the Continent: The Impact of Second World War Canadian and American Bases in Newfoundland* (1986), and he is currently writing a history of Memorial University College of Newfoundland.

Lynne Marks, a PhD candidate in History at York University, has published articles on the history of women's education in *Canadian Woman Studies* and *Ontario History*.

A.B. McKillop, professor of History at Carleton University, is the author of *Contours of Canadian Thought* (1987), *A Disciplined Intelligence: Critical Inquiry and Canadian Thought in the Victorian Era* (1979), and *A Critical Spirit: The Thought of William Dawson Le Sueur* (1977).

Barry M. Moody, associate professor of History at Acadia University, is the author of *The Acadians* (1981), editor of *Repent and Believe: The Baptist Experience in Maritime Canada* (1980), and co-editor of *The Journal of Henry Alline* (1982).

Diana Pedersen holds a Social Sciences and Humanities Research Council post-doctoral fellowship at Carleton University. Her articles have appeared in *Scientia Canadensis, Urban History Review*, and *Archivaria*.

Ruth Roach Pierson, associate professor of Feminist Studies at the Ontario Institute for Studies in Education, is the author of *"They're Still Women After All": The Second World War and Canadian Womanhood* (1986) and the editor of *Women and Peace: Theoretical, Historical and Practical Perspectives* (1987).

James Pitsula, associate professor of History at the University of Regina, is the author of *Let the Family Flourish: A History of the Family Service Bureau of Regina, 1913–1982* (1982) and *An Act of Faith: The Early Years of Regina College* (1987).

John G. Reid, associate professor of History at Saint Mary's University, is the author of *Six Crucial Decades: Times of Change in the History of the Maritimes* (1987), *Mount Allison University: A History to 1963* (1984), *Acadia, Maine and New Scotland: Marginal Colonies in the Seventeenth*

Century (1981), and *Maine, Charles II, and Massachusetts: Governmental Relationships in Early Northern New England* (1977).

Keith Walden, associate professor of History at Trent University, is the author of *Visions of Order: Canadian Mounties in Symbol and Myth* (1982).

ACKNOWLEDGMENTS

The editors gratefully acknowledge the financial and secretarial support provided by York University and Saint Mary's University while the manuscript was in preparation.

Paul Axelrod
John G. Reid

Introduction

Paul Axelrod and John G. Reid

In recent years there has been a remarkable flowering in the field of Canadian social history. Thanks to new work on the history of women, children, business, and the working class – written with increasing sensitivity to regional variations – Canadian historiography is richer, more ambitious, and more diverse than ever.

Educational history has shared in this renaissance. Once the domain of boosters and builders, preoccupied with administrative evolution and antiquarian detail, the historiography of Canadian education now embraces a wider range of issues and probes them more deeply. Studies of the relationships between education and social class, social control, and economic change have been augmented by critical, informative analyses of the motives and activities of school promoters and teachers. The social history of Canadian education has become a vibrant and promising field of inquiry. [1]

The historiography of Canadian higher education offers the same potential. Until recently much of the published work on universities was justifiably subject to severe criticism. [2] Fawning, celebrationist biographies of great individuals and impressive buildings, written by ex-administrators instead of professional historians, long inhibited the growth and sophistication of the historiography. Those few researchers committed to serious scholarship were both compelled to work in isolation and frustrated by the minimal interest shown by their colleagues in the field as a whole.

Mercifully, in recent years the situation has changed both in Canada and abroad. The two-volume essay collection edited by Lawrence Stone, *The University in Society*, published in 1974, demonstrated the fruitfulness of exploring further the social history of higher education, and a number of historians in Europe and the United States took up the challenge. In Canada such works as S.E.D. Shortt's *The Search for an Ideal* (1976) and A.B. McKillop's *A Disciplined Intelligence* (1979) not only made an important contribution to Canadian intellectual history but encouraged other historians to turn their attention to the history of university life. While still working at a formative stage in the field's development, a new generation of scholars has already redirected the course of higher educational historiography in Canada.[3]

The 1985 meeting of the Canadian Historical Association, which inspired this volume, offered a strong representation of this work. Papers from all parts of Canada addressed such issues as the social origins of students, the accessibility of universities to women, the culture of student life, and the social role of universities.[4] In addition, several recent histories of Canadian universities have successfully broken out of the stifling old-style institutional genre. They are sophisticated, well-written, and sensitive to cultural and regional milieux. The literature has also been enhanced by a number of theme studies, pushing the historiography beyond the administrative and institutional boundaries that have enveloped it. The historical writing on higher education finally shows signs of contributing significantly to the refinement and enhancement of Canadian social and intellectual history.[5]

Despite its vitality and quality, much of the newer work in the history of higher education remains unfamiliar to the historical community at large. Institutional biographies, whatever their quality, are seldom consulted by other social and intellectual historians, and are recognized more for their contributions to university lore than to Canadian historical writing. Theme studies, too, rarely reach a broad audience, sometimes being overshadowed by unscholarly, polemical works on university life.[6] While other aspects of the "new" history have entered the mainstream of Canadian historical discourse, the historiography of higher education remains, by comparison, undiscovered.

Why should others take notice of the history of higher education? Studying the university's past deepens our understanding of issues and themes current in social and intellectual history. Our knowledge of the dynamics of social class can be enhanced through an examination of the middle-class culture that Canadian universities appear to have embraced. What were the elements of that culture? How was it passed on, and how did it change? The important role that universities played in facilitating or inhibiting social mobility from one class to another or within classes can provide equally revealing insight into the ongoing problem of income and class disparity. Those interested in the history of work must turn to higher education to explore the emergence of professionalism in Canada. How have university students been prepared to enter the work force, and how have universities themselves decided what subjects and programs should be taught to meet social and economic demand? Universities, too, are both sources and transmitters of other influential intellectual and cultural values. For example, by examining the treatment and activities of female students, historians extend our knowledge about the heights attained by and limits imposed upon Canadian women in the past.

The study of student life in general adds immeasurably to our appreciation of the history and culture of a somewhat neglected group – Canadian youth. Finally, a number of the institutional histories have already contributed to the historiography of Canadian regionalism. Exactly what such work has offered to this and other fields of inquiry deserves wider acknowledgment and further study.

This volume's goal is to acquaint readers with new and stimulating work in the social history of higher education. It seeks to provide teachers of social and educational history easier access to ongoing research that is now dispersed or largely unknown. The book employs a variety of traditional and newer methodologies – literary, oral, and quantitative. By concentrating on aspects of the student experience, it offers a fresh perspective on the history of higher education, provides contemporary university students a unique insight into their own historical roots, and perhaps furnishes teachers with a useful tool for introducing students to Canadian social history. By highlighting original research, the book hopes both to bring the historiography of higher education closer to the mainstream of Canadian social and intellectual history and to encourage more work in a dynamic and growing area.[7]

But this book has more than a historiographical mission. It has a particular story to tell about the history of youth, university, and Canadian society. Beginning in the last quarter of the nineteenth century, it takes the reader through one hundred years of social change unleashed by the forces of industrial capitalism and rife with the competing tensions of religion and secularity, regionalism and nationalism, feminism and male domination, prosperity and depression, war and peace. These, of course, are themes familiar to students of twentieth-century Canada, but the following essays allow the observer to experience the impact of such pressures from an unusual perspective – that of Canadian students in the halls of higher learning. Those who see the university as merely an ivory tower, somehow levitating above the hard realities of Canadian society, will be surprised at how directly and powerfully the world has impinged upon university life.

The most conspicuous change during the hundred-year period from the 1870s to the 1960s was growth in the numbers of universities and of students. In the census year of 1871 there were seventeen degree-granting institutions. The five in Nova Scotia had a total student enrolment of 210. Only 76 students are known to have been enrolled in New Brunswick, though no evidence has survived for the Collège St-Joseph, one of the province's three institutions. The three in Quebec totalled 575 students, and the six in Ontario had 700. The 1,561 known students in Canada were drawn from a population of some 3.5 million. By 1971 the population had increased almost sixfold, to some 21.6 million, and 316,000 full-time students were attending fifty institutions spread across Canada.[8]

The increase in size and scale is an important indicator of change in Canada's universities. In the context of single institutions growth has often been portrayed lovingly by traditional university historians. Humble beginnings give way to crowded modern campuses. Buildings soar. Benefactors smile. Faculties expand. Students flock through the halls. From small acorns grow mighty oaks. However, the essays in this book show clearly that this whiggish approach cannot survive in the face of detailed analysis of the social history of higher education. Rather than celebrating growth, this volume explores the conditions, struggles, and dilemmas that generated and infused it.

The universities of the final decades of the nineteenth century were already grappling with the implications of social and intellectual change. In part the intellectual struggle was shared by universities throughout the Western world. The nature of knowledge itself was a matter of increasing controversy in the light of scientific developments, including the publication of Charles Darwin's major works, *Origin of Species* (1859) and *The Descent of Man* (1871). In Canada, with a strong tradition of church-associated higher education, the evolution debates posed a direct challenge to the comfortable assumption that knowledge and religious truth could not conflict. As scientists worked throughout the late nineteenth century to refine Darwin's initial insights, philosophers sought new syntheses that would preserve the moral significance of human knowledge while still accommodating scientific discovery. The most important Canadian product of the philosophical search was the idealistic vision propounded by John Watson, professor of philosophy at Queen's University. For Watson there was no contradiction between evolution and a moral view of humankind, for human society itself was constantly evolving towards an eventual ideal condition of unity and harmony in accordance with God's will. Thus, Watson could declare in 1888 that "the aim of the university is to produce noble, intelligent, unselfish men, and if it fails in that, it has failed of its highest vocation."[9] The concept of evolution could be turned to the service of morality and religion, and the implication was that universities and their graduates must participate in the continuing process of social improvement. They, like other Christian institutions and individuals, would serve the social gospel.

But the reorganization of knowledge in the late nineteenth and early twentieth centuries arose from more than the intellectual and ethical tensions between science and religion. It reflected critical changes in the economic and social development of Canadian society. The three decades following the introduction of the Macdonald government's National Policy in 1879 witnessed a quickening of the industrialization of eastern and central Canada, the exploitation of minerals and natural resources in the north, and the settlement of the west. While it retained its lofty moral purposes, the university found itself challenged by the utilitarian demands of industrial capitalist society. In the context of urban living, scientific management in large corporations, and changing agricultural technology, the classicist and the cleric increasingly shared the university stage with the engineer and the economist.

Academic specialization and the "culture of professionalism" penetrated the halls of higher learning. Servicing the small but growing number of managerial, supervisory, and other prestigious occupations, universities augmented the older professions of theology, law, and medicine with programs in dentistry, pharmacy, agriculture, engineering, and forestry. Seeking greater relevance in a complex world now inhabited by the visible poor and the struggling immigrant, several universities also began teaching in the field of social work before 1920. Increasingly, the other "helping" professions – nursing, household science, and secondary-school teaching – sought the prestige and specialized knowledge that universities were assumed to offer. In 1911–12, of some thirteen thousand university students, 55 per cent were enrolled in professional programs (excluding theology) and 45 per cent in arts and science.[10]

Training, service, and pragmatism affected all universities in Canada, though these influences were especially strong in the west. The universities of Saskatchewan, Alberta, and British Columbia, all established within the first two decades of the new century, provided core courses in the humanities but quickly expanded into new fields of teaching and research. Academics in these far from prosperous pioneering communities recognized that the universities' credibility and survival depended upon their willingness to contribute materially to economic and social development. They accepted state support for programs in "agricultural, technological, and professional training" on the assumption that it would foster within the universities a distinct utilitarian orientation. A leading exponent of this approach, Walter Murray, the founding president of the University of Saskatchewan, adopted the University of Wisconsin model of "scientists in service of the state" as his vision of the provincial university's role.[11]

University students prior to the First World War were a small, though increasing, minority in society at large. They entered college at a time when regional balances, class relations, capitalist consolidation, and gender roles in Canadian society were sources of tension and debate. The recruitment of university students from more diverse constituencies than before was one consequence of these economic and social changes. Another was the impact that strong social forces still dimly perceived and little understood would have on students' futures after graduation. The relevant articles in this volume give ample evidence of the debates over reform and ritual, the formulation of new ideals, and the volatile mixture of optimism and insecurity that prevailed through a time of major transition.

The essays by Judith Fingard and John G. Reid explore elements of these strains as they affected the Maritime provinces. Reid, while focusing more closely on later university-reform debates in the 1920s, illustrates the complex dilemmas evident in the relationship between higher education and society in the 1870s. The claim of the region's denominational colleges, and of the experimental federated University of Halifax, to be offering an effective general education to a rural clientele was contested by Scottish-trained reformers who argued that the concentration of specialized academic expertise must take priority over traditional notions of popular education. The results of the debate were inconclusive, but the fact that it had turned upon the relative importance of specialization and student access to universities was a sign of the social and intellectual developments that were already under way.

The question of access to universities, and its implications for the experience of the first two generations of women students at Dalhousie University, is also an important theme in the essay by Fingard. Women first enrolled at Dalhousie in 1881, and in the ensuing two decades they constituted 23 per cent of the students at the university. Most came from Halifax itself, with a large minority from elsewhere in Nova Scotia, and their origins tended to be middle class: business and clergy predominated among fathers' occupations. Some of these first-generation students were older than the usual college age and had teaching experience, and these women were the most likely to graduate. Many of the others – some 75 per cent of all the women students – did not graduate, whether because of economic restraints or because they had no intention of doing so. Their later careers were varied, involving employment or marriage (rarely a combination of the two), or living as unmarried adults in family surroundings. Like the students of the second generation, in the first two decades of the twentieth century, these early students had a high rate of out-migration from the Maritime region. The second generation, however, had more diverse social and geographical origins, and within the range of occupations that made up the accepted "women's sphere" had wider employment options upon graduation. The example of Dalhousie thus illustrates the general widening of university constituencies that proceeded from economic and social change, the role of gender in creating a distinctive student experience for women, and the cost to the Maritime region of the out-migration of able young people.

Chad Gaffield, Lynne Marks, and Susan Laskin explore related themes in their study of the experience of the just over one thousand students registering at Queen's University for the first time between 1895 and 1900. Their findings confirm the importance of late nineteenth-century change and provide further evidence that students of the era "were not only from elite backgrounds." Although the proportion of those of the conventional age-group who went to university remained very small, those who did attend came from more diverse origins than is often assumed: some 16 per cent grew up in working-class homes. As a group the students showed the effects of the increasing secularization of higher education, for by century's end more than half of the attendance at the Presbyterian institution was non-Presbyterian. Like the Dalhousie women – although at Queen's the trend was slightly more marked for men than for women – the graduates were geographically mobile. A bare majority stayed in Ontario, but usually not in the eastern part of the province, from which most students originated. A substantial minority went to the United States and a full 23 per cent to the Canadian west. University administrators at Queen's and elsewhere emphasized the role of higher education in the service of the nation, and the migration of graduates to the developing west could be cited to substantiate this claim.

Enthusiasm for the concept of national "service" was also reflected at English Canadian universities in the growth of militarism and self-conscious imperial sentiment before the outbreak of the First World War. The theme of militarization emerges strongly in the essay by A.B. McKillop on Ontario undergraduate culture. Even Christian missionary activities at home and overseas – which involved many graduates of Ontario universities – implied competition between denominations for the greatest number of converts. Martial ardour was also evident in the growth of "manly" sports and in the frequent equation of sporting success with prowess on the field of battle. The inauguration of the Canadian Officers' Training Corps at McGill in 1912 symbolized a more direct military role for universities. Although Ontario students had alternative diversions, serious or otherwise, the prominence of military values on pre-war campuses was an accurate foreshadowing of the student experience between 1914 and 1918.

Yet as Diana Pedersen notes in her discussion of "The YWCA and the Canadian College Woman, 1886–1920," the notion of national service could involve more than male-dominated militia activities. Influenced by the ideals embodied in feminism and the social gospel, the YWCA addressed the needs of both modern university women and the community as a whole with a program based on Christian activism. The First World War called into question the relevance and effectiveness of evangelical Christianity, leading to the demise of the college-centred YWCA, but the organization had helped to lay the foundations for a renewed burst of student idealism in the post-war period.

The significance of the First World War is considered in three other essays, those by Judith Fingard, Barry M. Moody, and Yves Gingras. Fingard illustrates the changes brought about by the war in the outlook and the later lives of many Dalhousie women students. Volunteer rescue work during the Halifax Explosion, for example, launched a number of careers in social work, public health, medicine, and dentistry. At Dalhousie as elsewhere, the war also removed many of the male students from the campus, leaving an uncustomarily high proportion of women. At Acadia University, as the essay by Moody makes clear, women in wartime occupied a homosocial world in which female friendships assumed major importance. Male students at Acadia had been quick to enlist. Imperial sentiment and the student magazines' frequent evocations of manly virtues had played their part in this, but even more influential on the predominantly Baptist students was the close identification of military service with Christian duty on the part of recruiters who conducted their rallies in the style of revival meetings. These were years of hardship and pain at Acadia, both for those students who went to war and for those who stayed behind, and yet the closing stages of the war saw a resurgence of optimism – of a sense, no matter how naïve later events may have made it seem, that those who survived would emerge strengthened from the conflict. At Acadia as at Dalhousie, future careers were profoundly affected by the wartime experience, and here too the women of this generation moved in growing numbers into traditionally male occupations such as medicine, university professorship, and the clergy. Women's "sphere" was slightly broadened, raising the spectre of gender equality on the Canadian horizon.

The First World War also brought an unprecedented effort by the Canadian government to promote the development of scientific research in Canadian universities. The essay by Gingras traces the uncertain beginnings of postgraduate scientific training in Canada. Although more piecemeal efforts were made by the larger universities in the late nineteenth century, the major stumbling-block was the lack of available financial support for graduate students. Many promising young Canadian scientists were lured away by the fellowships offered at American institutions such as Johns Hopkins University. But war enhanced the importance of scientific research, and the foundation of the National Research Council in 1916 was the result.[12] The following year the NRC inaugurated a program of national fellowships, a major initiative in the promotion and professionalization of academic science in Canada. While graduate students were no longer compelled to leave the country en masse to pursue their studies, "progress" in this area was scarcely evenly distributed. Just as the cities of Montreal and Toronto dominated the nation economically, so McGill and the University of Toronto, and to a lesser extent Queen's, were awarded the lion's share of the NRC fellowships over the first quarter-century of the program.

When the First World War ended, public attention turned towards domestic concerns, not the least of which was the state of the nation's youth. Historical mythology would have one believe that the world was turned upside-down in the 1920s. As school and college enrolments rose and as adolescence was "discovered," parents and educators would seem to have become obsessed with the vices and frivolities tempting their children in a prosperous and apparently irreverent era. According to the most anxious guardians of morality, automobiles, alcohol, dancing, petting, and jazz were threatening to corrupt youth in Canada, the United States, and Europe. From the society around them adolescents in schools and universities elicited hope, fear, and hyperbole.[13]

What legitimacy did the "flaming youth" model have in Canada in the 1920s? In his examination of student life at Regina College, James Pitsula finds little evidence of youthful insurgence. Admittedly, Regina's students were younger and subjected to more rules governing their religious and moral conduct than students at larger, non-denominational universities, but their normally accommodating behaviour was typical. On most campuses rules were occasionally broken – chapel was skipped, curfews were violated, liquor was discovered – but universities and colleges successfully socialized the youth placed in their charge.

The socialization process itself, however, was far from simple. Students were not mere pawns, and university authorities were not mere tyrants. As Keith Walden shows in "Hazes, Hustles, Scraps, and Stunts: Initiations at the University of Toronto, 1880–1925," ritual events like initiations were very important to students and were carried on despite the periodic objections of university administrators. These episodes fostered a group consciousness for youth entering an unfamiliar setting; they allowed males a physical outlet for their considerable energies, and they provided university youth at least temporary control over their environment. But even at their most uproarious these rituals upheld the conservative values of both the university and the middle-class professional world into which these youth were graduating. The students learned the importance of hierarchy, conformity, and deference. Rather than striking out in a sustained way against authority, they learned to internalize the stresses and insecurities created by the lofty expectations of their parents, their teachers, and the culture of professionalism. Walden's and Pitsula's accounts capture the tensions and complexities of the student experience in the age of the adolescent.[14]

Meeting others' expectations is a constant challenge for university youth. No era promised fewer rewards for hard work than did the depression-ridden 1930s. University students were hardly the most deprived members of their communities, but neither were they terribly indulged. While the fathers of 58.8 per cent of University of Alberta students in 1935 were professionals, businessmen, or supervisors, 11 per cent were white-collar workers, 12.4 per cent were skilled or unskilled workers, and 18 per cent were farmers.[15] Most students thus came from middle-class backgrounds, but during the Depression even they felt the effects of a ravaged economy. The salaries of professionals such as teachers and clergymen, already notoriously low, were cut further in the 1930s. Because their families were too poor to pay, one-third of the seventeen hundred students at the University of Saskatchewan had their tuition fees deferred in 1934–35.[16] Students cherished the experience of university, but the pleasures of graduation were offset by the prospect of an immediate future without work or security. For students, professors, and university authorities, the thirties was a period of diminished expectations.[17]

Why universities mattered to their members and sponsors, even in hard times, is illustrated in Malcolm Macleod's study of the student body at Memorial University College in St. John's, Newfoundland, between 1925 and 1949. At Memorial, as everywhere in neighbouring Canada, universities served local and regional constituencies. The costs of university away from home were often prohibitive, and for many Newfoundland youth "the first step in upward mobility ... needed to be less daunting and difficult than going into exile." Even where enrolments were low, universities in less prosperous areas of Canada were sources of local pride and periodically agencies of social service. During the 1930s the University of Saskatchewan's College of Agriculture provided some support for stricken wheat farmers, and educational reformers in Nova Scotia established an innovative system of adult and co-operative education. Against terrible financial odds, and with the aid of the Carnegie and Rockefeller foundations, applying the capitalist-philanthropic "gospel of wealth," universities in Newfoundland, the Maritimes, and the prairies survived – barely – the grim interwar years.[18]

In addition to experiencing the impact of economic change, universities were touched by the social values and the political tensions of the middle-class communities surrounding them. Through clubs, fraternities, sororities, and formal dances, young men and women met, courted, and often later married. The contacts and friendships made in the intimate university environment of the early twentieth century were frequently sustained in professional and business careers.[19] But the opportunities and rewards of the university experience were accompanied by the inequalities and prejudices that also pervaded middle-class culture. At Memorial, as MacLeod shows, "outport" students were often ostracized by "townies," and Catholics lived in peaceful though occasionally uneasy co-existence with Protestants. Across Canada, Jews and Blacks were the victims of discrimination in university admission policies and were barred from numerous campus fraternities.[20] Female students had won the battle for entry to universities, but the achievement of full sexual equality in classrooms, clubs, and professionals schools, as in Canadian society itself, had failed to materialize.[21]

Discrimination, economic disparity, the rise of fascism, the fear of war – there was no shortage of political issues to inspire the passions of concerned youth on campus. Universities have often been forums for the expression of critical, reformist, and even revolutionary ideas, and as Paul Axelrod discovers, there was a student movement in the 1930s. Its leading exponents were associated with the Student Christian Movement, and it was reinforced by the activities of socialist and communist youth. Axelrod explains why the fear of war more than the Depression itself prompted the campus movement and aroused the greatest concern among "average" students, but he also concludes that the vast majority of university youth distanced themselves from organizations promoting significant social change. The experience of the 1930s seems to demonstrate the ironic reality that youth become more conservative when social conditions become more severe.

The peace movement on campus and in the country at large was destroyed by the shattering experience of yet another world war. Universities attempted to carry on "normally" through the 1939–40 academic year, but neither conscience nor federal law would permit them to remain aloof. Compulsory training for male students, the suspension of inter-university athletic competitions, and the restructuring of academic programs to meet military requirements affected students and professors alike. The degree to which the war impinged on campus life at the University of Toronto is illustrated by Nancy Kiefer and Ruth Roach Pierson. They focus on the initiatives taken by female students for the right to participate meaningfully in war-related work. But even the demands of war could not alter the continuing marginalization of female students on campus. As the authors show, student activities in the Women's Service Training Detachment of the Canadian Red Cross Corps were unprecedented, impressive, and critical, but still limited by "social definitions of feminity" and "conceptions of women's social role." When women continued the battle for fuller participation in the social and cultural affairs of the university after the war, "their pleas and history of service were both ignored."[22]

War imposed the outside world on universities in sudden and direct ways. Less abruptly, more subtly, but no less acutely, the curriculum absorbed the impact of intellectual, cultural, and socio-economic changes in Canadian life. By the beginning of the Second World War universities and colleges had by no means abandoned their commitment to religious and moral training, but this mission had been augmented, and in many cases overtaken, by more secular goals and responsibilities. Surrounded by academic specialists and professionals, church-controlled colleges in English Canada disappeared, adapted, or bravely endured, while in French Canada curricular change occurred in institutions still bound to clerical authority.

The arts were increasingly influenced by new intellectual currents in the early twentieth century. Through its honours program, inaugurated in 1891, the University of Toronto introduced specialization into undergraduate arts, a movement that spread, though with somewhat less zeal, to other universities. Fresh from graduate training in England or the United States, "social" scientists increasingly replaced metaphysical and intuitive paths to truth with empirical methods employing observation and research.[23] The lines between idealists and empiricists, however, were not always clear or unbending. "Common Sense" philosophers, "regenerators," and social gospellers, among others, attempted to bridge the gap between the sacred and the secular worlds.[24] The road to modernity was always paved with good intentions.

Political economists and sociologists, for example, justified their service to the state or business in the noblest terms. Believing that all real knowledge, particularly that applied to the resolution of social problems, would improve the condition of humanity, they celebrated the university's social utility as enthusiastically as their predecessors in the nineteenth century had promoted the institution's denominational mission.[25] Notable critics of social science denounced the erosion of moral philosophy, the decline of the classics, the emergence of applied psychology, and the incursion of professionalism.[26] But such complaints were often overstated. In the arts, for example, English literature, the bastion of British North American – if not Western – civilization, preserved its paramountcy in English Canadian universities.[27] And in a variety of other ways, denominational and non-denominational colleges retained their high moral purposes. As Paul Axelrod shows, through censorship and sanctions they frequently took steps to protect the country's youth from "dangerous" ideologies. Even in the "modern" university, respectability and good citizenship still mattered.[28] Thus, by the Second World War universities both stood on guard for tradition and offered primarily middle-class youth the pragmatic training they required to maintain or eventually improve their social status.

The social sciences were accepted earlier and more readily in English Canadian than in French Canadian universities, where the educational authority of the clergy endured until the 1960s. But as Michael Behiels demonstrates, the struggle to legitimize social science in Quebec was initially engaged in the late 1930s by Father Georges-Henri Lévesque at Laval University. Father Lévesque sought to preserve the relevance of Catholicism in Quebec by infusing it with the principle of social action. Once the School of Social, Economic, and Political Sciences was created at Laval in 1938, its talented faculty walked a fine line between opponents in government and the church and secular critics who sought to free the discipline and the university from ecclesiastical authority. Out of this tension emerged a new intellectual movement whose members were instrumental in creating the ideology of the Quiet Revolution. While most recent historians have ably demonstrated the impact of social change upon the university, Behiels points to ways in which this process could also work in reverse.[29]

The remarkable social and economic changes in the post-war period touched virtually every sphere of Canadian life, and universities were no exception. Anxious to avoid the displacement experienced by returning soldiers at the end of the First World War, the federal government subsidized the tuition and living expenses of Second World War veterans interested in pursuing higher education. In 1946 alone thirty-four thousand veterans enrolled, doubling the student population and forcing upon the universities a period of "frantic improvisation," particularly with respect to the provision of housing and classroom facilities. Older and more worldly than their adolescent classmates, the veterans revitalized the academic and social life of Canadian universities and helped to liberalize, to a degree, a traditionally paternalistic campus environment.[30]

Having coped with the war and its aftermath, the universities experienced declining enrolments and continuing financial pressures at the end of the 1940s. Partial relief came from the implementation of a recommendation by the Massey Commission on National Development in the Arts, Letters, and Sciences (1951), which called upon Ottawa to support the development of indigenous culture. Direct federal funding to universities followed later that year (though it was refused for a decade by Quebec) and was buttressed in 1957 by the creation of the Canada Council.[31] As agents of national culture universities elicited a measure of public and political support. But the massive expansion of higher education in the 1960s owes its origins to less edifying, more utilitarian pressures. A combination of enrolment and economic demand fuelled an unprecedented period of growth. The post-war birth rate, which peaked at 28.9 per thousand in 1947, produced a generation that reached college age in the early 1960s.[32] Simply maintaining current post-secondary educational participation rates thus required extensive building. But even more was demanded. Convinced by what economists called the theory of human capital, which linked national economic growth to educational investment, parents, politicians, and businessmen zealously promoted the cause of higher education. Not only would university training put money in the graduate's pocket and raise the gross national product, but it would meet a variety of moral and ideological demands. The launching of the Soviet Sputnik satellite in October 1957 exposed inadequacies in Western scientific and technological development, stimulated the Cold War, and provided a rationalization for more educational spending. At the same time those favouring the democratization of capitalism argued that public funding of higher education would foster social mobility, help to redistribute wealth, and diminish class inequities. In an age of prosperity and promise, higher education appeared to be a public panacea.[33]

Both the exaggerated expectations and the ensuing disillusionment are captured in Patricia Jasen's account of student radicalism in the 1960s. While many writers have distorted the student movement with uncompromising damnation on the one hand or unyielding apologetics on the other, Jasen's more judicious interpretation is both sympathetic and critical.[34] She focuses on the New Left critique of the university arts curriculum and finds considerable merit in the contention that neither the student's nor Canadian society's intellectual and cultural needs were being adequately served in the university of the 1960s. Beset by the contradiction that "demanded allegiance to an ideology of social change while proclaiming the necessity of individual freedom," the radical analysis none the less raised important questions about an institution that "had become so obsessed with self-glorification and the necessity of its own growth that it was unwilling to acknowledge" its limitations and deficiencies.

In the two decades that followed there was no shortage of those willing to acknowledge the problems of higher education. In a period of prolonged recession and high unemployment the university's contribution to a growing public debt, to the pool of surplus manpower, and to the perceived decline of literacy and high culture roused frequent comment.[35] In an era of confidence and optimism it once seemed that universities and their students could do no wrong. In the latest age of diminished expectations they could, in the opinion of their most strident critics, do virtually nothing right.[36] With prudence and scepticism, the contributors to this volume explore the context of such extravagant – though not unprecedented – claims. The book offers a perspective on the social history of higher education that can be understood both thematically and chronologically. That higher education and society exert a mutual influence is obvious enough. The extent and the complexity of the interaction, however, have rarely been appreciated fully by historians or others. That it should be is essential not only for historical accuracy but also for the continuing health of universities.

NOTES

1 See Neil Sutherland, *Children in English Canadian Society: Framing the Twentieth Century Consensus* (Toronto: University of Toronto Press 1976); J.D. Wilson, ed., *An Imperfect Past: Education and Society in Canadian History* (Vancouver: University of British Columbia and CHEA 1984); George Tomkins, *A Common Countenance: Stability and Change in the Canadian Curriculum* (Scarborough, Ont.: Prentice-Hall 1986). Historians in western Canada have been particularly active in this field. For regional examples, see David C. Jones, Nancy M. Sheehan, and Robert M. Stamp, eds., *Shaping the Schools of the Canadian West* (Calgary: Detselig 1979); Nancy M. Sheehan, J. Donald Wilson, and David C. Jones, eds., *Schools in the West: Essays in Canadian Educational History* (Calgary: Detselig 1986); J. Donald Wilson and David C. Jones, eds., *Schooling and Society in 20th Century British Columbia* (Calgary: Detselig 1980); Jean Barman, *Growing up British in British Columbia: Boys in Private Schools* (Vancouver: University of British Columbia Press 1984). On Ontario, see Michael Katz and Paul Mattingly, eds., *Education and Social Change: Themes from Ontario's Past* (New York: New York University Press 1975); Neil McDonald and Alf Chaiton, eds., *Egerton Ryerson and His Times* (Toronto: MacMillan 1978); Alison Prentice, *The School Promoters* (Toronto: McClelland and Stewart 1974); Robert Stamp, *The Schools of Ontario, 1876–1976* (Toronto: University of Toronto Press 1982); Harvey J. Graff, *The Literacy Myth: Literacy and Social Structure in the Nineteenth-Century City* (New York: Academic Press 1979);

Chad Gaffield, *Language, Schooling and Cultural Conflict: The Origins of the French Language Controversy in Ontario* (Montreal: McGill-Queen's University Press 1987); Bruce Curtis, *Building the Educational State: Canada West, 1836– 1871* (London, Ont.: Falmer Press and Althouse Press 1988); *Ontario History* 78, no. 4, special issue on education (Dec. 1986). On Quebec, see Nadia Fahmy Eid and Micheline Dumont, eds., *Maîtresses de maison, maîtresses d'école: Femmes, famille et éducation dans l'histoire du Québec* (Montréal: Boréal Express 1983); Nadia Eid, "Éducation et classes sociales au milieu de 19ᵉ siècle," *Revue d'histoire de l'Amérique française* 22, no. 2 (sept. 1978): 159–79; Nicole Thivierge, *Histoire de l'enseignement ménager-familial au Québec, 1882–1970* (Québec: Institut québécois de recherche sur la culture 1982); Claude Galarneau, *Les Collèges classiques au Canada français, 1620–1970* (Montréal: Fides 1978). On the Atlantic region, see David Alexander, "Literacy and Economic Development in Nineteenth Century Newfoundland," *Acadiensis* 10, no. 1 (Autumn 1980): 3–34; Robert Nicholas Bérard, "Moral Education in Nova Scotia, 1880–1920," *Acadiensis* 14, no. 1 (Autumn 1984): 49–63; Judith Fingard, "Attitudes towards the Education of the Poor in Colonial Halifax," *Acadiensis* 2, no. 2 (Spring 1973): 15–42; Ian Ross Robertson, "The Bible Question in Prince Edward Island from 1856 to 1860," *Acadiensis* 5, no. 2 (Spring 1976): 3–25. For general historiographical accounts, see Chad Gaffield, "Back to School: Towards a New Agenda for the History of Education," *Acadiensis* 15, no. 2 (Spring 1986): 169–90; J.D. Wilson, "Some Observations on Recent Trends in Canadian Educational Historiography," in Wilson, *An Imperfect Past*, 7–29.

2 Paul Axelrod, "Historical Writing and Canadian Universities: The State of the Art," *Queen's Quarterly* 89, no. 1 (Spring 1982): 137–44; John G. Reid, "Some Recent Histories of Canadian Universities," *American Review of Canadian Studies* 14, no. 3 (Fall 1984): 369–73; Nancy M. Sheehan, "History of Higher Education in Canada," *Canadian Journal of Higher Education* 15, no. 1 (1985): 25–38.

3 For examples outside Canada, see Lawrence Stone, *The University in Society*, 2 vols. (Princeton, NJ: Princeton University Press 1974); Konrad Jarausch, ed., *The Transformation of Higher Learning, 1860–1930* (Chicago: University of Chicago Press 1983); Helen Lefkowitz Horowitz, *Campus Life: Undergraduate Cultures from the End of the Eighteenth Century to the Present* (New York: Knopf 1987); Colin Burke, *American Collegiate Populations: A Test of the Traditional View* (New York: New York University Press 1982), and the New York University Press series Education and Socialization in American History, gen. ed. Paul Mattingly; Paula Fass, *The Damned and the Beautiful: American Youth in the 1920s* (New York: Oxford University Press 1977); David O. Levine, *The American College and the Culture of Aspiration, 1915–1940* (Ithaca: Cornell University Press 1986); David Allmendinger, *Paupers and Scholars: The Transformation of Student Life in Nineteenth Century New England* (New York: St Martin's Press 1975); Steven Novak, *The Rites of Youth: American Colleges and Student Revolt,*

1798–1815 (Cambridge, Mass.: Harvard University Press 1977); Barbara Solomon, *In the Company of Educated Women: A History of Women and Higher Education in America* (New Haven and London: Yale University Press 1985); Louise L. Stevenson, *Scholarly Means to Evangelical Ends: The New Haven Scholars and the Transformation of Higher Learning in America, 1830–1890* (Baltimore: Johns Hopkins University Press 1986); Konrad Jarausch, *Students, Society and Politics in Imperial Germany: The Rise of Academic Illiberalism* (Princeton: Princeton University Press 1982); Charles McClelland, *State, Society and University in Germany, 1700–1914* (Cambridge: Cambridge University Press 1980); Geoffrey Giles, *Students and National Socialism in Germany* (Princeton: Princeton University Press 1985); *Historical Reflections / Réflexions historiques*, special issue on the history of higher education in France, 7, nos. 2 and 3 (Summer, Fall 1980); Sheldon Rothblatt, *Revolution of the Dons: Cambridge and Society in Victorian England* (London: Faber 1968); R.D. Anderson, *Education and Opportunity in Victorian Scotland: Schools and Universities* (Oxford: Oxford University Press 1983).

4 See Canadian Historical Association, *Historical Papers*, (1985): 235–8, for a list of papers presented.

5 For Canadian sources, readers are referred to the bibliography of this book and to the notes below.

6 For example, David J. Bercuson, Robert Bothwell, and J.L. Granatstein, *The Great Brain Robbery: Canada's Universities on the Road to Ruin* (Toronto: McClelland and Stewart 1984).

7 Readers will note that this collection focuses more on university life in Ontario and the Maritimes than on French Canada or the west, though the latter two regions are by no means ignored. This historiographical orientation reflects the current state of research on higher education, though it is hoped that this book will inspire new work in all areas of the country.

8 Robin S. Harris, *A History of Higher Education in Canada, 1663–1960* (Toronto: University of Toronto Press 1976), 623; E.F. Sheffield, "The Universities of Canada," *Commonwealth Universities Yearbook, 1973* (London 1973), 736, 745; Canada, *Census* 1870–71, vol. 1 (Ottawa 1873), table 1, p 83; Canada, *Census* 1971, vol. 1, p 1 (Ottawa 1974), table 1, pt 1–1.

9 *Queen's Journal*, 30 Oct. 1888, quoted in A.B. McKillop, *A Disciplined Intelligence: Critical Inquiry and Canadian Thought in the Victorian Era* (Montreal: McGill-Queen's University Press 1979), 200. See also Leslie Armour and Elizabeth Trott, *The Faces of Reason: An Essay on Philosophy and Culture in English Canada, 1850–1950* (Waterloo: Wilfrid Laurier University Press 1981), 216–30; Carl Berger, *Science, God, and Nature in Victorian Canada* (Toronto: University of Toronto Press 1983), 74–6; Ramsay Cook, *The Regenerators: Social Criticism in Late Victorian English Canada* (Toronto: University of Toronto Press 1985).

10 Harris, *A History of Higher Education in Canada*, 259–306, 628–9. See also Colin D. Howell, "Reform and the Monopolistic Impulse: The Professionalization

of Medicine in the Maritimes," *Acadiensis* 11, no. 1 (Autumn 1981): 3–22; Curtis Cole, "'A Hand to Shake the Tree of Knowledge': Legal Education in Ontario, 1871–1889," *Interchange* 17, no. 3 (1986): 15–27; James Struthers, "'Lord Give Us Men': Women and Social Work in English Canada, 1918–1953," in Canadian Historical Association, *Historical Papers* (1983), 96–112; Dominique Gaucher, "La Formation des hygiénistes à l'Université de Montréal, 1910–1975; de la santé publique à la médecine préventive," *Recherches sociographiques* 20, no. 1 (jan.–avr. 1970): 59–85; Jacques Rousseau, "L'Implication de la profession de travailleur social," *Recherches sociographiques* 19, no. 2 (mai–août 1978): 171–87; Jarausch, ed., *Transformation*, 28–32; Donald W. Light, "The Development of Professional Schools in America," in Jarausch, *Transformation*, 345–65; Alexandra Oleson and John Voss, *The Organization of Knowledge in Modern America, 1860–1929* (Baltimore: Johns Hopkins University Press 1979); Burton Bledstein, *The Culture of Professionalism: The Middle Class and the Development of Higher Education in America* (New York: Norton 1976); David Noble, *America by Design: Science, Technology, and the Rise of Corporate Capitalism* (New York: Knopf 1977).

11 Michael Hayden, *Seeking a Balance: The University of Saskatchewan, 1907–1982* (Vancouver: University of British Columbia Press 1983), chap. 1, p 65, and chap. 5. See also Patricia Jasen, "The English Canadian Liberal Arts Curriculum: An Intellectual History, 1800–1950" (PhD thesis, University of Manitoba 1987), 135; Mario Creet, "H.M. Tory and the Secularization of Canadian Universities," *Queen's Quarterly* 88 (1981): 718–36; Harry T. Logan, *Tuum Est: A History of the University of British Columbia* (Vancouver: University of British Columbia 1958), 48.

12 On developments in the application of scientific research to the Canadian pulp and paper industry, see James P. Hull, "From the FPL to Paprican: Science and the Pulp and Paper Industry," *HSTC Bulletin* 8, no. 1, (Jan. 1983): 3–13. See also Phillip C. Enros, "The University of Toronto and Industrial Research in the Early Twentieth Century," in R. Jarrell and A. Roos, eds., *Critical Issues in the History of Canadian Science, Technology and Medicine* (Thornhill, Ont.: HSTC Publications 1983), 155–66; and Yves Gingras, "Le Développement du marché de la physique au Canada: 1879–1928," in ibid., 16–30.

13 Robert Stamp, "Canadian High Schools in the 1920s and 30s: The Social Challenge to the Academic Tradition," in Canadian Historical Association, *Historical Papers* 1978, 76–93; Fass, *The Damned and the Beautiful*; John R. Gillis, *Youth and History: Tradition and Change in European Age Relations, 1770 to the Present* (New York: Academic Press 1981), chaps. 3–4.

14 For other accounts of student life in the 1920s, see relevant chapters of various institutional histories, and Gerald Friesen, "Principal J.H. Riddell: The Sane and Safe Leader of Wesley College," in Dennis L. Butcher et al., eds., *Prairie Spirit: Perspectives on the Heritage of the United Church of Canada in the West* (Winnipeg: University of Manitoba Press 1985), 250–64; Charles Johnston, John

Weaver, et al., *Student Days: An Illustrated History of Student Life at McMaster University from the 1890s to 1980s* (Hamilton: McMaster University Alumni Association 1986), 27–42; also Keith Walden, "Respectable Hooligans: Male Toronto College Students Celebrate Halloween, 1884–1910," *Canadian Historical Review* 53, no. 1 (Mar. 1987): 1–34.

15 Assembled by Paul Axelrod from reports of the board of governors and of the president of the University of Alberta, 1928–29 to 1939–40, University of Alberta Archives.

16 W.P. Thomson, *The University of Saskatchewan: A Personal History* (Toronto: University of Toronto Press 1970), 125.

17 See, for example, a personal account by H.S. Ferns, *Reading from Left to Right: One Man's Political History* (Toronto: University of Toronto Press 1983), 24–6. For accounts of the financial problems and students' experiences during the Depression, see Paul Axelrod, "Moulding the Middle Class: Student Life at Dalhousie University in the 1930s," *Acadiensis* 15, no. 1 (Autumn 1985): 84–122; Frederick W. Gibson, *"To Serve and Yet Be Free": Queen's University, 1917–1961* (Montreal: McGill-Queen's University Press 1983), 83–155; Charles M. Johnston, *McMaster University*, vol. 2, *The Early Years in Hamilton, 1930–1957* (Toronto: University of Toronto Press 1981), 39–83; Johnston and Weaver, *Student Days*, 43–60; Hayden, *Seeking a Balance*, 153–99; John G. Reid, *Mount Allison University*, vol. 2, *1914–1963* (Toronto: University of Toronto Press 1984), 60–143.

18 John G. Reid, "Health, Education, Economy: Philanthropic Foundations in the Atlantic Region in the 1920s and 1930s," *Acadiensis* 14, no. 1 (Autumn 1984): 64–83; Hayden, *Seeking a Balance*, 160.

19 Johnston and Weaver, *Student Days*, 59.

20 Axelrod, "Moulding the Middle Class," 109–10; Gibson, *"To Serve,"* 199–202; Stanley B. Frost, *McGill University: For the Advancement of Learning*, vol. 2, *1895–1971* (Montreal: McGill-Queen's University Press 1984), 128; Percy Barsky, "How Numerus Clausus Was Ended in the Manitoba Medical School," *Canadian Jewish Historical Society Journal* 1, no. 2 (Oct. 1977): 75–81; on the treatment of Japanese-Canadian students, see Elaine Barnard, "A University at War: Japanese-Canadians at UBC During World War II," *BC Studies* 35 (Autumn 1977): 36–55.

21 See articles in this collection by C. Gaffield et al., J. Fingard, A.B. McKillop, J. Pitsula, B. Moody, and N. Kiefer and R. Pierson. Also, Veronica Strong-Boag, "Feminism Constrained: The Graduates of Canada's Medical Schools for Women," in Linda Kealey, ed., *A Not Unreasonable Claim: Women and Reform in Canada 1880–1920s* (Toronto: Women's Educational Press 1979), 109–29; Lynne Marks and Chad Gaffield, "Women at Queen's University, 1985–1900: A Little Sphere All their Own?" *Ontario History* 78, no. 4 (Dec. 1986): 331–49; Peter E. Paul Dembski, "Jenny Kidd Trout and the Founding of the Women's Medical College at Kingston and Toronto," *Ontario History* 77, no. 3 (Sept.

1985): 183–206; Margaret Gillett, *We Walked Very Warily: A History of Women at McGill* (Montreal: Eden Press 1981); L. Groulx et C. Poirier, "La Place des femmes dans l'enseignement supérieur en service social au Québec," *Atlantis* 9, no. 1 (Fall 1983): 25–35; Judith Fingard, "Gender and Inequality at Dalhousie: Faculty Women before 1950," *Dalhousie Review* 64, 4 (Winter 1984–85): 687–703.

22 On the impct of the war on universities, see Gwendoline Pilkington, *Speaking with One Voice: Universities in Dialogue with Government* (Montreal: McGill University 1983), 23–48; Gibson, "*To Serve,*" chap. 8; Walter H. Johns, *A History of The University of Alberta, 1908–1969* (Edmonton: University of Alberta Press 1981), chaps. 13–14; Reid, *Mount Allison*, vol. 2, 152–9, 163–96; Johnston and Weaver, *Student Days*, chap. 5.

23 See, for example, S.E.D. Shortt, "Adam Shortt: The Emergence of the Social Scientist," in *The Search for an Ideal: Six Canadian Intellectuals and Their Convictions in an Age of Transition* (Toronto: University of Toronto Press 1976).

24 Shortt, ibid., chap. 7–8; Cook, *The Regenerators*, chaps. 7, 11.

25 Barry Ferguson and Doug Owram, "Social Scientists and Public Policy from the 1920s through World War II," *Journal of Canadian Studies* 15, no. 4 (Winter 1980–81): 3–17; Doug Owram, *The Government Generation: Canadian Intellectuals and the State, 1900–1945* (Toronto: University of Toronto Press 1986); Michiel Horn, "Academics and Canadian Social and Economic Policy in the Depression and War Years," *Journal of Canadian Studies* 13, no. 4 (Winter 1978–79): 3–10; Marlene Shore, *The Science of Social Redemption: McGill, the Chicago School, and the Origins of Social Research in Canada* (Toronto: University of Toronto Press 1987), and Shore, "Carl Dawson and the Research Ideal: The Evolution of a Canadian Sociologist," Canadian Historical Association, *Historical Papers* 1985, 45–73; Jasen, "The English Canadian Liberal Arts Curriculum," espec. chap. 5.

26 A.B. McKillop, *Contours of Canadian Thought* (Toronto: University of Toronto Press 1987), chap. 8; W.S. Learned, 1934, cited in Jasen, "The Liberal Arts Curriculum," Robert Hutchins, cited in Axelrod, "Moulding the Middle Class," 96.

27 See Watson Kirkconnell and A.S.P. Woodhouse, *The Humanities in Canada* (Ottawa: Humanities Research Council of Canada 1947), chaps. 3–4.

28 For other examples of censorship and restraints on academic freedom, see Frank Abbott, "Academic Freedom and Social Criticism in the 1930s," *Interchange* 14, no. 4 (1983–84): 107–23; Michiel Horn, "Professors in the Public Eye: Academic Freedom and the League for Social Reconstruction," *History of Education Quarterly* 20, no. 4 (Winter 1980): 425–48; Horn, "'Free Speech within the Law': The Letter of the Sixty-Eight Toronto Professors, 1931," *Ontario History* 72, no. 1 (Mar. 1980): 27–48.

29 See also Marcel Fournier, "Un intellectuel à la rencontre de deux mondes: Jean-Charles Falardeau et le développement de la sociologie universitaire au Québec," *Recherches sociographiques* 22, no. 3 (sept.–déc. 1972): 361–85.

30 Gibson, "*To Serve*," 243–72; Reid, *Mount Allison*, vol. 2, 206–8; Johnston and Weaver, *Student Days*, 73–80; Harris, *A History of Higher Education in Canada*, 456–7.

31 David Stager, "Federal Government Grants to Canadian Universities, 1951–66," *Canadian Historical Review* 54, no. 2 (Spring 1973): 287–97; J.L. Granatstein, *Canada, 1957–1967: The Years of Uncertainty and Innovation* (Toronto: McClelland and Stewart 1986), 139–68.

32 Frederick Elkin, *The Family in Canada* (Ottawa: Vanier Institute 1969), 17. See also W.E. Kalbach and W.W. McVey, Jr, *Demographic Bases of Canadian Society* (Toronto: McGraw Hill 1979), 96, and R. Bothwell, I. Drummond, and J. English, *Canada since 1945: Power, Politics, and Provincialism* (Toronto: University of Toronto Press 1981), 26–33.

33 Paul Axelrod, "Higher Education, Utilitarianism, and the Acquisitive Society: Canada, 1930–1980," in Michael S. Cross and Gregory S. Kealey, eds., *Modern Canada: 1930–1980s* (Toronto: McClelland and Stewart 1984), 186–95; Axelrod, *Scholars and Dollars: Politics, Economics, and the Universities of Ontario, 1945–1980* (Toronto: University of Toronto Press 1982), chaps. 1–3.

34 Useful treatments of the student movement include Kenneth Westhues, "Intergenerational Conflict in the Sixties," in S. Clark et al., eds., *Prophecy and Protest: Social Movements in Twentieth Century Canada* (Toronto: Gage 1975), 387–408; Cyril Levitt, *Children of Privilege: Student Revolt in the Sixties* (Toronto: University of Toronto Press 1984); "Idéologies et politique étudiantes," *Recherches sociographiques*, special issue, 13, no. 3 (sept.–déc. 1972). A romantic view is advanced in Myrna Kostash, *Long Way from Home: The Story of the Sixties Generation in Canada* (Toronto: James Lorimer 1980).

35 Axelrod, *Scholars and Dollars*, chap. 7.

36 See Bercuson et al., *The Great Brain Robbery*, espec. 147–56.

PART ONE

Region, Gender, and Social Class

CHAPTER ONE

Student Populations and Graduate Careers: Queen's University, 1895–1900*

Chad Gaffield, Lynne Marks, and Susan Laskin

Historians have approached the history of education in two distinct, though often complementary, ways. Some focus on the process of education itself, while others explore the relationships among schools, students, and larger social and economic forces. The latter approach has been employed primarily by historians of primary and secondary education interested in the role of schools as instruments of social reproduction. Through their studies of student populations in the late nineteenth century these scholars have examined the extent to which dominant ideologies and class, gender, and ethnic divisions have shaped emerging school systems.[1]

This investigative method can be applied fruitfully to the study of higher education, and much can be learned about the nature of Canadian society at the end of the nineteenth century through an examination of the experiences of both university students and graduates. As Canada was being transformed from a predominantly rural, small-town society to an urban, industrial nation, the university reflected patterns of both social continuity and social change. Women had gained entry to the halls of higher learning, yet universities remained male-dominated institutions. Religion continued to be an important component of higher education, yet the undermining of theological certainty brought about by Darwin and the Higher Criticism seemed to be pointing towards an increasingly secularized Canada.[2] While only a tiny minority of youth attended university, the composition of this group with respect to class and social origins merits further probing. The degree to which universities reproduced traditional elites or prepared new ones is a largely unexplored but important aspect of the social history of this period. Furthermore, as a number of scholars have shown, nineteenth-century Canada was a society in motion, and university students were among the migrants of the period, both in the institutions they chose to attend and in the careers they subsequently followed.[3]

Exploring these and other issues can tell us much about the backgrounds and experiences of university-bound Canadians, whose collective lives, particularly at the turn of the century, have rarely been the subject of systematic examination. Universities were becoming the "gate-keepers of the advanced technical-managerial society,"[4] and an analysis of who passed through the gate can offer valuable insights into the role of higher education at a critical moment of social and economic transition.

This chapter, a microcosmic examination of these issues, focuses on the 1,006 students who registered for the first time between 1895 and 1900 at Queen's University in Kingston, Ontario. Their identities and experiences have been reconstructed from two types of data: student records and alumni files. The students' records include information on gender, father's occupation, residence before attending Queen's, religion, and intended occupation, as well as notations for extramural students. The alumni files provide details of residences and occupations after Queen's. The data from students' records are quite complete, while alumni information is available for most graduates (85 per cent) but few non-graduates (12 per cent).

Queen's, like most other universities, was founded on the basis of religious affiliation. The school began in 1841 as a Presbyterian response to Anglican Bishop John Strachan's plans for a denominational university at Toronto.[5] By the end of the nineteenth century similar initiatives allowed students who wanted to attend denominational universities in Ontario to choose among the University of Ottawa (Roman Catholic), Western University (Church of England) in London, and the three Toronto institutions, the University of Trinity College (Church of England), Victoria College (Methodist), and McMaster University (Baptist).[6]

The major exception to this pattern was the non-denominational University of Toronto established in 1850. Initially, the creation of this "Godless" institution reinforced Queen's belief in the importance of an appropriate religious alternative for students of higher education.[7] By the late nineteenth century, however, Queen's attitude had evolved, and, as at other universities, denominational concerns began to fade. The Ontario government encouraged this development by effectively denying Queen's access to financial support because of its denominational status. Reflecting both the weakening of division among Protestant groups and the general secularization of Canadian society, Queen's began to sever formal ties with the Presbyterian church in the 1890s, officially completing the process in 1912. Queen's had never required religious tests of its students, but by the early twentieth century the university seems to have been moving further away from a Presbyterian student body, as evidenced by Queen's Principal Daniel Gordon's comment regarding the "open door policy with which [Queen's] welcomes all comers."[8] Although the university no longer defined itself in terms of denominational affiliation, the fact that Queen's principals continued to be clerics into the twentieth century suggests that the process of secularization was far from complete.[9]

Queen's open-door policy also seems to have reflected a certain commitment to accessibility, at least in regional terms. The Toronto-based University Federation movement of the 1880s met with firm resistance from Queen's. Administrators promoted Queen's as the regional university of eastern Ontario, whose residents would be severely jeopardized by the proposed centralization of higher education in Toronto. Queen's argued that the federation movement would put university out of the reach of those who could not afford to travel far from home to attend school. At the same time Queen's, under the nationalist-imperialist principal George Grant, developed larger ambitions.[10] Identity as either a Presbyterian or a regional university became only part of a grand vision encompassing the growing Canadian nation. One component of this vision involved Queen's moving beyond its regional base to provide education for aspiring university students of the newly developing west.

Queen's apparent commitment to accessibility was also indicated by its decision in 1878 to admit women, thereby becoming the first Ontario university to do so.[11] By the turn of the century women had gained access to most Canadian universities, but their numbers remained small in the face of the common ideology that viewed higher education as irrelevant and often damaging to women's ideal role as wives and mothers. Late nineteenth-century higher education remained a predominantly male experience at all universities despite a gradual widening of the boundaries of acceptable female behaviour.[12]

While the evolving gender ideology affected universities slowly, Canada's urban industrial development had a more immediate impact on institutions such as Queen's. In the early to mid-nineteenth century Ontario universities trained students for a very narrow range of occupations, particularly the ministry, and to a lesser degree medicine and teaching. By the 1890s, however, universities were beginning to provide training for a larger range of newly professional occupations. In this period the development of the School of Mines at Queen's and of engineering faculties and schools of librarianship at other universities indicated the expanding mandate of higher education.[13]

Increasingly, university officials spoke of the wide-ranging service their universities rendered to the nation through the training they provided for future professionals as well as for the next generation of moral Christian leaders.[14] In promoting universities as agencies of national service, administrators were also responding to and helping to shape the contemporary political agenda, which not only promoted industrial growth but also settlement of the west and the forging of a national identity. University administrators clearly saw one of their major roles as being the production of Canada's professional and religious elite, an elite that would in turn direct the creation and reproduction of the social and ideological fabric of the new nation. During George Grant's tenure as principal, Queen's rhetoric of national service became particularly strong.[15] By 1902 Grant's successor, Daniel Gordon, was explaining unequivocally that "however much we might desire to see our University renowned as a seat of learning or as a school of research, the test and touchstone by which it must be tried is the service it is rendering to the country."[16]

Behind the official discourse about the changing role of universities lay the continual arrival and departure of an increasing student body. The Queen's records permit us to explore the impact of both administrative ambitions and broad social and economic changes on those who passed through the university. Given Queen's origins, the starting point for consideration of these issues is the religious affiliations of the students. In an earlier study David Keane showed that the arts entrants in 1879–80 were still predominantly Presbyterian; almost all of the non-Presbyterian minority came from Kingston.[17] In other words, Queen's continued to reflect closely its denominational roots and status four decades after its establishment. Interestingly, however, the students of Queen's were quite heterogeneous by the end of the century. Despite the availability of a variety of other institutions with distinct denominational ties, Queen's attracted a majority of students who were not Presbyterian. Presbyterians made up only 45 per cent of all entrants between 1895 and 1900. This might reflect the effect of the open-door policy, but it may equally point to a more secular outlook among potential students for whom denominational affiliation was increasingly irrelevant to decisions about higher education.

While gradually moving beyond its denominational roots, Queen's continued to attract students primarily from eastern Ontario. We determined the university's catchment area (see Table 1) by using the location of the students' former schools to indicate their geographic origin.[18] Almost two-thirds of the students came from eastern Ontario, a region defined in this study as east of a line connecting Port Hope, Peterborough, and Pembroke. Of the other students, 28 per cent were from the rest of the province while 11 per cent came from elsewhere including England and the United States. In other words, most Queen's students did not have to travel far, if at all, between their homes and Kingston. This finding supports the administrators' argument that Queen's was playing an important service role for eastern Ontario. Of course, we cannot say whether or not these students would have gone to other institutions if Queen's had agreed to the centralization of higher education in Toronto; none the less, the data do suggest that the university was responding to a substantial local demand.

Queen's officials recognized, however, that a predominantly local student body had certain disadvantages for the university's ambitions to widen its geographical base, extend accessibility, increase revenues, and thus guarantee the continued viability of a university in Kingston. This recognition

Table 1

Geographic origin of Queen's students, intramural and extramural

Geographic origin	Intramural		Extramural		Total	
	No.	%	No.	%	No.	%
Kingston	181	24	4	2	185	19
Rest of eastern Ontario	352	46	35	21	387	42
Rest of Ontario	154	20	108	64	262	28
West	6	1	0	0	6	1
Quebec	22	3	11	6	33	4
Atlantic	23	3	1	1	24	3
United States	11	1	1	1	12	1
Europe	10	1	8	5	18	2
Other	5	1	0	0	5	0
Total	764		168		932	

contributed in the 1890s to Queen's pioneering role in the development of correspondence courses.[19] The university began providing tutors and examination centres in western Ontario so that students could complete courses without travelling to Kingston. Such students could also begin their academic careers extramurally and then travel to Kingston to complete their degrees. The extramural program at Queen's was unique in Ontario at this time, and it enlarged considerably the geographic scope of the Queen's population. Between 1895 and 1900 the Queen's student body included 186 extramural students. One-quarter of these students were from eastern Ontario, a proportion which suggests that even for students living near Queen's the extramural program increased university accessibility. For those living farther away from Kingston this program obviously provided increased access to higher education. Over 60 per cent of extramural students came from the rest of Ontario. Since many extramural students undoubtedly left high school several years before entering Queen's, residential addresses were also examined. This evidence shows that Queen's extramural program also served some students in western Canada. Nine registrants were at least temporarily living in the west, which gives limited support to Queen's claims of providing education beyond provincial boundaries.

In addition to its extramural program, Queen's above-average proportion of female students reflects the university's desire to expand its potential student base. Of the students who registered for the first time between 1895 and 1900, 20 per cent were female, compared with the provincial average of 13 per cent. Even at Queen's, however, higher education remained an

Table 2
Geographic origin of intramural students, by gender

Geographic origin	Male		Female		Total	
	No.	%	No.	%	No.	%
Kingston	117	20	64	39	181	24
Rest of eastern Ontario	285	47	67	41	352	46
Rest of Ontario	127	21	27	16	154	20
Other	71	12	6	4	77	10
Total	600		164		764	

experience primarily designed for men who required training for positions in the public sphere, a sphere incompatible with women's primary role in the home. The consequences of contemporary gender roles for the Queen's students are apparent in the registration data. Queen's women were registered only in the arts faculty, while men were enrolled in arts, medicine, theology, and engineering. An examination of geographic origin also provides a means of viewing the continued force of contemporary gender expectations. Queen's female population was far more local in origin than its male counterpart (see Table 2). Almost two-fifths of female intramural students came from Kingston, in comparison to half this proportion among males.[20] A further two-fifths of Queen's female students came from the rest of eastern Ontario, thereby leaving only one-fifth of their classmates from outside the region. The small catchment area for women at Queen's implies that parents were more willing to send daughters to university when transportation and boarding costs were not a financial burden. In addition, the supposed vulnerability and delicacy of Victorian women may have made some parents more reluctant to send daughters away from home.

The relative strength of the contemporary domestic ideology is further revealed by the gender distribution of extramural students. If the cost of travel and board are considered to have been the major factors in discouraging the attendance of women at university, a larger proportion of females would be expected to have enrolled in the extramural program. In fact, the proportion of women was somewhat smaller among extramural students (15 per cent) than among their intramural counterparts. This pattern emphasizes the consequences for higher education of the general perception that advanced learning was less suitable for females than for males. The university's extramural program did not, at least initially, alter these consequences.

Distinct geographic contexts thus characterized the Queen's students who were differentiated by gender and program (intramural / extramural). But

Table 3
Religion by geographic origin of intramural students, by gender

	Kingston		East Ont		Rest Ont		Other		Total	
	No.	%	No.	%	No.	%	No.	%	No.	%
All students										
Presbyterian	57	32	174	50	90	60	39	53	360	48
Non-Presbyterian	122	68	174	50	59	40	34	47	389	52
Total	179		348		149		73		749	
Male students										
Presbyterian	39	34	131	47	76	61	39	58	285	49
Non-Presbyterian	77	66	149	53	48	39	28	42	302	51
Total	116		280		124		67		587	
Female students										
Presbyterian	18	29	43	63	14	56	0	0	75	46
Non-Presbyterian	45	71	25	37	11	44	6	100	87	54
Total	63		68		25		6		162	

how did these distinctions intersect with the religious division of the registrants? Did the more heterogeneous denominational composition of the students in the 1895–1900 period reflect a generalized fading of Queen's religious identity? Or did Presbyterianism vary in importance among subgroups of the student population? These related questions can be considered by bringing together the data on religion and geographic origin for male and female students. These data make clear that while the overall percentages of Presbyterian and non-Presbyterian students were approximately equal, the denominational distinction was not spread proportionately over different groups of students.

Specifically, the majority of non-Presbyterian students came from within eastern Ontario or were extramural students (see Table 3). The proportion of non-Presbyterians was highest (two-thirds) among those students who had already attended school in Kingston. For these students the advantage of an established residence apparently outweighed any concern about Queen's denominational status. This pattern is consistent with Keane's evidence from 1879–1880, but the trend in the 1890s extended to all of eastern Ontario. In contrast to the earlier period, the majority of male students from the surrounding counties were also non-Presbyterian at the end of the century. A similar pattern has been found for denominational institutions in the Maritimes.[21] This evidence points to increased practical and secular concerns among students of the 1890s as well as the continued growth of university attendance. Not surprisingly, extramural students were more attracted by the unique academic opportunities of Queen's than by its denominational affiliation; only 42 per cent were Presbyterian.

At the same time, the religious composition of the student population coming to Queen's from outside eastern Ontario illustrates the continuing importance of the university's denominational status to certain students. Almost three-fifths of the intramural male students from outside the region were Presbyterian. Some of these students were clearly attracted to Queen's by ambitions to become clergymen, but the pattern among women implies that other factors were also at work. Non-Presbyterian women were in the majority only among female students from Kingston. Two-thirds of the women from the rest of eastern Ontario were Presbyterian. In total, over three-quarters of Presbyterian intramural women came from outside Kingston, in comparison to less than half of their non-Presbyterian counterparts. This evidence suggests that for both women and men who left home to attend university, religion was a major factor in the choice of the institution. Men's worlds were larger than women's in this period, and their decisions about university seem more secular. None the less, religion remained a strong force which could draw students away from the universities of their own regions.

In sum, the data on geographic context and gender suggest both the potential importance of religion to students and their parents and the extent to which its relevance could be outweighed by other factors, particularly proximity to a specific university. The evidence also demonstrates how the relative importance of each factor could differ among different students. For some students practical considerations were most important. They accepted higher education close to home despite the university's denominational roots. This attitude reflects the increasing secularization of higher education and of society as a whole. For other students, however, the values which had led to the founding of the denominational colleges in Ontario still prevailed. They, or their parents, chose their university on religious grounds, and they were willing to travel long distances to attend the appropriate institution. Like many other processes occuring in the 1890s, the choice of university thus demonstrated both the push of secularization and the continued force of religious concerns.

Decisions about attending university were, of course, reached in the context of material considerations. Choices of denomination or location were limited by the ability of families to afford different possibilities. Scholars of primary and secondary schooling have shown in detail the importance of economic factors in determining the educational experience of nineteenth-century youth.[22] Comparative findings for students of higher education are quite scarce. One explanation for the paucity of such research is the common assumption that university students represented a very select and therefore homogeneous minority of their age group. Indeed, only one-half of 1 per cent of all Canadians who were fifteen to twenty-four years old attended university in 1901, and, as we have seen, the vast majority were men. These students might be assumed to belong to an economic elite. School expenses would seem particularly likely to discourage participation from less materially secure families who lived outside university communities.

The very low participation rate emphasizes, however, that even youth from materially secure families did not usually attend university. Despite the clear financial obstacles, the tiny number who actually attended certainly represent only a proportion of those who could have, in fact, afforded higher education. Thus, the question arises of which financially able youth actually went to university. To what extent did they form a homogeneous sub-group within the total number of economically secure families?

Recent research in the United States has called into question the assumption that universities were simply reproducing a pre-existing elite, or at least part of this elite. David Allmendinger has examined the entrance to New England universities of students from relatively poor, and particularly rural, backgrounds. He sees an increase in the number of these students as a result of the declining position of New England farm families, who began to see college education as a means of achieving a more secure future for their children than that available through the family farm.[23] Colin Burke has also examined the socio-economic backgrounds of students in his study of colleges across the United States for the 1800–60 period. Using a comprehensive sample of twelve thousand students, Burke argues that there was an influx of less advantaged students into the universities and colleges in the ante-bellum period.[24]

In the case of Queen's, Hilda Neatby has similarly challenged the image of an elite student body in higher education. Fragmentary evidence leads Neatby to characterize nineteenth-century Queen's students as "poor and unsophisticated." She believes that "these young men and their parents were often sacrificing much in the cause of their education."[25]

The student records provide a key variable for actual analysis of the social and economic backgrounds of the Queen's registrants: father's occupation. The information is available for 65 per cent of the student body. Certain occupational titles occur quite frequently in the data, especially farmers, clergymen, merchants, and, to a lesser extent, physicians and manufacturers. Other titles are mentioned less often and have been grouped into four categories: other professional; manager, agent, and civil servant; skilled workers; and semi- and unskilled workers.

Table 4 shows that farmers' children made up the largest proportion (31 per cent) of intramural students. The economic position of these farmers is not known since the student records do not include any financial information. Similar research elsewhere suggests that some of the farm children may have come from modest backgrounds. Like farmers in New England, for

Table 4
Father's occupation by geographic origin of intramural students

Father's occupation	Kingston		rest E Ont		rest Ont		Other		Total	
	No.	%	No.	%	No.	%	No.	%	No.	%
Farmer	13	8	131	44	49	39	8	14	201	31
Clergy	19	11	26	9	9	15	10	18	74	11
Merchant	31	18	32	11	16	12	5	9	84	13
Doctor	5	3	10	3	6	5	4	7	25	4
Manufacturer	4	2	6	2	2	2	4	7	16	2
Other professional	34	19	8	3	6	5	10	18	58	9
Manager, agent, civil servant	34	19	41	14	11	9	7	13	93	14
Skilled	19	11	22	7	8	6	3	5	52	8
Semi- and unskilled	16	9	21	7	9	7	5	9	51	8
Total	175		297		126		56		654	

example, rural eastern Ontario parents may have saved carefully to send children (mostly sons) to university to escape dependence on the rocky farms of the region.

The clearest evidence of the heterogeneous nature of Queen's student body is that students from working-class backgrounds constituted 16 per cent of those attending the university.[26] The remainder of the non-farm students came from backgrounds that were at least middle class. Some of these students, including certain of the children of clergymen (11 per cent), may not have been wealthy. Others, such as the children of merchants and manufacturers, might be more readily characterized as members of an economic elite.

Not unexpectedly, more extramural students came from working-class backgrounds, with one-fifth of their fathers in skilled, semi-skilled, or unskilled occupations. Almost half of them came from farm families. Presumably, the extramural program allowed certain students to overcome financial barriers to university by enabling them to work while studying.

The continued force of the contemporary domestic ideology is reflected in the fact that women from wealthier homes were far more likely to attend university than those from more modest backgrounds. Indeed, the proportion of women attending Queen's who had working-class fathers was lower than that of men. As well, women were less likely than men to be from farm families (33 per cent of men, 21 per cent of women). Parents were more willing to sacrifice for their sons' education than for their daughters'. If financial resources were adequate, daughters might be sent to university; if choices had to be made, sons came first.

Table 5
Intended occupation by geographic origin of intramural students

	Kingston		rest E Ont		rest Ont		Other		Total	
Occupation	No.	%	No.	%	No.	%	No.	%	No.	%
Unknown	101	56	143	40	59	39	21	28	324	42
Minister	0	0	24	7	25	16	11	14	60	8
Doctor	41	23	102	29	17	11	19	25	179	23
Teacher	14	8	52	15	28	18	4	5	98	13
Lawyer	1	0	11	3	6	4	2	3	20	3
Engineer	22	12	22	6	14	9	19	25	77	10
Other	2	1	1	0	3	2	0	0	6	1
Total	181		355		152		76		764	

The relationship between socio-economic background and attendance at Queen's is further revealed by the data on geographic origin. Interestingly, these data do not suggest that "locals" and "boarders" formed distinct socio-economic groups. In fact, the distribution of parental occupations among students from different areas is remarkably similar. The data do not indicate that the expenses of travel and board primarily determined the social composition of the Queen's students. It is more likely that most people from less financially secure backgrounds simply could not forgo earning an income for the period of university attendance. Earning a degree extramurally while teaching was therefore probably the only option for many. The apparent result was that only a small proportion of students came from less materially secure families, regardless of their proximity to a university. In the case of Queen's, travel and board represented supplementary rather than primary financial determinants of the university population.

In addition to personal and family information, the student records provide fascinating evidence about the intended occupation of the registrants. Such explicit data on expectations are rare in all historical research and especially unusual in the study of education, where motivations must generally be inferred from circumstantial evidence. By stating an intended occupation, the Queen's students left direct testimony of their own ambitions and perceptions of higher education. Viewed in the context of the other information from the student records, this testimony provides an additional perspective on the character of Queen's University in the late nineteenth century.

The responses to the question of intended occupation also illustrate broader economic trends by identifying the positions for which university was considered to be necessary preparation at the turn of the century (see Table 5). The majority of male registrants (two-thirds) stated a specific intended occupation. These students most often planned to become physicians, ministers, teachers, or engineers. A small proportion intended to pursue law or other occupations. Unlike male students, most female students (71 per cent) did not specify an intended occupation. Their silence may have been based on an understanding that university would be a prelude to marriage and life in the private sphere.[27] Those women who did foresee paid occupations invariably anticipated teaching. Teaching was particularly important among the expectations of extramural students, who characteristically (75 per cent) specified an intended occupation. The data show that a majority of these students (59 per cent) planned to be (or already were) teachers. For those registrants with teaching experience, the Queen's extramural program provided an opportunity to upgrade their qualifications and thus, of course, to increase their salaries.

As with other aspects of the Queen's data, geographic context influenced the distribution of intended occupations among the university students. A clear correlation is apparent between distance from Kingston and the proportion of registrants who stated intended occupations. Less than half (44 per cent) of the local students registered with specific occupations in mind. However, the proportion of students with stated ambitions increased steadily among those from the surrounding region, the rest of Ontario, and outside the province. Specific ambitions seem to have been less important among university students already living in the host community. Those who left their homes to attend university would be more likely to require a specific ambition to draw them to Kingston.

These data also indicate the extent to which Queen's succeeded in attracting students to study particular disciplines. The fact that the percentage of students intending to be physicians was highest among those from eastern Ontario suggests that the Queen's medical faculty was not an effective magnet to those from other regions. In contrast, Queen's did attract students to study engineering, especially from outside the province. Such students benefited from the recently established School of Mines. Similarly, as one might expect, Queen's also drew students from beyond Kingston who intended to be ministers. In general, however, the data indicate that Queen's, as a regional university, had only moderate success in competing on academic terms with other universities who sought students outside eastern Ontario.

In sum, the data from the student records reveal a student body that felt the impact of a complex and contradictory array of social, economic, and ideological influences. Its denominational composition indicates that Queen's was influenced by secularization but at the same time continued to attract Presbyterians from across Ontario. The nature of female participation at Queen's reflects a widening of women's sphere but also the continued force of the contemporary domestic ideology. Both continuity and change can also be seen in expectations regarding the role of universities. Most students still attended to qualify for careers that had traditionally required university degrees, but some hoped to qualify for newly professionalized careers such as engineering. While Queen's was not simply reproducing a pre-existing elite, the nature of its student body makes it clear that a university education remained inaccessible to many Canadians.

What kind of an elite was being produced at Queen's? Were subsequent careers among graduates consistent with earlier ambitions or shaped by new social and economic forces within twentieth-century Canada? What happened to Queen's students after leaving university? Alumni records cannot be linked to all the students who registered between 1895 and 1900. As would be expected, data on prominent alumni are more complete than for those who were lesser-known graduates. [28] The alumni files thus present the post-Queen's experience in a favorable way; the data must be interpreted as the most positive estimate of the students' destinies.

The following discussion concerns two variables created from the alumni data: geographic destination and occupation. Some alumni files contain a list of addresses for former students, while others identify only place of death and perhaps one residence where the individual lived the greatest part of his or her life. In this analysis geographic destination is defined as either the location of the longest residence (if this information is available) or the last address. Similarly, the alumni files often document more than one occupation for graduates as they moved through their careers. Since multiple occupational information is quite usual in the files, data were collected in chronological order on up to three distinct occupations. The following discussion refers to each graduate's final occupational attainment.

Table 6 shows that the geographic destinations of Queen's graduates contrast sharply with their geographic origins. The most striking finding is the low percentage of graduates who stayed in Kingston or eastern Ontario. While Queen's catchment area was quite small, the university's graduates travelled far and wide, especially in the case of men. Over three-quarters of male graduates left the eastern corner of the province. Slightly more than one-half of these graduates did stay in Ontario, but substantial minorities went to western Canada (22 per cent) and to the United States (18 per cent). Female graduates were somewhat less geographically mobile than men. Over one-third remained in eastern Ontario, and almost two-thirds stayed in the province.

Assessing the specific contribution of the Queen's experience to this diaspora presents an intriguing challenge for which the required evidence is not available. Ideally, we would like to know where the students would have migrated had they not, in fact, gone to Queen's. Universities certainly strove to expand personal horizons. Principals such as Grant and Gordon hoped graduates would eventually become active members of both local and

Table 6
Destination of graduates by gender

Destination	Male		Female		Total	
	No.	%	No.	%	No.	%
West	110	22	26	25	136	23
Ontario	267	54	66	63	333	56
Kingston	(28)	(6)	(18)	(17)	(46)	(8)
rest of east Ont	(87)	(17)	(21)	(20)	(108)	(18)
rest of Ont	(152)	(31)	(27)	(26)	(179)	(30)
Quebec	14	3	1	1	15	2
Atlantic	8	2	0	0	8	1
United States	89	18	12	11	101	17
Other	7	1	0	0	7	1
Total	495		105		600	

national elites. The administrators' conscious promotion of national service encouraged students to leave the region in order to play a leading part in nation-building efforts of the time. Yet out-migration of young people, even from rapidly growing urban communities, was common, and in their emigration to western Canada and the United States, Queen's graduates conformed to national patterns. The data reveal the very limited extent to which Queen's affected Canada east of Ontario, with only small minorities of graduates moving to Quebec or the Atlantic provinces. Since this pattern is consistent with aggregate trends and since other evidence is not available, we cannot assume that the Queen's experience was itself responsible for the geographic dispersal of its graduates. Young people in Kingston who did not pursue formal education may have been just as likely as their university counterparts to leave the city as adults.

While the general residential pattern of the Queen's graduates does not attest to the role of the university in determining population distribution, the specific patterns associated with particular groups do indeed suggest that the university was influencing individual itineraries. In the case of women the evidence reveals that those who did not marry (and thus whose movements were generally defined by the small employment opportunities open to women) were less likely to leave the province than married female graduates. A far lower proportion of Queen's female students married than did their age cohort in the general population. The decision to attend university and the experience of higher education itself appears to have contributed to a frequent rejection of the contemporary definition of women as wives and mothers.[29]

Table 7
Last occupation of Queen's graduates

	No.	%
Education	125	25
Health	168	34
Clergy	56	11
Science	41	8
Law	24	5
Commerce	32	7
Government	30	6
Other	19	4
Total	495	

The Queen's data also suggest that post-university migration patterns related to the specific training and career choices of the students. While the occupations of the Queen's graduates are consistent with their late nineteenth-century intentions, they also reflect the new opportunities and changing occupational structure of early twentieth-century Canada. The small number of intended occupations specified by Queen's students became an array of more specialized occupational titles among graduates, whose career choices were shaped by the demands for services characteristic of urban industrial society.[30]

As they intended, the largest two groups of alumni worked in the fields of medicine and education (see Table 7). They were the products of the process of professionalization that influenced university development at the end of the century. The growth of science combined with the organized efforts of self-interested doctors to require from "legitimate" medical practitioners formal training within officially approved institutions.[31]

Similarly, the formal requirements for teaching steadily increased with the establishment and rapid development of school systems after the 1840s. By the early twentieth century university degrees were increasingly encouraged for secondary-school teachers and for principals of larger schools.[32] Along with the prominence of graduates in the health professions, the importance of educators emphasizes the ways in which Queen's was consciously training the elite professional groups of the early twentieth century.

Careers of Queen's graduates clearly reflect social change, but the continuing importance of graduates who entered the clergy indicates that universities were still discernibly traditional. In fact, the proportion of clergy among the graduates exceeded earlier expectations. Some of the entrants

who did not specify an intended occupation did become clergymen in subsequent years. At the time of registration only 8 per cent of the students
saw themselves as preparing for a religious vocation; in the end 11 per cent
of the graduates became ministers or priests. Thus, the secularization of
Canadian society did not mean that universities immediately and completely
lost their traditional association with formal religious training. Rather, the
relative importance of this association declined in the face of a conscious
attempt to prepare leaders in newly expanding fields. [33]

The most unanticipated groups among the Queen's graduates were those
working in occupations that had not even been mentioned among the intentions at registration. By the end of their careers 7 per cent of the graduates
were in commerce, while 6 per cent were in government. Neither possibility
had been specified by the university students, and, indeed, it would be
unreasonable to expect them to have done so. Historically, university training
had no real relevance to either the world of business or that of government.
However, the growth of these fields in the first half of the twentieth century,
and in particular their bureaucratization and greater complexity, led to a
demand for those with concrete and increasingly more extensive educational
qualifications. [34]

An appreciation of the diversity of the Queen's graduates' occupations
provides the basis for further analysis of the general pattern of post-university
migration. While the destinations of Queen's graduates clearly fit the larger
population movements of the time, occupational groups did indeed have
their own itineraries. The greatest contrast is between graduates in the two
dominant fields of health and education. Health professionals resembled the
general migration pattern in their avoidance of Quebec and the Atlantic region
and their participation in settling the west. Otherwise, they stayed in Ontario
far less frequently (38 per cent) and left for the United States, particularly
the northeastern states, more often (35 per cent) than did graduates in any
other occupation. The evidence under examination gives no hint why more
than one-third of Queen's graduates who worked in medicine did not stay
in Canada. Other studies imply that these graduates were responding to
better financial opportunities and more extensive and modern medical facilities in the United States. [35] Whatever the motivation, this alumni group
was travelling a path that has become characteristic in the twentieth century.
Those graduates who stayed in Ontario and who helped bring health services
to the developing west fulfilled Queen's promise to serve the nation; but
the substantial minority who moved to the United States indicate that graduates were responding to professional opportunities rather than national
ideology.

More than half (59 per cent) of the Queen's graduates who worked in
education stayed in Ontario. They became part of the continued expansion
of the public and secondary school system in the early twentieth century.
Since this expansion depended upon better-qualified teachers and a larger

proportion of administrators, university training became a valuable possession for those in the field, and the Queen's graduates did not have to travel
far to build their careers. At the same time, a higher proportion of educators
than of other groups did move west. This proportion (28 per cent) is consistent with the university's specific aim to provide teachers for the newly
settled communities of the prairies. The Queen's educators contributed to
the cultural dimension of "Empire Ontario" by reproducing the dominant
British Canadian values in one-room schoolhouses throughout the west.[36]
Their impact was reinforced by graduates with careers in law or the church.
All lawyers stayed in Canada, with most (54 per cent) contributing to the
judicial administration of the west. Similarly, almost all (85 per cent) of the
clergy disseminated ideals learned at Queen's in either Ontario or the west.

In contrast, those graduates with careers in commerce and government
reflect quite different geographic forces (see Table 8). Half the graduates
who worked in commerce stayed in Ontario, but one in four went to the
United States and the remaining quarter went equally to Quebec and the
west. Their migrations follow the industrial development of central Canada
and the United States, and, as for the health professionals, the national
border does not appear to have been a serious obstacle to career development.
In contrast, political boundaries were quite important to those who worked
in government. More than any other group (74 per cent) these graduates
stayed in Ontario, the province with the two largest government cities of
Toronto and Ottawa. Those in Ottawa joined other Queen's graduates who
played a central role in the development of a professionalized federal civil
service in the first half of the twentieth century.[37] Not surprisingly, no
Queen's graduate from the 1895–1900 years appears to have built a career
with the United States government, while only a small group participated
in government in Canada outside Ontario.

Taken together, the student records and alumni data from Queen's University contribute to an emerging social history of higher education and, at
the same time, provide insights into changes and continuities in broader
social and economic forces. The evidence lends support to recent studies
that have challenged the traditional image of homogeneous elite student
bodies. Not only did many materially secure children never attend university,
but those who went did not compose a uniform social group. Queen's may
have created elites, but it did not simply reproduce existing ones. University
did enable some individuals from less advantaged backgrounds, particularly
farmers' sons, to enter professional careers.

By providing the opportunity to attend university within one's own region,
Queen's and other universities may have increased accessibility in geographic terms. At the same time, however, the evidence points to the important role that the need to earn wages appears to have played in university
participation patterns. The chances of attending university for youths from
modest economic backgrounds were apparently not increased by the ability

Table 8

Destination of graduates by last occupation

Destination	Education No.	%	Health No.	%	Church No.	%	Science No.	%	Law No.	%	Commerce No.	%	Government No.	%	Other No.	%	Total No.	%
West	35	28	36	21	13	23	5	12	13	54	4	12.5	6	20	2	10.5	114	23
Ontario	74	59	64	38	36	64	28	68	10	42	16	50	22	74	12	63	262	53
Quebec	1	1	2	1	2	4	2	5	0	0	4	12.5	1	3	3	16	15	3
Atlantic	0	0	3	2	0	0	2	5	1	4	0	0	1	3	0	0	7	1
U.S.	15	12	58	35	4	7	3	7	0	0	8	25	0	0	2	10.5	90	18
Other	0	0	5	3	1	2	1	3	0	0	0	0	0	0	0	0	7	1
Total	125		168		56		41		24		32		30		19		495	

to remain at home. The financial cost of going to university was far greater than the price of tuition and books.

The Queen's evidence also helps to flesh out other facets of the background and motivations of students who travelled to university at the turn of the century. Between the late 1870s and the mid-1890s the Queen's student body lost its predominantly Presbyterian character. This denomination remained the most important single religion, but by the end of the century more than one-half of the students had other affiliations. The new religious diversification demonstrates the forces of secularization both in higher education and in society as a whole.

The distinct university experiences of men and women also arose from broader social trends. The minority female patterns were not simply smaller versions of the majority. Rather, the backgrounds, aspirations, and subsequent experiences of university students reflect society's differential treatment of men and women during the transformation at the turn of the century.

The great contrast between the students' intended occupations and their subsequent experiences emphasizes the extent to which Queen's students participated in these decades of social and economic change. Their expectations had been created in a predominantly rural society. In contrast, their careers developed in the complex urban world of the twentieth century, in which professionalization and a growing emphasis on educational qualifications meant that a university education was increasingly valued in a wide range of occupations. The graduates' paths followed broad population movements but also distinct occupational patterns. For some, residence after university was consistent with Queen's promotion of nation-building, but the itineraries of other graduates indicate that for many the perception of professional opportunity was the real motivating force.

At the turn of the century the processes of secularization and professionalization contributed to a changing social role for universities in which the formation of new elite groups led to diverse destinations for graduates. Their diaspora was not random but rather was associated closely with gender and occupation, as well as with general population flows. Like other institutions, universities were thus reflecting and contributing to social change while at the same time helping to ensure that dominant ideologies retained their primacy within the rapidly developing nation. The complexity of these relationships attests to the importance of analysing the history of education within the larger historical process of Canada's evolution.

NOTES

* This research was originally undertaken for the *Historical Atlas of Canada / Atlas historique du Canada*, which is funded by the Social Sciences and Humanities

Research Council of Canada. We would like to thank Anne MacDermaid and her colleagues at Queen's University archives and the staff at Queen's University alumni office for their assistance. We would also like to thank John Blakely, P.J.S. LaPierre, the anonymous readers, and the editors of this volume for their comments.

1 See, for example, Michael Katz, *The Irony of Early School Reform: Educational Innovation in Mid-Nineteenth Century Massachusetts* (Boston: Beacon Press 1970); Ian Davey, "Educational Reform in the Working Class: School Attendance in Hamilton, Ontario 1851–1891" (PhD thesis, University of Toronto 1975); and Alison Prentice, *The School Promoters: Education and Social Class in Mid-Nineteenth Century Upper Canada* (Toronto: McClelland and Stewart 1977).

2 The nature and process of secularization in English Canada remains largely unexplored. An important recent contribution to our understanding of this process is Ramsay Cook, *The Regenerators: Social Criticism in Late Victorian English Canada* (Toronto: University of Toronto Press 1985).

3 The relationship between migration and university participation has heretofore received very little attention. The importance of this topic is emphasized by George Weisz in "The Geographical Origins and Destinations of Medical Graduates in Quebec, 1834–1939," *Histoire sociale / Social History* 19, no. 34 (May 1986): 93–119.

4 Michael Katz, "The Moral Crisis of the University, or, the Tension between Marketplace and Community in Higher Learning," in W.A.W. Neilson and Chad Gaffield, eds., *Universities in Crisis: A Mediaeval Institution in the Twenty-First Century* (Montreal: Institute for Research on Public Policy 1986), 9.

5 Hilda Neatby, *"And Not to Yield": Queen's University, 1841–1917* (Montreal: McGill-Queen's University Press 1978), 11–28.

6 Robin Harris, *A History of Higher Education in Canada, 1663–1960* (Toronto: University of Toronto Press 1976). There were also a number of theology schools, including Knox College in Toronto, which was Free Church Presbyterian and was competing with Old Kirk Queen's for students who wanted to become Presbyterian ministers. In fact Old Kirk and Free Church had united in 1875, but divisions remained.

7 Neatby, *"And Not to Yield,"* 104–5.

8 Principal Gordon, "Inaugural Address," *Queen's University Journal* 30 (1902–03): 20.

9 Doug Owram, *The Government Generation: Canadian Intellectuals and the State, 1900–1945* (Toronto: University of Toronto Press 1986) 10.

10 For a discussion of George Grant's nationalism see Carl Berger, *A Sense of Power* (Toronto: University of Toronto Press 1970).

11 Some uncertainty does appear to surround the precise origins of Queen's admission of women; see P.J.S. LaPierre, "Women at Queen's," unpublished research paper, University of Toronto 1986.

12 For a discussion of women's experience at Queen's, see Lynne Marks and Chad Gaffield, "Women at Queen's University, 1895–1905: A 'Little Sphere' All Their Own?" *Ontario History* 78, no. 4 (December 1986): 331–50. Nicole Neatby discusses a later period in "Women at Queen's in the 1920s: A Separate Sphere" (MA thesis, Queen's University 1986). A comparative perspective is offered by John G. Reid, "The Education of Women at Mount Allison, 1854–1914," *Acadiensis* 12, no. 2 (Spring 1983): 3–33.

13 For a discussion of the professionalization of engineering, see David Noble, *America by Design* (New York: Knopf 1977).

14 On the changing social context of higher education, see Mario Creet, "H.M. Tory and the Secularization of Canadian Universities," *Queen's Quarterly* 88, no. 4 (Winter 1981): 718–36; and Burton Bledstein, *The Culture of Professionalism: The Middle Class and the Development of Higher Education in America* (New York: Norton 1976).

15 Neatby, *"And Not to Yield,"* 240; and A.B. McKillop, *A Disciplined Intelligence; Critical Inquiry and Canadian Thought in the Victorian Era* (Montreal: McGill-Queen's University Press 1979), 218–19.

16 Principal Gordon, "The Installation Address," *Queen's Quarterly* (1903): 323.

17 David Ross Keane, "Rediscovering Ontario University Students in the Mid-Nineteenth Century" (PhD thesis, University of Toronto 1981), 848.

18 Geographic origin can be explored in the student records by way of two types of information: residential address and the address of the school attended prior to Queen's. Unfortunately, the data on residential address are quite problematic. Students were asked to provide this address at the time of enrolment. However, registrants sometimes listed a temporary location where they were employed rather than their "home." In contrast, certain students clearly did list their parents' address. In either case, the actual meaning of the data is difficult to define, especially given the constant population turnover characteristic of the nineteenth century. The address of the pre-Queen's school is more satisfactory for analysis since the question was interpreted in the same way by the students who responded in almost all cases (93 per cent). Moreover, this information corresponded closely with parents' addresses when these data were also provided.

19 Edward A. Dunlop, "The Development of Extension Education at Queen's University, 1889–1945" (PhD thesis, University of Toronto 1981). In the following discussion the category of extramural students does not include those who studied full time in Kingston but took extramural courses on other occasions.

20 A similar pattern has been identified among women students at the University of Saskatoon in the early twentieth century. See Michael Hayden, *Seeking a Balance: The University of Saskatchewan, 1907–1982* (Vancouver: University of British Columbia Press 1983), 62.

21 John G. Reid, *Mount Allison University*, vol. 1, 1843–1914 (Toronto: University of Toronto Press 1984).

22 Michael B. Katz, Michael J. Doucet, and Mark J. Stern, *The Social Organization of Early Industrial Capitalism* (Cambridge, Mass.: Harvard University Press 1982); and Davey, "Educational Reform and the Working Class."

23 David Allmendinger, *Paupers and Scholars: The Transformation of Student Life in Nineteenth Century New England* (New York: St Martin's Press 1975).

24 Colin Burke, *American Collegiate Populations: A Test of the Traditional View* (New York: New York University Press 1982).

25 Neatby, *"And Not to Yield,"* 193. Paul Axelrod has argued that at Dalhousie University in the 1930s, while some students were of the elite, the majority represented a broad range of middle-class and modest economic backgrounds. Paul Axelrod, "Moulding the Middle Class: Student Life at Dalhousie University in the 1930s," *Acadiensis* 15, no. 1 (1985): 84–122.

26 Students with fathers who were skilled workers composed 8 per cent, while those with fathers who were semi- and unskilled formed the same proportion of all students' fathers. Some of the skilled workers may in fact have been small employers and therefore not working class. As a result, we may overestimate the proportion of university students from working-class backgrounds.

27 See Marks and Gaffield, "Women at Queen's."

28 As mentioned earlier, there are alumni data available for 85 per cent of the graduates and 12 per cent of the non-graduates. The following discussion therefore includes a small number of students who did not graduate.

29 Marks and Gaffield, "Women at Queen's." Of Queen's women students, 58 per cent married, compared to 88 per cent of women in their age cohort. Canada, *Census of Canada* 2, 1921, table 29. For a discussion of marriage patterns among American women graduates, see Roberta Wein, "Women's Colleges and Domesticity, 1875–1918," *History of Education Quarterly* 14, no. 1 (Spring 1974): 31–47; and Anne F. Scott, "The Ever-Widening Circle: The Diffusion of Feminist Values from the Troy Female Seminary, 1822–1872," *History of Education Quarterly* 19, no. 1 (Spring 1979): 3–25.

30 In assessing the careers of graduates, it should be remembered that not all graduates furnished information to the alumni archives and, although the coverage is remarkably good, we have no way of assessing the bias in the data. Perhaps the complete absence of farmers and manual workers in the alumni data, for example, is explained by a reluctance of such graduates to keep in touch with their alma mater.

31 R.D. Gidney and W.P.J. Millar, "The Origins of Organized Medicine in Ontario 1850–1869," in C.G. Roland, ed., *Health, Disease and Medicine: Essays in Canadian History* (Toronto: Hannah Institute of the History of Medicine 1984): 65–95; J. Bernier, "La Standardisation des études médicales et la consolidation de la profession dans la deuxième moitié du XIXe siècle," *Revue d'histoire de l'Amérique française* 37 (1983): 51–65; and Colin D. Howell, "Reform and the Monopolistic Impulse: The Professionalization of Medicine in the Maritimes," *Acadiensis* 11, no. 1 (Autumn 1981): 3–22.

32 Marta Danylewycz and Alison Prentice, "Teachers, Gender, and Bureaucratizing School Systems in Nineteenth Century Montreal and Toronto," *History of Education Quarterly* 24 (Spring 1984): 75–100; and Glen Graeme Langston, "Teacher Training at Dalhousie University, 1924–1970" (MA thesis, Dalhousie University 1972).

33 The evolving ideology of higher education is discussed in Patricia Jasen, "The English Canadian Liberal Arts Curriculum: An Intellectual History, 1880–1950" (PhD thesis, University of Manitoba 1987), and Marni De Pencier, "Ideas of the English-Speaking Universities in Canada to 1920" (PhD thesis, University of Toronto 1978).

34 See Owram, *The Government Generation*; David O. Levine, *The American College and the Culture of Aspiration 1915–1940* (Ithaca, NY: Cornell University Press 1986), 45–67; and Sanford M. Jacoby, *Employing Bureaucracy: Managers, Unions and the Transformation of Work in American Industry 1900–1945* (New York: Columbia University Press 1985), 126–9.

35 The distinct itineraries of the medical graduates in Quebec are examined by Weisz in "Geographical Origins and Destinations of Medical Graduates."

36 A.B. McKillop argues that "a far greater proportion than the population of Queen's warranted became teachers throughout the country and sought to live up to the moral example set them by Grant and Watson." McKillop, *A Disciplined Intelligence*, 218–19. For a discussion of Ontario's desire to reproduce the west in its own image, see Doug Owram, *Promise of Eden: The Canadian Expansionist Movement and the Idea of the West 1856–1900* (Toronto: University of Toronto Press 1980).

37 Owram, *The Government Generation*; and J.L. Granatstein, *The Ottawa Men: The Civil Service Mandarins, 1935–1957* (Toronto: Oxford University Press 1982).

CHAPTER TWO

College, Career, and Community: Dalhousie Coeds, 1881–1921*

Judith Fingard

In the decades spanning the turn of the twentieth century Dalhousie University attracted students because of its Halifax location, its Presbyterian ambiance, and its professional programs. The enrolment of women increased gradually, from two in 1881 to 166 in 1921, the latter figure being equal to the total student enrolment for 1881. A qualitative change also occurred in women's participation. By 1921 coeds had gained admission to all the existing courses, including medicine (1888), dentistry (1914), law (1915), commerce (1920), and engineering (1921). Unlike most of its contemporaries, however, Dalhousie offered very few "female" programs: only music was available among the ornamental subjects, and the one applied program designed to attract women was a short-lived course in public-health nursing. The social sciences were non-existent. Despite the "male" orientation of the curriculum, women held their own in the classroom, capturing an impressive share of the honours in proportion to their minority percentage of the student population. Half of the Avery Prize winners – the graduating students with the highest grades in the general degree programs – were women.

A study of the first two generations of Dalhousie women enables us to set their participation rates and levels of performance within the context of continuity and change in the patterns of higher education and career choices for women. The approach adopted here is a group biography of the 1,270 women who began formal study between 1881 and 1921. It enables us to explore three questions for each generation: who went to college, what kind of social environment they encountered, and what happened to them as alumnae.[1]

THE FIRST GENERATION

During the first generation, which includes registrations from 1881–82 to 1900–01, 392 women went to Dalhousie; they formed 23 per cent of the student body. At the time of their attendance, 265, or two-thirds of the women were residents of Halifax, the largest rural contingent coming from eastern Nova Scotia, particularly the Scottish Presbyterian communities in Pictou County. Less than 2 per cent of the women were non-Maritimers. Rural women were more likely to complete degrees than were Halifax women and often had some teaching experience. As a rule college women of the first generation were older than those who followed them. For their programs of study they chose arts, letters, science, or medicine. As for their family background, most of our sketchy information on occupations of parents and guardians relates to the Halifax residents. Businessmen, ranging from shop-keepers to bankers, were the most numerous among the fathers, but given the close connection between religion and higher education, it is not sur-prising that the single most common occupation represented by the identified fathers was that of clergyman.

While parental interest and encouragement were important factors in de-termining female attendance at university, the first generation included a large proportion of women who were self-motivated. With no tradition of higher education for girls, the pioneer female students, particularly those from the country, tended to be women of ambition with clear-cut goals and a degree of independence. Financial resources often determined the length and frequency of their undergraduate study. Slightly older women like Mar-garet Newcombe, the first graduate, and Annie Hamilton, the first medical graduate, who were both twenty-eight on graduation, came from modest rural backgrounds. Both were orphans by the time they started college. Being normal-school graduates who had taught for several years, they put themselves through college with the aid of savings, scholarships, and oc-casional teaching.[2]

But for many first-generation women, study at Dalhousie was a luxury which did not culminate in a degree. The attitude of Lucy Maud Montgomery of *Anne of Green Gables* fame is instructive in this regard. She was able to afford one year at Dalhousie, in 1895–96, and left initially with regret. By 1910 she had overcome her disappointment. "Looking back on my life with the insight which comes from riper experience." she wrote in her diary, "I think my going to Dalhousie was a mistake – a waste of time and money. I do not think I received any good whatever from that year as far as edu-cational value went." Moreover, the year did not help her to find the job she wanted as a journalist or, failing that, a better teaching position. "It is not because I did not enjoy it that I consider it a wasted year," she concluded. "It is simply because I do not think it advanced me in any way."[3] Despite Montgomery's retrospective rationalizations, it seems likely that the high proportion of non-graduates to graduates among the first-generation women (3 to 1) was related in part to regional economic conditions which were unfavourable not only to prolonged periods of leisure for study but to con-tinued residence within the region itself.

Financial circumstances were not the only factor determining the shape
of the undergraduate career for women. If we look at some of the wealthier
families, we find that the graduate was still the exception. The same applied
to most daughters of clergymen, fathers with modest means but influential
standing in the community. None of the ten daughters of two of Halifax's
leading Presbyterian divines, R.F. Burns and P.G. MacGregor, who attended
in the 1880s, took degrees, though half of them were around the college
halls long enough to do so. Since daughters of wealthy or high-status families
were not expected to have to earn their own livings, they could dabble in
intellectual pursuits to a far greater extent than those women who were
motivated by the idea or the necessity of a vocation. Because they lived in
the city, it was easier for such women to attend part time or intermittently.
They treated Dalhousie more like a library or a club than an educational
institution. Late nineteenth-century ideas about the adverse effect of mental
activity on a woman's physical constitution may also have played a part in
discouraging some women from studying for degrees. Even graduates were
patronizingly coddled. Sarah Archibald, the first female Avery Prize winner
in 1892, was described by the *Dalhousie Gazette*, after graduation, as en-
joying – and, by implication, needing – "a well-merited season of rest at
her home." Dr Martha A.L. Philp, who became a medical missionary in
west China, was, during the summer after her graduation in 1902, reported
to be "resting at home in Middleton after the terrible strain of examinations."[4]

Although it was the more exceptional, self-motivated or career-oriented
women who completed their degrees, this is not to suggest that non-graduate
women were dilettantes or failures. Many of them pursued activities after
leaving college that did not depend upon the professional qualification of a
degree, which was of little real advantage to women in many teaching jobs,
in nursing, or in social service. Their attitude to college was quite utilitarian,
especially when they could not afford to study solely for study's sake.
Frances Theakston, who studied science at Dalhousie during 1896–97, eventually became principal of LeMarchant Street elementary school. Mabel H.
Parsons, an arts student in the early 1890s, devoted her life to educational
work among black women in the southern United States, first as principal
of the high school associated with the Spelman Seminary in Atlanta and
then as dean of Hartshorn Memorial College in Richmond. Georgina Paton,
an arts student for two years in the 1880s, trained as a nurse in the Boston
Homeopathic Hospital before joining the Grenfell Medical Mission in Labrador. After her marriage to a physician, she and her husband established
their own hospital in Mexico. Hedwig D. Hobrecker, who attended in arts
between 1897 and 1901, took a course in Christian service work at the YWCA
training school in New York and returned to Halifax as the secretary, in
charge of work for girls, at the local YWCA. In 1930 she became national

executive secretary of the YWCA. Other non-graduates completed their degrees elsewhere. Wilhelmina Gordon, for example, left Dalhousie after three years in arts at the turn of the century to graduate from Queen's, where she subsequently became the first female faculty member and taught in the English department for forty-one years.

The Dalhousie college to which the first generation of women students came in the nineteenth century was a small, intimate institution where men and women attended classes together and where, until almost the end of the century, the women shared in a number of the men's extra-curricular activities. The main college society, the Philomathic Society, was a mixed organization of the 1890s. Women also joined the staff of the college newspaper, the *Dalhousie Gazette*, then largely a literary journal. With only 11 per cent of the degrees going to women between 1885 and 1900, their presence in the college was not construed as a threat to its male character. They were in no position to object to their exclusion from student politics and debating.

Family solidarity worked against gender hostility. Many of the girls were related to the boys in the programs, and enough of them came from the coed public schools to take for granted the integrated nature of the college. The houses of Halifax students were continually open to the female and male friends of the local students. Out-of-town girls frequently resided with Halifax relatives or friends, though some institutional accommodation was available with the establishment of the Presbyterian Ladies' College in 1887. One of the Dalhousie boarders was L.M. Montgomery in 1895–96. Her year at the Halifax Ladies' College provides us with some insight into the day-to-day life of the college women.[5] Although she was not a regular undergraduate, in that her goal was a short-term one and her program would not lead to a degree, she entered fully into the spirit of college life, right down to writing all the Christmas and end-of-year examinations that she was not required to do. We find her also active in the Philomathic Society, in the missionary meetings of the Y, in the socials and at homes, and even attending incomprehensible football games.

At the Ladies' College L.M. lived with six other Dalhousians on the Dalhousie floor known as "the third-and-a-half." Like L.M., Alberta Victoria Reid and Margaret (Rita) Perry left Dalhousie without taking a degree. L.M.'s favourite was Margaret H. Chase, a first-year, seventeen-year-old from Onslow. Daughter of the Reverend J.H. Chase, Dalhousie's first graduate in 1866, and a product of the Colchester County Academy at Truro, Chase completed her BA in 1899. She left immediately for California, where her ailing father had gone to restore his health. There she nursed him, taught English, eventually completing an MA at the University of California in 1915, and became assistant director of the California Polytechnic School, where she spent the rest of her teaching career.

Three of L.M.'s contemporaries were in their senior year, and L.M. attended their graduation ceremonies in April 1896. Bessie Cumming had come to Dalhousie straight from Pictou Academy at the age of sixteen in 1891 but, like many of her contemporaries, had been out of college for a year, in this case between her first and sophomore years. The daughter of a Pictou County clergyman, Cumming returned to Dalhousie in 1896–97 for graduate study before undertaking a teaching job at the School for the Blind in Halifax. She married the Reverend A.F. Robb in 1901 and went with him to Korea as a missionary teacher, where they worked for over thirty years. She was one of the fifteen overseas missionaries among Dalhousie's first generation of women.

Elma Baker was also a graduate of Pictou Academy. She had entered Dalhousie at the age of eighteen in 1892 and studied for four consecutive years in the arts program. After graduation she taught at North Sydney High School, being appointed vice-principal in 1898, and in 1901 became Bessie Cumming's successor at the School for the Blind. Shortly thereafter she moved permanently to British Columbia, like fifteen other Dalhousie women of the first generation, and eventually married the inspector of public schools in Vancouver.

Nina Elizabeth Church, the other 1896 graduate, came from Bedford and resided at the HLC only during her last undergraduate term. She was an older woman, having entered Dalhousie at the age of twenty-five in 1892, a product of the county academy in Halifax. Church continued her education by taking MA degrees at Dalhousie in 1899 and Radcliffe in 1903 and a PhD in English in 1914. Her subsequent career was principally as dean of women at Oklahoma University, the type of administrative position through which many women in both the first and second generations got a foot in the door of a coed college.

For the out-of-town girls without family nearby, the Halifax Ladies' College served as a home away from home, but L.M. resented the "bossing" that she encountered from the HLC old-maid administrators. As she later wrote, "I did not quite like boarding at the Ladies' College. Accustomed as I had been for two years to much greater personal freedom I found the restrictions irksome and the unmitigatedly feminine atmosphere rather stifling."[6] Despite its imperfections, L.M. still might have preferred HLC to the other institutional accommodation in town provided at the very end of the century by the YWCA, that hostelry established by maternal feminists in most Canadian cities to protect unaccompanied young women from the evils and temptations of the impersonal urban environment. When L.M. stayed there briefly as a working journalist in 1901, she found as one of her roommates, in "a big barn-like apartment" which "looked as much like a hospital ward as anything you can imagine," Stella Messinger, a second-year medical student, for whom the hospital-ward ambiance must have seemed entirely appropriate.[7]

Few of the Dalhousie women of the first generation were as prominent as L.M. Montgomery or as easy to trace in their subsequent lives. Yet we know a fair amount about their marital status and their migration patterns after college. Of the 392 women who attended Dalhousie between 1885 and 1900, at least 41 per cent and perhaps as many as 55 per cent remained single. Of the 174 who are known to have married, 63 had Dalhousie husbands. Geographical mobility was a major feature of the lives of both single and married women of the first generation, especially as young adults, and much of the mobility occurred outside their native Maritimes. The whereabouts of 65 per cent (64 of 98) of the first-generation graduates was known in 1937, when all of them would have been over fifty. A large proportion of the remaining 35 per cent were by then deceased. Of these surviving first-generation graduates, 61 per cent (39 of 64) lived outside the Atlantic region in 1937. Others, who were Nova Scotia residents in 1937, had spent their most productive and reproductive years outside the region before returning on their own retirement or that of their husbands. Grace Burris had taught school in British Columbia for over thirty years before retiring to Nova Scotia in 1936; Bertha Hebb had lived in South Africa for twenty-five years before settling in Nova Scotia with her husband; Ethel Muir, a philosophy professor at Mount Holyoke and later Wellesley colleges, had returned permanently to the Halifax area by 1937.

Among the reasons for leaving home, intellectual and evangelical pursuits ranked high. Dalhousie was slow to develop graduate programs. Although nearly 20 per cent of the women graduates took master's degrees at Dalhousie, beginning in 1892, and another 10 per cent undertook some graduate work there, the most gifted had then to look outside Halifax and outside the region for opportunities for further study. The first generation of women went to the United States, often to women's colleges. Sixteen of the ninety-eight graduate women are known to have pursued graduate studies in arts or science soon after their Dalhousie years at Bryn Mawr, California, Columbia, Harvard, Princeton, Radcliffe, or Wellesley. Four of the sixteen completed doctoral studies. Not all of the women who engaged in post-graduate study remained in the United States, but those who did were able to follow careers which would have been impossible in the Maritimes.

Religious evangelicalism attracted thirteen Dalhousie female graduates to foreign missions, which became a lifetime commitment for six of them. Bessie Cumming and Catherine Mair, with their Dalhousie clergyman husbands, dedicated their lives to Korea, as did Ellen Maxwell and Mary O'Brien with theirs to India and China respectively. To India also went Jemima MacKenzie, MD, while Annie Hamilton, MD, spent the twentieth-century portion of her life in China. Others made temporary forays into foreign lands, motivated by the spirit of British imperialism which informed turn-of-the-century Canadian nationalism. Five Dalhousie women volunteered in 1902 to teach in the concentration camps in South Africa, a venture which drew four of them permanently from the region.

A large proportion of the out-migration was dictated by marriage, and in cases where the husband was also a Maritimer (usually a Dalhousian), such marriages deprived the region not of one talent but of two. Prominent among the emigrating Dalhousie husbands were clergymen, doctors, lawyers, and professors. Winnifred Braine and Martha Brown, both MDs, each married a Dalhousie physician. The Braine-Reynolds medical team settled in Montana; the Brown-Shaw team chose Oregon, where they were in 1897 "said to have a large and lucrative practice."[8]

The patterns of migration among the women who attended Dalhousie but did not graduate were not dissimilar. The same sources provide information relating to place of residence in 1937 for 38 per cent (112 of 294) of the first-generation non-graduates, which indicates that nearly half spent their productive and reproductive years elsewhere. Marriage drew the non-graduates away slightly more than it did the graduates. The Dalhousie clergymen-husbands chosen by some of these women were particularly mobile because of population stagnation at home. Elizabeth Creelman, who attended classes in the mid-1880s, and Edith Sutherland, who was forced out of college through ill health in 1899, both married missionaries. Two other nineteenth-century students who married Dalhousie Presbyterian ministers were Lillie Calkin, to whom belongs the distinction of being the first woman enrolled in the degree program in 1881, and L.M. Montgomery. Both couples settled in Ontario.

If the high proportion of non-graduates among university women was one distinguishing feature of the first generation, a second was their degree of dutiful obligation to family as adults, especially among the city-bred. Daughters of the well-to-do and even the not-so-well-to-do often remained within or returned to the family circle to become companions to parents or sisters, or helpmates to brothers. Two striking examples are afforded by the experience of the Stewart and Ritchie families of Halifax. Anne Amelia Stewart, the eldest Stewart daughter, graduated in 1886 at the age of twenty-seven with a Bachelor of Science degree. For the next fifteen years she studied at Bryn Mawr and Cambridge and taught in girls' schools in the United States and central Canada before returning to Halifax as a private tutor engaged in preparing students for university entrance. She lived in the family home on South Street with her brother and two sisters, both of whom had also attended Dalhousie (Maria L.J., 1886–88, and Elizabeth H., BSc 1900) but neither of whom went out to work. The Stewart sisters, daughters of the Reverend Murdoch Stewart of Pictou County, tended always to be known as the sisters of Dr John Stewart, dean for many years of the Dalhousie medical faculty, the brother who pursued a career while they led a genteel but modest existence befitting the maiden daughters of a Presbyterian divine.

The Ritchies were also family centred. Eliza, the youngest of three daughters at Dalhousie, was the only one to graduate, at the age of thirty-one in 1887, and after completing a PhD in philosophy at Cornell in 1889, she taught philosophy and psychology at Wellesley College for ten years. In 1899 she quit her job and returned to Halifax. Supported by an inheritance, she wrote, lectured, organized, and promoted the advancement of women, including Dalhousie women. She gave non-credit art lectures to raise funds for Forrest Hall, the first university residence for women, to which she also donated one year of her services as warden, and she subsequently became the first female member of the board of governors. In the community her energies were devoted to the suffragist cause, to the promotion of art appreciation, to the encouragment of young writers. She was an active member of many organizations, including the local Council of Women. She lived with two of her sisters (Mary W., 1882–88, and Ella A., 1884–86) and their brother George, a barrister, at Winwick on the North West Arm. Their way of life was seldom repeated in the second generation, when not only did paid work become a suitable pursuit for respectable young ladies but also, except for those with a religious vocation, marriage became the only socially acceptable alternative.

For those first-generation women who worked, the occupation of teacher was pursued by at least seventy. We can infer that many of the women who married within a few years of leaving college were also teachers in the interim. Other forms of educational work were pursued by at least ten more of the women who are known to have had occupations. Health care was the second most prominent area of endeavour, with eighteen doctors, four nurses, and three other health workers as well as three social workers identified. For the rest whose occupations are known, business and writing or some combination of these undertakings with teaching round out the picture. But for 283 of the 392 women we have no reliable information. For most of them, early death, genteel spinsterhood, or the domestic world of marriage and family were the likely fates. Only a very small number of women were able to combine work and marriage – mainly the writers, and some of the physicians – but many of the married women worked alongside their husbands without special remuneration or recognition in the mission field, the manse, the business, or the drawing room.

THE SECOND GENERATION

The second generation of 878 women, who entered between 1901–02 and 1921–22 and who constituted 26 per cent of the student body, was, like the first, still drawn overwhelmingly from Halifax, though the proportion of city women dropped from two-thirds to one-half. The ties with the Scottish Presbyterian strongholds of eastern Nova Scotia were strengthened as their percentage increased from 15 to 20. The other major increase occurred in the percentage of women coming from Cape Breton, from 1 to 7.5 per cent, reflecting the impact of urbanization on that area. Still very few students came from outside the Atlantic region, perhaps 2.5 per cent. None the less a number of the girls had only recently moved to the area. Esther MacKay was the elder daughter of the Reverend Duncan O. MacKay, a graduate of 1890, who returned to Nova Scotia from Ohio so that his children could also be educated at Dalhousie. Phebe Christianson was born in Glace Bay but educated in Alberta, where her father's highly mobile occupation as a mining engineer had taken him before he accepted a job in Sydney Mines after she finished high school. Catherine E. Read went to Moose Jaw Collegiate after her clergyman-father moved his family to Saskatchewan in search of a more healthy climate than that of northern New Brunswick. But her father's death in an accident in 1919, her last year in high school, sent the rest of the family back to her mother's family home in Truro, where maiden aunts offered to help support the widow and her children.[9] And then there was the unique case of the student nuns from Mount Saint Vincent, about half of whom were American-born and -raised but found themselves in Halifax, often permanently, because it was the location of a Sisters of Charity motherhouse serving an international region.

Despite a slight broadening of the ethnic composition of the student body, the college remained essentially Presbyterian, with a large number of Mcs and Macs to confirm the ancestry of the students. Although data on fathers' occupations are only slightly better than for the first generation, the predominance of clergymen had apparently passed, and the daughters of business and professional men constituted over 30 per cent of the students. Both farmers and workers contributed at least 6 per cent each to the female population of the college. With almost 30 per cent of the occupations unknown, however, an accurate assessment is impossible. A significant number of the women came from female-headed households – as many as 10 per cent, and this is bound to be an under-representation, since occupations were sometimes reported for fathers who were in fact dead.

The students of the second generation, both those with family experience of college and those without, included girls whose eventual attendance at university was taken for granted. The demystification of "college" owed a great deal to the respect for education that was engendered in Nova Scotia, where, to this day, a larger percentage of the eighteen- to twenty-one-year-old population attends university than in any other province save Prince Edward Island. In many cases at Dalhousie it was the Scottish heritage that determined the matter-of-fact acceptance of university attendance as part of the rites of passage: "school and college along with the porridge."[10] Parents who were determined to do the best for their children often made great sacrifices in order to enable them to participate in the expanding opportunities for higher education. A remarkable number of them appear to have been as generous in their encouragement of their daughters as of their sons. On a salary of $750 a year the Reverend Robert Murray and his wife Jessie sent their two daughters and four sons to Dalhousie between 1913 and 1931, both girls graduating with MDs. Robert Murray's sister Catherine and her husband, Graham Creighton, oversaw the college education of their four daughters and two sons between 1911 and 1927, two of the girls becoming school teachers, one an artist, and the fourth an ophthalmologist. The Colquhouns, Scottish immigrants to Halifax, provided for the education of their eight children, including five girls, at Dalhousie in the first three decades of the century. Whatever strains the years of study might have placed upon the family budgets of a country clergyman, a school inspector, and a marine engine superintendent, the impact must have been even greater for single parents such as Mrs J.R. Henry of River John, Pictou County, the widow of a collector of customs, whose five children, all girls, graduated from Dalhousie between 1912 and 1921. In return for their encouragement, the parents of the second-generation women found their daughters anxious to use their education to earn an independent living. Indeed, the young women often felt compelled to get a job as soon as possible in order to repay their debts. For this reason, budding post-graduate careers were sometimes cut short by the guilt of obligation to self-sacrificing parents.

But the corollary of parental enthusiasm was parental ambition for particular careers. Edith Creighton, the eldest in her family, wanted to be a nurse, but her father absolutely forbade it and expected his four daughters to teach; yet the youngest girl, Anna, was able to persuade him to allow her to pursue a medical degree. Jacob Resnick, the first Jewish father to send his children to Dalhousie, had a family of three girls. He encouraged the eldest to be a doctor, the next a lawyer, and the youngest a teacher. His plans worked out only for the eldest, the first child often bearing the major burden of parental designs. Sister Francis d'Assisi also went to college at the behest of her superiors, though in her case it was a mother superior and a director of sisters' education, not her natural parents. She and seventeen other Sisters of Charity were chosen for academic training through segregated instruction after intelligence testing was used to determine their native ability. Once embarked upon a college program, they had no choice in course selection.[11]

The recruitment of second-generation students from a wider socioeconomic background meant that the student body now included daughters of workingmen like Merle and Marjorie Colpitt, whose father was an electrician, Louise and Helene Sandford, whose father was a mason, and Sister

Monica Nearing, whose father was a miner. A number of other girls were
drawn from poor or marginal farming homesteads. Bessie Turner, for example, came from a farm in Westphal on the outskirts of Dartmouth. Similarly, Margaret Kuhn was raised on a not very successful farm at Cole
Harbour dyke, east of Dartmouth, an isolated location where her mother, a
former teacher with normal-school training, educated her seven children at
home, Margaret until the tenth grade. Esther Crichton came from a farm in
Annapolis County, where her city-born father died just as he was beginning
to succeed in his agricultural ventures. Both Bessie Turner and Esther Crichton had relatives in Halifax with whom they resided while attending school
and college.[12]

Until the opening of Shirreff Hall, the women's residence, in 1923, other
out-of-town girls boarded in private houses or institutions. Bessie Hall, the
Avery Prize winner of 1916, spent her first academic year at the YWCA on
Hollis Street, where she met Emelyn MacKenzie, a lifelong friend during
their respective professional lives as social worker and corporate lawyer in
the United States. The YWCA had not improved much since L.M. Montgomery described it ten years before. Emelyn MacKenzie claimed it was
"a shabby place" with poor food, but "it had one cardinal recommendation
and that was that room and board was only $3 a week," an important
consideration for a poor girl from Cape Breton who never seemed to have
a cent to spend.[13]

About the same time, Jessie MacDougall, the Avery Prize winner of
1914, lived at the Halifax Ladies' College, which was still the most important
hostelry for Dalhousie women, but she did not like being an HLC boarder
any more than L.M. Montgomery had and left to board instead for five
dollars a week in the house of a comfortably placed widow. According to
the correspondence of medical student Florence Murray, the discipline at
HLC had relaxed since L.M. Montgomery's days. She described a late-night
feast shared by twelve Dalhousie women in October 1915 that was interrupted shortly after midnight by the house mistress, who reported them to
the headmistress, Dalhousie pioneer Margaret Newcombe. Widow Trueman,
as Newcombe was then, told the Dalhousie girls that their "conduct was
shocking and she was inexpressibly grieved ... Then," according to Murray,
"we all had to promise on our honor that we would not speak over the
telephone for more than two minutes at a time, would not take any outsiders
to our rooms, and would not go to anyone else's room after ten o'clock at
night."[14]

With the opening of Forrest Hall on South Park Street by the alumnae
association in 1912 and, after the war, of its successor Marlborough House,
a number of women left accommodation in other institutions to live at this
semi-official residence. The residences were closer to the campus and had
an exclusively Dalhousie ambiance, in contrast to the boarding accommo-

dations among schoolgirls and working girls. During the academic year 1915–16, the sixteen women who lived at Forrest Hall ranged in age from seventeen to twenty-seven and in experience from "freshettes" to seniors.[15] All were products of the region's public-school system; at the time of their attendance at Dalhousie five of them came from Pictou County, another three from Cape Breton Island, two from Lunenburg County, one each from Colchester, Yarmouth, Cumberland, and Hants counties, and one each from Prince Edward Island and New Brunswick. Their family backgrounds were generally modest. Four were widows' daughters. The occupations of the fathers of the other twelve were entered in the registration books as two farmers, two lumbermen, a locomotive engineer, a bookkeeper, a bookseller, a fuel inspector, a merchant, a clergyman, a druggist, and a retiree. All but four of these wartime students completed their degree programs at Dalhousie. One of the four, Frances Vickery, was called home to Yarmouth at the end of her first year to help in her father's bookstore when her brother went overseas. Subsequently she went to Mount Allison and took a degree in home economics.[16]

Nine of the women embarked on long-term careers, four as teachers, one as a dentist, one a librarian, one a druggist, one an office executive, and one a social worker. As might be expected, the career women tended to remain single. The exception was Arabella MacKenzie, the dentist, who continued to practise after her marriage. The other seven married within the space of one to ten years after leaving Dalhousie, and in the interim several of them worked in schools or the civil service. The marriage rate for this group of women was very similar to that for the second generation as a whole.

Only six of the women remained in the region. The others travelled in various directions. Edith "Monty" Montgomery, a niece of L.M.'s, spent most of her teaching career in British Columbia, where thirty other second-generation women could be found in 1937. Three of the women joined the considerable exodus of college students to the United States. Sib Metherall went to New York as a teacher, as did Jean Ross as a librarian. Bessie Hall, a PhD of Bryn Mawr, practised her social-work skills, principally in Baltimore. Ontario attracted four of the married women as it did sixty other women of that generation by 1937. Annie Fraser spent most of her teaching life in Montreal, one of forty-eight Dalhousie women who could be found in the province of Quebec in 1937. Lily Bayne, a wartime bride, went overseas. She died in England of influenza in the post-war epidemic which carried off several Dalhousie women.

While this survey of 1915–16 Forrest Hall girls indicates that some widows' daughters could afford to live in residence, not all out-of-town mothers had the means or inclination to send their daughters to such institutions. Widow Henry of River John moved to Halifax every winter and rented a house in which her five daughters could live under her nurturing care. After the death in Sydney Mines of the father of Phebe Christianson, an only child studying medicine, Mrs Christianson sold their house and moved to Halifax, where she rented a house on the edge of the Studley campus and took in as boarders a number of her daughter's female classmates. Similarly, Joyce Jamer's mother, widowed in 1913, came to Halifax from Andover, New Brunswick, in her daughter's junior year and for two years "rented houses and took college students as roomers." [17]

The experiences of the second-generation women, beyond the boarding house, the classroom, and the socials, were characterized by three influences: the intensification of women's activities in their own separate sphere; the eagerly pursued religious experiences of Bible study, the Student Volunteer Movement, and the Student Christian Movement; and, for those women whose university careers overlapped with the 1914–18 period, the war.

The division of the male and female students into separate spheres emerged as a prominent feature of college life at the turn of the twentieth century. Before that the women were too few in number and too single-minded in their studies to spend time forming female societies. But the increasing numbers of women reinforced their sense of exclusion, before the war, from the principal societies run by the men: the student council and the debating societies. As a result the women formed a society called Delta Gamma in the autumn of 1899. Never exclusive like a fraternity, the organization nevertheless developed its own rituals, with an autumn initiation of new girls and a wide range of activities – social, intellectual, and political. Florence Murray described a meeting of Delta Gamma in a letter to her mother in October 1915: "The chief business of the evening was the initiation of the freshettes. All the new girls were asked to retire to the hall, from which they were taken a few at a time and made to sing together each singing something different, or to give a two minute address immediately upon a specified subject, etc., etc. Then each girl was blindfolded, told to open her mouth and given a piece of cold macaroni to eat. After that she was presented to the president and received into the society." [18] Lighthearted though these jinks seemed to be, they could be quite intimidating to shy girls, like Margaret Kuhn, who was initiated into Delta Gamma in 1919. The subject of her address was kissing, which she proclaimed, in her embarrassment, to be unsanitary. [19]

The major serious activity was debating, in which the topics ranged from the romantic to the economic, from "It is better to have loved and lost than never to have loved at all" to "Women should receive equal wages with men for equal work performed." In 1917 the members of Delta Gamma contemplated forming a suffrage society, but, like women in the wider community, the students were so overwhelmed with volunteer work in the aftermath of the Halifax Explosion that they scarcely had time to notice their own enfranchisement in the spring of 1918. [20]

Delta Gamma was a good training ground for college politicians. In 1916 the first woman was admitted to the student council, though Bessie Hall's only function was to organize a dance and attend one meeting to report on her progress.[21] The debating prepared women for their first participation in faculty and inter-faculty debates during the war and for the formation of an intercollegiate debating team after the war. Another all-female club was the college YWCA, organized in the late 1890s. Although its activities included some social-service work, like visiting the poor-house and talking to factory girls, its main contribution was to prepare the way for the intensification of spiritual and evangelical life on campus.

One of the most striking phenomena of college life during and after the war was the preoccupation of many Protestant students with interpreting and promoting the Bible. The religious climate had always been strong at Dalhousie, but the second generation was subject to the influences of the social gospel, the foreign-missionary movement, in which their predecessors were playing such a prominent role, the national Student Christian Movement, which grew out of the college YMCAs and YWCAs, and H.B. Sharman's *Records in the Life of Jesus*, the primer of the Dalhousie Bible study groups which flourished during the period. Bible study was sustained by faculty interest, particularly by the work of H.L. Bronson, a physicist whose scientific training led him to challenge fundamentalism but not to question the tenets of Christianity.

Participation in the Bible study groups and the Student Volunteer and Christian movements had as much, if not more, influence over the subsequent lives of many of the women as did the classroom lectures. Among those who responded most fully to spiritual activities were women whose ambitions to follow a religious vocation were frustrated by their sex. Florence Murray, for example, had wanted to become a Presbyterian minister and went into medicine only as a second choice when her request was refused by the church authorities. Her years of medical training at Dalhousie were filled with spiritual preparation for the years ahead. She was one of Professor Bronson's Bible study group leaders, and she was active in the college YWCA and the campus Student Volunteer group.[22] Another enthusiastic supporter of the Student Christian Movement, which replaced the college Ys in 1921, was Margaret Kuhn, who felt inspired to become a deaconess and opt for overseas mission service. Family obligations precluded these ambitions, and she eventually "went into the ministry" as a minister's wife, in common with thirty-five other women of her generation, not including those who married missionaries. While at college she was a regular Bible student, relishing the liberation from her fundamentalist background which Bronson's tutelage provided.[23]

With professors leading the movement, the students found little opportunity for scepticism. Yet Florence Murray became aware in 1916 that some of her classmates were having "intellectual difficulties." Bessie Hall, then in her senior year, was one of them. Although she was a Bible study group leader and a YWCA worker, she told Murray that "she couldn't believe much of the old testament and couldn't get over the difficulty of the miracles in the new testament." Murray continued, in a letter to her father, her description of Hall's doubts:

If miracles ever happened, why don't they happen now? How could the story of Jonah be true? It was utterly impossible for the sun to go backward. Other religions had traditions just like the stories in our Bible and it was probably mostly tradition too, and so on. I am sure Bessie is in earnest and wants to know the truth but what could you say to all that stuff? I did my best but she knows so much philosophy and other things I don't know the names of to quote at me that she leaves me feeling rather helpless and inadequate for the task. Sometimes it is hard to know just how much is literal and how much is figurative, isn't it? And some things are quite impossible to understand. [24]

Despite the heavy dose of Bible study and the evangelical influence, a much smaller percentage of women in the second generation joined the foreign-missionary movement than in the first. A number of reasons can be suggested. Girls of modest means and humble backgrounds might have dreamed of foreign missions but were tied to more prosaic goals: for them missionaries were to be admired, not emulated. Other women who were active in the Christian organizations on campus now had opportunities in social work, specialized medical training, and health professions with which to make their contribution to humanity at home. And in so far as missionary work had represented a liberation from the constraints of a male-dominated society, many second-generation Dalhousie women could pursue a more independent life, free from the restraints of the traditional Victorian family, without removing themselves from their own culture.

Of the eleven women attracted to the foreign-mission field from the second generation, only two were physicians: Murray went to Korea and Elizabeth Thurrott to India. The rest were missionary teachers, most of whom stayed for about five years, including Grace Baker in India, Harriet Bligh and Jean Foote in Korea, Isobel McCurdy with her husband in China, and Mabel MacKay in British Guiana (Guyana). Longer terms of service were put in by Gwen Fraser with her husband in Turkey, Janet MacDonald and her husband in China, Jessie Maxwell, who went to India to work with her first-generation Dalhousie missionary-aunt Ruth Maxwell Cock, and Pearl Young, who served for many years in China.

Although the religious inspiration of the early twentieth century did not produce an abundance of missionaries, neither did it produce pacifists among the women during the First World War, an event that profoundly affected the outlook and careers of many of the second-generation women. The percentage of women in the university rose from 23 at the outbreak of the war to almost 40 in 1917–18, before returning to pre-war levels in 1920–21. With the slump in the enrolment of men Florence Murray found her second-year medical class halved in 1915–16, with the prospect that by the following year "Dalhousie will be a ladies college." At her stage of medical study Florence had little hope of getting overseas, but from the safe distance of Halifax she speculated that she would "rather go behind a gun than peaceably in a hospital."[25] The irony was that Halifax was far from safe, and Florence Murray would soon get her chance to exercise unpractised medical skills in the devastation of the war.

In the meantime, the bustle of wartime Halifax meant excitement, volunteer work, and uncertainty for the college women. The troops training near Forrest Hall included brothers, sweethearts, and friends of the coeds. The girls found the soldier boys very appealing. As one woman of that period wrote: "When the Band would play and the Boys went marching by who could concentrate?"[26] Dalhousie women engaged in Red Cross work, making bandages and so on, established a knitting program to produce socks and mittens, collected Christmas treats to send to all Dalhousie boys overseas, and adopted a Nova Scotian prisoner of war.[27] Jean Ross, who entered Dalhousie at the beginning of the war in 1914, remembers the students' impression was that "surely it would be over in five or six weeks! Then we decided well, it was taking a bit longer but surely by Christmas? Soon we settled down to blackouts at night. And in the early morning the tramp tramp tramp of soldiers going to board the ships waiting in the Harbor. And aloft the sound of the Dawn Patrol returning. All too soon we went to the newspaper offices to read the casualty lists ... our male classmates left us, some never to return."[28]

Any innocence not destroyed by the casualty lists was surely shattered to smithereens by the Halifax Explosion of 6 December 1917, when a collision and fire involving a munitions ship in the harbour devastated part of the city. With the college closed, Dalhousie girls, like others, rallied to the cause, and nursed and succoured the mutilated and homeless of the north end of the city. Florence Murray, then in her fourth year in medicine, reported for duty at the YMCA emergency hospital run by the military. Answering in the affirmative when asked if her class had undergone training in anaesthesia, despite the fact that she herself had not, she was sent to the operating room to give anaesthetics. Her first case was a six-year-old child whose eye reflexes to the anaesthetic might have provided her with the dosage guide she needed had the eyes still been present in the little head. She acquired enough experience on the job that day to be appointed official anaesthetist for the hospital the following morning.[29]

The rescue work that Dalhousie girls undertook and the general relief scheme itself encouraged involvement in social work. Self-sacrificing jobs

at low pay which satisfied the social conscience became for the first time
an alternative to foreign missionary work for activist graduates of the period.
Catherine C. Colquhoun, for example, was described as "one of the most
enthusiastic of the workers" after the explosion. She joined the staff of the
Relief Commission and was later transferred to the Halifax Bureau of Social
Services. According to the *Dalhousie Gazette*, "she had positive genius for
this sort of work and a woman prominent in local philanthropic circles said
that she had never met anyone with so much sympathy and tact." Shortly
after she went to New York to engage in settlement work, only to be cut
off in her prime during the post-war influenza epidemic.[30] The rescue work
created a number of positions that Dalhousie women filled and that may
have launched their careers. The pioneer dentists, for example, were first
employed by the Massachusetts-Halifax Relief Commission: Arabella
MacKenzie, followed by Roberta Forbes. As a result of the establishment by the Imperial Order Daughters of the Empire of a home for children
orphaned by the explosion, Eliza Brison, one of Dalhousie's earliest female
medical specialists, was given the rare opportunity among medical women
of pursuing her career in her native province. A psychiatrist, she became
the resident physician for the Home for Feeble-minded Girls, which grew
out of the original explosion scheme, and later the first woman doctor with
a residency at the Victoria General Hospital in Halifax. Subsequently she
was appointed the provincial psychiatrist.

The explosion also created a different category of female graduate when
a public-health nursing course was introduced at Dalhousie for several years
in the early 1920s. The twenty-nine women who had registered by 1921–
22 represented a new type of woman in university. Not only were they
experienced, trained nurses, but most of them were at least thirty years of
age and some of them in their late forties. Several had distinguished war
service to their credit. Apart from the women in nursing, the enrolment in
programs during the second generation included 736 in arts, 41 in music,
35 in medicine, 30 in pharmacy, 13 in law, 11 in science, 6 in dentistry,
3 in commerce, and 1 in engineering, with at least 54 taking graduate degrees
in arts and science. Yet the percentage of Dalhousie female post-graduates
fell, both at Dalhousie and elsewhere, a reflection perhaps of enlarged
opportunities at professional schools but also an indication that even the
women in the purely academic programs were becoming more career-
oriented and anxious to find a place in the work-force.

A more interesting question is why so many more women were now
completing their degrees: 51.2 per cent compared to only 25 per cent in the
first generation, or one-third of the total graduates between 1901 and 1925,
in contrast to 11 per cent in the first generation. To some extent the increase
reflects the upgrading of qualifications in areas of prime interest to women,
particularly in teaching. Margaret King insists that her two reasonably well-

paid teaching jobs in Nova Scotia in the 1920s, one at Edgehill, a private boarding school for girls, the other at the Imperial Oil Company school for the children of the refinery workers at Imperoyal, outside Dartmouth, both required degrees.[31] Second-generation women, like their first-generation foremothers, flocked to the teaching profession. Although we lack specific career information relating to the second-generation women, we have identified at least 223 school teachers. In descending order, the other most prominent occupations were nursing, medicine, business and secretarial work, college teaching and administration, librarianship, and such health professions as pharmacy and dietetics.

But to ascribe to many women a single occupation is singularly misleading. Second-generation women enjoyed considerable occupational and geographical mobility. Multiple occupations were common. Physicians became university professors and administrators, as did nurses, pharmacists, and writers. Art and writing were often combined with teaching. Women changed their occupations both early and late in life as a result of new training, travel, war, or growing confidence. A case in point is Jean Bayer of the class of 1908, the secretary of Walter Murray, the founding president of the University of Saskatchewan. Described as Murray's "right-hand man" and as "a sort of fairy godmother" to the university, she wanted a more independent role, which she achieved by pursuing graduate study at the University of London and returning to Saskatchewan as a professor of English.[32] Jean McDonald, a teacher of academic subjects in British Columbia and Nova Scotia, mastered two business courses when she was young and kept up her secretarial skills until she decided finally to combine the two interests formally within her profession. At the age of fifty she went to Columbia University, where she qualified for teaching business subjects, an expertise she then pursued in a rural high school in Nova Scotia during the last seventeen years of her employment.[33]

Multiple locations for work were even more common than multiple occupations. It was a roving generation. Women were finally as free of chaperones as of restrictive clothing. They travelled; they drove their own cars; they sought out challenging opportunities at home and abroad. It was the period of the peripatetic school teacher who moved from job to job. Edith Creighton, who graduated in 1915, taught variously in public and private, secondary and post-secondary institutions in Halifax-Dartmouth, Manitoba, New York, Hamilton, and St John's. Marion Elliott, a BA of 1925, taught in rural Nova Scotia, at Havergal in Toronto, then the American Academy in Shanghai; then, after her marriage, in South Africa during the Second World War, Malaya after the war, and, after her husband's death, at Elmwood in Ottawa and Branksome Hall in Toronto.[34]

It appears that only about 55 per cent of the second-generation women married, and 6 per cent of those women only late in life. As with the first generation, very few of the women were able officially to combine paid work and marriage. The most successful in this regard were women in the male-dominated professions: medicine, dentistry, university teaching. For Anna Creighton, who married five years after securing her MD in 1922, there was never any question of giving up her work. She felt she had taken a place in her profession as an eye specialist which had been keenly sought by her male counterparts: she could not fail to carry it through, having already deprived a man of the opportunity of a residency. The moral commitment sustained her through the disapproval she encountered from those who were not averse to telling her that her duty lay in another direction – and her critics included her own mother, who strongly disapproved of the way she brought up her two children. [35]

Gender discrimination was often the lot of women who continued to work until retirement age, married or not. Women in the professions found they could not compete with the men for the more lucrative positions despite their identical training at university. Their quarrel was not with the university but with society, which allowed them to think of themselves as equals during the years of their education and then consigned them to job ghettos once they entered the work-force. Mona Flemming, for example, a pharmacy graduate, was for many years the pharmacist for the Halifax Visiting Dispensary. Her pay was a pittance in this semi-public position. No male pharmacist would have done the job: the men ran the private-enterprise drugstores; the women got the low-salaried institutional positions with charities and hospitals. [36] In the field of medicine, Anna Creighton's ophtalmological practice in New York, beginning in the late 1920s, was dependent on low-paid surgery on the public hospital wards. For at least twenty years the general practitioners of the city would not give her the referrals she needed in order to build up even a modest private practice, a handicap she attributes solely to her sex in a male-dominated profession. Work-place segmentation by gender was as common a phenomenon among professional women as it was among their working-class sisters.

For those women who chose or were forced to stay at home, we must not underestimate the importance of the educated married woman's role within the community. Isabel Grant's experience is a case in point, as well as an example of the new opportunities that opened up to second-generation women on graduation. An honours mathematics graduate of 1911, she was recommended by President John Forrest for a job as an actuary with the federal government in Ottawa. The family anecdote claims that Grant applied using her initials only, got the job, and surprised her employers by turning up in skirts. They decided to give her a chance as the federal government's first female actuary and insurance expert. Subsequently she married another civil servant, and thereafter as an Ottawa resident she practised her political skills as a school-board member and became a women's rights activist, which culminated in her founding and chairing the first Canadian committee on the status of women, where her special concern was bringing to light tax discrimination against women. By the end of her life she had served two successive terms as president of the National Council of Women.[37]

Isabel Grant's prominent contribution to the status of women in Canada was made from her residence in Ottawa. She was one of the 45 per cent of the second-generation women, both graduate and non-degree, who were known to have resided outside the region in 1937. Although this figure tends to suggest that second-generation women did not leave the region in such overwhelming numbers as did the nineteenth-century students, it still emphasizes that the human resources of the Maritime region were being siphoned off to enhance more prosperous and developed areas and that comparable opportunities simply did not exist at home. The level of outmigration was unacceptably high, not only in terms of loss of talent to the region but also to Canada itself. Almost half of the emigrants were living in the United States in 1937. The reasons for leaving were more varied but not significantly different in substance from those influencing the first-generation migrants.

Single women often left initially to pursue training that was not available in the Maritimes and, for those who went to the States, not open to them in the rest of Canada. This applies to training in librarianship. The only program in Canada was at the Toronto Public Library and subsequently at the University of Toronto, where the director, Winifred Barnstead, a first-generation Dalhousie graduate, certainly welcomed Dalhousie graduates such as Esther Crichton, whose training led to jobs in Toronto and Ottawa. Whatever encouragement Maritime women may have felt at Toronto, the inability of that program to guarantee employment to all the applicants meant that a significant proportion of Dalhousie women who became librarians were trained in the United States. Jean Ross, one of a number who went to the Brooklyn Public Library training program, did so only after the administrators of the Toronto program made it clear to her that job recommendations would go first to Ontario residents.[38]

Americans never seem to have discriminated against Maritime women. Graduates of Dalhousie found opportunities for study and good jobs not only as librarians but as nurses and medical and dental specialists and educators. Roberta Forbes, a Springhill girl who had been very active in student affairs when she was taking dentistry, became interested in orthodontics as a result of her work with children under the aegis of the post-explosion Massachusetts-Halifax Health Commission. To specialize in this field she was admitted to the Eastman Dental Dispensary in Rochester, New York, as was Angela Magee, one of her contemporaries. This was after Forbes had considered working in Nova Scotia as a school dentist, but the very small salary there and the lack of access to private practice did not appeal to her. She felt she had to go to the United States, not only to train but also to make a living, and so she stayed, working first at Rochester and then in Florida.[39] Other women were essentially too well qualified to find a job at home. Mabel Morrison, one of the handful of second-generation women who went on to complete PhDs, found that there were no jobs for women in Canadian colleges and therefore moved to the United States, where the large number of women's colleges – both junior and degree granting – absorbed a significant number of female faculty.[40]

While Mabel Morrison went to the United States alone, others went in family groups when hard times hit the Maritimes in the 1920s. Joyce Jamer, a teacher, settled permanently with her mother and sister in the United States, where her mother, a practical nurse, easily found a job.[41] The three Hoben sisters – Grace, Lou, and Marion – attended Dalhousie along with their brother Rainnie between 1911 and 1924. Children of a merchant who had moved to Halifax from Saint John around the turn of the century, they all packed up and moved to Atlanta, Georgia, in 1926. Thelma Smith, daughter of a lumber merchant, was in her junior year at Dalhousie when her family moved to Boston, where she joined them on her graduation in 1922, never to return.

The largest proportion of Dalhousie women who left the region permanently were not career oriented or family centred but rather tied their fortunes to those of their husbands. In 15.5 per cent of the cases the migrant women's husbands were Dalhousie men, whose areas of work included the law, the church, higher education, science, technology, and business. Marriages in the mid-1920s provide us with a number of illustrations of the out-migration of newly trained engineers from the deindustrializing Maritimes. Mary Kirkpatrick and Laura Smith married electrical engineers who found employment in central Canada. Other Dalhousie women and their engineer-husbands went to the United States. Gladys Lewis, for example, married Arnold Smith, a mechanical engineer and fellow native of Colchester County. They moved to the United States only after extensive efforts to find engineering employment in Canada had failed.[42]

Taken together, the most striking continuing feature of the first two generations of Dalhousie women is the high rate of out-migration. Since as many as two-thirds of the female Avery Prize winners left the region, the brightest students appear to have migrated in greater numbers than the average students. The region bore the expense of training the minds that then abandoned it, often reluctantly, sometimes to contribute to the development of underdeveloped regions in Canada and the Third World but more often to gravitate to prosperous areas of central Canada and the United States.[43]

Another feature that remained constant, despite the gradual broadening of the socio-economic and geographical intake to include the daughters of marginal farmers and socially mobile artisans, was the number of students from the same families. Among the 1,270 women surveyed in this paper, about 1,000 nuclear families are represented on the basis of female sibling relationships alone. If daughters, female cousins, and grand-relatives could be taken into account, we would find that the number of discrete families would be reduced again by as much as 20 per cent. With university education costing proportionately no less in the early twentieth century than it does today, the decision to educate children imposed a considerable strain on family resources and must have represented choices that crippled family finances during a difficult transitional period in the Nova Scotia economy. At a time when community and career opportunities in the region were exposed to the disintegrating effects of deindustrialization and economic decline, the college years provided a rewarding experience to cherish.

For women of the second generation greater opportunities materialized in terms of the programs they followed. Their options on graduation, however, no longer included the genteel spinsterhood of the first generation. Paid work or marriage were the alternatives. Most women saw their choice of careers as teaching, nursing, or office work. Ironically, therefore, they were not very different from non-university women in the general work-force except in their training for a more senior or better-paid job. For the women in the "male" professions of medicine, dentistry, and law, university proved to be poor preparation for the real world. As Dr Eva Mader recalls: "It was not until after I graduated and found things were refused me because I was a woman that I realized we were different. In Nova Scotia and at Dalhousie I did not feel this. In other parts of Canada it was much more difficult to get the education you wanted if you were a woman."[44] Only further research will tell us if in fact it was easier in Nova Scotia. If it was, that does not mean the environment was more liberating; it means that the export of brains was a serious industry requiring the best of the raw materials, female as well as male.

In the Maritimes as elsewhere, university women comprised a tiny proportion of the female population.[45] They shared with their counterparts in American and Australian coed colleges similar class origins, age profiles, undergraduate experiences, and career patterns.[46] They differed from non-university women in their high mobility rates and their low marriage rates. They were among the first women in Canada to have a real choice: the female world of marriage and domesticity or the male world of career and independence. They were certainly the first to be able to combine the two. In two generations they graduated from the pioneer era, when female Dalhousie graduates were self-motivated older women or cloistered city women, to the Great War era, when coeds were drawn from a broad spectrum of the social scale with similarly broad and varied degrees of dedication and ambition. While both generations were conditioned and influenced by the traditional oppressors of women – the family and the church – they were also liberated by those same institutions, which encouraged their intellectual development, their entry into the professions, and their socialization with men. At the same time, their sense of identity as women, and hence their female culture, were reinforced by their living together, associating with each other in female organizations, and competing with each other in debates and games. In other words, the familiar dichotomy in women's experience, of wanting to be both equal with men but separate from them, was strengthened rather than weakened in Dalhousie and other coed colleges at the turn of the century.

NOTES

* The author gratefully acknowledges the financial assistance of the Social Sciences and Humanities Research Council of Canada and the research assistance of Samantha Brennan, Sue Brown, and Rebecca Veinott.

1 The student population of 1881-1921 is derived from the matriculation and registration books located in the Dalhousie University Archives, the annual calendars, and directories of former students published in 1925 and in 1937. For the purposes of this paper, every woman whose name appears in the official registration documents has been included. Most of these names also occur in the 1937 directory. Less reliance was placed on the calendars and the 1925 directory, especially as they included for 1891–92 and 1892–93 the names of one hundred women who attended Dalhousie as "special" students to take one class, possibly in the summer. They have been excluded from the data-base in order to avoid severely skewing the statistics. The data do, however, include the special students listed in the registration books, many of whom were part-timers. Most of the biographical information on individual women is derived from registration and alumnae records, including the *Dalhousie Alumni News*, which appeared (initially irregularly) from the 1920s to the 1980s, and the *Dalhousie Gazette*, which published alumnae news till the 1920s. Only quotations and additional sources are footnoted. Maiden names are used throughout except where a married name is necessary for clarification.

There is no history of Dalhousie, but Paul Axelrod has explored one aspect of its social history: "Moulding the Middle Class: Student Life at Dalhousie University in the 1930's," *Acadiensis* 15, no. 1 (Autumn 1985): 84–122. I have discussed another side of women's experience at Dalhousie in "Gender and Inequality at Dalhousie: Faculty Women before 1950," *Dalhousie Review* 64, no. 4 (Winter 1984–85): 687–703.

2 See Harry Bruce on Margaret Newcombe: "How did she get into the picture?" *Dalhousie Alumni Magazine* 1, no. 2 (Winter 1985): 7–8; Arthur Lindsay on Annie Hamilton, "Knox Church, Brookfield, Nova Scotia: A History of the Congregation," 1976.

3 Mary Rubio and Elizabeth Waterston, eds., *The Selected Journals of L.M. Montgomery*, vol. I; *1889–1910* (Toronto: Oxford University Press 1985), 390–1.

4 *Dalhousie Gazette*, 10 May 1892 and 1 July 1902.

5 *Journals*, I:136, 144–61.

6 Ibid., 391.

7 Ibid., 264–5.

8 *Dalhousie Gazette*, 9 Nov. 1897; 10 Feb. 1902.

9 Esther MacKay Ross to the author, 12 Feb. 1986; Phebe Christianson Thompson to the author, 12 Mar. 1986; C. Eunice Read Hawkins to the author, 15 Mar. and 2 Apr. 1986, and interview, 12 May 1986.

10 Interview with Edith Creighton, 22 Aug. 1984; Nova Scotia, *Report of the Royal Commission on Post-Secondary Education* (Halifax 1985), 111–14.

11 Jessie MacDougall to the author, 27 Jan. 1986, and interview, 8 June 1986; interviews with Rebecca Resnick Glass, 1 Aug. 1984; Edith Creighton, 22 Aug. 1984; Anna Creighton Laing, 25 Oct. 1985; and Sister Francis d'Assisi (Margaret MacCarthy), 28 Apr. 1986; Anna Creigton Laing, *My Father's Reply* (New York: Vantage Press 1984), 1.

12 Bessie Turner Nickerson to the author, 27 Jan., 20 Feb. 1986; interviews with Margaret Kuhn Campbell, 23 Apr. 1986, and Esther Crichton, 19 June 1986.

13 Reminiscences of Emelyn MacKenzie, *Ansul* 7, no. 4 (Jan. 1976): 5–6.

14 Interview with Jessie MacDougall, 8 June 1986; Florence Murray to her mother, 23 Oct. 1915, Dalhousie University Archives (DUA) MS-2-535-A9.

15 The sources do not quite agree on the Forrest Hall residents in 1915–16, but they have been immortalized by three of the boarders: Bessie Hall, "Life at Forrest Hall," *Dalhousie Gazette*, 14 Jan. 1916; Annie I. Fraser, "The Girls of Forrest Hall" (a poem); Clara Smith, "Forrest Hall: The Palace of Art" (a poem).

16 Frances Vickery Goudey to the author, 19 Jan. 1986.

17 Interview with Florence Henry Sperry, 2 Feb. 1986; Phebe Christianson Thompson to the author, 12 Mar. 1986; E. Joyce Jamer to the author, 26 Jan. 1986.

18 Florence Murray to her mother, 23 Oct. 1915, DUA, MS-2-535-A9.

19 Interview with Margaret Kuhn Campbell, 23 Apr. 1986.

20 *Dalhousie Gazette*, 15 Dec. 1917, 9 Nov. 1921, Graduation number, May 1922.

21 Bessie Hall to her mother, postmarked 13 Jan. 1916, Public Archives of Nova Scotia, MGI, vol. 661.

22 Florence Murray to her mother, 23 Oct. 1915, DUA, MS-2-535-A9; *Dalhousie Gazette*, 27 Nov. 1918; Florence J. Murray, *At the Foot of Dragon Hill* (New York: E.P. Dutton 1975), viii–ix.

23 Interview with Margaret Kuhn Campbell, 23 Apr. 1986. On the SCM at Dalhousie in this period see P.B. Waite, *Lord of Point Grey: Larry Mackenzie of UBC* (Vancouver: University of British Columbia Press 1987), chap. 3.

24 Florence Murray to her father, 3 Mar. 1916, DUA, MS-2-535-A10. Even faculty sceptics like historian George Wilson led Bible-study groups.

25 Florence Murray to her father, 17 Sept. 1915, 3 Mar. 1916, DUA, MS-2-535-A10.

26 Frances Vickery Goudey to the author, 19 Jan. 1986.

27 *Dalhousie Gazette*, 3 Dec. 1917; Murray, *At the Foot of Dragon Hill*, ix.

28 Jean Ross to the author, 21 Jan. 1986.

29 Murray, *At the Foot of Dragon Hill*, x.

30 *Dalhousie Gazette*, 12 Jan. 1918. Interview with Marjorie Colquhoun Keddy, 27 June 1986.

31 Margaret King to the author, 2 Feb. 1986.

32 *Dalhousie Gazette*, Oct. 1911, Dec. 1912; Michael Hayden, *Seeking a Balance: The University of Saskatchewan, 1907–1982* (Vancouver: University of British Columbia Press 1983), passim.

33 Jean McDonald to the author, 21, 29 Jan. 1986.

34 Interviews with Edith Creighton, 22 Aug. 1984; Marion Elliott Campbell, 30 July 1986.

35 Interview with Anna Creighton Laing, 25 Oct. 1985.

36 Interview with Mona Flemming, 31 Jan. 1986.

37 E. Margaret Bentley to the author, 26 July 1985.

38 Jean Ross to the author, 21 Jan., 11 Apr. 1986; interview with Esther Crichton, 19 June 1986.

39 Roberta Forbes to the author, 18 June 1986.

40 Mabel Morrison to the author, 15 May 1986.

41 E. Joyce Jamer to the author, 26 Jan., 16 March 1986.

42 Laura Smith Ross to the author, 27 Jan. 1986; L.F.H. Smith (on his mother's behalf) to the author, 27 Jan. 1986.

43 Alan Brookes, "Out-Migration from the Maritime Provinces, 1860–1900: Some Preliminary Considerations," *Acadiensis* 5, no. 2 (Spring 1976): 26–56; Patricia A. Thornton, "The Problem of Out-Migration from Atlantic Canada, 1871–1921: A New Look," *Acadiensis* 15, no. 1 (Autumn 1985): 3–34; John G. Reid, *Mount Allison University*, vol. 1, 1843–1914 (Toronto: University of Toronto Press 1984), 179.

44 Eva Mader Macdonald to the author, 4 June 1986.

45 Lynne Marks and Chad Gaffield, "Women at Queen's University, 1895–1905: A "Little Sphere" All Their Own?" *Ontario History* 78, no. 4 (Dec. 1986): 336.

46 Farley Kelly, *Degrees of Liberation: A Short History of Women in the University of Melbourne* (Parkville, Victoria: Women's Graduate Centenary Committee 1985), 1–77; Barbara Miller Solomon, *In the Company of Educated Women: A History of Women and Higher Education in America* (New Haven and London: Yale University Press 1985), 1–140.

CHAPTER THREE

Parade Street Parade:
The Student Body at Memorial
University College,
1925–49*

Malcolm MacLeod

Of the major universities in Atlantic Canada, Memorial University of New-foundland has the most recent foundation. Students were first admitted to the non-degree program of Memorial University College (MUC) in 1925, four years after an ongoing operation for interdenominational teacher training – which eventually blended into Memorial's offerings – had been started. The government policy that brought the college into existence was prompted in part by a desire to honour the war dead with a new institution to serve the living. It was also a response to the wish of Newfoundland's leading educators to develop a more highly qualified corps of teachers for the coun-try's several church-run school systems, and generally to make advanced learning more accessible for the ambitious and scholarly inclined. Previ-ously, the only recourse for would-be students after graduation from the St John's colleges – denominational high schools with residential facilities – was to go abroad to Canada or Britain.[1] Financial assistance from the Carnegie Corporation of New York helped to establish Memorial University College in an impressive building on Parade Street on the "higher levels" above downtown St John's.

The first quarter-century, 1925–49, makes a natural period in the study of Memorial. This was the time of junior-college immaturity, before the institution was elevated to degree-granting status in the year of Newfound-land's confederation with Canada. Those two and one-half decades saw wild fluctuations in the general affairs of Newfoundland. During the late 1920s and early 1930s came the last blossoming of Newfoundland independence, before pride and economic diversification sickened into widespread dole-subsistence and public bankruptcy. The years 1934–39 saw the inauguration of the Commission of Government, a benevolent dictatorship marked by many, often fruitless, attempts at modernization and reform, while little recovery was made from the Great Depression. The 1940 discovery of the island's strategic utility, by both Canada and the United States, ushered in

Table 1
Enrolment at selected universities, 1925–47

Academic year	Mount Allison	Dalhousie	Acadia	St FX	MUC
1925–26	301	800	431	202	57
1931–32	355	[1016]*	637	268	158
1935–36	449	884	490	305	272
1940–41	[568]*	678	680	312	254
1946–47	881	1569	890	870	434

Sources: See n 3.
* Previous year's figure.

a new era of plentiful military spending, which for a time eliminated unemployment and brought relative prosperity to ordinary families as well as
to the government.[2]

The pulses and pauses in Newfoundland life were reflected, sometimes
tardily, in the enrolment history of Memorial University College (see Table
1). From 57 registered in the first year, the plateau of 100 students was
reached in 1929, and 200 five years later. Then depression and war slowed
growth. Four times between 1933 and 1944 the enrolment was less than it
had been the previous year. In 1936, 255 students registered; in 1943 there
were 254. After that, registration began to increase rapidly. Returning veterans with special assistance from government raised the attendance level
to a peak of 434 in 1946–47. Three years later, the veterans having departed,
it slumped to 307. In the following year, in normal conditions once more,
it rose to 400 and continued thereafter to rise. Newfoundland's total population increased from about 270,000 in 1925 to 350,000 in 1949. Thus the
participation rate at Memorial, per 10,000 of population, increased from 2
to 7 students by the mid-1930s, then stalled at between 8 and 9 (except in
the immediate post-war years) for the remainder of the college era.

Throughout the pre-Confederation years, total enrolment at Memorial was
small, not only by the standards of later eras but also by comparison with
several of the closest universities on the Canadian mainland. Acadia, Dalhousie, Mount Allison, and St Francis Xavier were much older institutions
and had long-established constituencies. Nevertheless, even Dalhousie in
some years had only three or four times the number of students in Memorial's
abbreviated program, and there was a time in the late 1930s when the St
John's college almost equalled St Francis Xavier in size, before falling off
to half the enrolment when the veterans arrived.[3] In the post-Confederation
era Memorial, with its chartered monopoly on providing university services
to a captive and increasing population, would outstrip in student numbers

Table 2

Location of home address for students entering Memorial, academic years
1928, 1938, and 1948

	1928–29 %	1938–39 %	1948–49 %	Proportion of Nfld pop. in that area[1] %
Northern areas[2]	9	5	12	12
Central Nfld[3]	8	5	7	6
Bonavista Bay	8	8	3	8
Trinity Bay	2	5	9	8
Conception Bay	28	23	13	15
St John's metropolitan area	40	36	39	20
Placentia Bay & southern Avalon	4	4	5	10
South coast[4]	—	7	9	10
Western Nfld	2	5	3	12
Labrador	—	—	—	2
United Kingdom	—	1	—	

Source: Memorial University, Registrar's Records.
1 Average of figures in the 1935 and 1945 censuses.
2 From Cape Bauld to Lumsden (on the "Straight shore" east of Fogo).
3 The Exploits River system from Red Indian Lake to Bishop's Falls.
4 From Cape Ray to Fortune.

all of these Maritime institutions. The early foundations of this expansion
lie in the ambitions, achievements, and demography of the first generation
of Memorial students. Where did they come from? Why did they choose
to attend Memorial? How were their lives as students affected by such
questions as religion, age, gender, and social class? How representative of
Newfoundland society were these early marchers in the Parade Street parade?

Memorial University College did not give equal service to all parts of
Newfoundland. Analysis of the home addresses reported by entering students
(see Table 2) shows that twice as many came from the St John's metropolitan
area as the area's proportion of the overall population would warrant. Conception Bay – close to St John's and, like the capital city, prosperous compared
with many other parts of the island – was similarly over-represented in the
beginning, although in the late 1940s it declined to a normal share of the
student body. The most under-represented areas, by contrast, were those of

Placentia Bay, the southern part of the Avalon peninsula, and western Newfoundland. These territories sent only one-third as many students as might
have been expected from the general distribution of population.[4] Placentia–
southern Avalon, it seems, was the part of Newfoundland where satisfaction
with traditional low levels of schooling, or disinterest in higher education,
was greatest. Western Newfoundland, however, was a very different case.

Communities on the west coast were at least five hundred kilometres from
Memorial. On the Newfoundland Railway, serpentine proof of the island's
modernization, there were eight hundred kilometres of distance and expense
between St. John's and Corner Brook. From Corner Brook, Antigonish and
therefore St Francis Xavier University were just as near. Not only that, but
a good proportion of pre-paper-mill settlers in western Newfoundland belonged to families whose forebears had migrated into the area from Nova
Scotia during the 1840–60 period.[5] For many of those families St Francis
Xavier, as a centre of Catholic and Celtic learning, was not only the closest
but also their own university. The indications are that the university participation rate in western Newfoundland was relatively high compared with
that of most other parts of the country, but the region's students were more
likely to be at St Francis Xavier or some other nearby mainland college than
at Memorial. While only 3 or 4 per cent of Memorial students came from
this populous region, there were years when nearly half of all Newfoundlanders at St Francis Xavier hailed from the west coast.[6] Although a publicist
of MUC noted in 1932 that "Corner Brook was the first school to start a
leaving scholarship tenable for two years at this college," it is clear that
even such encouragements had little effect on the people of western Newfoundland in the pre-Confederation era.[7]

In other areas, however, Memorial was more successful in increasing
student clientele when the Depression slackened. These included the northern
reaches beyond Bonavista Bay – from the Straight shore and Fogo Island
as far north as St Anthony – and the whole stretch of the south coast from
Fortune westward. Under-representation of these areas became progressively
less evident, until by the 1940s they produced the same fraction of MUC
students as they did of Newfoundlanders in general. Trinity Bay residents
also felt this growing attraction. The overall picture shows Memorial very
slowly winning the loyalty and attendance of the country's furthest regions.
Northern, western, and south-coast Newfoundland, with about one-third of
total population, began in the 1920s by contributing only one-tenth of Memorial students, but by 1948–49 these areas were home for one-fourth of
them.[8]

Despite this expansion of the college's clientele, analysis of students'
home addresses (see Table 3) also reveals that the experience of Memorial
students remained essentially insular. First-time registrations in three years
– 1928, 1938, and 1948 – were studied. Labrador, St Pierre, and contiguous

Table 3
Home address homogeneity at Memorial, Dalhousie, and Mount Allison

Home address	Dalhousie, 1930s* %	Mount Allison, 1938–39 %	MUC new students, 1938–39 %
Newfoundland	5	3	99
Maritime Provinces	82	88	—
Rest of Canada	3	6	—
United States	9	1	—
Britain	negligible	—	1
Other	1	2	—

Sources: Memorial University Registrar's Records; Axelrod, "Moulding the Middle Class," 88; Mount Allison University Calendar, 1939–40, 140–53.
* Based on figures from 1930, 1935, and 1939 in Axelrod, "Moulding the Middle Class," 88.

parts of the Canadian mainland were all unrepresented. Only one student gave a non-Newfoundland address – his family lived in Bedfordshire, England.[9] This consistency of geographical origins was different from the mixtures of regionalisms and even nationalities found in the universities of the nearby Maritime provinces. At Dalhousie in the 1930s, for example, 9 per cent of the students came from the United States and another 6 per cent from other foreign countries, including Newfoundland. Every Canadian province was represented. Similarly, at Mount Allison in the same period, one student in eight was from outside the Maritime region. Rubbing strange elbows broadened the education enjoyed at those colleges; Memorial lacked this advantage.[10]

For all that, the Memorial students had a variety of reasons for registering for higher education. Interviews with former students, conducted during the oral-history phase of the Memorial College history project, provide some indication of this diversity. One question put to the interviewees was whether the decision to go to college had been essentially their own or somebody else's. Reactions were mixed. Over half the group remembered quite clearly that it had been their own decision. Included among these self-motivated were all of the older students who came back to college after spending several years in the adult work-force. After working for several years as a teacher and lay minister, one recalled that "I said with five or six hundred dollars in the bank, which was a lot then, I'll take a chance on going to university. I had written to Mount Allison, I had written to Memorial ... I decided well Memorial is Newfoundland, it is home."[11] There were also self-reliant youngsters. "Each of us ... was expected to make his or her

Table 4
Programs chosen by students entering Memorial, academic years
1928, 1938, and 1948

Programs	1928–29 %	1938–39 %	1948–49 %
Arts & Science A (Arts emphasis)	26	13	20
Arts & Science B (Sci. emphasis)	59	15	3
Pre-medicine	9	7	20
Pre-engineering	—	15	15
Teacher training / Education	—	47	41
Special / other	6	4	1

Source: Memorial University Registrar's Records.

own decisions, pretty much, about education and about the future," said one member of the class of 1940. [12]

The next-largest group – about one-quarter – knew it had been a parent's decision. "I think it was taken for granted in the family," remarked one interviewee, "that we would [go to college], peculiarly, perhaps, because no one in the community had ever gone to college except my mother. Now mind you, our sights were not set terribly high ... We were destined to be either teachers or preachers." [13] A further 10 per cent indicated a vague recollection of family expectation although no conscious decision had been taken, while another small but significant group were influenced by teachers or other non-family members. Only a minority of those interviewed knew of previous college graduates in their immediate families: two dozen of the fifty-four who answered this question had one or both parents, or an older sibling, who had undertaken post-secondary study. A few had more distant relatives who had gone to college, but half indicated that in three known generations of two families, reaching back to the parents of both their parents, they were the first to do so. In this group were found examples of the families of fishermen or semi-skilled workers helping the next generation to climb the socio-economic ladder to white-collar careers.

Whether their registration was an outcome of long family tradition and firm expectation or of a newly seized and unprecedented opportunity, what did the students come to Memorial to study? Analysis of the programs for which entering students registered in 1928, 1938, and 1948 (see Table 4) indicates thaat the most popular choices that emerged in the middle 1930s were, in order of priority, preparation for teaching and studies in science and medicine. The pre-engineering option drew about 15 per cent of each year's new crop of students from then on, while those selecting arts /

humanities / social-science options – many of them teachers at one stage or another – fluctuated at about the same proportion.[14] Of all the students, a substantial proportion would have been unable to go to college if Memorial had not been established. When the oral-history respondents were questioned on this point, only a very few were unable to answer. The number who said decisively yes – they would have gone away to an institution outside Newfoundland – was exactly balanced by those who emphatically realized they never would have gone on to post-secondary study if the extra expense and initiative of leaving their own country had been required. Many could never have afforded it; to others it would not have seemed a reasonable ambition. The first step in upward mobility, for them, needed to be less daunting and difficult than going into exile.

Once at Memorial University College, the students joined a community that was far from homogeneous and one where divisions in society at large were reflected clearly enough to produce similar division and at times animosity within the student body. The students were diverse in many important respects. One of these was the large and increasing spread between the ages of the youngest and the oldest students. The 1928 intake group ranged from age 14 to 26; ten years later the range was from 15 to 33; and in 1948–49 it reached a spread of 33 years, from 15 to 48. In part this resulted from the acceptance of academically precocious students from the hothouse programs offered by church-run residential upper schools in St John's. Although the normal rule was that an entrant must be 16 full years of age, exceptions were obviously made for some applicants.

More important in producing changes in the age structure were two long-term trends. First, there was a tendency for women to enter the college at a young age. Most new women students in 1928–29 were aged about 17.5, though the presence of a small group of mature students lifted the overall average to 18.4. Ten years later it was virtually unchanged at 18.5, but had fallen to 17.3 by 1948. The explanation of this change lies in the characteristics of the teaching profession. Since the integration of the normal school into MUC in the early 1930s, a large number of teachers in training had been attending the college. Of the women education students the average age in 1938 was 19.5, whereas by 1948 it was 17.5. It had become more common for women who intended to teach to come to the college for some professional preparation, before exposing themselves to classroom rigours, than had previously been the case. This aspect of the college-age profile reveals the professionalization of teaching as well as indicating the wartime prosperity that permitted a large group to pass on to post-secondary education without needing to pause and earn employment income first.

Among the men the average age was rising, and this was the second trend influencing the general age structure. Male entering students in 1928 averaged 18.3 years; by 1938 the average had risen to 20, and was maintained thereafter at the higher level. The increase can be accounted for by the growing number of mature students: the ages of the men were always more widely distributed than were those of the women, who tended to cluster more closely around the average age. Detailed analysis of male students who were over 21 years of age on entering Memorial reveals that they tended to be Protestant (United Church and Salvation Army), from Bonavista and Trinity Bays and the south coast rather than St John's, of lower-class origin, and enrolled in science. Many were teachers, taking advantage of the college to strengthen their general education and improve career prospects. Other were preparing for a career change, as in the case of Arthur Butt, a twenty-nine-year-old former fisherman who had resumed his education after experiencing a religious conversion, and eventually became a minister.[15] Except for some concern about the preparedness of the very youngest students, this mixture of generations and experiences from the most tender and naïve to gnarled veterans of fishery, classroom, and pulpit worked well, and no doubt each age-group contributed to the general education of the others.

Not always so harmonious was the relationship between urban and outport students. The division between "townies" and "baymen" – St John's vis-à-vis the outports – is well recognized in Newfoundland society. It was faithfully reflected at Memorial. The degree to which actual social barriers resulted was a matter on which recollections of former students yielded conflicting opinions. Most town students, not surprisingly, recalled no such divisions. "To my knowledge," wrote one, "there were no town versus outport barriers to sociability among the students ... We were at Memorial with a purpose – "to do well" – we had the same aim – there was no time for any divisions – we were at unity."[16] Another town student called the relationship between the St John's and outport students "very cordial" but went on to note that "there were times when we'd probably rib them because of their accents. Of course we had accents too, but their accents were peculiar and they seemed to lack confidence."[17]

Such attitudes were remembered more feelingly by the outport students themselves. The first MUC student from a tiny Notre Dame Bay community recalled that "we were regarded a little bit below the sod, we had to prove ourselves. They were the elite, they had gone to Bishop Feild College and Methodist College and all that, so we had to be on our mettle." Most student officeholders, he added, were from St John's: "We stayed in the background."[18] Some of the outporters even found universities they attended subsequently – institutions in a foreign country – more friendly and congenial than the Newfoundland college was: "It seems to me that I never did become a real part of Memorial College in the same sense as I became a part of Mount Allison. I was at home there. As much as I appreciate the many good things that Memorial College did for me, I never acquired the warmness for the institution that I acquired for Mount Allison. The town versus outport

Table 5
Health of Memorial students, 1944

Defects found	Teachers in training	Academic students
Active pulmonary TB	1	1
Suspicion of TB	1	—
Dental	23	15
Vision	14	12
Tonsils	5	6
Orthopedic	4	5
Skin	3	1
Hearing	—	3
Heart	—	2
Miscellaneous	5	7
Total no. of defects	56	52
No. of students examined	66	139
Ratio of defects to students	5/6 (85%)	2/5 (37%)

Source: Leonard Miller to Commissioner for Public Health and Welfare, 12 June 1944, Provincial Archives of Newfoundland and Labrador (PANL), GN 38, s3-4-1, file 7.

barrier existed at Memorial and perhaps had something to do with this."[19] Another student who was also at MUC in the early 1940s and at Mount Allison thereafter "found that I got along and fitted in better with students from New Brunswick, Prince Edward Island, and Nova Scotia than I did with the people in St John's, because I was an outport bay noddy and they were townies."[20]

College authorities were aware of practical and educational as well as social differences among their two groups of clients. "I know," wrote one observer, "the members of the Board ... appreciate the fact that many of our outport students are seriously handicapped because of the impossibility of staffing small schools" or providing them with much in the way of teaching aids.[21] Conditions in outport areas were very harsh, leading to colonial tuberculosis and infant-mortality rates that were 4 times and 1.5 times the Canadian average respectively.[22] In the worst years of the 1930s one person in four was on public relief. Children who were undernourished and inadequately clothed became visible once compulsory education was introduced in 1942.[23]

Brutal evidence of outport disadvantages came to light indirectly when towards the end of the 1943–44 academic year the Department of Public Health arranged for complete physical examination and chest X-ray of the whole student body. The results, presented in two reports (see Table 5), showed that students enrolled in Memorial's Department of Education, for professional preparation as teachers, were much less healthy than others. Education was the program that outport students dominated by about four to one, whereas students from St John's – who through their youth had had easier access to high-quality health care – constituted about half of the "academic" students. No doubt this explains the latter group's much lower incidence of tooth decay, eye problems, and potentially fatal diseases such as tuberculosis. In the same year the board of Governors considered a thoughtful memorandum: "The morale and tone of the college must of necessity depend very much upon the adjustment of the personal problems of the students. It may reasonably be surmised that at the MUC these difficulties present rather a special problem in the case of students from outside St. John's ... [Those from] remoter outports must be expected to have a somewhat restricted view of education in the life of a University student."[24]

Despite their lack of preparation for urban living, however, outport students achieved more academically than their colleagues from St John's. The first college president, J.L. Paton, was quoted by an interviewee as remarking that he had "never come across students anywhere with such a hunger for learning and education as outport Newfoundland students."[25] Former outport students confirmed his impression. The town students, commented an outporter, "didn't have so much riding on it, living at home and coming from a different level of society, I mean financially. They didn't have the financial worries that we had and in some cases they were just going ... to university because it was the thing to do." Another, who attended college over a decade later, had a similar analysis: "Many of the outport students did quite well in university because often times they had [learned] to work much harder ... Many of the outport schools in those days had three and four classes in the same room, and in order to get a good education you really had to work at it so by the time you came to university you were well able to work."[26]

A comparison of the academic achievement of town students and those from the most benighted outport areas confirms this impression. Northern Newfoundland and the stretch of south coast from Port aux Basques to Fortune surely includes communities as isolated and disadvantaged as any on the island. The scholastic record of students who entered Memorial from those areas in 1928, 1938, and 1948 was compared with the record of St. John's entrants in those same years. Academic achievement of the outporters was more steady and successful both in the first term, when the shock of city life was the greatest, and in students' final set of Memorial examinations. In the first September-January term St John's freshmen's average mark was 49 per cent (that is, 9 marks above the old MUC pass of 40 per cent). Outport students, however, scored an average of 52.3 per cent. Also, it is worth noting that about one in twelve of city students did not write that first set of examinations, while marks were recorded for all the outport students. Moving to the grades at college-leaving, one finds that both groups improved their scholastic standing. At this stage the average mark of a town student was 51.1 per cent, and of an outport student 56.3 per cent. During their first year at the college 10 per cent of St John's students but none of the outporters had dropped out.

One of Memorial's early students, now permanently enshrined in Newfoundland literature, is Art Scammell. He had already written his famous "Squid-Jiggin' Ground" before coming in from Notre Dame Bay for college. One of the pieces he wrote while at MUC is "The Haunted Lab," a poem in rhyming couplets in the style of Alexander Pope, written after the class studied "The Rape of the Lock" in English 2. Scammell chuckled when describing the impact that his work made on his sometimes crusty professor, Alfred Hunter: "It won his admiration; he read it out in class, and he praised me a bit. The townies were sort of flabbergasted – to think that a chap from Change Islands could – could outdo Pope, you know."[27]

If the town-outport distinction was evident in student life at Memorial University College, then so too were the religious differences that were also deep-seated in Newfoundland society. Memorial itself had been created as a non-denominational capstone for the Newfoundland educational system, which at every lower level was riven along religious lines into separate systems. The college catered to all of the large and small religious groups in the country, and church affiliation was a standard item of information sought by the registrar when students enrolled. Analysis of the stated affiliations of entering students in 1928, 1938, and 1948 shows that the relative strength of religious groups was reproduced at Memorial. The Anglican, Salvation Army, Pentecostal, Presbyterian, and even the tiny Seventh Day Adventist and Jewish segments were all represented in numbers corresponding well with their share of general demography. Participation of Roman Catholics – they comprised one-third of potential college clientele – declined from 32 per cent in 1928 to 23 per cent in 1948. The only denomination consistently over-represented was the United Church of Canada. Representing one-quarter of the general population, Methodist / United Church families provided between 35 and 44 per cent of the student body and thus demonstrated their strong attraction to the use of higher education as a ladder for social mobility.

Oral history evidence suggests that, while religious differences did not obstruct social interaction, awareness of such distinctions remained pervasive. In part this was attributed to the attitudes of an older generation. "It made a little bit of difference to some of the parents," one woman recalled; "I was Catholic; maybe one of my parents might say, well, I don't know if you should go out with him, he is a Protestant."[28] Another example was given by a Protestant aspirant for a Rhodes Scholarship, who knew that in

1940 he must defer his application by a year because "the year before another Protestant had received it so I knew that I wouldn't stand a chance." It was now the turn of a Roman Catholic.[29] Consciousness of religious divisions among the students themselves was noted by informants, although most agreed that they rarely interfered with social activity. Although there were Jewish students at Memorial, recalled one interviewee, "we didn't know it ... We were aware that we were educated either by Church of England, United Church, Roman Catholic, Salvation Army, or whatever, but it didn't make any difference, none at all."[30] A Jewish former student of the early 1930s was only slightly less emphatic. "Anti-Semitism was present," he remarked, "but I felt no more than inter-Christian antagonism. I was in no way disadvantaged."[31] An especially poignant example of religious distinction, cited by another informant, also indicates acceptance rather than animosity: "One thing that still sticks in my memory is what happened when one of the students died. We all went in cap and gown to attend the funeral service. It was an Anglican student, so we paraded down to the Anglican Cathedral. The RC students fell out, they didn't go inside the church. They waited until the service was over. [Were they criticized by other students for doing that?] I wouldn't use the word criticized ... It was a novel experience rather than something you criticized."[32]

Differences in gender roles were also evident at Memorial, as in society in general, and were capable of resulting in restriction of women's academic options and, at times, of their participation in student ceremonies. The proportion of male to female students at MUC fluctuated widely. The entering students of 1928–29 included one-third who were women, a proportion similar to those at nearby universities on the Canadian mainland.[33] Ten years later women made up 44 per cent of the entering students, an increase that reflected in part the absorption of the normal school. Of 100 students taking teacher training at Memorial in 1938–39, 60 were women; in the other college programs women retained their previous proportion of about one-third. By 1948 the proportion of women had fallen steeply, to only 22 per cent. While it would be easy to guess that the explanation lay with the Second World War, the causes were in fact more subtle. By 1948 the large "bulge" of male veteran students had gone through: Memorial, with its two-year programs, had a shorter experience with the veterans than did the degree-granting mainland universities. Women's outnumbering stemmed in reality from the development and popularity of professional programs at Memorial. Whereas in 1928 just 10 per cent of college entrants selected the pre-medical course, and pre-engineering had not begun, by 1948 as many as 131 of the 329 students were enrolled in those two male-dominated fields. In the other college programs 31 per cent of the students were women. Therefore, the study of the male-female ratio shows that women were a rather consistent one-third of students in the core program, while ratios in the overall college registration waxed and waned according to the gender-related requirements, and popularity, of professions.

This statistical analysis indicates that at Memorial women students met interference in their choice of a program of studies. One, attempting to enrol for geology, remembers being given to understand that tramping out on wild lonely expeditions in search of outcrops and samples, or floundering across bogs, was not within the range of ladylike behaviour.[34] In professional preparation, with the exception of studies in education, the college certainly catered more to men. The household-science program had been created with women in mind, but very few enrolled. The pre-engineering clientele – representing more than one-fifth of the student body from the mid-1930s on – was exclusively male; no female engineering student appeared at Memorial until the 1960s. This was typical of the times. At Mount Allison, for example, the 1944 presentation of an engineering diploma to a woman was an aberration not repeated for almost twenty years.[35] Memorial did have women enrolled in pre-medical studies – 5 out of 38 in the first year in 1948–49, for example – but the completion rate was low. It may be speculated that many of these students entered pre-medicine more as an introduction to scientific study than with the ambition of actually becoming physicians. One who did complete the two-year program in 1937, however, encountered a slight from fellow-students at graduation time that indicated the potential for outright gender discrimination: "I heard afterwards that all the pre-meds, there must have been 12 or 13 of them or something like that, had someone take their picture and I wasn't included ... I got after those fellows for years about it ... I said well you dirty mean things – talk about discrimination against females, I said, what chance would I have in medical school when the pre-meds wouldn't even have me in their picture?"[36]

Such an overt snub was the exception rather than the rule. A study of Dalhousie in the 1930s found there a condescending attitude to women as mere social butterflies, and sex-differentiated supervision of living arrangements and leisure-time schedules.[37] These particular manifestations of gender stereotypes were not reported by informants on the conditions in Newfoundland. One female former student, asked whether she encountered any lingering feeling that women should not really aspire to a college education, replied, "I never got that impression." She added that President Paton had given leadership in this regard. On one occasion he had intervened angrily in a student singsong to halt the singing of "My Darling Clementine," on the grounds that the final words of the song – "I kissed her little sister, and forgot my Clementine" – were demeaning to women.[38] Nevertheless, it is clear from the evidence that women faced restrictions. There were, to be sure, thriving women's activities included in student life and culture, an example being the tradition of a women's ice-hockey team.[39] Yet when it came to student officeholding, women were not necessarily regarded as equal to men. The president of the students' representative council, for example, was invariably male. Gender divisions, while not always finding open expression, were deep-seated in the student community and in the university as a whole.

The student body of Memorial University College can also be analysed according to socio-economic class, although some serious difficulties immediately arise in such an investigation. First, the concept of class is complex and endlessly debatable. Secondly, previous studies of class structure – in Newfoundland, or in the student body of nearby Canadian universities – provide little help.[40] Finally, the information base on which to build the analysis is slender, consisting merely of the father's occupation reported by approximately four-fifths of the students at the time of registration. In general terms social class is determined by the extent and security of a family's grasp upon a portion of the wealth which society produces. Particular indicators include breadwinner's income and type of occupation, nature and location of residence, years of schooling, and church, ethnic, or other affiliations.[41] Accordingly, a scale of Newfoundland's class structure was constructed on the basis of occupational-income data reported in the 1945 census. The scale was then applied to the "father's occupation" data for Memorial students, and a table drawn up to compare the proportion of students originating in each of four occupation income groups with the percentage of the total work force that these constellations of jobs represented.[42]

The resulting figures, in Table 6, show that the class composition of Memorial students was skewed in an elitist direction. Over the three decades of the 1920s, 1930s, and 1940s, students from the upper and upper-middle classes, which constituted only 10 per cent of Newfoundland society, made up nearly half of the college student body. The lower class was no means excluded, but this group, which consisted of two Newfoundlanders out of every three, was represented in the halls of higher learning by fewer than one in three of the students. Nor do we see convincing evidence of greater participation by the lower class as time passed. What is striking, however, is the increasing attendance of lower-middle-class students. They made up one-fifth of the study body in the late 1920s but increased to one-third twenty years later. This growth was balanced by a falling away of upper and upper-middle-class representation to the point where students from these classes were only four times as likely to be in the college as their population in Newfoundland society would suggest, rather than six times as likely, which was the situation in 1928–29.

An additional perspective can be obtained by comparing Memorial's class structure with that of an institution elsewhere (see Table 7). By adopting for Newfoundland students the same method of analysis employed in a recent study of Dalhousie University, it can be suggested that Memorial was draw-

Table 6
Apparent socio-economic class of students entering Memorial in three
academic years, based upon parent's occupation

Occupational Class*	1928–29 %	1938–39 %	1948–49 %	Proportion of Nfld workforce (1945 census)
Upper – highest-paid professionals, owners, managers, etc., average income over $2,500	13	11	10	1.4
Upper middle – highly skilled occupations, average income $1,500–2,500	45	34	32	8.9
Lower middle – lowest-paid professional, many semi-skilled occupations, average income $900–1,500	19	25	33	24.9
Lower – occupations requiring common, low-level skills, average income $475–900	23	30	26	64.7

* See n 42.

Table 7
Father's occupations of new students at Memorial, 1938

Category	Known cases %	Dalhousie University, 1930s, for comparison %
Professional	20	28
Business	14	31
Supervisory	4	11
White collar	14	9
Artisan-skilled	13	8
Semi- and unskilled	11	6
Farmer, fisherman	25	8

Sources: Memorial University Registrar's Records; Axelrod, "Moulding the Middle Class," 91.

ing upon a more comprehensive cross-section of the population than did the most developed of Nova Scotia's institutions.[43] From the three first-listed categories of professional, business, and supervisory occupations – generally considered higher-status occupations than the others – Dalhousie drew 70 per cent of its student body, but MUC only half that proportion. All the humbler walks of life were much better represented at the Parade Street campus in St John's than at Dalhousie in Halifax. To a degree these figures reflect the fact that the Nova Scotia economy was more fully developed than that of Newfoundland. They also remind us that Dalhousie's substantial professional programs in law, medicine, dentistry, and pharmacy drew upon a generally city-bred and upper-crust clientele. Memorial in 1938 – with teacher-training, the most popular part of its curriculum, drawing a big outport response – bore an appropriately more rural, accessible image.

So, while privileged classes were over-represented at MUC, the humblest families had greater participation rates in college studies than was sometimes the case at other colleges in the region. "You will like the students," a prospective faculty member from Britain was told in 1948; "they come from all over the island, often from very humble homes and poor schools, but are very easy to get on with; most likable people."[44] Although the statistics give no credence to the hardy myth that Newfoundland's higher social class looked down on Memorial and preferred institutions elsewhere, they also show that the existence of the university program in St John's contributed to upward mobility through education, especially for the lower-middle class.

In sum, the analysis of the Memorial University College student body between 1925 and 1949 reveals elements of both change and continuity. The group was always small, homogeneous in nationality, and composed, about half, of individuals in whose families post-secondary education was previously unknown. It was heterogeneous in terms of religious affiliation and social class, and this diversity contributed, along with differentiated gender roles and the tension between urban and outport students, to the existence of divisions that could at times produce antagonism. In all these respects the quarter-century is a single period in the institution's social history. Yet important changes did occur: in the fluctuating ratio of women to men, the average age of both, and the relative strength of upper-, middle-, and lower-class contingents. Geographical distribution changed also. By the late 1940s some of the island's distant coasts and corners were much more significantly represented than during the early years of the college, although the St John's metropolitan area continued to provide about double its proportionate share of the students. The Depression, wartime prosperity, and the changing requirements of professions for which MUC students were preparing themselves were factors influencing these changes.

Despite all the limitations that stemmed from geography, age, religion, gender, and social class, Memorial functioned as an agent of change in Newfoundland by providing individuals with opportunities that had not existed before. The college was an entry into the wider world of higher education. The interwar period was a time when post-secondary institutions in all Western countries were being refashioned by forces of economic development, social aspiration, professionalization, and state policy.[45] What happened in Newfoundland – Memorial's registration by 1930 was 5 students per 10,000 of population, compared with over 25 per 10,000 in Canada and 175 in the United States[46] – was a tardy, small-scale response to profound influences operating internationally.

Memorial's founding represented the filling of a localized need by a characteristically North Atlantic response. The student community in St John's was never wholly representative of Newfoundland society, nor did it lack internal tensions. Nevertheless, for Newfoundland as a whole and for many individuals, the establishment of the college at the apex of the country's educational system succeeded in opening vistas of higher education that might not otherwise have been glimpsed.

NOTES

* Frank O'Leary gathered and processed from old students' records much of the data used for the tables in this study, and Jeannie Howse helped to assemble other data. Their assistance was made possible by a research grant from the Social Sciences and Humanities Research Council of Canada, gratefully acknowledged.

1 See Malcolm MacLeod, "Students Abroad: Preconfederation Educational Links between Newfoundland and the Mainland of Canada," Canadian Historical Association, *Historical Papers* 1985, espec. 174–7.

2 The best general account of the period is S.J.R. Noel, *Politics in Newfoundland* (Toronto: University of Toronto Press 1971). For economic developments, see several articles by David Alexander, especially "Economic Growth in the Atlantic Region 1880–1940," *Acadiensis* 8 (Autumn 1978): 47–76. On the 1940s see Malcolm MacLeod, *Peace of the Continent: The Impact of Second World War Canadian and American Bases in Newfoundland* (St John's: Cuff 1986).

3 See Table 1. Sources for Table 1: Mount Allison University calendars; John G. Reid, *Mount Allison University*, vol. 2, *1914–1963* (Toronto: University of Toronto Press 1984), 449; Dalhousie University calendars; Paul Axelrod, "Moulding the Middle Class: Student Life at Dalhousie University in the 1930s," *Acadiensis* 15 (Autumn 1985): 87; Robin S. Harris, *A History of Higher Education in Canada, 1663–1960* (Toronto: University of Toronto Press 1976), 473; correspondence, J. Cockayne, assistant registrar, Acadia University, to M. MacLeod, 30 June and 31 July 1986; St Francis Xavier University calendars; Memorial University, registrar's records.

4 See Table 2.

5 Rosemary Ommer, "Highland Scots Migration to Southwestern Newfoundland: A Study of Kinship," in John J. Mannion, ed., *The Peopling of Newfoundland: Essays in Historical Geography* (St John's: Institute of Social and Economic Research 1977), 215.

6 MacLeod, "Students Abroad," 184, table 6.

7 "College Notes," *Daily News* (St John's), 29 Oct. 1932, in MUC Scrapbook, Centre for Newfoundland Studies, Memorial University of Newfoundland.

8 See Table 2.

9 Ibid.

10 See Table 3.

11 Interview with Rev. R. Humby, Dayspring, NS, 14 Aug. 1984.

12 Interview with Dr Ian Rusted, St John's, 1 Feb. 1983.

13 Interview with Dr Leslie Harris, St John's, 28 June 1983.

14 See Table 4.

15 Interview with Rev. A.S. Butt, Glovertown, Nfld, 13 Mar. 1983.

16 Mrs Olive Field Dawe to M. MacLeod, 23 May 1983.

17 Interview with A.C.L. Hudson, St John's, 13 Jan. 1983.

18 Interview with A.R. Scammell, St John's, 6 Nov. 1982.

19 Harold Loder to M. MacLeod, nd [Feb. 1983].

20 Interview with Dr David Pitt, St John's, 18 Oct. 1982.

21 A. Frecker to Secretary, MUN Board of Regents, 6 Jan. 1951, MUN Board of Regents Office, file "Appointments, 1948–51."

22 R.A. MacKay, ed., *Newfoundland: Economic, Diplomatic and Strategic Studies* (Toronto: Oxford University Press 1946), 158, 170–1, 200.

23 See Table 5.

24 MUN Board of Regents Office, Board of Governors Minutes, 10 Jan. 1944, 1–3.

25 Interview with Stuart Godfrey, Ottawa, 3 May 1983.

26 Interviews with M.O. Morgan, St John's, 21 Sept. 1984; and Rev. David Genge, Saint John, NB, 1 Oct. 1983.

27 Interview with A.R. Scammell, St John's, 6 Nov. 1982.

28 Interview with Mrs Kathleen Hanley, St John's, 29 Nov. 1982.

29 Interview with Horace Hall, Saint John, NB, 2 Oct. 1982. The Second World War then intervened, and no awards were made from 1941 to 1946.

30 Interview with Mrs Margaret Sanford, Vancouver, 16 Oct. 1983.

31 Dr H.D. Rosenberg to M. MacLeod, 12 Aug. 1983.

32 Interview with M.O. Morgan, St John's, 21 Sept. 1983.

33 For example, at Mount Allison in 1928–29, women were 36 per cent of the students (post-graduates, seniors, juniors, sophomores, freshmen, and special students). Mount Allison University calendar, 1929–30, 120–30. At Dalhousie in 1930–31, 28 per cent were women. Axelrod, "Moulding the Middle Class," 87.

34 Interview with Mrs Iris Power, St John's, 24 Nov. 1982.

35 Interview with Professor Jack Facey, St John's, 17 Nov. 1982; Reid, *Mount Allison*, vol. 2, 188.

36 Interview with Mrs Kathleen Hanley, St John's, 22 Nov. 1982.

37 Axelrod, "Moulding the Middle Class," 111–14.

38 Interview with Mrs Audrey Stirling Norman, Kingston, Ont., 5 May 1983.

39 Photographs of women's ice-hockey teams, sent to the author by Mrs Gertrude
   Facey Rees (1928) and Mrs Betty Christian Parsons (1935–38). Women's
   hockey was also popular at Canadian universities during these years. See S.F.
   Wise and D. Fisher, *Canada's Sporting Heroes* (Don Mills, Ont.: General Pub-
   lishing 1974), 46, 53, 186; and C.M. Johnston and J.C. Weaver, *Student Days*
   (Hamilton, Ont.: McMaster University Alumni Association 1986), 38.

40 Reid, *Mount Allison*, 2:447, uses the scale constructed by B.R. Blishen, "Construction and Use of an Occupational Class Scale," *Canadian Journal of Economics and Political Science* 24 (1958): 519–31, which lists some 350 male and
   female occupations, using data from the Canadian census 1951. What Reid's
   "Group 1,2,3," etc., signify is not apparent in the book. Since Blishen's scale
   ranks jobs using an elaborate formula composed of income and years of schooling
   – and therefore excludes wealthy merchants of no particular education from the
   top class – it was not appropriate for Newfoundland. Paul Axelrod, "Moulding
   the Middle Class," takes a different approach from Reid and includes a long note
   (23) which describes how he constructed his occupational scale. The scale again
   has seven categories: professional, business, supervisory, white collar, skilled,
   semi- and unskilled and farming / fishing. It would have been possible to use this
   for the students at Memorial, and I was tempted, but the range of incomes included in each grouping dissuaded me. In Newfoundland in 1945, for example,
   professionals ranged from male physicians ($4,721, the top of the list) to female
   librarians ($882) and teachers ($712) – which means that persons in this professional category were spread across more than 90 per cent of the full range from
   highest to lowest income. Since income is a very important consideration when
   students are trying to scrape together funds to cover tuition and other expenses, I
   decided that a scale based on income alone was the most significant and revealing. See, however, Table 7.

41 Blishen, "Construction and Use of an Occupational Class Scale"; J.A. Kahl and
   J.A. Davis, "A Comparison of Indices of Socio-economic Status," *American
   Sociological Review* 20 (1955): 317–25; J. Tuckman, "Social Status of Occu-
   pations in Canada," *Canadian Journal of Psychology* 1 (1947): 71–4; D.J.
   Treiman, *Occupational Prestige in Comparative Perspective* (New York: Aca-
   demic Press 1977).

42 See Table 6. It should be noted that the information used for the table is not as
   complete as the data used in previous analyses of the students by home address,
   age, religious background, etc. A sizeable minority of the students did not respond to the question about father's occupation – 11 per cent of the entries in
   1928, 25 per cent in 1938, and 16 per cent in 1948. These holdouts reveal a
   pattern: in most cases, a mother rather than father is given as next of kin. Presumably, when these fathers died or disappeared, the family's standard of living

was lowered. Pertinent though this is as an attempt to assess class origins, there was no legitimate way to include these cases in the statistics.

Several simple steps were taken to establish Newfoundland's class structure during the quarter-century of Memorial University College. An occupational-class scale was constructed, based solely upon income as reported in the detailed 1945 census. This report is far superior, for every statistical or interpretative purpose, to the only other census, that of 1935, taken in the period.

The 1935 document lists only 37 male and 18 female occupations with total earnings, the men amounting to just 78,000 workers, although there were an additional 12,000 or 20,000 in that Depression-racked work-force. When we abandon that 1935 table ("total number in *selected* occupations") and move on to the 1945 report, much carefully tabulated information appears.

The 1945 Newfoundland census lists 260 occupations in 16 useful groupings and provides such depth of detail on incomes that when there is only one worker in a particular category, the income of that individual is sometimes reported as the average for the group. The male occupations in this impressive tabulation were ranked according to income, and then, using no technique more sophisticated than common sense, they were divided into four occupational classes.

The highest-paid occupations comprised 12 categories of professionals, including accountants, doctors, and eight Memorial professors, the St John's wholesale princes, and proprietor-managers in the manufacturing industry. The next level – termed here "upper-middle-class" occupations – was 19 categories of workers in "manufacturing and mechanical" (paper-makers, machinists, foremen), additional professionals and managers of more modest means, and the highest-paid operatives in the transportation, construction, and utility industries. The lower-middle class included many construction trades: plumbers, painters, and glaziers; foremen; metal workers; several transport categories such as teamsters, truck drivers, and longshoremen; and, occupying the same pay-range, the humblest professional occupations, including 317 clergymen. These allocations left chiefly lumbermen, common labourers, and 31,000 fishermen to be termed occupationally the lower class.

The greatest difficulty was encountered in trying to decide where best to draw the line between lower-middle and lower-class jobs. The decision was made to extend the lower-middle class down far enough on the income list so as to include in it carpenters and telephone linemen. It was thought the degree of skill and even theoretical knowledge required by these occupations justified a ranking higher than lower class, even though such workers were often outdoors in bad weather, doing work that involved a degree of risk, and were paid just one-fifth of the average income earned by physicians and surgeons. If we then include, as lower-middle class, occupations with average income in 1945 between $900 and $1,500, the questionable judgments become those concerning coopers and independent shoemakers. Since their average incomes were closely bracketed with those of mining labourers and janitors, they were placed in the lower class.

43 See Table 7.

44 A.C. Hunter to Rev. W. Rees-Wright, 16 Aug. 1948, MUN, President's Office,
Hatcher Papers, file "Appointments 1948."

45 The transition in the Western world generally – which is the proper context
for understanding developments in Newfoundland – is well described in K.H.
Jarausch, ed., *The Transformation of Higher Learning, 1860–1930* (Chicago:
University of Chicago Press 1983); see especially the editor's summary essay,
pp 9–36. Details for Canada are found in Robin S. Harris, *A History of Higher
Education in Canada, 1663–1960.* United States developments are well studied in
J.S. Brubacher and Rudy, *Higher Education in Transition: A History of American
Colleges and Universities 1636–1976* (New York: Harper & Row 1958, 1976);
B. Clark, ed., *Perspectives on Higher Education* (Berkeley: University of Cali-
fornia Press 1984); and W.C. DeVane, *Higher Education in 20th Century Amer-
ica* (Cambridge: Harvard University press 1965). See also David O. Levine, *The
American College and the Culture of Aspiration, 1915–1940* (Ithaca: Cornell Uni-
versity Press 1986).

46 The participation rate in Newfoundland was more in line with that in Britain,
where the number of students per 10,000 population was 8.7 in 1920. Calcula-
tions based on figures in Murray Ross, *The University: The Anatomy of Academe*
(New York: McGraw-Hill 1976).

PART TWO

Student Life and Culture

CHAPTER FOUR

Marching as to War: Elements of Ontario Undergraduate Culture, 1880–1914

A.B. McKillop

Student life outside the lecture halls of Ontario universities reflected the growing complexity of Ontario society in the late nineteenth and early twentieth centuries. By 1900 a discernible student culture was beginning to emerge, with undergraduates engaged increasingly in activities that went beyond academic requirements. Just as the curricula offered by universities and colleges underwent a division of labour as professors and administrators sought to provide a degree of scholarly order to the expanding realm of knowledge, so too did student life witness an expansion of extra-curricular activities.

Increasingly students identified with some form of social group rather than, as in the past, with the Christian self seeking moral nurture or conversion. These group activities tended to be focused in two areas, and to a lesser extent in a third. With the presence of women on university campuses, usually in the faculties of arts, male undergraduates met the challenge of their presence by turning to aggressive, "manly" activities in the form of organized sports that helped to preserve their sense of a domain of male exclusiveness. Women in turn gravitated towards an interest in missionary work and were aided in doing so by conventional social definitions of the women's role as well as by an ardent desire, shared by the turn-of-the-century male, to engage in some form of useful social service. Finally, by the early twentieth century a degree of military presence existed, in the form of appeals for organized martial training on the university campus.

In the intellectual and social climate of late Victorian Ontario, the values and assumptions associated with each of these clusters of activity – sports, missions, and the military – at times converged. Sports were often portrayed as a form of warfare; Christian missions to "heathen" nations took on military precision and required no less dedication; and, most tragic of all, warfare was seen as a deadly serious, manly game to be played with missionary zeal. The student generation of 1914, university authorities, and the public were debating the sexual implications of the tango. By the end of the next school term, with the first undergraduates beginning to fall in Flanders, the matter had become a source of silent embarrassment. The autumn of 1914 was no time to dance.

The student ambiance at different colleges and universities varied. Yet the growth of organized student activities in the late nineteenth century, at times unrelated to curricular concerns or the wishes of their professors, indicates that an important common element in the turn-of-the-century life of students was their desire to gain a measure of autonomy over their own affairs and activities. In 1890 the editor of the *Queen's Journal* lamented the "spirit of individualism" among students that threatened to "zap out all true college spirit" by subordinating collective social life to studies; but only four years later, life at Queen's had changed dramatically with the appearance of a host of campus organizations, including a "Banjo Club of twenty members."[1] By 1910 the individualism of 1890 that cared little for student collective activity had become a pluralistic democracy of interests that threatened to get out of control. "We hear much of the 'democracy' which prevails at Queen's," wrote the *Journal*'s editor; "However, there is a growing danger that this 'democratic spirit' may run riot among a countless number of organizations and societies. That society which will have for its object the 'elimination of most of the existing organizations' is the one that is urgently needed."[2]

At University College in Toronto, in spite of its internal difficulties, a similar range of student activities existed. In response to an 1899 accusation by the Toronto *Mail* that "there was not the proper unanimity and heartiness" that should prevail at University College" (the article cited a lecture given by Morley Wickett on city government attended by only two faculty members and not many more students), President Loudon replied by noting that there were more than forty literary, scientific, musical, social, and athletic societies at the institution. By 1910, with Loudon and much of the tension of the 1890s gone from the scene, the Toronto *Star* could note the "multiplicity of events in university life" at Varsity. It continued: "It is not an exhaustive list by any means. There are many other functions, class meetings, 'frat' meetings, and private social affairs. It all goes to show that university life is not narrow, but that it includes almost every branch of activity. The university, in fact, is a city, a community unto itself. It has its work and its play, its humdrum and its excitement."[3] Even at the smallest of institutions the diverse range of student interests was reflected in numerous organized activities in which students could occupy their extra-curricular time, and at each university the common seasonal rhythm of twentieth-century campus life developed. "The average ... student's life," wrote one journalist, "can safely be divided into three periods. In the fall the social development has the floor and city manners and every-day culture is absorbed. In the winter sports and social events are less freely indulged in and time becomes more valuable. In the spring cramming, plugging, grinding become the keenest desire of the most lackadaisical."[4]

Within the dynamic of provincial student life, organized activities in the years prior to the Great War ranged from those embodying high seriousness to others aimed at simple amusement and social intercourse. At Queen's University and at Victoria University, students demonstrated their awareness of and concern for the problems of national and international life. They complained about "blind adherence to party" in national politics; they recognized that "socialism," while perhaps "chimerical," was "a very plausible remedy for the ills of humanity"; they railed at the fact that the prohibition question, which had begun as a moral movement, had become "more and more a football for secondrate politicians, and a subject for mockery by men who have no faith in morals"; they decried the social costs of industrial combines.[5] Invariably, a major theme of student editorialists was one that sought to define what the essential responsibility of the modern student should be: active participation in the search for amelioration of such problems or temporary disengagement from them in order to pursue their academic studies and participate in extra-curricular social events.[6]

One of the first and most important organized student activities in Ontario universities, found at virtually all of them, was that of Christian missions. With the "opening up" of the Canadian west in the 1870s, the extension of evangelism into the "heathen nations" of the Orient in the 1880s, and the discovery of the "New Ontario" of mining towns and logging camps early in the twentieth century, the major Protestant denominations in Canada sought to extend their religious influence. Denominational colleges were a major source of recruitment. At Queen's University, Victoria University, and McMaster University missionary societies were early and continuing outlets for student energy and Christian conscience.[7] Moreover, since relations between women and men were distant and formal after the admission of the former into higher education, missionary organizations proved to be one social arena in which mutual interests could be shared. Actual recruitment of missionaries, whether for foreign or home service, largely involved men; but the hundreds of articles on various aspects of missionary activity that appeared in student newspapers from the 1880s until the Great War indicate that equal interest existed on the part of college women. In years when the occupational spheres of both sexes continued to be distinctly separate, the widespread interest in missions provided a common forum and a measure of equality. Moreover, if Canadian women interested in missionary work were like their American counterparts, women thus engaged could gain a measure of personal and vocational independence from men while not having to abandon their beliefs in Christian gentility and Victorian "womanliness."[8] In any event, the first joint society of men and women at

Victoria University was its Missionary Society, at which the sexes united in 1891.[9] On its executive board the next year were three men and two women.[10]

By the twentieth century a number of organized agencies existed for the generation of interest in missions and the recruitment of missionaries. The missionary departments of the separate denominations, the Young People's Forward Movement for Missions, the YMCA and YWCA, and the Student Volunteer Movement, as well as alumni who had become missionaries, provided a steady stream of speakers to campus organizations on conditions, folkways, and opportunities in China, Japan, Africa, and Canada itself.[11] The appeal for Christian missionary service worked. By the second decade of the twentieth century Ontario denominational colleges had provided scores of missionaries for overseas and home service – in Korea, India, and China, as well as in poverty-stricken districts of Canadian cities. Others devoted themselves to service as labourer-instructors for the "Frontier College" that the Queen's arts and theology graduate of the late nineteenth century, Alfred Fitzpatrick, had founded in 1899 to provide basic literacy skills (as well as political socialization) for the continental European immigrants who so largely populated the lumber and mining camps of northern Canada.[12]

The missionary spirit among students reflected a genuinely altruistic sensibility on the part of those who took part, directly or indirectly; but actual missionary activity involved a great deal of competition on the part of the different denominations for the heathen souls that constituted a source of moral capital for them – resulting in a seasonal count of converts whose numbers were compared, favourably or unfavourably, with those of competing denominations. Yet in the late nineteenth and early twentieth centuries the Christian soldiers who marched into benign missionary warfare for converts were not the only ones who imbued the spirit of competition with moral attributes. A second major form of extra-curricular student activity in Ontario universities was that of organized sports. And as with missions, such sports were conducted and justified within the framework of an informal moral code derived from the muscular Christianity of mid-Victorian England.

Late Victorian and Edwardian university sports in Ontario were conducted with a mixture of missionary zeal and martial ardour, and, in a complementary inversion of the way in which the Christian soldiers of the period were "marching as to war" in their attempt to convert other races and to Canadianize the European immigrants within Canada, so did rugby and hockey players do manly battle in the name of moral virtue. The very term "rugby" came from the English public school of that name. The school and its famous nineteenth-century headmaster, Thomas Arnold (father of critic and poet Matthew Arnold), became closely identified with the phrase "muscular Christianity" and the games-playing that was such an integral part of an English public-school education. [13] In the middle decades of the nineteenth century, sporting activities could be found on Ontario campuses, but these were usually conducted as occasional social events: students of Trinity might challenge the Toronto Cricket Club to a match, or students of Queen's compete for prizes offered by citizens of Kingston on their annual field-day. [14] Organized sports such as football could be found in Ontario by the early 1870s, but it is perhaps significant that real enthusiasm for the sport did not take place until the 1880s – in fact, precisely when women began to gain entrance to universities.

The *Queen's Journal*, for example, noted that a "Foot-Ball Club" was founded in the 1871–72 year, and by 1874 an Athletic Association had been formed; but on several occasions in 1879 student journalists found it necessary to remind the student body that the team and the Association still existed. Said one writer: "Before the interest in Athletic sports has vanished entirely would it not be well to organize an active and living Athletic Club, one not merely in name but in reality?" [15] But by 1885, just after Elizabeth Smith and her two female colleagues convocated as the first women graduates in medicine at the university and with a growing number of women enrolled in arts at Queen's, male interest had picked up considerably. The editor of the *Queen's Journal* welcomed the opening of a new gymnasium in that year: "If a man be weak and puny in body, he will, in nine cases out of ten, be weak and puny in his studies." [16]

From the mid-1880s on, organized athletic competition became an increasingly major part of extra-curricular life, and rugby football matches between Queen's, McGill, and Toronto were regular occurrences by the end of the decade, under the auspices of the Ontario Rugby Football Union until the Intercollegiate Rugby Football Union was formed in 1898. By then it was necessary to establish rules of eligibility preventing those not regularly "in attendance at lectures" from playing. Hockey was played at Victoria College by the last of its Cobourg years (the early 1890s); it had made its appearance at Queen's in the mid-eighties, but no organized club existed there until 1888. Soon, formal co-ordinating campus athletic associations began to be organized. The Trinity College Amateur Athletic Association was founded in 1892, four years after the women's residence of St Hilda's College was opened; at Victoria an Athletic Union appeared in 1894. At Queen's by the early 1890s informal student political parties developed within the Alma Mater Society. They were known as "the Sports" and "the Christians." [17] By the early twentieth century university sports such as hockey and rugby football were major public entertainment events.

In the world of Thomas Arnold, to be "muscular" meant also to be "manly," and the public-school "games ethic" of which such traits were a part was of enduring influence within the British Empire, including Canada, well into the twentieth century. [18] Yet the nearly simultaneous growth of

interest by male undergraduates in organized extramural sporting competition
and the appearance of women on campus may also be linked. Scholars of
American history have noted that the cult of manliness occurred at a time
when "genteel culture" was in the process of being "feminized," with the
sentimentalism of the liberal arts increasingly equated with feminine attributes.[19] Novelist Henry James captured the fear of male members of the
American gentry when, in his 1886 novel *The Bostonians*, one of his characters complained that "the whole generation is womanized; the masculine
tone is passing out of the world; it's a feminine, a nervous hysterical,
chattering, canting age, an age of hollow phrases and false delicacy and
exaggerated solicitudes and coddled sensibilities, which, if we don't look
out, will usher in the reign of mediocrity, of the feeblest, and flattest and
the most pretentious that has ever been seen."[20] Within such an anxious
milieu, in which Victorian males were increasingly uncertain how best to
assert themselves as "men," the cult of games and the articulation of the
characteristics of "manliness" were of therapeutic value. In such a context
manliness was less the opposite of childishness than it was of femininity.[21]

Charles W. Gordon ("Ralph Connor"), a student at the University of
Toronto in the 1880s, made the connection between organized sports, "manliness," and "femininity" in his autobiography, *Postscript of Adventure*. By
1879, he recalled wistfully, "a keen rivalry" existed between the "boys"
of Toronto, McGill, and Queen's in sporting as well as in academic matters.
"I say 'boys' for up till 1882 the sacred portals of universities in Canada
had not been opened to female students. While I personally voted for the
extension of university privileges to women I was conscious of a secret
feeling of which I was somewhat ashamed, that something of the lofty
splendor of university life had departed with the advent of women. It was
a little like playing baseball with a soft ball ... Though we found the young
ladies charming, if somewhat exclusive in their ways, there remained an
indefinable regret at the passing of a certain virility from University at the
coming of 'the skirts.'"[22]

"There was a time," wrote a Victoria University senior in 1904, "when
the popular conception of a college man was a near-sighted and spindle-
shanked individual, wearing a brow 'sicklied o'er with the pale cast of
thought,' and carrying in his hand some volume of the classics or of philosophy. *Tempora mutantur* and to-day the mental picture most readily called
up ... is, perhaps, that of a husky fellow in a padded suit with a rugby ball
under his arm." By then, the "athletic and social" side of university life
was threatening, in this student's view, to "overshadow the scholastic
side."[23] But the impulse towards athletics and action threatened more than
that: it also threatened the status of the clergy in the way it portrayed them
as physically weak and emotionally overwrought. By the latter part of the
nineteenth century, what had occurred rather earlier in America was also

happening in Ontario. The image of the clergy – and for that matter of the "artsman" – was becoming feminized. As historian Ann Douglas has demonstrated, the early nineteenth-century American minister and lady had been appointed by their society as "the champions of sensibility." But as the century progressed, as "genteel culture" was challenged by the harbingers of a more materialistic and crass socio-economic order, such virtues had become faults in men. In this way, "in what seemed the flush tide of American Protestantism, [ministers] often appeared as the laggards, hesitant promulgators of feminine virtues in an era of militant masculinity, strangers in the promised land ... Cut off at every point from his masculine heritage, whether economic, political, or intellectual, the liberal minister was pushed into a position increasingly resembling the evolving feminine one ... [He] was losing his role among his society's leaders; his place was increasingly in the Sunday School, the parlor, and the library, among women and those who flattered and resembled them."[24]

One woman student at Western University in 1908 created a fictionalized "girl-meets-boy" scene for her student newspaper column on "Western Girls." After "playing a lone hand nearly all evening" at the university's conversazione, a young man summons up courage and strikes up a conversation with a beautiful young lady. "He stopped for want of breath, thus giving the girl the chance to ask 'You aren't another of those Meds., are you?' Deeply humiliated by her tone he had to reply, 'Oh, no Miss, worse than that – I am divinity student, but I assure you I have some redeeming points."[25] By the end of the century ministers in Ontario were conscious of their tarnished image and their damaged status, and some sought to rectify matters. "The day is long gone by," said one student in *Acta Victoriana*, "when an unhealthy frame and physical weakness are part of the stock in trade of the ministry." He went on to stress the physical demands made on the ministry, the "commanding physical appearance" of ministers of yesteryear, and urged his readers to acquire, if necessary, the physical stature necessary to command respect: "The necessary elements are ... an upright carriage – square shoulders, bright eye and clear complexion – those outward signs which tell of steady nerve and good blood."[26]

By the early twentieth century students writing on "Athletics and Religion" could approvingly quote President Theodore Roosevelt's statement that athletics at Harvard were valuable because they helped turn out "vigorous men" instead of "mollycoddles." Moreover, continued the student, athletics and religion were compatible because both cultivated virtuous habits: courage, self-confidence, control of temper, and, above all, "the idea of fair-play,"[27] that cardinal virtue of muscular Christians. Ontario students often talked of their sporting activities along such lines. "Let the game be played for its own sake," said a McMaster student in 1914, "and if a victory cannot be gained by fair means, then surely it should not be gained at all."[28]

American college students' attitudes towards athletic competition, stressing victory rather than the cultivation of "character," often came under heavy criticism. "In Canada we are happily almost entirely free from such practices..." (such as the wearing of padded uniforms), said one smug Queen's student of the nineties. "Football is not a bowls, but a game in which hard knocks must be given and taken. Nevertheless in Canada it is as yet, we are glad to see, a manly game, and as such wholly free from the caddish tactics which disgrace American football. We hope that it will long be so, and that any changes which may be made in the Canadian game will be toward the British style of play, and the British spirit of honest, manly sport, rather than toward the American spirit, which in effect says: win, fairly if you can, but if not, win at any cost."[29] Symptomatic of the crassness of the American approach to organized athletics was the appearance of the "professional coach" on its campuses, thereby undermining the assumption that organized "manly games" should best be left to gentleman-amateurs. The innovation was roundly condemned in Canadian college circles for many years,[30] but by 1913 schools originally critical, such as Queen's, were coming to change their views, especially after suffering defeats by scores of 49–2.[31]

The cultivation of a spirit of fair play was fine, but by the early twentieth century students also recognized that the "real world" of careers in business and commerce was a harsh and competitive one. Advocates of manly sports also stressed that student athletics prepared young men for such a world. The old image of the university student as "a wizened old book-worm shut up in the gloomy recesses of a dingy library, familiar only with a race of dead men" increasingly reflected a reality of university life that was perceived to be passing out of existence. "Students are now trained for the battle of life rather than polished to meet the requirements of drawing-room society."[32] The successful man was one who embodied the resources made possible by physical education – "courage, endurance, aggressiveness," the ability to make "quick and accurate judgment, who is able to sacrifice himself, and who can 'honor while he strikes him down, The foe that comes with fearless eyes.' Not one of the qualities named but is developed by physical culture and athletic games."[33]

Such "foes" were perceived to be not only one's occupational competitors. In the international imperial rivalry among nations it was all the more imperative to develop a healthy and vigorous citizenry. "One of the most serious problems that confronts the British Empire," an American expert on physical education told the students of Queen's in 1907, "is the physical deterioration of the people in her towns and cities." In order to prevent such national inferiority and vulnerability, a few broken bones or forced joints were seen to be a price that must be paid, for in the process of engaging in strenuous athletic activities the student would learn

To set the cause above renown,
   To love the game beyond the prize,
To honor while you strike him down,
   The foe that comes with fearless eyes,
To count the life of battle good,
   And dear the land that gave you birth
And dearest yet the brotherhood
   That binds the brace of all the earth.[34]

In this way, to the notion of sport as an essentially male affair characterized by fair play in the heat of competitive battle, was added the idea of male bonding, as well as the suggestion that athletics was a peaceful substitute for the ultimate manly game: war.

Games as war, wars as game: the rhetoric of the fifteen years that preceded the Great War reflected the perceived affinities. The use of such elevated diction often carried with it, as in England,[35] an innocent, romantic, pseudo-medieval imagery, whether expressed in the context of athleticism or of military action. When students of Queen's left Kingston to play the University of Toronto in football, they "went forth ... to enter the lists with the Blue Knights of Varsity"; when they returned from such competition, it was a "sturdy band of warriors" that was welcomed home.[36] Sports columns at Western University carried inspirational poems, similar in their martial imagery, derived from the presumption of personal control, Christian self-abnegation, and purity of purpose: "I will go forth among men, not mailed in score. But in the armor of a pure intent."[37] University sermons were given on "The Game of Life," extolling the virtues of playing it "fairly and worthily" and urging that young men put their "best self" forward. "To play the game," the Reverend Professor S.W. Dyde told an audience of Queen's students, meant following the example of the English schoolboy. "To play the game is for him to subordinate himself to the team, to be manly, straightforward, fair to the other side." To illustrate his point, Dyde quoted from a poem in which, he said, "the ideal, kept before the English boy in the cricket-field, stood him in good stead afterwards in the sterner field of battle." One stanza went:

The sand of the desert in sodden red, –
   Red with the wreck of a square that broke; –
The gatlings jammed, and the colonel dead,
   And the regiment blind with dust and smoke.
The river of death has brimmed its banks,
   And England's far, and Honour a name,
But the voice of a school-boy rallies the ranks,
   "Play up! play up! and play the game!"[38]

The idealism that was so vital a part of nineteenth-century university life in Ontario could be put to many purposes, and Dyde as well as others in positions of power and responsibility played not only upon the students' spirit of youthful enthusiasm and their willingness to dedicate themselves to a righteous cause but also upon the meaning of a university itself. "It is an ideal working in them; it is the spirit of devotion to truth and goodness; it is a mystic and invisible society of truth-seekers."[39] It was such a conception of war, of games, and of the university, that Queen's history professor J.L. Morison embodied when, in arguing for military training at the universities in 1910, he declared: "Military training for defensive purposes is our purer duty, a privilege to be demanded as a right, and one of the manliest and most fascinating forms of recreation."[40] And students assimilated such values. "Our business in the field of fight," quoted the 1913–14 sports editor of the *McMaster University Monthly* in an epigraph to his column, "is not to question but to prove our might."[41]

By then the imperial spirit, dedicated to martial vigour, had already taken its place in the Ontario school system, both in the classroom and on the playing fields. The 1910 edition of the *Ontario Fourth Reader*, long used in the public schools of the province, was suffused with the ideology of imperial loyalty and personal sacrifice. "On the flyleaf," writes historian Robert Stamp, "beneath a beautifully coloured Union Jack, appeared the motto, 'One Flag / One Fleet / One Throne.' The first page was Kipling: 'Oh Motherland, we pledge to thee / Head, heart and hand through years to be.' There were verses from Henley: 'Mother of Ships whose might / England, my England.' There was a hymn of empire by Scott: 'Strong are we? Make us stronger yet; / Great? Make us greater far.' There was Thomson's 'Rule Britannia,' Campbell's 'Ye Mariners of England,' Macaulay's 'The Armada,' Byron's 'The Eve of Waterloo,' and Tennyson's 'Funeral of Wellington.'"[42] And so forth, for more than four hundred pages. As early as the 1890s provincial legislation had allowed for classes in military instruction in public schools. By 1900 thirty-three Ontario schools had established corps of military cadets, and the creation in 1909 by Lord Strathcona of a half-million-dollar trust fund for physical and military training in Canadian schools, combined with widespread public interest in Canada's military preparedness, increased pressure for a military component in the field of public education. The federal militia, which controlled the Strathcona Trust, naturally emphasized the military side of the physical-military coin. This was particularly the case after the 1911 appointment of Sam Hughes, brother of Ontario Superintendent of Schools James Hughes, as federal minister of Militia.[43]

Athleticism and militarism were also supported in university circles. In 1911, upon the election of a federal Conservative government intent upon increasing Canada's military capacity, Canadian universities formally considered the formation of an officer-training program to be patterned after the Officers' Training Corps, created in England in 1908. After negotiations with the Canadian government McGill University formed a unit of the Canadian Officers' Training Corps (1912). At Queen's, after an offer of private funding by Major R.W. Leonard, Principal D.M. Gordon, while professing his abhorrence of war, actively promoted a scheme to build a residence for COTC recruits on the university grounds. Under Leonard's proposal the residence would be superintended by a military officer, and military discipline would be expected. O.D. Skelton, for one, objected privately to the "cheap bribery of bed and board offered to induce students to join," stressing the divisive effect such a scheme would have on the student body: "It would do much to shift the whole centre of gravity of the university." Deeply disturbed by these developments, Skelton could find no defence for them on either "physical or moral grounds: a university which cannot train a man in self discipline & self control otherwise than by teaching him the goose step has failed in its mission."[44]

Nevertheless, well-known university officials such as Principal William Peterson of McGill University continued to urge, in speech after speech, the necessity of military preparedness by wedding the English-Canadian identification with British imperial spirit to the future of Canadian national integrity. Experts in the humanities also told of the virtues of empire. James Cappon, professor of English at Queen's University, eulogized the British Empire in a way that bore testimony to the Hegelian idealism he had learnt at the feet of philosopher John Watson's mentor, Edward Caird, when he was at university in Glasgow. "The Empire," said Cappon early in the century, "represents an ideal of high importance for the future of civilization, the attempt to assemble in a higher unity than even that of nationality the forces which maintain and advance the white man's ideals of civilization, his sense of justice, his constitutional freedom, his respect for law and order, his humanity." On the eve of the Great War classicist Maurice Hutton, principal of University College, Toronto, set forward a similar idealistic imperial vision that portrayed British imperialism as the world's defender of Christian ethics and political liberty. Wars, he told his students, "were fought by professional soldiers full of love of fighting, full of joy of adventure, full of a certain honourable spirit and chivalry about the rule of fair fighting, full of a very real and universal feeling of sportsmanship and fairplay."[45]

To portray student life before the Great War as being dominated completely by athletics or martial ardour would, however, be to misrepresent it. By 1914 a rich variety of activities quite distinct from those of the classroom or the library was available to Ontario university students, and the evidence suggests that they took advantage of them. No longer was it possible to portray a distinct student type, whether in moral attributes or in dress. "As a matter of fact," a London journalist had written in 1903, "the university youth branches into as many branches and sub-varieties as the diligent botanist may find among the festive fungi of autumn. The only type not found among our freshmen is the Gibsonesque mummy whom school girls worship in the pages of American magazines."[46] The Gibson Girl – the creation of lithographer Charles Dana Gibson and first appearing in *Life* magazine in the mid-1890s – marked a departure in the portrayal of American feminine beauty in mass magazines. "Tall and commanding, with thick, dark hair swept upward in the prevailing pompadour style," her figure was more slender than that of the voluptuous woman of the Victorian era. She was small of mouth, with a snub nose, but was generous in bosom and hip. For some feminists she embodied the image of the New Woman, for she was often portrayed in situations where either her independence and athletic capacity or her social graces were evident.[47]

Campus newspapers in Ontario did not reflect the impact of the Gibson Girl to any direct extent in the first few years of the twentieth century, but papers such as *Varsity* and *Queen's Journal* did portray the bewildering complexity of campus life. They also changed from a magazine to a newspaper format. (*Varsity* did so in 1908, the *Journal* in 1911). Now less forums for discussing ideas and for publishing "serious writing," the new-look student newspapers reflected the discovery of fashions and fads by students and of the university student as consumer by retailers. Display advertising increased dramatically, and students were bombarded with pitches for underwear, hats, coats, dry-cleaning, cooking ranges, shoes, sporting goods, pianos, flowers, and books. By 1914 at Queen's, advertisers in its newspaper were attempting to sell "Society Brand Clothes" by means of lithographic portrayals of Gibsonesque types dressed in the height of sartorial elegance at formal social events.

Woman's perceived social role was still relatively circumscribed, but now it had expanded beyond the domestic sphere and into forms of service to the state. The female undergraduate continued to be channelled, however, into particular academic departments and faculties. At Queen's University in 1912–13, for example, of two hundred and fifty women registered intramurally, two hundred and thirty-three were in arts and the remaining seventeen were in education. A year earlier, of thirty-two students enrolled in education, twenty-three were women.[48] "Women's Department" columns in student newspapers, as often as not, supported and justified such limited roles, with the essence of "womanliness" portrayed as "a divine quality which subtly reveals itself in tone, glance, and act."[49] It may be that at times, faced with the increasingly aggressive, "manly" persona projected by male undergraduates as a social image, females found comfort, security, and a degree of camaraderie in the cultivation of distinctly "feminine" traits. In this sense, a tea party could be a political act.

Yet the female undergraduate of the early twentieth century was by no means placid and submissive. At times she took exception to condescending male vocabulary. As one irate coed wrote: "And about 'fairness' and 'beauty' – when will the masculine mind grasp the fact that girls don't live and move and have their being on pretty speeches! The average man thinks that if he says something neat on 'beauty' or 'grace' that no sane girl can withstand him. We would like to educate you out of that. If you really mean them, and feel you *must* give expression to your feelings or expire, all well and good, but don't think that we cherish them and value them for anything more than they are really worth. Their economic value, even at election times, is comparatively small." By 1914, when these sentiments were expressed, women at McMaster refused to accept the design of a pin suggested by the men as a university emblem. Male students feared an overly "feminine" design for the pin and declared that they would "never consent to adorn their bosoms with filigree and seed pearls." For women students the issue was essentially a political one: when decisions were made, they wanted an equal voice.[50] The year 1913, noted the editor of the Women's Department of the *McMaster University Monthly*, had been one of "great advances" in the "Women's Cause," especially with respect to the suffrage. "But for us," she said, "'Woman's Cause' has the wider meaning – the opportunity for the expression of women's newly-found selves. Woman is an individual, else why were two beings created instead of one? Individuality is her birthright; and so is the expression of this individuality."[51]

This new-found freedom was not simply a manifestation of the "battle of the sexes." It was, perhaps, more a manifestation of an important relationship between them. Historian Peter Ward has argued persuasively that during the nineteenth century English Canadian young adults consistently enlarged the "social space" in which courtship took place. While chaperonage continued throughout the century, youths – especially women – increasingly assumed control over the organization of their social lives. "By the later nineteenth century the sexes held much courtship territory in common. The parlour remained women's courting preserve, but men and women had greater access to one another in public spaces, spaces free of restrictions on entry and free of close oversight."[52] In this context college activities involving a mixing of the sexes can be seen in part as the necessary social rituals leading to the possibility of courtship, and they involve many of the same tensions between youths and chaperones inherent in the alteration of the forms of social space noted by Ward.

The new individuality on campus was expressed in many ways, but none more so in the years prior to the Great War than the resistance of students to the quasi-parental control by university officials of their social activity. After 1910 both sexes were willing to express their desire for more social contact, and this usually meant pressure on authorities for an increased number of dances. In 1911, 285 students from the Ontario Agricultural College and the Macdonald Institute petitioned the minister of Agriculture to rescind the prohibition on mixed dancing in Guelph. "This has resulted," they complained, "in a great deal of wholesome pleasure being lost to the students, and has made our social functions very lacking in enjoyment." The same year a major issue at Queen's was whether the university's senate would continue to permit two dances per month. Students at the University of Toronto worried in 1912 whether the demolition of the old gymnasium would result in an absence of facilities for the Union Dance, the Rugby Dance, the Medical "At-Home," the Arts Dance, and the School of Applied Science Dance.[53]

The craze for dancing was a major issue in the university and daily press in Toronto during the last few months of lingering Victorian innocence. The fact was, however, that the sense of innocence existed less at the universities than it did in the expectations of the public. In December 1913 the Toronto News broke the story that a "Tango Party," involving five men and "some chorus girls," had apparently been held in the North Residence Building of the University of Toronto.[54] From that point on during the academic year both the News and the Toronto Telegram kept a watchful eye on campus life, reflecting their readers' fears of possible sexual impropriety on the part of students, who were expected to be models of youthful innocence. Organized dances were closely observed by the press, and, sure enough, students were seen to be doing the tango. In an earlier era the waltz had been condemned because it provided the possibility of public bodily contact between the sexes. Now, it appeared, on campuses in the United States and Canada, young men and women prized the waltz – with its "look but do not touch" image – less than they did the one-step, the bunny hug, and other dances that "allowed a lingering close contact."[55] In this context, fear of the tango represented the fear of society that previously well-defined sex roles, particularly that of the sexually antiseptic, angelic woman, were disintegrating. The tango was not a dance; it was a threat.

The Toronto daily press portrayed the "tango craze" in tones combining sarcasm and titillation. "That naughty yellow-haired maiden, the Tango," wrote a Star reporter, "is having a sort of peekaboo dance around the college halls this winter, and every time she gets up quite close to the patronesses and professors they discreetly close their eyes and pretend they don't see her." President Robert Falconer of the University of Toronto denied in reply that student dances were "indelicate" and assured the public that they were "in the hands of the patronesses," who, he was certain, "would not countenance such a dance as the Tango." Varsity also came to the aid of student virtue, but in terms that scarcely reassured the public: "The Tango, as everyone knows, includes a great number of dances, some of which are objectionable and some are not. If the Tango maid mentioned in the Star is to represent all the modern fancy dances, they are quite right in saying that the Tango maid has appeared around the college halls."[56] By February of 1914 even students were caught up in the near hysteria. The University of Toronto Undergraduate Committee, in charge of dances and being lobbied intensively by both male and female students, banned the wearing of corsages on the grounds that it had become necessary to curb the "unreasonable custom of young ladies being decorated in a semi-barbarous manner with vivid bouquets at all the dances." The *News*, which carried the story, added that the committee, "acting under advice of certain of the University authorities, 'have found it essential to issue an injunction against the indulgence in the new dances.'"[57]

By then not even the Methodist atmosphere of Victoria College was immune to the dance craze. At officially sanctioned "promenades" some imaginative student organizers managed to position the orchestra on the landing of the second floor of the residence, where the promenade was held. Then, with music wafting up to the third floor, "many couples ... danced to their heart's content while clergymen and Methodist supporters paced the lower floors in blissful ignorance." But in the end, Methodist discipline prevailed. The student body as a whole, as well as the Women's Literary Society, passed resolutions banning student dancing in the college. The result, by the spring of 1914, was "a barricaded stairs, and a dark third floor."[58]

The third floor, the floor of youthful joy, would remain in darkness for four bleak years.

NOTES

1 *Queen's Journal*, 8 Nov. 1890, 2; 10 Dec. 1890, 34; 1 Dec. 1894, 48.

2 Ibid., 16 Nov. 1910, 93. In the official report from the Queen's Department of History for the academic year 1911–12, Professor Morison wrote: "I could wish that apart from definite examination and essay work, there was more real interest in reading for its own sake; apart from that want on the part of the students, which concerns not History alone, but all the Departments, I have no reason to complain. If anything could be done to cut down social functions, work would greatly gain." Queen's University, *Report of the Principal, 1911–12* (Kingston 1912) 10.

3 "Enthusiasm in the University – An Interview Criticized by President Loudon," Toronto *Mail*, 18 Nov. 1899; "Varsity's Big Program Ready for Next Week – Lectures and Tennis Tournament Begin Monday – Receptions to Freshies and Freshettes Follow – the Difficulties of Enrollment – Students Awed by Display of Faculty Robes," Toronto *Star*, 1 Oct. 1910.

4 "The Week at Varsity," Toronto *Telegram*, 6 Feb. 1911.

5 On *partyism*, see *Queen's Journal*, 20 Mar. 1891, 145; 20 Jan. 1892; "Political
  partyism at Queen's," 27 Nov. 1913. On *socialism*, see *Queen's Journal*, 4 Apr.
  1896, 172; review of Agnes Maule Machar's *Roland Graeme, Knight*, 21 Jan.
  1893, 74–5. On American *expansionism*, see "American Expansion," *Queen's
  Journal*, 24 Dec. 1898, 56–7. On *prohibition*, see "The Present Phase of the Prohibition Question," *Queen's Journal*, 1 Apr. 1899, 152–3. On *combines*, see
  "Editorial," *Queen's Journal*, 12 Feb. 1914, 4–5. Although illustrations have
  here been drawn from Queen's University, other universities also exhibited degrees of social concern. See, for example, W.A. Lamport, "Is the Baptist Position in Reference to the Manitoba School Question Consistent?" *McMaster
  University Monthly* (Apr. 1896): 296–304; George J. Menge, "The Social Problem," ibid., (Mar. 1901): 255–60. For Victoria University, using *Acta Victoriana*
  as a source, see "Looking Backward" [review of Edward Bellamy's *Looking
  Backward* (1888)], *Acta Victoriana* (Jan. 1890): 14–15; "Editorial" [re Labour-
  Capital relations] (Dec. 1892): 3–4; W.G. Watson, "Christian Socialism" (Feb.
  1894): 154–9; W.J. Conoly, "Compulsory Arbitration" (Dec. 1894): 84–6; A.H.
  Sinclair, "Labour and Capital" (May 1896): 380–4; J.B. Gibson, "Prohibition as
  a Problem of Individual and Social Reform" (Dec. 1890): 105–11, and (Feb.
  1901): 248–56; F.L. Farewell, "The Church and Social Problems" (Oct. 1903):
  31–8; W.E. Gilroy, "Christian Socialism" (Dec. 1903): 224–9. The list could be
  extended greatly for the years prior to the Great War.
6 See, for example: "The Student's Attitude toward the Everyday World," *Acta
  Victoriana* (Nov. 1900): 71–2; "What a College Course Should Be," ibid. (Feb.
  1899): 367–70; R.H. Bell, "Some Manifestations of Our College Life," ibid.
  (April 1899): 455–62; "The Student's Attitude to College Activities," ibid. (Oct.
  1902): 37; "Student Life at Victoria," ibid. (June 1905): 556–9.
7 "Missionary Association," *Queen's Journal*, 22 Nov. 1873, 6; "Queen's College
  Missionary Association," ibid., 16 March 1886, 122–3; "Intercollegiate Missionary Alliance," *Acta Victoriana* (Dec. 1887): 6–7; "The Sixth Annual Convention
  of the Canadian Inter-Collegiate Missionary Alliance," ibid. (Dec. 1890): 19–21;
  "Ninth Annual Report of the Fyfe Missionary Society," *McMaster University
  Monthly* (Nov. 1891): 69–73; "Thirteenth Annual Report of the Fyfe Missionary
  Society," ibid. (Jan. 1896): 170–7; "Canadian Inter-Collegiate Missionary Alliance, Thirteenth Biennial Convention," ibid. (Dec. 1900): 121–5.
8 See Jane Hunter, *The Gospel of Gentility: American Women Missionaries in
  Turn-of-the-Century China* (New Haven: Yale University Press 1984).
9 C.B. Sissons, *A History of Victoria University* (Toronto: University of Toronto
  Press 1952), 197.
10 "Re-organization of the Missionary Society," *Acta Victoriana* (Jan. 1892): 19.
11 Each issue of every student newspaper contained missionary notices, but see, for
  example: "The Origin of the Young People's Forward Movement for Missions,"
  Acta Victoriana (May 1902): 446–8; "Great Convention of Students Will Meet in
  Toronto," ibid. (Jan. 1902): 239–40; A.B. Williams [Students' YMCA Secretary for

Canada and the East], "A Significant Student Movement," ibid. (March 1903): 401–3; J.G. Hume, "The Canadian Colleges' Mission," ibid. (Dec. 1907): 198–200; "A Summer in New Ontario," in *In Cap and Gown* [Western University], 19 Feb. 1908, 102–4; "Intercollegiate Y.M.C.A.," *Queen's Journal*, 19 Nov. 1906, 88; "Peregrine Preachers or Practical Experiences in New Ontario," ibid., 15 Jan. 1907, 209–11; "Protestant Missions," ibid., 1 Feb. 1907, 317–18; "The Student Volunteer Band," ibid., 16 Nov. 1910, 95; "University Service – Rev. J.D. Byrnes, Supt. of Missions, Gives Us a Vivid Account of Conditions in Great North Country, and Future Prospects – An Appeal for Help," ibid., 26 Jan. 1914, 1.

12 Alfred Fitzpatrick, *The University in Overalls* (Toronto: Hunter-Rose 1920).
13 See David Newsome, *Godliness and Good Learning* (London: John Murray 1961), 80–2.
14 *Trinity 1852–1952* (Toronto: Trinity College 1952) 28; Hilda Neatby, *"And Not to Yield": Queen's University, 1841–1917* (Montreal: McGill-Queen's University Press 1978), 143.
15 See "The Foot-Ball Club," *Queen's Journal*, 31 Oct. 1874, 7; also 5 Apr. 1879, 1; 25 Oct. 1879, 1; 20 Dec. 1879, 50.
16 *Queen's Journal*, 25 Nov. 1885, 30.
17 *Trinity 1852–1952*, 27–34; Sissons, *Victoria University*, 202–3, 212–13; Neatby, *"And Not to Yield,"* 200, 212–13; D.D. Calvin, *Queen's University at Kingston* (Kingston: Queen's University 1941), 277–87.
18 See J.A. Mangan, *Athleticism in the Victorian and Edwardian Public School: The Emergence and Consolidation of an Educational Ideology* (Cambridge: Cambridge University Press 1981); and Mangan, *The Games Ethic and Imperialism: Aspects of the Diffusion of an Ideal* (New York: Viking 1986).
19 See Ann Douglas, *The Feminization of American Culture* (New York: Avon Books 1977).
20 Quoted in Stow Persons, *The Decline of American Gentility* (New York: Columbia University Press 1973), 275.
21 Joseph F. Kett, *Rites of Passage: Adolescence and Youth in America, 1790 to the Present* (New York: Basic Books 1977), 173; David I. Macleod, *Building Character in the American Boy: The Boy Scouts, YMCA, and Their Forerunners, 1870–1920* (Madison: University of Wisconsin Press 1983), 44–5, passim; Michael Rosenthal, *The Character Factory: Baden-Powell's Boy Scouts and the Imperatives of Empire* (New York: Partheon Books 1986), 88–107, passim; Carol Christ, "Victorian Masculinity and the Angel in the House," in Martha Vicinus, ed., *A Widening Sphere: Changing Roles of Victorian Women* (Bloomington: Indiana University press 1980), 146–62.
22 Charles W. Gordon, *Postscript to Adventure: The Autobiography of Ralph Connor* (Toronto: Macmillan 1975), 39–40.
23 Senior, "First Things in College Life," *Acta Victoriana* (Oct. 1904): 27.
24 Douglas, *Feminization of American Culture*, 12, 23, 48–9.

25 "The One Who Peeped," "Western Girls – Beware of Cosy Corners," in *In Cap and Gown* (March 1908): 150–1.
26 A.P. Addison, "The Ministry and Athletics," *Acta Victoria* (Apr. 1897): 361–2.
27 R. Pearson (1904), "Athletics and Religion," ibid. (March 1907): 366–70.
28 N. Davies (1914), "Athletics," *McMaster University Monthly* (Feb. 1914): 222.
29 *Queen's Journal*, 2 Dec. 1893, 35.
30 See, for example, "Professional Coaching in Football," *Queen's Journal*, 19 Nov. 1906, 84; "The Rugby Situation," ibid., 21 Oct. 1913, 2, 5.
31 "The Failure of Our Rugby Team – The Sporting Editor gives His Views – Advocates Recognition of Athletes by Faculty, More Liberal Financial Support, and the Hiring of a Professional Coach," ibid., 16 Oct. 1913, 1.
32 "The College Man and Business," *Acta Victoriana* (Feb. 1904): 333.
33 "Editorials – Physical Education," *Queen's Journal*, 1 March 1907, 342.
34 R. Tait McKenzie, MD, professor of Physical Education and director of the Department of Physical Education, University of Pennsylvania, *Queen's Journal*, 1 Feb. 1907, 247. See also W.H.M., "A History of the Gymnasium Movement in Queen's," ibid., 1 Feb. 1907, 243–6.
35 See Paul Fussell, *The Great War and Modern Memory* (New York: Oxford University Press 1975), 18–23, passim.
36 *Queen's Journal*, 9 Nov. 1900, 50; 7 Dec. 1900, 85.
37 "Intercollege Football," in *In Cap and Gown* (Dec. 1907): 41.
38 Rev. S.W. Dyde, "University Sermon – 'The Game of Life,'" *Queen's Journal*, 9 Dec. 1899, 66–7.
39 Ibid., 67.
40 *Queen's Journal*, 16 Nov. 1910, 89–90.
41 N. Davies (1914), "Athletics," *McMaster University Monthly* (Dec. 1913): 129. See also Michael Pearlman, "To Make The University Safe for Morality: Higher Education, Football and Military Training from the 1890s through the 1920s," *Canadian Review of American Studies* 12 (Spring 1981): 137–56.
42 Robert M. Stamp, *The Schools of Ontario, 1876–1976* (Toronto: University of Toronto Press 1982), 93.
43 Ibid., 93–4.
44 O.D. Skelton to D.M. Gordon, 17 Dec. 1913, D.M. Gordon Papers, box 3, section A, Queen's University Archives. Gordon's eighteen-page unpublished speech, "University Military Training," undated but clearly written around this time (in the same source), provides an elaborate rationale for extensive military training on campus. See also: Neatby, *"And Not to Yield,"* 292; Hartley Munro Thomas, *The History of the UWO Contingent, COTC* (London: University of Western Ontario 1956), 3–6.
45 William Peterson, *Canadian Essays and Addresses* (London: Longmans 1915), 87–154; Cappon and Hutton quoted in S.E.D. Shortt, *The Search for an Ideal* (Toronto; University of Toronto Press 1976), 74–5, 91. See also Allan Franklin Bowker, "Truly Useful Men: Maurice Hutton, George Wrong, James Mavor and

the University of Toronto, 1880–1927" (PhD thesis, University of Toronto 1975), 50–71; Carl Berger, *The Sense of Power* (Toronto: University of Toronto Press 1970), passim.

46 "Students Are Back to Work – Organizing Societies at Western University," University of Western Ontario Scrapbook 1 (1903–06), University of Western Ontario Archives.

47 See Lois W. Banner, *American Beauty* (New York: Alfred A. Knopf 1983), chap. 8, "The Gibson Girl," 155–74. See also Lynn B. Gordon, "The Gibson Girl Goes to College: Popular Culture and Women's Higher Education in the Progressive Era, 1890–1920," *American Quarterly* 39 (Summer 1987): 211–30.

48 "A Splendid Address – Principal Gordon Thinks Women's Sphere Has Now Extended to the State," *Queen's Journal*, 19 Jan. 1912, 3; Queen's University, *Report of the Principal, 1912–13* (Kingston 1913), 14–15; Queen's University, *Report of the Principal, 1911–12* (Kingston 1912), 23.

49 *Queen's Journal*, 3 Dec. 1906, 144.

50 "Editorial Notes," *McMaster University Monthly* (March 1914): 255; "Women's Department," ibid. (April 1914): 315–16.

51 Miss Mary Fowler (1914), "Women's Department," ibid. (Feb. 1914): 7.

52 Peter Ward, "Courtship and Social Space in Nineteenth-Century English Canada," *Canadian Historical Review* 68, no. 2 (Mar. 1987): 56, 60–61.

53 "Students Plead for Dancing at the Agricultural College – Largely Signed Petition Urging Its Permission Sent to the Minister of Agriculture," Toronto *Mail and Empire*, 9 Jan. 1911; "About Our Social Affairs," *Queen's Journal*, 4 Dec. 1911, 1; "Students May Dance at the University School," Toronto *Globe*, 9 Oct. 1912.

54 "Tango Party Reprimanded – President Falconer Is Preparing at Statement," Toronto *News*, 6 Dec. 1913.

55 See Ellen K. Rothman, *Hands and Hearts: A History of Courtship in America* (New York: Basic Books 1984), 211–12; Paula S. Fass, *The Damned and the Beautiful: American Youth in the 1920s* (New York: Oxford University Press 1977), 23–5.

56 "No Objectionable Tangoing at Varsity – Report of 'Toronto Star' – Fancy Dances at Varsity Are Not of Indelicate Kind – President Falconer's Opinion," *Varsity*, 17 Dec. 1913.

57 "Flowers and Tango under Student Ban – 'Sentimental Corsages' Will Not Be Allowed at the Undergraduates' Dance," Toronto *News*, 5 Feb. 1914; "Cold Shoulder for Tango," Toronto *Telegram*, 14 Feb. 1914.

58 "When Students' Fancies Clash With Religion – What Will Methodists Do About Dancing? – Victoria College Craze," *Montreal Star*, clippings, Dec. 1913, in "Student Activities – General," vol. 20, file 1, University of Toronto Archives.

CHAPTER FIVE

Hazes, Hustles, Scraps, and Stunts: Initiations at the University of Toronto, 1880–1925*

Keith Walden

Over the past decade there has been a marked shift in the writing of university history to take into account the experiences of students as well as those of faculty and administrators.[1] This has derived in part from broader investigations of youth as a distinct social category,[2] but it is also a product of the reorientation of social history to recover the perspective of those who have been ignored heretofore in historical accounts. The effort to reincorporate the experiences of forgotten people, who often left no written records of their own, has led some historians to a new appreciation of the significance of social actions. Using anthropological approaches, they have tried to decipher the meaning embedded in various forms of communal activity. In particular, rituals and other kinds of festive life have attracted notice because they help to order society while simultaneously revealing tensions arising from that order.[3] They perform important functions in and of themselves but also convey messages which are acted rather than spoken.

While many individual students were not mute historical participants, there is more uncertainty about the evolving nature of their experience as a collectivity. Especially after the founding of school papers in the latter part of the nineteenth century, collegians could pontificate at length about their circumstances, but whether the few who wrote expressed representative views or identified all areas of concern is open to question. With students as well, then, it is useful to consider the rituals they performed. These were an important, time-consuming part of undergraduate life, uniting many individuals in common activity. Moreover, since the continuities of these symbolic performances usually were consciously considered, they provide a more coherent focus for probing the long-term expansion of the university from the perspective of those on its bottom rungs than would merely dipping into school papers from decade to decade.

Collegians had many rituals – parades, dinners, sports events, and dances, to mention just a few – but one of the most prominent was initiation. Most campuses had procedures to incorporate newcomers into their midst, procedures that were memorable because they involved unusual forms of behaviour and influential because they were performed by impressionable people trying to assimilate the norms and conventions of an unfamiliar milieu. Initiations were important not because they changed participants in and of themselves but because they made manifest particular sets of relationships, values, and concerns. As symbolic demonstrations they were just as relevant to upper classes as to first year. Because they attempted to communicate something fundamental about student culture, because they were premeditated, their forms were deliberate and considered. No other ritual conveyed more effectively the essence of the students' view of their collective existence, and yet virtually no effort has been made to investigate them.

The purpose of this study is straightforward. Using the University of Toronto between 1880 and 1925 as a case study, it attempts to answer two sets of questions. First, what form did initiations take; how did they evolve, and how did university authorities respond to them? Second, why were these rituals performed, and what do they indicate about the changing circumstances of student existence? The paper will trace the rites of male and female students at University College, largest of Varsity's affiliated units, and to a lesser extent those of medical and engineering students.[4] These events, it must be admitted, are somewhat elusive. Because they were often secret or semi-secret, because they seemed so removed from consequential affairs of the world, records of what was done were not kept in any consistent way. What was vital got passed along by action and oral tradition. For the most part it is impossible to say who or how many participated, though the message of these social dramas was not limited to those directly involved. However, by examining administrative records, city dailies, and especially college papers, it is possible to get a clear sense of their formal aspects and thereby grasp a great deal of their meaning.

The years from 1880 to the mid-1920s were years of profound change for North American higher education. In the nineteenth century the university emerged, in the words of Burton Bledstein, "as the seminal institution within the culture of professionalism."[5] Acquiring specialized expertise became a prominent middle-class career strategy, and colleges took on the job of dispensing formal credentials. Getting an education became a much more serious business. With increased demands for their services, universities began to grow like topsy, expanding both the size of classes and the range of offerings. Women forced the gates of academe in growing numbers, recasting the character of campus society, but male clienteles changed as well. As degrees became prerequisite for certain careers, more high-school graduates moved on immediately to higher studies, lowering the relative age of student bodies. On top of this, colleges had to respond to intellectual developments such as Darwinism, which had an enormous impact on curriculum, indeed on the whole rationale of higher education.[6]

Varsity was no exception to all this. University College, for example, had a student body of 113 when it opened in 1853. By 1880 it had tripled to 349, and at the turn of the century, sixteen years after women were admitted to degree programs, it was up to 556.[7] The First World War eventually did crimp enrolments, but only temporarily: in 1924, 1,286 were attending.[8] This pattern was repeated not only in the other arts colleges but also in professional faculties for medicine, engineering, education, and forestry, which had been organized in the 1880s and after. Growth had advantages, especially for those who wanted to study new subjects like political economy, English literature, and psychology, but it was concomitant with higher degrees of competition, heavier intellectual demands, and the necessity of adjustment to an institution that was in constant flux.[9] All these had an impact on students. Initiations became a key instrument for generating group consciousness, inculcating the values of college society, and pinpointing the anxieties of student life. They facilitated an acceptance of changing conditions, but they also provided a focus for resistance to disturbing aspects of industrial capitalist society.

Much of what is known about the character of early initiations stems from an incident that occured in 1881.[10] Perhaps untypical in some respects, it does confirm a general pattern suggested by other bits and pieces of evidence from the period. In mid-November it became known that the Glee Club was rehearsing a number containing disparaging remarks about freshmen for an upcoming Literary and Scientific Society gathering. An attempt by the first year to thwart the intended insult was forestalled by seniors, who kidnapped four ringleaders and locked them into a third-floor residence room. Though one of the instigators managed to escape through a window with tied sheets, the rest of the class did nothing to disrupt the program. After the meeting the remaining prisoners were produced, tried, and ordered to sing the offending ditty. Having performed "after the manner of an ancient Pistol eating his leek," they were released. Fifteen seniors were hauled before the college council and made to promise that such proceedings would not recur, but the press got wind of the story and loudly decried what the *Globe* described as "the most disgraceful outrage that has ever yet occurred in College circles in this city." The reaction was overblown, for, as "A Third Year Man" pointed out in a letter to the *World*, this was just one of a long series of such acts in recent years.[11] Besides confirming that hazing was already well established, the incident points up a number of features of initiations in the 1880s. First, it reveals the central role of the University College residence. So strong was the connection that one student immediately denounced its "bullying inmates" for acting without the support of those who lived outside. This was flatly contradicted by four upperclassmen, who insisted that over two-thirds of the eighty-five men at the trial and full three-quarters of its presiding officials were non-residents. It was, they protested, "a concerted action of the senior years, and all sections of the undergraduates were represented."[12] Nevertheless, the residence, which housed about forty boarders, was obviously a convenient, relatively private site for student capers, and frosh who lived there were more likely to be targeted for hazing pranks.[13] They could be seized more easily, but also they were under more intense scrutiny by their betters. However, non-residents, lured to the campus by Literary Society meetings or fraudulent team lists, certainly were not immune.[14]

Second, the 1881 affair reveals that many of the proceedings were highly structured, usually based on the format of a trial presided over by a Grand Caliph or Mufti. In 1885, for example, a post-Literary Society assembly

resolved itself into Mufti, solemnly arrayed, a dozen true and honest-looking jurymen, learned counsel for and against the prisoners, the zealous crier, ushers sturdy and watchful, ubiquitous reporters, and, finally, eager and all-attentive spectators. The mysteries of the orthodox knee-drill, grovellings, gallops passings, together with diverse other arcanal rites, were duly inculcated into the delinquents after their case had been more or less carefully and leniently considered by the court. And it must not be imagined that the eminent counsel for the defence left a stone unturned to secure their acquittal. But the odds were against him, for, not to talk of the vigilance on the part of the prosecution, the plea of mental aberration on which much reliance had been laid was preemptorily disposed of by his lordship.

Not all hazings were this elaborate. Victims were often dealt with singly and by much smaller groups. Campus wit "Jay Kobb" recalled a nocturnal visit by Mufti and his "muffled gang," who made him "dance a horn-pipe on the bed" and "made the floor with foamy substance shine." It was unnecessary, apparently, to convene a full court on all occasions.[15]

Mufti was a figure of some significance, and yet little is known about who occupied the position or why. The only detailed clues about the nature of this august personage relate to William Beattie Nesbitt, who, according to President Daniel Wilson, filled the role in 1887. Nesbitt, later a prominent Conservative, was twenty-one at the time, in his third year. He owed his authority to an imposing physical presence, a reputation for recklessness and fun, and an ability to organize. His service with the 1885 Saskatchewan expedition, which crushed the Riel Rebellion, did no harm. Probably, Mufti was chosen by his fellow students from among those who lived in residence, but the position was not tied strictly to seniority.[16] Magnetism and conviviality were likely given a heavy weighting.

Mystery surrounding the Mufti points up a third feature of these initiations – the effort to maintain secrecy and surprise. This was easily accomplished when single individuals were targeted. "Sir Cheekie Freshman," roused from a sound sleep by hideous figures who carried him into the college tower, was obviously caught completely off guard. Elaborate proceedings were more difficult to shroud, but rumours of their imminence may have been deliberately spread. Seniors, no doubt, took delight in the anticipatory anxiety of their quarry. *Varsity*, the student paper, had no compunction about reporting in January 1881 that a "Conspirators Club" had been formed, the laudable object of which, "an open secret," would become known by light of events soon to take place. Large or small, these happenings tended to occur at night in settings that, if possible, were cramped and eerie, and hinted of danger. The unfinished, earthen-floored cellars beneath the college's convocation hall were a favourite location, as were the banks of Taddle Creek, which ran through the campus. Completing the emphasis on mystery was the effort to persuade victims to make "solemn declarations of secrecy" so the impact of future ceremonies would not be diminished.[17]

A fourth feature was the careful selection of victims. The freshmen involved in 1881 were not randomly plucked. Apologists often justified initiations as necessary for the correction of character and behavioural faults. "No sooner do the freshmen enter college," observed N.H. Russell in 1886, "than a hungry watch is set on them to determine who shall be hazed." Misdeeds included disgusting eating habits, mutilating lecture benches, putting on airs, and usurping privileges deemed to be the prerogative of seniors, like sporting canes, escorting ladies, or sitting at certain tables in the library.[18] Punishments varied according to the crime. Mufti Nesbitt, for example, convinced a militant anti-smoker to paint and paper his room, and promptly invaded it with a dozen fuming cronies who scented the walls and carpets beyond repair. Granted, some newcomers were goaded or tricked into committing transgressions, and just being fresh was excuse enough for treatment, but it seems clear that hazing was not applied uniformly or indiscriminately.[19]

Because they were often tied to specific irritants, there was no precise schedule for initiation events. They occurred whenever seniors got sufficiently agitated and found a suitable opportunity to act. Mufti's court in 1885 adjourned "with orders that the next session should be holden whenever the state of the docket would call for another general gaol delivery."[20] Corrective action could be taken at any time during the year, not just the beginning of term. In fact, since people's faults took time to appear, delay was normal.

A final dimension of initiations revealed by the 1881 affair was that student opinion was divided over their utility. The four seniors who claimed in that instance that 80 per cent of their fellows were sympathetic to the proceedings may have been correct, but some were vociferous in their condemnation. Their concern was about methods, not purposes. The point, wrote a third-year student to the *Globe*, was not whether freshman insolence would be condoned but "whether we are going the countenance as a part of the necessary social machinery of University College a procedure which is a highly punishable criminal offense – nabbing, or kidnapping if you please."[21] This particular tempest soon blew out, but the controversy lingered, as occasional letters to *Varsity* over the next half-decade indicate.[22]

In the winter of 1887–88 a dispute over initiation erupted again, dividing the student body as never before. It is not clear what sparked it, but in December of 1887, anti-hazers, as they called themselves, began a concerted attack. Arguing that it survived only through majority indifference, they denounced hazing because it violated personal liberty, destroyed college fellowship, was dangerous, uncontrollable, ungentlemanly, and unfair. Nor did it stop freshman impudence. There was simply no valid reason for it.[23]

Pro-hazers were hard pressed to respond. Besides trying to emphasize the harmlessness and fun of the practice, and its character-forming aspect, they defended it as a grand old college tradition that provided relief from the intellectual rigour of student life.[24] Of course, supporters may have felt little pressure to respond in writing to their opponents. As long as they could keep doing it, why worry about a few letters in *Varsity*?

Their critics also realized that the battle would not be won by words alone. In late January thirty-seven of them signed a petition reiterating their arguments and calling for a mass meeting on the subject. They claimed to be "in no way motivated by feelings of hostility to the friends of hazing," but they were determined to do more than air pieties. When the rhetoric subsided in Moss Hall on the first of February, 127 of the 200 people present had enrolled in the new Non-Hazing Union.[25]

Little seems to have followed this organizational burst. Pro-hazers perhaps hoped that the union would disintegrate over the summer if they kept quiet. It was not to be. When they indicated in the fall that they would not desist willingly, the campus began to seethe. *Varsity* warned that serious trouble was brewing – "serious for the bitterness and ill feeling that must result from a continuance of a state of affairs in which one party in the college defies the opinion of the other, that other in its turn exercising an unfriendly surveillance over the actions of its opponents." The two sides lashed at each other throughout the term; by mid-December a confrontation was imminent. "During the past week," wrote a correspondent to the *Mail*, "the atmosphere around the college has seemed charged with a sort of electrical expectancy that always tells of the approach of the fateful hazing night. Meetings have been held in different boarding houses, and groups of prominent hazers may be noticed in the corridor holding whispered conversations, and the sh-h-h of inviolable secrecy can be heard by ... their opponents who chance to pass by. Nothing definite has yet been done, but it is evident that a crisis is at hand."[26] The next evening, before a Literary Society meeting, it broke.

Pro-hazers armed with heavy canes congregated by the entrance to the hall. The first year, in response, kept tightly together and tried to push inside. Efforts to detach one or two of them sparked a general row that spread out over the college lawn, but the hazers regrouped, rushing towards a stout freshman who became the prize in a tug of war that lasted a half-hour, despite faculty entreaties to stop. Eventually frosh carried their class-mate to safety, then returned to ensure that no one else had been captured. The contenders eyed each other suspiciously but gradually dispersed.[27]

Though hazers protested that they had not instigated the brawl, their cause was irreparably damaged. The union's critique had been confirmed; the university had been disgraced, and the college council was prodded into passing a calendar regulation forbidding interference with the personal liberty of any student. Hazers quietly caved in. By February *Varsity* reported that the treatment of freshmen could once again be discussed in calm tones. "The somewhat stupid and barbarous hazing of the past," it asserted, "is no longer possible."[28]

The demise of Mufti was remarkably swift. The 1881 incident, far more serious than anything after, had subsided quickly; seven years later hazing was emphatically rejected. What accounts for this rapid change? Perhaps there was a sudden increase of Christian idealism among the students. Too little is known about the YMCA at Varsity in this period, but, as friction grew, a few traditionalists complained that the age of chivalry had been succeeded by that of "calculators, economists, namby-pambies and YMCA men."[29] This was, after all, a seedtime of revivals.

Administrative pressure undoubtedly had some effect. By the mid-1880s council was refusing to let students use college buildings for their rites, and besides any ethical rethinking this encouraged, it had the practical effect of making proceedings less comfortable. At one affair in December 1886, where the court had "rather a cold time of it," the trial was short and sentences quickly carried out.[30] If there was less fun to be had, fewer students may have been inclined to defend the custom. Clearly, though, the admin-istration followed the students' lead. Only after the union had paved the way did faculty feel bold enough to demand respect for individual freedom. Also debilitating was the decline of residence spirit. By the end of the 1880s the future of this centre of student activity was in doubt. Rumours that it was about to be closed or converted to teaching space[31] perhaps eroded the confidence of those best able to rally support for the old traditions.

Finally, the increased size of the student body may have rendered hazing ineffective and disruptive. Larger first-year cohorts made it more difficult to impress everyone by making an example of a few. At a time when diminishing esprit de corps was a common lament at Varsity, the possibility that freshmen could be oblivious to a pivotal moulding process was dis-turbing. Larger senior classes were equally problematic. Combining efficient secret organization with inclusive participation was no longer easy. Those relegated to the fringes of planning and execution may have channelled resentment into a critique of the whole procedure. What is clear is the

emergence in this period of class years as the basic units of student association at University College. Supporters of the Literary Society complained
after the first year-executive appeared in the fall of 1888, but within two
years *Varsity* had decided they were "most helpful adjuncts to the pleasure
and benefit to be derived from college life, and have apparently come to
stay."[32] As students began to rethink the framework of their interaction,
the format of initiation must have been questioned as well.

While the speedy rejection of hazing is not easy to explain, its abolition
was not as radical as might first appear. Many who opposed the pointless
humiliation of freshmen were not against initiations per se. Even the most
active members of the Non-Hazing Union, according to *Varsity*, favoured
some kind of ceremony. Seniors were still anxious to deflate bumptious
frosh and defend their prerogatives.[33] And so, while the tug of war over a
fat boy on the college lawn ended a tradition, it bore a striking resemblance
to the sorts of rites that began to predominate thereafter. The haze was gone;
hustle had arrived.

Hustling was not new. The administration of "sundry cuffs and kicks to
freshmen in the corridors" was an established practice.[34] If those imposed
upon resisted, as often happened, inter-year fights erupted. This procedure
now began to be encouraged. Some complained that these contests were not
nearly as effective in disciplining frosh as the older method. "We have mist
the haze for sometime now," went the punch line of a campus joke. For
most, though, the hustle represented a felicitous compromise between hazers' desire to maintain college traditions and non-hazers' concerns about
liberty and decency. Andrew Dumbarton's "Song" captured the central
features of the practice as well as the satisfaction and delight of those who
participated:

Gin a body meet a body
  Comin' down the stair,
Gin a body shake a body
  Need a body care?
A' the laddies get put through it,
  Naebody need cry;
Lassies may escape the hustlin',
  Laddies needna try.[35]

At first, hustles were conducted in the college corridor. On a Friday
afternoon in mid-November of 1890, for example, seniors waited on men
of the first year emerging from a lecture and "escorted them through the
building" during a pleasant half-hour. Several notebooks and fragments of
wearing apparel were left behind "owing to an unavoidably hasty departure,"
but otherwise a good time was had by all. Faculty were less enthusiastic,

for, as *Varsity* put it, "modern furniture seems ill-designed to meet the forces of manhood." When the hustle occurred in 1892, President Loudon turned on fire hoses, which only scattered contestants more widely through the building. More effective was his warning that participants in future struggles would be suspended.[36] A different location and occasion had to be found.

Fall convocation, which officially began the university term, had long been a cherished undergraduate event. Students would mass in the gallery at the back of the hall to razz the speakers and make general commotion. It was also customary on this occasion for the president to introduce the incoming class, calling freshmen to the front of the balcony. In 1893, forbidden the use of college corridors, the students simply adapted convocation to their purposes. They had their usual boisterous fun during the ceremony, and when it was over, "became somewhat familiar" with their new associates.[37] The frosh were driven into one corner of the balcony and held until the audience departed. Once the seniors had ranged themselves up and down the stairway, their prisoners were allowed to descend in an appropriate manner – shoved side to side until they landed in the mud outside. One freshman so deposited discovered "that I had taken the crease out of my trousers, had had my neat, new four-in-hand necktie nearly torn to pieces, and that my hat was somewhat damaged."[38] A subsequent parade through the streets may have lifted his spirits.

Though council fined some of those involved, students were not deterred. Similar proceedings occurred in 1894, when Mackenzie King, then a senior, knocked down the college registrar three times to prevent interference. King apologized in writing immediately after and the practice continued unabated.[39]

By 1896, when convocation was held in the gym on campus, experience and convenient facilities persuaded the sophomores to dress more suitably for the occasion – in football clothes. Freshmen also learned. Two years later the new class met a few days before the hustle, devised a counter-strategy, and appointed a commander-in-chief. They arrived en masse at the ceremony, but organization only made them easier to get at. Still, they persevered with planning efforts, and in 1899 were so keyed up they instigated the fun.[40]

By this time, not only were university authorities applying heavy pressure but student criticism was mounting as well. Not everyone was convinced that being pushed downstairs and into the mud cured freshman conceit or fostered esprit. Prodding from both groups perhaps led to a realization that since the hustle had evolved into a competition between two prepared sides, it might as well be treated as an athletic event.[41] Sports, while just reaching the peak of importance that has lasted throughout the century, still had strong associations with schooling. Casting initiation in this form combined a modern sensitivity with an effort to sustain the distinctiveness of the college experience.[42]

Next year, instead of assaulting frosh at convocation, sophs presented them several days later with a large green flag, then "scrapped" to get it back. A tickled *Varsity* proclaimed that the "flag rush" would supercede the hustle. So it did. For the next six years variations on this format were played out. In 1901 the two groups fought over a Spaulding bat. In 1902 they staged a rugby match. In 1904 the prize was a banner with three white geese.[43] These good-natured brawls through the parks and ravines about the college, lasting an hour or two, were popular spectacles, so popular that the audience began to join in. School of Science students who intruded in 1905 gleefully battled both sides. A year later their intervention inspired a general exodus on to city streets, where trolleys were stopped and ice wagons looted.[44]

Some artsmen had complained before that the flag rush was tame and bloodless. Now, the combination of outside interference, administration displeasure, and public criticism led more people to question it. The college literary society debated its utility and voted to end it, perhaps influenced by a request from President Falconer. There was no official hustle in 1907. To compensate, sophs disrupted first-year elections at the end of October, smashing several desks and destroying much clothing.[45] Clashing in the corridor was not a forgotten art.

The prospect of no initiation was disconcerting, though, so the second-year class of 1908–09 tried to find a more acceptable alternative. Instead of an outdoor scrum that could get out of control, it decided to sponsor an indoor athletic meet featuring individual encounters between members of the first two years. The events included boxing, wrestling, tug of war, basketball, and various kinds of races.[46] Once more the centre of the arts initiation moved inside, this time to the gym floor.

However manly, these matches did not satisfy all the longings of the upper year; proceedings immediately began to get more raucous. Next year, before the sports, frosh were required to chase a greased pig. Two years later they were forced to run a gauntlet between a double line of sophs wielding canes, brooms, and sticks. Those who declined could do a skit later on or take an ice-cold shower. *Varsity* insisted that good will prevailed, but many minor scuffles had broken out and subsequent initiations were toned done. The crop of 1913 had to contend only with flour, eggs, flypaper, boot polish, and the like before proceeding to sports and refreshments.[47]

As the rites became more rigorous, enthusiasm could not be contained in the gym. The 1911 evening was concluded with a street parade past various ladies' colleges. In 1912 two hundred students marching down Yonge Street disrupted streetcars and clashed with police. Predictably, the administration got anxious and pressured the student parliament to consider alternatives.

A few suggestions were put forward over the next few years, but tradition prevailed. The initiation of 1914 took the form of a flag rush and athletic meet, followed by refreshments. However, to guarantee order, it was agreed that events would be sanctioned beforehand by SAC, the new Students Administrative Council, and umpired by the university's security force.[48]

This was probably not as much of an innovation as it seemed, but affirmation of the principle of supervision symbolized the increasing effectiveness of efforts to regulate initiations and pointed the way to the future. So did the appearance of hazing elements after 1910. It was not the old kind of haze. It could not be. Hustling and its spin-offs had altered too many things. Mufti's court often did not materialize until the late fall; after convocation became the venue, timing was fixed to the beginning of term. Before, all the upper years had participated; now it had devolved upon sophomores alone to maintain the seniors' honour. This hazing was more standardized, its application indiscriminate, but its fundamental character was clear. From the turn of the century men's initiations at University College had been athletic contests in which both sides had a chance. Even the hustles of the preceding decade had had a sporting, free-for-all ambiance. The attempt to demean freshmen with unpleasant surprises, to inflict indignities without receiving them, marked a turn away, one that would became much more pronounced later on.

Though the evidence for them is much sketchier, initiations at Toronto's professional schools in the two or three decades before the war seem to have had a similar character. They were rougher and dirtier, but still essentially games. Sawbones, like artsmen, moved their rites out of doors. The joy of Trinity Medical students in the 1890s and before, especially on the first day of term, was the "old-time custom" of "elevating": "Any student of the first year who was bold enough to take a front seat in the amphitheatre was suddenly pounced upon by his 'superiors,' some of whom would endeavor to hoist him up to the back benches while others would struggle to keep him down. In this way the poor innocent would almost be torn limb from limb." There was a festive tone to the practice, a fact underlined in 1893 when an organ grinder was hired to strike up every time a body was raised.[49]

Perhaps the lecturer shoved off the stage on that occasion was responsible for pushing initiations out of the classroom. By 1897, at any rate, the hustle took place in a corridor, and by 1902 it had moved completely outside, where the point of elevating evaporated. Well before the war all reference to it had disappeared, and the meds' performance, like most others, had become a scrap. Now, sophomores dressed in cast-offs and armed with large supplies of gunk ambushed freshmen coming from class. Torn clothing and blackened faces soon gave everyone the appearance of South Sea islanders.[50]

School of Practical Science rites were similar, although engineers had a penchant for inks and dyes, and also a stronger tendency to sustain rivalry throughout the year. Their ancient custom, dousing offending heads under a faucet, or "tapping," proved to be more durable than "elevating," perhaps because it could be accomplished in smaller groups. It was done throughout the year, but wholesale scraps cropped up unpredictably as well.[51]

While artsmen moved indoors in the years just prior to the war, medical and sciences students remained outside. In part this may reflect a desire to emphasize the manly, rugged character of their fellowship and to impress more firmly class and professional solidarity. "The gym and the gridiron are too tame," reckoned one science grad in 1912. "They are not peculiar to university life. 'Mixing it up' has a savour that will always be sweet to a strong, virile student body." As well, greater rigidity of professional-school curricula made it simple to corral the freshman year. Scraps were easily arranged by upper classmen, hard for freshmen to avoid. In arts, enormous timetable variations meant that events had to be scheduled more precisely and incentives given to participate.[52] Allowing people to save their wardrobes was perhaps one concession, and since surprise was impossible, there was less reluctance to move from the playing field.

Despite these differences, medicine and science initiations in the pre-war period, like those of University College males, were essentially games with a high degree of equality in the proceedings. Sophs were dressed more appropriately but they got bashed about just as much as freshmen, and got just as dirty. To them, a blackened face was more a mark of accomplishment than of abasement. After the war they were much less willing to be vulnerable.

Women's initiations at University College naturally were more decorous. For many years the central event was a formal reception hosted by the Women's Literary Society at which freshettes were introduced to a variety of campus groups, including faculty wives and female graduates, both of whom were invited. Autumn Tea, as it came to be known after it was instituted in 1890, was a pleasant but conventional social occasion.[53] Some ladies must have felt it was too refined, for it began to be supplemented with less orthodox ceremonies. The first of these on record, a mock trial and guessing game, occurred in 1895, twelve years after Varsity first admitted females. A year later neophytes were treated to a dainty supper, then summoned before the Literary Society executive, warned of the difficulties besetting them, reminded of "the things which, from time immemorial, it has been forbidden for a freshette to do," and made to promise not to offend against these regulations. There is no clue as to what was prohibited. In 1904 slightly more participation was demanded of the novices. One by one in a large, dimly lit room, they were confronted by shrouded figures representing wisdom, love, and fame. Each girl chose among the three and thereupon received a few words of warning or encouragement from her ideal. The didactic intent misfired, for "these momentous decisions were taken, in the vast majority of cases, rather flippantly." If similar performances were organized in other years, they were unreported in *Varsity*.[54]

What ensured the continuity of this style of event and displaced the primacy of Autumn Tea was the establishment of Queen's Hall, the college's first women's residence. In 1907, a year and a half after it opened, initiation took place during a Guy Fawkes party and dance. This was a popular format, surviving more or less intact right through the war. The affairs were masquerades. Freshettes were required to dress as babies, while upper years sported more dignified costumes. The number who chose to come in some variety of male attire is striking. At the first event, for example, colonial dames and Greek maidens appeared, but so did Johnny Canuck and Buster Brown, football players, and English squires. In 1912 there were rugby players, members of the Queen's Own Regiment, and gentlemen in full evening dress.[55] As well as refreshments these evenings normally featured singing, college yells, and stunts put on by the upper years. The latter varied from short visual jokes, like rowing a boat with matchsticks, to more extended productions like enactments of "Young Lochinvar" or humorous commentaries on the passing scenes of college life.[56]

Much of the entertainment, though, revolved around the newcomers, who gradually became subject to more and more ragging. In 1907 they were asked only to repeat two oaths, to the king and to the seniors. In 1910 they were given verses that had to be sung to tunes of their own devising. The tests were conducted both individually and ensemble. In 1913, upon entering a judgment hall where doom was pronounced upon them by shrieking ghouls, they were coated with green paint and sand. The year after they were showered with breadcrumbs and wet sawdust.[57]

During the two decades after 1895 this part of women's initiations at University College became much less restrained. Strictures regarding females were loosening in society generally, but thirty years of accomplishment at Varsity reduced the need to justify their presence by genteel behaviour. Equally important was the acquisition of their own space. Within the protective bounds of Queen's Hall inhibitions were shed more easily, and as the girls began to frolic with paint and sawdust, their fun began to resemble the boys'. However, there were important differences. Usually, though not always, coed occasions took place well into November rather than October. Having had more time to adapt to school, freshettes underwent their trials with somewhat more confidence. Furthermore, women's rites required more preparation: costumes had to be made, decorations arranged, skits devised and practised. Planning for these was a useful way of forging close bonds.

While male initiations became increasingly freshmen-sophomore affairs only, female ones continued to involve all years. Seniors continued to run them. No doubt smaller numbers made such inclusion possible, but there may well have been a greater sense of community among women students, a deeper recognition of the need for mutual support; certainly their inter-year rivalries were much less intense. Women's initiations, attended by faculty wives and other invited guests, were more carefully supervised. They were always held indoors and concluded at a reasonable hour. Because it was virtually impossible for them to get out of hand, they engendered almost no controversy. However, women's initiations were not necessarily less demanding than men's. The women had to invent amusing entertainments, demonstrate singing and acting skills, and perform for a wider audience than their student peers. The hustle put a premium on strength, women's stunts on artistry and poise.

During the war the Guy Fawkes party changed very little, though baby costumes and men's wear gave way to a variety of new themes. In 1916 coeds dressed as Indians, a year later as pirates.[58] Inoffensive and low key, there was little here that could be objected to. Male initiations were another matter. Those disruptive foofaraws now seemed a waste of energy and resources, a mockery of grimmer conflicts elsewhere. At the outbreak of war men abolished inter-year scraps. Three years later *Varsity* lauded the success of this policy, noting "an almost entire absence of the old-time scenes of wildness" during the past two sessions. Yet official cancellation had not clamped down the lid completely. At University College in 1916 four sophs were suspended for participating in a cloakroom attack on the frosh. A year earlier meds sophs had been unruly during a banquet and theatre party held to compensate for the absence of a hustle. They also continued to stage informal inter-year fights.[59]

By 1917 restraint was crumbling even more. "Light skirmishes" between first and second years were a daily occurrence through early October. Hats, collars, and ties were stolen, water fights begun, windows broken. A small rumpus by medical students attracted city-wide attention.[60] Before the policy of abolition became a farce, the Student Administrative Council accepted reality. A scrap was acceptable, it decided, if good spirit – a euphemism for restraint – prevailed. Engineers quickly picked up on the formula. With SAC permission they put on an extensive program that included decorating faces and subjecting frosh to ordeals like the "gauntlet," the "torture chamber," and the "black hole." Next fall University College initiated its frosh for the first time since 1914, working green paint, molasses, axel-grease, lampblack, and castor oil into a variety of torments based on a medical motif.[61] The organization of these two events around particular themes suggests a heavy influence from women's initiations. After all, by 1918 coeds had more experience with these things.

War muted male initiations and drove them partly underground but did not eliminate them. Even before victory was secured, they surfaced with renewed vitality. Athletics had dominated the spirit of the pre-war hustle. While they did not disappear, post-war initiations had a much different character. It was not entirely new. The arts initiations of 1913 and 1914, as well as the affairs approved by SAC near the end of the conflict, presaged it. Now the essence of initiation was not a contest between more or less equals but a series of affronts borne by freshmen alone. Frosh rules, frosh clothing, and unpleasant ordeals all indicate that with the revival of initiations came a return of the haze.

Prohibitions for first-year students were old hat, but after the war they became more conspicuous and more rigorously enforced. Many colleges and faculties formally codified their directives. SAC itself thought this so appropriate that it struck a committee to recommend suitable strictures. Generally, rules were not onerous. The School of Science decreed in 1921, for example, that during initiation frosh had to enter the building through the basement and remove their hats while inside. Throughout their first year they could not use the east door, could not wear spats or a Derby hat, and had to be available to the Engineering Society for fatigue duty. At University College in the fall of 1924 frosh were forbidden to use the front door and to wear spats or a bow-tie until initiation was over.[62] It was not simply that large post-war enrolments required the writing down of what used to be passed on orally. The emphasis on restrictions had faded greatly after Mufti's fall. Moreover, reports on their new imposition gave no indication that these were honoured traditions. It did not seem to matter what rules were applied so long as newcomers were sufficiently cowed.[63]

Freshman ordinances often specified the wearing of distinctive articles of clothing. There were precedents in college life for the identification of particular groups by certain kinds of dress, but the heavy insistence on initiation costumes was a post-war innovation.[64] Every faculty had a device. In 1921 science regulations called for green ties, arts for red and white caps, which could not be removed even when off campus, and meds for red ties. Freshettes at University College were not exempt. Their initiation guide that year stipulated the wearing of a bright green hat with ribbons under the chin as well as one black and one white stocking. Seniors took these requirements seriously. In 1921 two meds frosh who refused to wear the designated tie were dumped into a pail of grimy water. A year earlier three frosh caught without regulation skull-caps had their heads dipped in tar. For men, at any rate, there were strong incentives to conform to the dress code.[65]

Rules may have caused inconvenience and clothing embarrassment but physical tests remained the most exacting part of post-war male initiations. The proposed 1922 School of Practical Science program (SPS), authorized by the dean and student executive, was obviously considered acceptable. Each frosh was to be undressed and coated in food dye.

He would then sit on a circle of wire and get a shock from that – I think it was a Ford coil. He would go out of that room and around the corner. There was a barrel of glucose, and a man would take a handful of this and put it in his hair. After that a man would put a handful of sawdust in his hair. He would then go down two steps and through a hole into the big room, and as he came out of the hall he would have lamp black sprinkled on him. He would run the gauntlet around the room between two rows of Sophs – I just forgot what the obstacles were, but one was in the form of crawling through a barrel; another was going up a greased plank and jumping down the other end – I think the next one was going through an automobile tire suspended about 2 feet off the ground, and next his rolling an onion through lamp black sprinkled on the floor. Then he would crawl up through a sheet of canvas made up of bags dipped in water. When he came on the other side of that, he would go through another hole from this big room, and would climb up some steps to a chute – the chute was about 5 feet high at one end, and it led down into a box about 8 × 3 of flour and lamp black sprinkled through it, and when he came to the top of this chute he would be told to close his eyes and shut his mouth for fear he would get some flour in. Then he would be shot down the chute; someone would catch him at the bottom, and he would be lifted out and put on a bench. They would then give him a mouthful of bitter aloes or some kind of salts or both.

Plans were disrupted when frosh refused to accept their fate. They trapped the sophomores in the gym, cut the lights, and dripped ammonia down through the roof, almost asphyxiating those inside. When the reception committee finally emerged and caught its breath, it went wild, attacking the perpetrators with barrel staves, then forcing them to proceed with the scheduled events.[66]

Severe criticism over the affair put a damper on subsequent SPS initiations, but other faculties kept up the search for disagreeable surprises. In 1925 arts and meds frosh both were stripped, blindfolded, coated with paint and grease, and made to slide down a chute on their stomachs into piles of animal entrails procured from a local slaughterhouse. Again, SAC and Caput, Varsity's disciplinary committee, chewed out the respective organizers, who agreed they had gone too far.[67] These physical ordeals had a much different character from that of pre-war hustles. Though sports sometimes followed these trials, they were no longer the central events. In the parts that really mattered frosh were given no chance to prove themselves. When they tried, as the new engineers did in 1922, sophomores were inordinately displeased.

While post-war initiations for women were nothing like the work-outs for men, the earlier trend of making things more difficult for freshettes continued. At University College in 1919 neophytes dressed as corpses had to take part in a pillow fight and also had to pick up pennies with lard smeared

on their noses. In 1922, dressed as insects, they were doused with water
and made to eat mysterious things. When a new style was inaugurated the
following year, perhaps in response to the sps fiasco, the format was a show
put on by freshettes alone.[68] Perhaps there were too many coeds now for
all the years to perform, but probably few seniors complained about being
pushed out. Passive enjoyment was more in keeping with their dignity.

The rigours of post-war initiations stimulated student debate about their
utility. The issue was raised so often that *Varsity* finally organized an opinion
poll in 1923. A vast majority supported the tradition; of 1,131 replies, only
136 urged abolition. Arguments for and against had changed little since the
1880s. Those in favour said they fostered discipline, humility, and loyalty
to class and school. Those opposed claimed they were childish, useless, and
motivated only by revenge. Critics were not completely isolated, though.
Many on the majority side were not averse to reform. Their suggestions
included better control over events, a de-emphasis on physical aspects with
a corresponding increase in distinctive badges or clothing, and more shows
of frosh solidarity in parades, sports, and stunts.[69]

While students debated, faculty fretted. sac's review of plans was not
effective in stopping spontaneous outbreaks nor in preventing participants
from getting carried away in the heat of the moment. Its censures and fines
were not sufficient to discourage transgressions. As the severity of initiations
increased, therefore, the administration began to intrude more heavily into
their conduct.

Through the early 1920s, despite great concern, President Falconer was
reluctant to act. He admitted to the principal of Queen's in 1923 that he did
not want to take a position that would be difficult to enforce. Instead, he
urged faculty at the various schools to keep as firm a grip on things as
possible. By the fall of 1924, however, he was willing to test the waters.
Caput passed a resolution disapproving of the excessive use of distinctive
badges or apparel and invited the co-operation of sac to restrain their use.[70]
It was a suggestion, not an order. A year later Caput's confidence had
grown. When public opinion became greatly exercised by the use of offal,
Falconer had an excuse to act.

In November, after "consulting" with the sac executive, Caput issued a
two-pronged directive. First, no ceremony "involving physical violence,
destruction of property, interference with personal liberty, or personal dignity, or in any way discreditable to the University" was to take place, on
penalty of suspension or expulsion. Second, initiations were to be prepared
by a committee of the senior class in each faculty and approved by a joint
committee of Caput and sac. The administration now had the right to intervene directly in all of the planning. This was followed up before the end
of the academic year with an instruction requiring college or faculty permission to make frosh wear special items of dress. They could be asked to

wear a tie or skull-cap but not both; if the former, it had to be of standard shape and size with no special design or name on it. There were few objections to all this, and when Falconer reiterated the regulations to the 1926 incoming class, *Varsity* heartily endorsed the end of the "shampoo with axel-grease ... meal of castor oil" era.[71]

The effectiveness of these measures in practice is debatable, for tie clipping soon became a fad. Ties could be snipped for infractions of frosh rules, and since it was easy to manufacture infractions, the sophomores' goal was to cut every tie. Freshmen began to travel in packs for protection, while groups of seniors lay in wait for them. Scraps became common, a disturbing development, since scissors or knives were necessary to do the cutting. The spontaneity of these encounters made them hard to control.[72] As Falconer knew, initiations were remarkably resilient. They would continue for a long time to come. Still, even if he had not done away with them altogether, he had greatly reduced their capriciousness.

From 1880 to 1925 initiations were a prominent feature of Varsity life despite ongoing administrative disapprobation. Faculty was uneasy, for though these rites promoted a useful school loyalty, they were, as Principal Taylor of Queen's put it, "unquestionably a constant possibility of serious trouble."[73] Just as consistently, students perpetuated their cherished custom. Sometimes there were quarrels about the format of the ceremonies; sometimes they were redesigned. Never was there a serious possibility of abolishing them, and even when pressures against them were most successful, ways were found to subvert restrictions.

Rarely, however, did students explain why they performed these rites, and any rationales offered were usually perfunctory and formulaic. What sustained the tradition? The answer, in some ways, is obvious. These initiations, like any other, served to induct novices into a new situation, indoctrinate them with its values, express tensions arising from it, and relieve pressures that were diagnosed.

Initiations are designed to instil or make manifest a group consciousness. In universities this was problematic because each year a substantial block departed while a new one arrived, composed of people from varying social, economic, and geographic circumstances, most of whom were accustomed to family intimacy. Re-establishing social equilibrium and fostering a common spirit called for an impressive display that would help to shatter old loyalties and forge new ones. The antics of one short afternoon or evening would not effect a complete transformation, but they could have a considerable impact. Some of the process may have been designed to correct behaviour flaws, but much more important was the wish to mould a collective outlook.

Some anthropologists suggest that there are two main types of initiation

– those used to admit recruits into secret societies, and those used to advance individuals to new stages of the life-cycle.[74] Varsity rituals encompassed both, though increasingly they veered toward the latter. Colleges were not secret societies, but especially in the nineteenth century they were remote from the experience of most and often were attended by older people seeking entry to more rewarding careers. Hazings in the 1880s, focused on special individuals and conducted by an august potentate, resembled the rites of many organizations at the time.[75]

As the relative age of students dropped and starting university often became synonymous with leaving home, initiation seemed more like a rite of passage to adulthood. Fixing it to the beginning of term in the 1890s intensified this impression. Still, the desire to implant a feeling that collegians were special no doubt remained strong. As Burton Bledstein has pointed out, emerging professional groups in nineteenth-century America lacked the cohesion, camaraderie, and consciousness of a traditional class.[76] College provided something of a corporate sensibility, and initiation symbolized the entry of freshmen into a privileged circle.

Initiations did more than admit newcomers. They also attempted to teach proper values. Again, this is a normal function of such ceremonies. These values were not necessarily at odds with those of wider society; in fact, since most Varsity students were respectable middle-class children, their outlook was bound to be conventional. Still, university was unfamiliar terrain for frosh. They looked for advice about how to dress, how to act, how to think. Initiations were not the only information conduit, but, because they were performed at such an impressionable stage and in such a prominent manner, their ability to imprint was strong.

Messages were broad ranging, and many were ambiguous. It would be difficult if not impossible to compile a complete list. Some things, however, were made crystal clear, notably the structure of student society. Separate initiations by college and faculty demonstrated where internal loyalties were expected to rest. Especially in the professional schools, this was likely a deliberate career orientation. Separate initiations by sex clarified murky questions about gender roles and expectations. Though male and female rites came to resemble each other more closely, there were wide differences between them. Men's events were always physically more strenuous. The advent of hustles and, later, athletic contests, may have been partly a response to a more obvious female presence: countering any impression that collegians were effeminate called for public demonstrations of rigorous manliness.[77] Gender division was dictated by conventional propriety, but it also reflected different priorities in bonding. After 1890, especially, men emphasized the unity of each class year; women attempted to draw together the whole female university community, including faculty wives. The separation of spheres is hardly surprising, but it does reaffirm that the college experience of the sexes was not identical.

Besides faculty and gender divisions Varsity initiations also underlined the importance of hierarchy in college life.[78] Upper years were anxious to entrench a status ladder that put freshmen firmly on the bottom rungs. Even during the more purely athletic phase of men's rites the resolution of less numerous sophomores was intended as a practical demonstration of their superiority. This responsibility of challenging the first-year class helped to fix their position on the ladder as well. The decline of these free-for-alls, though, was coincident with a growing impulse to reinforce the principle of hierarchy, a desire that became clearly evident after the war with the return of hazing to men's rites and its creeping inclusion into women's. Twentieth-century hazing was more routinized, more anonymous, more restricted in time than that of the 1880s, yet the basic impulse to degrade freshmen through unpredictable, unpleasant trials was the same. What accounts for the effort to fortify these rigid divisions?

Hierarchy was appealing when social norms and expectations were in flux, and not just to students. The young were perhaps especially sensitive to these shifts, though, because they felt under pressure to act in modern ways. While some students responded enthusiastically to changing conditions, not all wanted to participate in new possibilities, were able to participate, or felt completely comfortable when they did participate. Changing standards bred uncertainty, confusion, and insecurity, if not outright reaction.

In these circumstances, initiations that entrenched year distinctions may have been very satisfying. Not only did their time-honoured observance provide a sense of continuity, a connection with the seemingly fragile past; they also reinforced a framework that made the student experience comprehensible, one that conformed to a dominant feature of industrial capitalist organization. Moreover, as individual worth came to be judged more fully on the basis of personality and congeniality,[79] they affirmed a non-individualized criterion of status. Individuals comparing their own dull circumstances to the glamorous mass-media image of student existence derived comfort from the simple device of seniority. If they felt deficient in looks, charm, wealth, or style, at least they got recognition for academic success. The emphasis on hierarchy helped to buffer the brunt of change and buttressed the self-respect of many ordinary students.

The entrenching of hierarchy demonstrates that initiations also addressed tensions underlying university life. Victor Turner and other anthropologists have pointed out that festive life is more than a means of establishing order, more than a safety-valve that distracts attention from unpleasant realities. It also allows comment on societal arrangements and their inherent vexations. Whether or not the end result is accommodation to dominant forces, it exposes concerns.[80] If real life is embedded in ritual, then, what do initiations reveal about the students' own view of their situation?

It should be noted that all the dominant forms of Varsity institutions were rooted in the ancient custom of misrule, which turns normal social structures and relationships topsy-turvy so that their legitimacy can be commented upon, alternatives posited, and different roles experimented with, all in a play context that helps to defuse the possibility of backlash.[81] This ludic rearrangement was obvious in women's rites. Modelled primarily on the theatre and music hall, coed stunts may have been conceived as burlesques of grander shows going on downtown.[82] What really cued the intent of inversion, though, was the celebration of Guy Fawkes night, a traditional occasion of misrule. Costume, with freshettes dressed as babies and many seniors as men, confirmed it. When the infant motif was shucked, gender disguise remained in pirate, Indian, and devil masquerades.

The earlier phase is particularly intriguing. It simultaneously affirmed and disputed conventional ideas of women's roles. Taking care of babies represented acceptance of maternal responsibility; male dress, an awareness that sex status was distinctly unequal. The appropriation of trousers was a demand for the highest respect from new members of the community as well as a prod at male pretensions, justified, apparently, only by the cut of cloth. However, it was also a way of commenting on women's anomalous position in an institution, indeed a society, dominated by men. For some, the gist was self-mockery, ridiculing the presumption that women could trespass outside their sphere. For others, disguise was a gentle challenge to male hegemony, asserting a right to more social authority and offering an opportunity to practise a role they planned to adopt more fully. For all it was means of bolstering resolve in an environment where they felt vulnerable and somewhat alien. Mothering instincts and mutual support were the keys to survival. The move away from infant costume and gender disguise during the war and after was a sign that coeds felt increasingly comfortable at Varsity.

Women were not alone in celebrating misrule. It was also the basis of male rites. Mufti and his court parodied judicial procedures. Hustles and scraps lampooned the well-defined rules of regular sports. Post-war hazings derived from the assembly line and perhaps from military induction procedures. Frosh were processed one by one in a travesty of the efficiency techniques of scientific management; like stamped-out products, they were simultaneously individualized and diminished. Significantly, features unique to university life, like exams or lectures, were not burlesqued. Attention was focused beyond the campus, an indication perhaps that Joseph Kett has over-emphasized the degree to which collegians developed an insular mentality.[83] Initiations did bespeak a detachment from the workaday world, but they embodied a recognition that reattachment was inevitable.

While these rites generated confidence about that eventuality by permitting practice of authority roles to be taken up in earnest later on, they also point to anxieties, especially an awareness that isolated individuals could easily be manhandled by an indifferent, even hostile social apparatus. If independent selfhood was risky or impossible, the solution was to build networks of mutual support and advantage. Initiations, of course, were designed to help forge those bonds, and the changes that began to occur after 1889 – the increasing strenuousness, the shift in timing to the beginning of term, the insistence that all frosh participate – indicate a growing sense of urgency in this regard.

While initiations fit into a strategy of coping with industrial capitalism, they also posited a different set of values. Life should be more than an unrelenting drive for efficiency and success. It was also something to enjoy. This was a message intended especially for college authorities. Misrule was a way of resisting the rising insistence that learning be a serious, full-time, competitive pursuit. It was a way of resisting the growing imperatives of professionalism within the institution. Through initiations, as well as other activities, students proclaimed that the purpose of university – their purpose – was to have fun and to get to know their fellows, not just to acquire knowledge. These traditions expressed opposition at the same time that they created group solidarity. Their beauty was that they allowed students to assert independence without having to confront authorities directly. True, a desire to test official will or reach may have figured in some performances, but for the most part faculty were extraneous. Initiation was not an end-run around their restrictions as much as a game played on a different field.

It is in this context – the usefulness of initiation in allowing students to articulate their own values and mould college to their own ends – that the changes of the 1920s become fully significant. Though students continued to shape their own rituals to some extent, they became much more effectively controlled. Earlier, faculty sometimes imposed discipline after the fact, if culprits could be identified, but for the most part they had relied on student common sense to ensure that things did not get out of hand. In the 1920s, when this no longer seemed sufficient, they insisted on the right to regulate the initiation process and impose strict limits on conduct. Nominally they acted conjointly with student government, but in fact the impetus for the clamp-down came from Caput, tired of being treated like freshmen – surprised and humiliated.

Given the enormous post-war concern about the "problem" of youth, administrative efforts to increase control were probably inevitable. Public sensitivity to the supposed hedonistic recklessness of the young encouraged prevention of any potentially embarrassing incidents. What is striking is the lack of student opposition to this intervention. The absence of any complaint in *Varsity* or elsewhere suggests a greater willingness by males to tolerate the kind of supervision that females usually accepted. This may be another example of coed influence, or perhaps it was a consequence of the altered composition of the student body. As the university became a logicial continuation of high school and undergraduates a more homogeneous adolescent group, there may have developed a more unquestioning acquiescence to authority that was perceived to be *in loco parentis*. It also may be, however, that many students were disturbed by aspects of so-called "modern" behaviour and desired more rigorous controls.

In her influential book *The Damned and the Beautiful* Paula Fass argues that by the 1920s the affectionate family and extended school system had produced a distinct culture of youth, centred around universities. The new generation was more tolerant in attitude, freer in behaviour. As the tension between modern and traditional modes of thought was played out after the war, "the young turned readily to what was new in the culture, they did it with a delight and excitement ... The young could adjust, were forced to adjust, and were eager to adjust. And as they did so, they drew the culture with them."[84] Students, according to Fass, were self-confident, forward-looking pioneers, pulling the rest of society towards modernity. Some, especially women, no doubt were.

However, what the increasing emphasis on hierarchy and growing administrative control over initiations point to is the appearance of, not a self-confident peer society busily defining new standards of permissiveness and augmenting the authority of the young, as Fass would have it, but a conservative, insecure group increasingly susceptible to adult pressures. Although much evidence suggests that student culture had a continental frame of reference, it may be that Varsity's experience was exceptional or that Canadian circumstances were different from the American ones she describes. These trends seem logical, though. Industrial capitalist society was not likely to concede any real power, except consumption, to such a potentially volatile group as the young. Any cultural authority it did grant would be tightly circumscribed by other forces, internal and external.

Initiations, for most students, were brief episodes of frivolity, but they were also important social dramas that marked the attainment of maturity, delineated the structure of campus life, and displayed concerns about past and future prospects. They were more than signposts; they constituted a practical response to pressures they identified. They facilitated acceptance of industrial capitalist society, with its culture of professionalism, yet also embodied resistance to its encroachments. Respect for hierarchy represented both an adherence to a fundamental tenet of bureaucratic organization and a defence against modernity's destablizing effects. The unity they engendered was valuable both in quests for successful careers and in efforts to withstand what was unpalatable. Even though their resistive potential was whittled down, they remained pivotal ceremonies in university life. No wonder! They attached students to a romantic past and girded them for an uncertain future. As ever, actions spoke more loudly than words.

NOTES

* The author would like to thank Harold Averill, Marion Wyse, Sharon Larade and the rest of the staff at the University of Toronto Archives for their help and hospitality.

1 In the Canadian literature, for example, see Paul Axelrod, "Moulding the Middle Class: Student Life at Dalhousie University in the 1930s," *Acadiensis* 15, no. 1 (1985): 84–122; Lynne Marks and Chad Gaffield, "Women at Queen's University, 1895–1905: A 'Little Sphere' All Their Own?" *Ontario History* 78, no. 4 (1986): 331–49; F.W. Gibson, *"To Serve and Yet Be Free": Queen's University, 1917–1961* (Montreal: McGill Queen's University Press 1983); John G. Reid, *Mount Allison University*, vol. 1, *1843–1914*; vol. 2, *1914–1963* (Toronto: University of Toronto Press 1984).

2 See, for example, Paula Fass, *The Damned and the Beautiful: American Youth in the 1920s* (New York: Oxford 1977), and Joseph Kett, *Rites of Passage: Adolescence in America, 1790 to the Present* (New York: Basic Books 1977).

3 See, for example, Natalie Z. Davis, *Society and Culture in Early Modern France* (Palo Alto: Stanford University Press 1975); Rhys Isaac, *The Transformation of Virginia, 1740–1790* (Chapel Hill: University of North Carolina Press 1982); Susan G. Davis, *Parades and Power: Street Theatre in Nineteenth Century Philadelphia* (Philadelphia: Temple University Press 1986).

4 At the University of Toronto, known colloquially as "Varsity," initiations were conducted not only by colleges and faculties but also by residence and fraternities. Evidence relating to the latter two types is fragmentary.

5 Burton J. Bledstein, *The Culture of Professionalism: The Middle Class and the Development of Higher Education in America* (New York: Norton 1976), 121.

6 A.B. McKillop, *A Disciplined Intelligence: Critical Inquiry and Canadian Thought in the Victorian Era* (Montreal: McGill-Queen's University Press 1979).

7 [W.J. Alexander], *The University of Toronto and Its Colleges, 1827–1906* (Toronto 1906), 261.

8 University of Toronto, *President's Report for the Year Ending 30th June, 1925,* 3.

9 There is no recent comprehensive history of the University of Toronto, but useful information can be found in the following: W. Stewart Wallace, *A History of the University of Toronto, 1827–1927* (Toronto: University of Toronto Press 1927); Claude T. Bissell, ed., *University College, A Portrait 1885–1953* (Toronto: University of Toronto Press 1953); Anne Rochon Ford, *A Path Not Strewn with Roses* (Toronto: University of Toronto Press 1985). On the declining age of Varsity students, see David Ross Keane, "Rediscovering Ontario University Students of the Mid-Nineteenth Century: Sources for and Approaches to the Study of the Experience of Going to College and Personal, Family and Social Backgrounds of Students (PhD thesis, University of Toronto 1981), 495, 847.

10 There is some evidence of initiation-type activities earlier. See the *White and Blue* (first student newspaper at Toronto), 14 Oct. 1879; Hilda Neatby, *"And Not To Yield": Queen's University, 1841–1917* (Montreal 1978), 195. Other hints about the reception of freshmen in the 1860s and 1870s can be found in W.J. Loudon, *Studies of Student Life*, vol. 5, *The Golden Age* (Toronto: Macmillan 1928).

11 Toronto *World*, 19 Nov. 1881; Toronto *Evening News*, 22 Nov. 1881. Toronto *Globe*, 23 Nov. 1881; Toronto *World*, 22 Nov. 1881. See also *Varsity*, 25 Nov. 1881. One of those kidnapped was Lyman Duff, later Canada's chief justice. See David Ricardo Williams, *Duff: A Life in the Law* (Vancouver: University of British Columbia Press 1984).

12 Toronto *World*, 22 Nov. 1881; Toronto *Globe*, 23 Jan. 1881.

13 The *White and Blue*, for example, reported that residence freshmen had been forcibly shaved and their hair burned in the quad. See 31 Jan. 1880.

14 See, for example, *Varsity*, 4 Dec. 1886, 79, and Fred J. Steen letter, *Varsity*, 3 Dec. 1887, 65.

15 A Grad, "Ixion's Caverns," *Varsity*, 12 Dec. 1885, 90–1; Jay Kobb [W. Allister Murray], "O Atticum Roomum," *Varsity*, 27 Oct. 1891. See also Ah Sin, "A Freshman's Experience, no. 2: Initiation," *Varsity*, 18 Dec. 1880, 100; "That Worry – Sir Cheekie Freshman's Version," *White and Blue*, 15 Nov. 1879.

16 U of T Archives, Langton Papers, Sir Daniel Wilson Diary, B65-0014/004, 22 June 1887; Toronto *Star*, 1 Feb. 1913; letter from Ubique, *Varsity*, 10 Dec. 1887, 79. The last and only other identifiable Mufti, Peter White, held the post in 1892, when it was solely a residence position. White became a prominent lawyer. See F.G. Griffin, "Hazing a Real Barbaric Art at Varsity Thirty Years Ago," Toronto *Star*, 15 Mar. 1924.

17 "The Worry of Sir Chee Kiefreshman," *White and Blue*, 8 Nov. 1879; Patriarch, *Varsity*, 29 Jan. 1881, 145; "Ixion's Caverns."

18 Russell letter, *Varsity*, 27 Nov. 1886, 65; "Ordeal Lasted until March," *Varsity* 26 Jan. 1923, 3; "A Fresh Tragedy," *Varsity*, 2 Dec. 1881, 76–7; *White and Blue*, 14 Feb. 1880; Loudon, *Studies of Student Life*, 67–8.

19 Toronto *Star*, 1 Feb. 1913; Fred J. Steen letter.

20 "Ixion's Caverns." See also "Ordeal Lasted until March."

21 Toronto *Globe*, 23 Nov. 1881; J. MacKay letter, Toronto *Globe*, 24 Nov. 1881.

22 See, for example, *Varsity*, 12 Dec. 1885 and 27 Nov. 1886.

23 See, for example, letter in *Varsity* from the following: J.J. Ferguson, 10 Dec. 1887; J.H. Chewitt, H.J. Cody, H.C. Boultbee, and A.T. DeLury, 21 Jan. 1888; Mondarmin, 8 Jan. 1888.

24 See, for example, Ubique letter, *Varsity*, 10 Dec. 1887.

25 *Varsity*, 4 Feb. 1888, 135; Toronto *Mail*, 2 Feb. 1888.

26 "The Hazing Question," *Varsity*, 3 Nov. 1888, 5; Toronto *Mail*, 14 Dec. 1888.

27 Toronto *Mail*, 15 Dec. 1888.

28 "The Non-Hazing Union," *Varsity*, 9 Feb. 1889. Mufti remained as a residence figure until 1893, when three students were expelled for hazing. After 1888,

though, he did not have wider college authority. See U of T Archives, Loudon Papers, "Hustling and Hazing Affairs," A72-0030, box 4, file H27.

29 Ubique letter. See also letters cited above from Russell, Steen, and Mondarmin.
30 Wilson Diary, 12 Dec. 1885; *Varsity*, 4 Dec. 1886, 79.
31 See, for example, *Varsity*, 2 Feb. 1889, 84–5.
32 *Varsity*, 21 Oct. 1890, 7. On concerns about diminishing esprit de corps, see *Varsity*, 23 Oct. 1886, 4 and 13 Nov. 1886, 44. On the controversy over year organizations, see *Varsity*, 31 March 1888, 229; 16 Feb. 1889, 101; 2 March 1889, 101.
33 "The Hazing Question"; "A College Court," *Varsity*, 26 Jan. 1889, 76; N.F. Coleman, "Our Annual Hustle," *Varsity*, 23 Nov. 1898, 75.
34 See Cody and DeLury letters.
35 *Varsity*, 15 Mar. 1892, 240; *Varsity*, 27 Oct. 1891, 35; "Song," *Varsity*, 16 Dec. 1890, 131.
36 *Varsity*, 18 Nov. 1890, 94; *Varsity*, 3 Nov. 1891, 55; "Hustling and Hazing Affairs."
37 Toronto *Mail*, 11 Oct. 1893.
38 Toronto *World*, 11 Oct. 1893; "First Impressions," *Varsity*, 15 Nov. 1893. The event was held that year in the auditorium on Queen Street. University College was being rebuilt after the 1891 fire, but its convocation hall had become too small anyway.
39 "Hustling and Hazing Affairs"; Toronto *World*, 6 Oct. 1894; Toronto *Mail*, 6 Oct. 1894; W.L.M. King Diary, 5 Oct. 1894; Toronto *World*, 7 Oct. 1896; "Moral Stories – II," *Varsity*, 2 Dec. 1896, 88.
40 L.M.M., "A Reminiscence," *Varsity*, 4 Nov. 1896, 39; "Moral Stories – II"; Toronto *World*, 7 Oct. 1896; *College Topics*, 18 Oct. 1898; "Convocation," *Varsity*, 19 Oct. 1894, 4; *Varsity*, 17 Oct. 1899, 10.
41 Coleman, "Our Annual Hustle"; W.C. Good letter, *Varsity*, 2 Nov. 1898, 36.
42 Brian Dobbs, *Edwardians at Play: Sport, 1890–1914* (London: Pelham Books 1973), 18; J.A. Mangan, *Athleticism in the Victorian and Edwardian Public School: The Emergence and Consolidation of an Educational Ideology* (Cambridge: Cambridge University Press 1981), 9.
43 "The Hustle," *Varsity*, 11 Oct. 1900, 7; *Varsity*, 16 Oct. 1901, 4; Toronto *Mail*, 7 Oct. 1902; "The Hustle," *Varsity*, 12 Oct. 1904, 7.
44 "The Hustle," *Varsity*, 12 Oct. 1905, 19; *Varsity*, 11 Oct. 1906, 24; *Varsity*, 18 Oct. 1906, 37; Toronto *Star*, 9 Oct. 1906.
45 "The Passing of the Hustle," *Varsity*, 14 Oct. 1902, 8; Stroller, "Week by Week," *Varsity*, 14 Oct. 1903, 5; *Varsity*, 17 Oct. 1907, 22; Toronto *Telegram*, 29 Oct. 1907.
46 *Varsity*, 9 Oct. 1908, 1.
47 *Varsity*, 12 Oct. 1909, 1; *Varsity*, 18 Oct. 1911, 1; *Varsity*, 29 Oct. 1913, 1.
48 *Varsity*, 18 Oct. 1911, 1; Toronto *World*, 22 Oct. 1912; Toronto *Telegram*, 11 Oct. 1913; *Varsity*, 13 Oct. 1913, 2; *Varsity*, 16 Oct. 1914, 1. SAC, established in

1914, was the student governing body for the whole university. It evolved from the student parliament founded in 1908. Each faculty and college had its own student council as well.

49 Toronto *Mail*, 8 Oct. 1890; Toronto *World*, 11 Oct. 1893. Trinity Medical School, to which most of the early evidence relates, did not amalgamate with U of T's medical school until 1903. Varsity medical students also practiced elevating. See "Medical Notes," *Varsity*, 27 Oct. 1891, 43.

50 In 1902 frosh were lifted over a bar and deposited in the school basement. Brief references to 1905 and 1906 events make no mention of anything like this. A.E. McFarlane, "The Hustle: From an Undergraduate Standpoint," *Varsity*, 21 Oct. 1897, 19; *Varsity*, 14 Oct. 1902, 14; *Varsity*, 19 Oct. 1905, 48; *Varsity*, 11 Oct. 1906, 29; *Varsity*, 4 Oct. 1911, 1.

51 *Varsity*, 6 Oct. 1911, 1; *Varsity*, 24 Nov. 1904, 121; *Varsity*, 20 Nov. 1900, 93; *Varsity*, 4 Feb. 1903, 239.

52 In 1911, for example, UC frosh were urged to turn out for initiation in newspaper notices and in personal invitations. *Varsity*, 16 Oct. 1912, 1; *Varsity*, 11 Oct. 1911; *Varsity*, 16 Oct. 1911.

53 *Varsity*, 16 Oct. 1901, 4; *Varsity*, 14 Oct. 1902, 7; *Varsity*, 27 Oct. 1904, 45.

54 *Varsity*, Dec. 1904, 147; *Varsity*, 21 Oct. 1896, 16; *Varsity*, 10 Nov. 1904, 79.

55 *Varsity*, 14 Nov. 1907, 90; *Varsity*, 11 Nov. 1912, 3.

56 *Varsity*, 11 Oct. 1910, 4; *Varsity*, 10 Nov. 1913, 1.

57 "Guy Fawkes Party," *Varsity*, 14 Nov. 1907, 90; *Varsity*, 11 Oct. 1910; *Varsity*, 10 Nov. 1913, 1; *Varsity*, 9 Nov. 1914, 3.

58 *Varsity*, 13 Nov. 1916, 2; *Varsity*, 14 Nov. 1917, 3. Also *Varsity*, 11 Oct. 181, 1.

59 *Varsity*, 10 Oct. 1917, 2; U of T Archives, University College Council Minutes, A69-0016, 2 Nov. 1916; *Varsity*, 27 Oct. 1915, 1; Med letter, *Varsity*, 12 Oct. 1917, 2.

60 *Varsity*, 5 Oct. 1917, 3; *Varsity*, 12 Oct. 1917, 1.

61 *Varsity*, 12 Oct. 1917, 2; *Varsity*, 17 Oct. 1917, 1; *Varsity*, 16 Oct. 1918, 1.

62 *Varsity*, 28 Sept. 1921, 2; *Varsity* 28 Jan. 1921, 1; *Varsity*, 1 Oct. 1924, 4.

63 See, for example, *Varsity*, 21 Feb. 1921, 2.

64 At Victoria University in the late nineteenth century, for example, each year wore ties of a special colour. See *Acta Victoriana* (Nov. 1878): 9.

65 *Varsity*, 28 Jan. 1921, 1; *Varsity*, 3 Oct. 1921, 1; *Varsity*, 5 Oct. 1921, 1; Toronto *Telegram*, 20 Oct. 1920.

66 U of T Archives, Papers of University Historian, Report of SAC Investigatory Commission, 24 Jan. 1923, A 83-0036/022, file Caput 1906–32.

67 Ibid. Robert d'Arcy, chief constable to A.D. LePan, 23 Oct. 1925.

68 *Varsity*, 17 Oct. 1919, 4; *Varsity*, 20 Oct. 1922, 1; *Varsity*, 18 Oct. 1923, 1.

69 *Varsity*, 7 March 1923, 3; *Varsity*, 30 Oct. 1922, 2. See also *Varsity*, 21 Feb. 1921, 2; *Varsity*, 26 Jan. 1923, 2; *Varsity*, 2 Feb. 1923; 6; *Varsity*, 9 Oct. 1923, 2, 4.

70 Papers of University Historian, Falconer to Taylor, 20 Feb. 1923; University College Council Minutes, 3 Oct. 1919; *Varsity*, 6 Oct. 1924, 1.

71 *Varsity*, 19 Nov. 1925, 141; *Varsity*, 17 Oct. 1928; *Varsity*, 1 Oct. 1926, 2.

72 *Varsity*, 30 Sept. 1929, 2.

73 Papers of University Historian, Taylor to Falconer, 19 Feb. 1923.

74 See, for example, J.S. LaFontaine, *Initiation: Ritual Drama and Secret Knowledge across the World* (Harmondsworth: Penguin 1985). Both types employ similar devices, including oaths, distinctive dress, tests, and mutilation of the body.

75 Gregory S. Kealey, *Toronto Workers Respond to Industrial Capitalism, 1867–1842* (Toronto: University of Toronto Press 1980), 41–2; Russell Hann, *Some Historical Perspectives on Canadian Agrarian Political Movements* (Toronto: New Hogtown Press 1973), 6–7; Eric Hobsbawm, *Primitive Rebels* (Manchester: Manchester University Press 1959), 150–74.

76 Bledstein, *Culture of Professionalism*, 127.

77 On the importance of manliness in this period, see Morris Mott, "The Winnipeg Vics 1890–1903: The Meaning of Hockey at the Turn of the Century," in School of Physical and Health Education, University of Toronto, *Proceedings, 5th Canadian Symposium on the History of Sport and Physical Education* (Toronto 1982), 1–10.

78 John Reid has made the same point in *Mount Allison University*, 1:191.

79 Warren I. Susman, "'Personality' and the Making of Twentieth-Century Culture," in *Culture as History: The Transformation of American Society in the Twentieth Century* (New York: Pantheon 1984), 271–85.

80 Victor Turner, *The Anthropology of Performance* (New York: PAJ Publications 1986), 75, and *Process, Performance and Pilgrimage* (New Delhi: Concept 1979), 21, 64, 94.

81 Davis, *Society and Culture*, 130.

82 When Guy Fawkes parties began, it was a long-standing custom of male U of T students to frequent the theatre on Hallowe'en. Since women could not participate in those often disruptive affairs, they perhaps viewed the party as a substitute. See K. Walden, "'Respectable Hooligans': Male College Students in Toronto Celebrate Hallowe'en, 1884–1910," *Canadian Historical Review* 68, no. 1 (Mar. 1987): 1–34.

83 Kett, *Rites of Passage*, 174–5.

84 Fass, *The Damned and The Beautiful*, 367–8.

CHAPTER SIX

Student Life at Regina College in the 1920s

James M. Pitsula

The discovery of adolescence in the first two decades of the twentieth century focused the concern of North Americans on the special needs and problems of youth.[1] In the 1920s concern escalated to alarm as books, magazines, and movies reported the antics of "flaming youth." The youth of the 1920s initiated a sexual revolution, not a revolution resulting in a dramatic increase in sexual intercourse but a revolution growing out of new patterns of sex-play – dating, necking, and petting.[2] Young people flouted convention by smoking and drinking in public, and the dances they enjoyed most were the ones most criticized by adults. "The dancers were close, the steps were fast, and the music was jazz."[3] Anxiety about the wild behaviour of a generation, who seemed addicted to booze, sex, and fast cars, spread to Canadian campuses. Many of the First World War veterans returning to Queen's brought back habits of smoking and drinking, dancing and gambling, which younger students were happy to imitate. The attempt to control unruly behaviour and maintain the good name of the university led to a major student strike in 1928.[4] Although the atmosphere at the University of Saskatchewan was more conservative and subdued, the president received complaints about students' drinking and smoking; the faculty passed a resolution condemning the playing of jazz music at undergraduate parties, and the student newspaper dispensed the following advice:

> Neck and the world necks with you
> Be a prude and you're all blue
> There are plenty of girls in Saskatchewan Hall
> So why should you neck alone.[5]

During the 1920s at Mount Allison University in New Brunswick the students showed their independence by refusing to attend chapel services and by demanding an end to the ban on dances. In both instances the university authorities gave way.[6] Even the high schools worried about rebellious youth: "Increases in productivity, affluence and leisure time all contributed to making what came to be called the flapper age or the jazz age. Large numbers of youth who were brought up in comparative affluence, free of concerns about involvement in production, began to develop a different style of life around the new technology of the twentieth century ... To many veteran school personnel and other upholders of traditional moral values, all this seemed to be leading youth straight down the path to hell."[7]

Contemporaries probably exaggerated the unorthodoxy of allegedly flaming youth. Opinion polls taken in the United States in the 1920s failed to turn up any significant differences in fundamental beliefs between middle-class youth and their parents, apart from differing levels of tolerance for petting and necking.[8] The youth culture of the 1920s was mainly a matter of style and naughty flirtation rather than a deep-seated revolt.[9] Middle-class youth created a sub-culture by adopting "norms, customs, modes of dress, and language fads different from those of adults," but not a counter-culture, which requires "the presence of an ideology that defends deviant behaviour in the name of some progressive ideas."[10]

Students at Regina College, a residential high school and junior college established by the Methodist Church in 1911, did not participate, except in a minor way, in the youth sub-culture of the 1920s. The comprehensive nature of the curricular and extra-curricular program, the type of supervision and discipline, the relative isolation of Regina from the sources of metropolitan culture, and the socio-economic background of the students all predisposed them to accept adult norms and values. Young people at Regina College were not afraid to break the rules on occasion and make mischief, but there was no pattern of self-conscious rebelliousness.

Initially, the academic program did not go beyond grade twelve (senior matriculation), which at that time was the equivalent of first-year university. In 1925, however, the college was affiliated with the University of Saskatchewan and began to offer second-year arts. Students were now able to take the first two years of the four-year arts degree. The Regina institution provided an important service for rural Saskatchewan, where high schools were scarce. Parents preferred to send their children to a residential school rather than have them board in a private home in a strange city. The college enforced discipline and lived up to the slogan displayed in its advertisements, "Your boy or girl will be safe in Regina College." As educational facilities improved in rural parts of the province, fewer young people had to leave home in order to attend high school, particularly for grades nine and ten. The enrolment at Regina College, as shown in Table 1, was increasingly concentrated in the higher grades and in the university courses.

The students who came from Regina attended the college for reasons different from those of the rural students. Some parents liked the prestige

Table 1
Academic students attending Regina College
1920–30

Year ending	Prepa- ratory	Grade 9	Grade 10	Grade 11	Grade 12 (First- year arts)	Second- year arts	Total
1920	33	37	47	54	32	—	203
1921	18	28	40	61	33	—	180
1922	8	26	31	47	24	—	136
1923	9	20	40	53	32	—	154
1924	10	20	24	53	51	—	158
1925	6	9	23	56	47	—	141
1926	0	22	27	64	63	36	212
1927	7	19	22	65	87	38	238
1928	3	17	22	58	82	41	223
1929	8	13	35	65	69	49	239
1930	2	9	26	56	57	54	204

Source: University of Regina Archives, 7516, Report of the Registrar to the Regina College Senate, 1932.

of a private school, which they considered a cut above the public collegiates. Others sent their children for disciplinary reasons: "There were some very high spirited students – especially the day students who lived in Regina and made up the rest of my class. They had been sent to College as a last resort because they boasted they had been kicked out of every collegiate in Regina. Their chief aim was to disrupt the class and the teacher so much that no work could be done – and they did make it very difficult to accomplish much in many of the classes ... They did achieve the nervous breakdown of one teacher by Christmas."[11] After 1925 a larger percentage of the student body came from Regina because many chose to take second-year arts at the college rather than attend a university and pay for board and room.

None the less, Regina College remained, throughout the 1920s, mainly a residential school (in 1925–26, 69 per cent of academic students lived in residence).[12] Non-residential students, with their stories of evening adventures, could have a disturbing influence on the residential students, who spent every evening in study hall. The rules therefore prohibited out-of-town students from taking room and board in a private home if space was available in the residence. The students were about equally divided between boys and girls (104 girls and 108 boys in 1925–26). About 70 per cent of them were between 16 and 19 years old, but the range of ages was surprisingly wide. The youngest student in residence in 1925–26 was 13 and the oldest 29, the large variation attributable to the policy of admitting older men and women who had been unable to attend school at the normal age or who wished to upgrade their qualifications. [13]

As one would expect in a college run by the Methodist Church, most of the students were of that denomination. After church union in 1925 the United Church predominated (78.4 per cent), followed by Anglicans (9.4 per cent), Presbyterians (4.7 per cent), and a sprinkling of Lutherans, Baptists, Roman Catholics, Jews, and Christian Scientists. [14] Additional information about the backgrounds of the students was obtained from a questionnaire filled out in 1984 by 49 students who attended the college during the 1920s. Interviews were conducted with another 10 students, for a total sample of 59 (45 women and 14 men). The large majority came from outside Regina (51). Fathers' occupations were as follows: farmer, 38; storekeeper, 4; real-estate / insurance agent, 2; clergyman 2; lawyer, 2; Regina College faculty, 2; business executive, 2; salesman, 1; druggist, 1; butcher, 1; station agent, 1; medical doctor, 1; parents deceased, 2. Regina College students in the 1920s were mostly the sons and daughters of farmers with a relatively small admixture from the business and professional classes.

In answer to the question "Was going to Regina College a financial strain?" 26 replied "yes"; 3 "probably"; 5 "somewhat"; 5 "don't know"; and 18 "no". Many students helped to pay their way by working on the family farm: ploughing, seeding, cultivating, binding, stooking, racking, threshing, hauling, milking, butchering, and cooking and baking for the threshing crew. Ernest W. Stapleford, president of the college from 1915 to 1934, cited the example of a girl who earned four dollars an acre breaking up a new quarter-section of land. Others took summer or part-time jobs as book sellers, piano teachers, orchestra musicians, section hands for the CPR, sales personnel, and office clerks. The college hired needy students as librarians, nurses' assistants, laboratory workers, janitors, and dining-room waiters. Landing a job often made the difference between being able to enrol or not. While a small minority belonged to wealthy and prominent Regina families, the majority came from modest backgrounds. Extravagance was discouraged, and parents were reminded that "a large amount of spending money is injurious to students." Allowances had to be paid through the college bursar, not directly by the parents, the amount of money having been approved by the dean. [15]

The aim of Regina College was to build character and create good citizens by providing a well-rounded education. The program was intended to foster the spiritual, intellectual, physical, and social development of young people. Religious training consisted of compulsory Sunday church attendance, daily chapel, religious-education classes, and voluntary Christian student organizations. The girls from the residence walked to Metropolitan Methodist (later United) Church "in line" – that is, in pairs, with one teacher in front and another at the back. The only acceptable excuse for non-attendance was illness, verified by a note from the nurse. The boys, who did not have to walk in line, had an easier time avoiding church: "To avoid church you probably stayed in bed till after breakfast. Somebody brought you a few slices of buttered toast. When the last call for church was made, you were probably in the tub having a prolonged bath. Then, as soon as the coast was clear, you and the gang sneaked out the east entrance, down Hamilton Street to the White Spot Cafeteria."[16]

During the week the morning classes were interrupted by a twenty-minute chapel service consisting of hymns, prayers, and a short talk. One of the faculty members usually presided, but on occasion a special guest – for example, Bliss Carman or Nellie McClung – would address the students. Not all of the speeches were strictly religious. The chief of the fire department gave advice about fire prevention, and the Methodist Social Reform Secretary described the physiological harm caused by even moderate consumption of alcohol.[17] Pranks were played, such as planting an alarm clock inside the speaker's lectern or jamming the piano keys with hymn-books. Boys diverted themselves by rubbing their seats on the wooden benches, generating enough static electricity to "spark" the girls.[18] Students tried to skip out, but there was no attempt to have compulsory attendance abolished. A yearbook poet even celebrated the mid-morning break from classes:

'Mid the bang and the pang of college life,
  'Mid the trials and troubles and all the strife,
'Mid the hustle and bustle of college years,
  There's one bright light that helps us to steer
Through all that is wrong and would lead us astray,
  And that is the morning chapel each day.[19]

The religious-education classes occupied two half-hour sessions per week. The courses surveyed the Old and New Testaments, incorporating the results of modern Biblical scholarship (moving one student to complain, "Religious education classes were interesting except that sometimes they explained away the miracles").[20] The listing of Walter Rauschenbush's *The Social Principles of Jesus* as one of the textbooks suggests the continuing influence of the social gospel.[21] On a Sunday in March designated College Sunday the religious-education instructor appealed to the students to make a definite personal commitment to Christianity. In 1923 he was dismayed by the result: "Investigation later suggested that one chief difficulty we have had to contend with this year has been the lack of the best type of leadership among our students ... [It is suggested] that great care be exercised in dealing with student offenders against the fundamental standards of our college life, so that it be seriously considered in the fall term especially, whether such offenders, after being put on trial, should not be dismissed for the sake of the common welfare of the student body."[22] The response of the following year, when the challenge to lead a Christian life was made in a small classroom rather than a large hall, was much better: "A large majority of students in each form recorded decisions to begin the Christian life or be more loyal to it, to undertake the means necessary to sustain that life and to go back to their communities with the idea of service dominant."[23]

Compulsory church attendance, chapel services, and religious-education classes were supplemented by voluntary student associations. The college YMCA presented programs in 1924–25 on such topics as "Choosing a Vocation," "The Race Problem," "Hygiene," and "Something Every Boy Should Know," and debated on the theme "Resolved that Preparation for War is a Guarantee of Peace."[24] The YMCA and the YWCA were united in 1925 in the Student Christian Movement, which busied itself with a regular Sunday-evening fireside hour of readings and singing, sleigh rides, and teas to raise money for the International Student Service.[25] Both the SCM and its predecessors organized small discussion groups where students could talk about issues of personal concern. The YMCA in 1925 covered such topics as "playing square, clean speech, habit, boasting, petty gambling, tobacco, camouflage, girls, the making of a real man, work, making good, and friendships."[26] In 1929 over 50 per cent of the residential students signed up for the discussion groups.[27] The SCM focused upon the personal development of students rather than on politics or social causes. This may have reflected the relative youth of the student body compared with that of a university campus.

Religion was an important part of student life at Regina College. Despite occasional disobedience by individuals, most young people accepted compulsory religious observances and gave the SCM considerable support. Students made no concerted demands for change and showed no signs of wanting to "liberate" themselves from religious beliefs and practices.

The college operated on the premise that spiritual growth and character development went together with intellectual training. The women's dean stated in 1925, "The work of the classroom has been given first place," a sentiment that also found favour with the men's dean. "One of the fine things with regard to our sport is that it does not interfere with the students' studies ... We believe in a place for everything and everything in its place."[28] Classes were scheduled from 8:40 A.M. to 12:00 noon and from 1:30 P.M. to 4:00 P.M. Spares were spent studying, with residence students attending compulsory study hall every evening, Monday to Friday, from 7:30 P.M. to 9:45 P.M. The second-year arts students and those with averages above 60 per cent were allowed to study in their own rooms, while a teacher patrolled the halls to make sure everyone was working. At about 8:30 a bell announced a fifteen-minute break, and a box of apples appeared.

The faculty met once a week to review examination results in order to identify the students who needed extra tutoring and encouragement. Students were expected to work in a disciplined way:

It was an excellent school with good teachers. I learned how to apply myself and how to study for the first time while there. I felt afterward that I owed a great deal to this training and to learning for the first time what it meant to be a "student" ... To sum up my feeling about Regina College, I think what I learned about good study habits had a marked effect upon my later life, even influencing the way our children were educated. When we found at the Junior High level in Burnaby that no good study habits were formed (they were called "squares" if they so much as did their homework) and that they had no experience in writing final exams, we had each of them attend a private school where there was a much greater incentive for them to work. [29]

Academic achievement was measured by formal examinations at Christmas, Easter, and at the end of June. Most extra-curricular activities came to a halt soon after the Easter break to allow sufficient time to prepare for finals. The marks were published in a Regina daily newspaper, giving recognition to the successful and providing an incentive for the less successful.

Although the athletic director complained in 1929 of being unable to persuade his colleagues that physical education belonged on an equal footing with academics, the college had a comprehensive athletic program in which all students participated. [30] Girls in residence did "setting-up exercises" before breakfast, as well as "corrective exercises for curved spines and round shoulders." After breakfast, they went ourdoors for a brisk twenty-minute walk "in line," as when they walked to church. The boys could do as they liked, perhaps a game of tennis or a run around Wascana Lake. [31] Students received a minimum of one hour and as much as three hours per week of instruction in physical education during regular class time. Grades were assigned and used in the calculation of students' averages for the term reports. The full range of intramural and intercollegiate sports was offered: hockey, rugby, basketball, volleyball, baseball, tennis, boxing, swimming, hiking, track and field, and skating. [32]

Extra-curricular activities also catered to students with a literary bent. A newspaper appeared irregularly, but the major publication was the yearbook. The Drama Club staged elaborate productions, which always received rave reviews (regardless of their quality, one suspects). The Boys' Literary Society held mock parliaments and debated such resolutions as "Resolved that Canadian boys should receive military training in colleges and high schools and military camps" and "Resolved that the doctors should be paid by the Community." [33] The Latin club played Latin games, sang Latin songs, and listened to lectures with titles like "A Visit to Horace's Farm." [34] A short-lived Historical Society attempted intellectual discussions ("many diverse opinions were painfully extracted from the would-be historians").[35] Aspiring college Carusos joined the boys' glee club, and the girls' chorus practised weekly. The student orchestra was much in demand at social functions. A sorority, the Pente Kai Deka, brought together all the girls in second-year arts who wished to join.[36]

The college had social events to mark the beginning and end of the term. The faculty hosted a formal fall reception, complete with receiving line, to welcome the students. Games were played to break the ice: "The guests were divided into groups according to birthday months. Each group was required to compose a song, the rendering of which was in all cases very amusing ... After being allotted partners, a contest involving the knowledge of trees was conducted."[37] The college banquet in March, a formal affair with toasts, speeches, and musical entertainment, capped the school year. During the year there were Hallowe'en, Valentine's, and other parties. Movie and theatre excursions were organized: "After a hectic, but successful attempt to arrange satisfactory partners, the third Form sallied forth to the Capitol Theatre. After listening for two hours to the soul-disturbing cries of one Al Jolson for his mammy, they returned to the College, amusing themselves on the way back by making awful attempts at imitating the said Mr. Jolson."[38] At skating parties the girls filled out skating cards similar to dance cards, listing their partners for the evening. The college did not allow dances until 1925, and even then the privilege was extended only to those in second-year arts. Some of the younger students resented the ban:

I always felt that we should have been able to dance with boys. I remember one nite we went to the library – someone played the piano and we turned out the lights. Some of the boys dropped in and we were dancing up a storm and on went the lights. A teacher had heard us. One boy was so scared he jumped out the window and broke his leg. That ended his College career. We were a little scared it might end ours too. They were pretty strict with us.

Our grade 12 graduation was held on the campus. It was a beautiful summer nite. All the girls in their Grad dresses and the boys so handsome. The College had hired a band and the music was beautiful! One of the tunes I remember was "Linger Awhile." But we were not allowed to dance.[39]

The strictures against dancing were gradually relaxed. Although the faculty in 1928 gave the right to grade twelve, a similar motion for grades nine, ten, and eleven was defeated the following year. A motion allowing grade-eleven students to dance was then introduced and passed by a slim margin. School dances were, of course, well-chaperoned and ended before midnight.[40]

In addition to attending formal social events organized by college organizations, the students practised their own initiation rites, not unlike those described by Keith Walden in his essay in this volume on student life at the

University of Toronto. Initiation for Regina College boys in the 1920s began when the Grand Demon, dressed in a flowing brown robe, his face painted a bright red, entered the dining hall at suppertime firing shots from a Colt .38. He ordered the freshmen to change to old clothes and then come to the chapel. They were blindfolded and escorted through the tunnel to the gymnasium, where they were brought before the Grand Demon for trial, found guilty, and "shot." Their lifeless bodies were taken to the balcony of the gym and dropped to the floor below. The corpses were embalmed in fluids. The Grand Demon revived the bodies by administering a mild electric shock. Each boy swore the oath of allegiance to the Brown Brotherhood Goblet.[41]

The girls had a tamer initiation. The newcomers were required to appear at supper with middies on backwards, skirts upside down, faces painted, and hair in small braids. With great green bows added to their hats, they marched downtown to the Capitol Theatre and took front-row seats. At the end of the movie the words "Welcome Freshettes of Regina College" flashed on the screen. The spotlight turned on the girls, who stood up and faced the audience while the orchestra played "Hail, hail, the gang's all here." Back at the college the "freshettes" were forced to run the gauntlet of "Devil's Alley," after which they could consider themselves full-fledged members of the student body.[42]

Extra-curricular activities came under the jurisdiction of their respective student directorates: social, literary and dramatic, athletic, Student Christian Movement, and yearbook. Representatives from each of these directorates, together with executive officers elected by the student body as a whole, made up the student council. The students were permitted a limited form of self-government under the watchful eye of the faculty. A faculty adviser was attached to each student directorate and two faculty members sat on the student council. In addition, the returning officer for the elections was always a teacher.[43] Each of the residences had student committees to advise the deans and bring forward questions and complaints. Generally speaking, however, the deans did not trust these student bodies with much power. The dean of men sized up the situation: "I have found that in this body certain boys have a high sense of responsibility but that others have not. For this reason I have been unwilling to entrust much executive power to them as far as residence discipline is concerned."[44] The student committees could be used in such a way as to strengthen the authority of the deans. If the dean had the support of respected student leaders, the rank and file were more likely to fall into line and obey the residence rules.[45]

Regina College was not a democratic community. The lines of authority were clear, and there was no question who was in charge. Not only did the faculty give constant supervision and guidance, but they also knew what they wanted to accomplish. Their purpose was to help young people develop into capable, well-rounded citizens of good character. The entire college program – religious, academic, athletic, and social — was dedicated to that end. What the college was teaching was not confined to the classroom or the organized extra-curricular activities. The faculty, in addition to being experts in their respective academic disciplines, were expected to serve as role models exemplifying good character. The college had something of the atmosphere of a family, with the faculty taking the role of benevolent, though strict, parents.

The residential nature of the college guaranteed that students and faculty spent a great deal of time together. From "lights on" at 7 A.M. to "lights out" at 10 P.M. students were under almost constant supervision. They had little opportunity to break away on their own or "get into trouble." The girls in particular were carefully watched. If they wished to leave the college grounds, they needed to obtain the permission of the women's dean and sign a register when they left and again when they returned. On a Saturday afternoon girls might go shopping downtown, but only in a group, not by themselves.[46]

At the beginning of the school year a girl's parents were asked to supply a list of people whom the girl might suitably visit. Invitations to dinner or other social events were approved only when the name of the hostess appeared on the list. The hostess, or someone representing her, picked the girl up at the college and brought her back at a prearranged time. Early leave expired at 9:45 P.M. and late leave at 11 P.M.; weekends away from the college were granted sparingly. Girls had the privilege of receiving callers at the residence at certain specified times, from 5 to 6 P.M. on weekdays, from 2 to 6 P.M. on Saturday, and from 4 to 5 P.M. on Sunday. "Gentlemen callers" were required to bring with them a letter of introduction from the girl's parents or guardian. Girls who were at least seventeen years of age could go out with boys on Saturday afternoon, provided, of course, that they had the permission of the girl's parents and the women's dean. In 1929 the calendar for the first time mentioned that a girl could accept an invitation from a boy for Saturday night. However, the calendar hastened to add that a Regina College girl could not attend a public dance and that "motoring" was permissible only with adult friends on the visitors' list or in a motoring party with an approved chaperone.[47] Clearly, the college authorities feared the possibilities created by riding in a boyfriend's car.

Compared to the girls, the boys at Regina College enjoyed considerable freedom to come and go as they pleased. The rules about chaperones and staying in groups did not apply to the boys. They could leave the college premises more easily, except during class time or study periods. Although the outside doors were locked at 10:30 P.M., boys made their entry through the coal-chute or unlocked basement windows.[48] The girls could not help but notice the contrast between their regimentation and the latitude given the boys: "We never understood why girls required so many 'musts' and boys went free!"[49]

Most of the students from farms and small towns were anything but sophisticated. They were given instruction in polite manners and the social graces. At mealtimes one faculty member sat at the head of each table of eight. Students who did not know what a bread and butter plate was, or did not wait until everybody at the table was served before beginning to eat, were promptly corrected. Rough farm boys had to be told laboriously "which forks and spoons to use and to cut meat one piece at a time and convey that solo piece to your mouth with your fork hand before you cut another."[50] The college also insisted upon certain standards in dress and grooming. The girls lined up in pairs for inspection before entering the dining room. Girls with uncombed hair, untidy stockings. or crooked hemlines were sent back to their rooms to make themselves presentable. Boys had to wear a suit-jacket and tie.[51]

Girls were continually reminded what "ladies" did and did not do. Ladies did not go downtown without wearing a hat and gloves ("You don't go down the front steps putting on your gloves; they must be on before leaving"); ladies did not buy jewellery at the fifteen-cent store, and they did not wear gaudy make-up.[52] Rooms were inspected and the state of closets and drawers commented upon. After one particularly enjoyable party, the women's dean delivered a stern lecture: "Apparently, our fun had been too noisy and un-lady-like."[53] For girls "the tea" was an important institution. They learned how to "pour" and to conduct themselves properly as hostesses. Board of governors' wives invited the girls to their homes, affording the students a glimpse of the higher levels of Regina society.[54] The injunction to "behave like a lady" was a continual theme: "All were encouraged to be ladies at all times. One thing I remember was 'If you must chew gum go into your closet and shut the door' ... The College was almost a 'finishing school.' I came from College feeling able to conduct myself as a lady ... [The dean] wanted everyone of her girls to be 'ladies' and for the most part I think we went along with her ideas."[55]

The faculty made sure that boy-girl relationships did not get out of hand. Students were allowed to play tennis as couples as long as the courts were well supervised from the windows above. A boy might carry his girlfriend's skates down to the lake and skate with her, but if they wandered too far away by themselves, they were breaking the rules.[56] Boys and girls walked in pairs on "progressive hikes," changing partners every time the whistle blew. In the 1920s one night a week was set aside for dignified courtship:

Tuesday evenings are gala nights for the students of Regina College. About five o'clock Mr. Willey [the janitor] can be seen inspecting the lights of the Reception Room and also the springs of the chesterfield. Mrs. Truman arduously flourishes a duster over certain stiff-backed chairs which are only used on this one occasion. Miss Theal [the matron] also celebrates – the menu – onions, liver, and bacon, but no one minds for every little heart is palpitating in anticipation of the great event. Two young ladies, obviously embarrassed, stand at the tower room door and receive the braver members of the other sex, while every other fair maiden in the residence hangs over the bannister of the first floor landing waiting anxiously for her name to be called. The gentlemen having arrived, everyone proceeds to take full possession of the few precious moments, with the anxious eyes of the Faculty alternating between the chesterfield and the clock. At seven ten, the harsh ringing of the bell brings us to earth again and with languishing glances and last words of farewell, everyone moves to the tower room door. They are gone! The night is over and we once more settle down to the routine of college life.[57]

The instruction given on matters of sex was, as would be expected of the time and place, very discreet. The women's dean held a "dean's hour" every Saturday after the noon lunch when she talked to the girls about etiquette, deportment, and personal hygiene. The topics ranged from "not reading others' letters to never using a toothpick."[58] One day the dean announced that the subject of the following week's discussion would be "BFS." The girls waited in a state of some bewilderment, until they in due course learned that BFS were boyfriends.[59] The men's dean also gave talks to the boys about good manners and suitable vocabulary. Embarrassment surrounded the sex lectures: "The pamphlet he distributed, which had to be returned, was read, usually after lights out, by aid of a flashlight and with a great deal of snickering."[60]

Despite the best efforts of the faculty, boys and girls found ways to spend time together and contrived unauthorized communications: "Girl Watching – (a very important part of our education!) I seem to recall after hours, or during study periods, hanging out windows to look across the way to the girls' residence, signals exchanged; and whispered conversations through the steel doors that separated us from the tower room."[61] Items printed in the college yearbook hinted of couples testing the bounds of propriety:

  Girl: 'No, now we mustn't, didn't you see the Deans have decided to stop necking?'
  Boy: 'Great Scott! First thing you know they'll want students to stop too.'[62]

In one famous episode that achieved almost the status of a legend, three boys and three girls took a room for the weekend in the Hotel Saskatchewan. They might have escaped punishment had they not made such a mess of the room, causing the hotel manager to complain to President Stapleford. All six were immediately expelled.[63]

Boys were expected to be "gentlemen," and girls were expected to be "ladies," although the latter seemed rather more important than the former. The "flapper," "what this age would call a very modern girl,"[64] was decidedly not a lady. A symbol of the exuberant "roaring" twenties, the flapper "smoked, drank, wore a lot of make-up and short dresses, and 'slept around.'" Many Regina College girls imitated flapper styles and fashions, but only a few carried the imitation to the extent of sleeping around.[65] Two girls created a sensation at the college in 1916 when they bobbed their hair,[66] but by the 1920s bobbed hair was commonplace. Girls were experimenting with the "shingle," the "buster brown," marcel waves, spit curls, and little back-combed bushes covering the ears called "cootie garages."[67] Make-up was permitted, but only in modest amounts. The students poked fun at those who used too much:

> When Smarty took her in his arms
> The color left her cheek
> But on the lapels of his coat
> It showed up for a week.[68]

Clothing styles showed the flapper influence. Girls wore sleeveless dresses with the low-waist design. They rolled their stockings below the knee in keeping with the popular song, "Roll'em, roll'em down and show your pretty knees!" While a girl's party dress might be in the flapper style ("Brief skirt, long waist, wide belt and beads, gold shot taffeta and black beads"), everyday wear consisted most often of a middy, with a red or blue tie, and a skirt.[69] Regina College kept a tight rein on flapperdom: "Some girls tried to emulate them [flappers] but this was frowned on ... There was no encouragement of flappers in Regina College under Dr. Stapleford ... We were aware [of flappers] but our styles of dress were watched. I don't think we ever disgraced the college."[70]

Flappers were part of the libertine spirit of the jazz age. Even Regina, isolated from the major cities, experienced some of the general cultural influences of the 1920s. Newspapers, movies, and magazines spread the latest fads and trends. Playing in a Regina theatre in 1931 was a movie with the slightly risqué title "Confessions of a Co-ed: A Flaming Diary of Flaming College Youth." (Predictably, this 1920s movie didn't arrive in the city until 1931.) The film dealt with "the lives and loves, hopes and ambitions of the most interesting people in America today, the young College students. Its startling exposures ... will amaze you ... an exciting procession of girls' clothes, proms, dances, dating and week-ending in fashionable mountain resorts."[71] The moviegoer was tantalized with revelations about the glamorous life-style and uninhibited sexual behaviour of modern youth.

Jazz was the official music of youthful rebellion. The Regina newspaper, the *Leader*, published an alarmist story in 1922 warning that the "Empire May be Undermined by Spirit of Jazz."[72] Dan Cameron, instructor at the Regina College Conservatory, fulminated against the music's allegedly pernicious influence. He composed some facetious program notes for a jazz concert: "Petting parties, with club variants, were a significant feature of cave-man life. The untrammelled ego has been stimulated to a remarkable degree since the war by modern concepts of what freedom means. For this reason, the simple and vigorously direct emotional reactions of our primitive forebears are appreciated now as never before."[73] Cameron hit upon a major theme of 1920s culture, the discarding of conventional restraints as a result of disillusionment and disorientation caused by the First World War. Jazz was associated with primitive instincts and sexual freedom. Regina College students listened to and played jazz, but not to the exclusion of everything else. They danced the Charleston, but also the waltz and the two-step. The picture of a young generation out of control does not really fit.

Like jazz, public smoking and drinking were symbols of defiance and rebellion. Students at Regina College smoked on the sly, puffing while hanging out of windows so that there would be no odour left in their rooms, and standing on one side of a building or the other, depending on the direction of the wind. The furtive smoker might be able to sneak a drag in the laundry room or in the garden shed.[74] Detection was easier to escape away from the college grounds: "Fell's café was a no-no, but we went into its secluded booths, and, after buying a 10-cent package of cigarettes, practised smoking."[75] If smoking was considered bad behaviour, drinking was much worse. Drinking among Regina College students was not common, but boys were usually more daring than the girls. Only the very few girls labelled "fast" were reputed to drink. The boys took more chances, some even keeping bottles under the mattress or in a suitcase. Five boys were suspended in 1925 for drinking a small quantity of liquor on the college grounds.[76]

Students tried other forms of recreation not exactly in keeping with the norms of a Methodist church college. James M. Minifie, a student from 1919 to 1921, learned algebra by an unconventional method: "My other mathematical mentor was Blake Harper, a youth from Rouleau, on the rich Soo Line, who came to Regina College with a pork-pie hat and a pair of dice. He taught me how to use quadratic equations, and the theory of probability. Both quadratics and galloping dominoes, he pointed out, worked out on a plus or minus formula, whereas the theory of probability was a one-way street. The best way to learn crap-shooting, he held, was to lose twenty dollars betting on probability."[77] Crap-shooters could be found even in the girls' residence: "Oh yes, I learned to play poker at Regina College, Lola Murphy and I. We played for matches, as we didn't have money for anything like that. After a few hands the girl who was teaching us decided that it would be a good idea to play for 'Eats.' We'd had a nice 'care' package from home. Lola was too smart for that though. So she straightened out our would-be teacher and we kept our eats."[78] Most of the infractions of the rules were relatively innocuous. For sheer girlish excitement nothing could match the "midnight feed": "The lady teacher who was on duty for that day would come to each room, open the door and say 'Goodnight, Miss —.' So any mischief would have to be postponed until after she had made the rounds. From time to time a pupil would receive a parcel of food from home – often a chicken and other goodies. Friends would be invited in, then the key hole plugged, a blanket put at the bottom of the door so no light could be seen from outside. These were very special and memorable occasions."[79]

The students generally accepted, even though they did not always obey, the rules. Young people at Regina College may have been troublesome and high-spirited on occasion, but there was no general pattern of rebellion to suggest the existence of an independent youth culture. Most of them had come right off the farm and had little money to spare. A boarding-school education was a privilege not to be taken lightly. Parents at home were making financial sacrifices, and many of the students themselves waited on tables or worked as harvest labourers to pay the fees. As one student put it, "We were full of beans, but we weren't really bad. Our parents were having a tough time, for heaven's sake!"[80]

Even if students had been inclined to defy adult authority in a systematic way, they would not have had an easy time of it. The college filled the students' days with adult-controlled activities. Education was not something that happened only in the classroom but in the chapel, the study hall, the dining hall, the recreation room, on the playing field, and in the corridors. Regina College was not teaching academic subjects so much as it was teaching young people how to live. A youth sub-culture depends for its existence upon the influence of peers to establish norms different from those of the adult world. Peer influence was weak because the environment was at all times dominated by the faculty, who demanded, and generally received, obedience and respect. Absences from the college grounds were carefully regulated; students were rarely out of the sight of a dean or teacher.

Regina College youth in the 1920s exhibited few of the traits supposedly typical of the flaming youth of the roaring decade. Saskatchewan farms were a great distance, in more ways than one, from the urban purveyors of mass culture. The Methodist Church established Regina College "to impart to students not only the desired scholarship but at the same time the refinement and Christian character which is so essential to the full-orbed man or woman."[81] In the 1920s the college appears to have been doing just that.

NOTES

1 See Joseph F. Kett, *Rites of Passage: Adolescence in America, 1790 to the Present* (New York: Basic Books 1977).

2 Paula S. Fass, *The Damned and the Beautiful: American Youth in the 1920s* (New York: Oxford University Press 1977), 262.
3 Ibid., 301.
4 Frederick W. Gibson, *"To Serve and Yet Be Free": Queen's University, 1917–1961* (Montreal: McGill-Queen's University Press 1983), 68, 75.
5 Michael Hayden, *Seeking a Balance: The University of Saskatchewan, 1907–1982* (Vancouver: University of British Columbia Press 1983), 144–9.
6 John G. Reid, *Mount Allison University*, vol. 2, *1914–1963* (Toronto: University of Toronto Press, 1984), 99–100.
7 Robert M. Stamp, "Canadian High Schools in the 1920s and 1930s: The Social Challenge to the Academic Tradition," Canadian Historical Association, *Historical Papers 1978*, 79.
8 Kett, *Rites of Passage*, 262.
9 Fass, *The Damned and the Beautiful*, 376.
10 Kett, *Rites of Passage*, 258, 262.
11 Kathryn Milligan Biller, 1928–29, Regina College questionnaire.
12 University of Regina Archives (URA), Regina College, attendance summaries, 1925–26 to 1931–32, academic department, 75-2, 1900, box 9.
13 URA, 7516, report of the registrar to the Regina College senate, 1926–30; report of dean of men's residence, 1925–26.
14 URA, 7616, report of the registrar to senate, 1926–27.
15 URA, Regina College calendar.
16 Alva Samuel Haggerty, 1927–29, Regina College questionnaire.
17 URA, Regina College Register, Dec. 1923; Ethel E. Malone, 1923–27, questionnaire; Mary A. Garnons-Williams, 1922–26, questionnaire.
18 Bartlett Humbert, 1919–23, interview, 26 July 1984; Estella E. Kempton, 1924–25, questionnaire; Lloyd G. Gray, 1928–31, questionnaire.
19 URA, Regina College Register, 1929–30.
20 Pearl Kinney, 1915–19, questionnaire.
21 URA, 7516, report of the religious education instructor to senate, 1921–22.
22 Ibid.
23 Ibid.
24 URA, Regina College Register, 1925.
25 Ibid., 1929–30.
26 Ibid., 1925.
27 URA, 7516, report of the religious education instructor to senate, 1928–29.
28 URA, 7516, report of the dean of women's residence to senate, 1924–25; report of the dean of men's residence to senate, 1921–22.
29 Kathryn Milligan Biller, 1928–29, questionnaire.
30 URA, 7516, report of the physical-education instructor to senate, 1928–29.
31 URA, 7516, report of the physical-education instructor of the girls and the teacher of expression and drama to senate, 1921–22; Howard H. Lucas, 1926–29; R. Harold Batty, George L. Culham, 1928–30, questionnaire.

32 URA, 7516, report of the girls' physical-education instructor to senate, 1923–24; report of the academic dean to senate, 1921–22.
33 Regina *Leader*, 17 Jan. 1920; 13 Mar. 1920;1 Mar. 1924.
34 URA, Regina College Register, 1929–30.
35 Ibid.
36 Dorothy E. Van Cleave, 1929–30, questionnaire; URA, Regina College Register, 1929–30.
37 URA, Regina College Register, 1928–29.
38 Ibid., 1928–29.
39 Alma May Faraasen, 1922–24, questionnaire.
40 URA, 7516, academic faculty minutes, 22 Nov. 1929.
41 URA, Regina College Register, 1928–29.
42 Ibid., Dec. 1923.
43 Ibid., 7 Nov. 1929; 23 Sept. 1931.
44 URA, 7516, report of dean of men's residence to senate, 1925–26.
45 URA, 7516, report of dean of women's residence to senate, 1924–25.
46 URA, 7516, Regina College Calendar, 1924–25; Doris Brogden Dakin, 1920–21, 1923–24, interview, 16 Aug. 1984.
47 URA, 7516, Regina College Calendar, 1929–30.
48 Alva Samuel Haggerty, 1927–29, questionnaire.
49 URA, Kathleen R. McKenzie, "A Backward Look," in *Glimpses of the Last Fifty Years* (Regina: University of Saskatchewan 1961).
50 Mabel Emerson Geddes, 1927–28, questionnaire.
51 Pearl Sproule, 1929–30, interview, 23 July 1984.
52 Mona Fielding, 1930–31, questionnaire; Frances L. Hansen, 1927–31, questionnaire.
53 Georgie May Haggerty, 1926–28, questionnaire.
54 Eloise Mabel Metheral, 1926–29, questionnaire.
55 Lena Myrtle Taylor, 1917–18, Edythe M. Brown, 1926–26, Vera E. Weddige, 1926–27, questionnaire.
56 Ruth (Willsey) Wilkinson, 1914–16, interview, 27 May 1986.
57 URA, Regina College Register, 1928–29.
58 Lila May Staple, 1922–26, Phyllis M. McGirr, 1922–25, Alice E. Morrow, 1927–29, questionnaire.
59 Marion F. Grayson-Bell, 1933–34, questionnaire.
60 James E. McCann, 1934–36, questionnaire.
61 Alva Samuel Haggerty, 1927–29, questionnaire.
62 URA, Regina College Register, 1925.
63 Elsie Stapleford, 1926–27, questionnaire.
64 J. Albert Trew, 1915–16, questionnaire.
65 Pearl Sproule, 1929–30, interview, 23 July 1984.
66 J. Albert Trew, 1915–16, questionnaire.

67 Estella E. Kempton, 1924–26, Frances M. Oliver, 1926–28, Frances L. Hansen, 1927–31, Mabel Emerson Geddes, 1927–28, questionnaire; Evelyn Froom Lewis, 1929–30, interview, Aug. 16, 1984.

68 URA, Regina College Register, Mar. 1923.

69 Amelia Fedje, 1925–27, Kathryn Milligan Biller, 1928–29, Beryle Catherine Maxwell, 1926–28, Lily May Staple, 1922–26, questionnaire.

70 Marion Grayson-Hall, 1933–34; Anne May Engel, 1926–28, Edythe M. Brown, 1925–26, questionnaire.

71 Regina *Leader*, 7 Nov. 1931.

72 Ibid., 13 Nov. 1922.

73 Dan Cameron, "In the Music World," Regina *Leader*, 19 Dec. 1925.

74 Doris Riddell, 1928–30, interview, 31 July 1984; Roy Eckhoff, 1928–29, interview, 26 Sept. 1984.

75 Frances L. Hansen, 1927–31, questionnaire.

76 George Lloyd Culham, 1928–30, questionnaire; URA 7516, report of men's dean to senate, 1924–25.

77 James M. Minifie, *Homesteader: A Prairie Boyhood Recalled* (Toronto: Macmillan 1972).

78 Alma May Faraasen, 1922–24, questionnaire.

79 Marie Peterson, 1920–21, 1922–24, questionnaire.

80 Evelyn Froom Lewis, interview, 16 Aug. 1984.

81 URA, Regina College Tenth Anniversary Yearbook, 18.

PART THREE

The Campus at War

CHAPTER SEVEN

Acadia and the Great War*

Barry M. Moody

At 5:30 A.M. on Monday, 11 November 1918, a startled Acadia University was awakened by the incessant ringing of the college bell, which in the past had summoned students and faculty to classes, calamity, and fire. This time it rang to announce the end of the Great War, in fact the end of all wars, or so the optimists believed. [1]

In the months that followed many Acadia students would attempt to explain what impact the war had had upon themselves and their institution. [2] The valedictorian in June 1919 commented: "The war has accomplished its work. Its lessons are stamped indelibly upon our lives and now, recognizing past mistakes and failures, we are better able to face this new dawn." [3] On two things most students could agree: that they stood at the beginning of a new era, and that the old ways of living and thinking must be buried forever. As one editorial in the student newspaper observed: "Now we must set our faces to a new future, for none to whom the war has been a reality ... can reconcile themselves to the attitudes and ideas of pre-war days." [4]

Although naïve in their optimism about the future, the students were right to recognize the momentous changes that had taken place in their lives and in their college. Acadia and Acadia students had made a remarkable contribution to the war effort; both had been transformed in the process.

When war was declared in August 1914, Acadia University, a Baptist institution in Wolfville, Nova Scotia, was in the midst of the most expansionist period in its history. [5] Between 1908 and 1915 seven new buildings were constructed on campus to accommodate the rapidly expanding student population. Record enrolments were achieved almost every year until the dramatic declines of the war period. The demands of the war years on both student and material resources sapped the strength ot the university; the lean years of the 1920s and 1930s allowed no time for recovery. In stark contrast to the seven new buildings of the immediate pre-war period, only six were constructed in the next forty years, and half of those were to replace buildings destroyed by fire. The rapid growth and improvement of the university had been brought to a sickening halt by the twin calamities of war and economic depression.

The optimism of that pre-war period is clearly revealed in the minutes of the board of governors. In 1913 and 1914 nearly thirty thousand dollars had been expended on property purchases alone. An ambitious building program was under way,[6] and in May 1914 all professors' salaries were augmented by one hundred dollars, which represented a 7 per cent hike.[7] As late as December 1914 an increase was granted to the salary of William Oliver, janitor; his forty dollars per month plus house was now to include free fuel and lights.[8] By the spring of 1915 the financial picture was no longer as rosy, nor the future of the college as secure.

As early as March 1915 the first of a succession of faculty resignations for "war reasons" began when Miss Beatrice Langley, teacher of violin in the Ladies Seminary, thanked the board for her reappointment but felt that "in consequence of her brother being at the front she ought to return home."[9] For the rest of the war there would be a steady stream of faculty, especially from the Collegiate Academy, leaving for the front.[10]

Although these changes were serious, they tended to have a greater impact on the academy and seminary than on the university itself. Far more critical was the partial defection of the president of Acadia, Dr George B. Cutten, as more and more of his time and energies were siphoned off for war work. As the war progressed, Cutten spent an ever-larger portion of his time in recruiting throughout the Maritime provinces. Unlike their fellow evangelicals the Methodists, the Baptists of the Maritime provinces had no deep-rooted pacifist traditions that would cause mental conflict for Cutten or most of his co-religionists.[11] No ambivalence, public or private, concerning student enlistment and training is observable at Acadia as it was at Mount Allison University in nearby New Brunswick.[12] In February 1916 Cutten asked the board for a leave of absence to enable him to pursue recruitment full time. The board proved sympathetic, granting a leave until the fall.[13] On Cutten's request this was later extended to June 1917, with Dr J.F. Tufts acting as chairman of the faculty in the interim.[14] In December 1917 Cutten rushed off to help a stricken Halifax cope with the aftermath of the explosion. This was followed by a further request for a leave of absence from May to September 1917, to help with the rehabilitation work in that city. It was with greater reluctance that the board agreed once again to free Cutten from his Acadia responsibilities.[15]

Clearly Cutten's almost total commitment to the war seriously undermined Acadia's ability to cope with the crisis she faced during these crucial years. Cutten's very great sense of responsibility to Acadia and to education in general had to be temporarily set aside in the face of what many believed to be the looming threat to freedom and democracy posed by Kaiser Wilhelm.

Cutten probably realized that his preoccupation with the war would have serious repercussions for Acadia, but to him and many others nothing could be as important as winning the struggle with Germany.

As the war continued, Acadia faced serious problems on almost all fronts. As early as the fall of 1914 the conflict began to have its effect on student enrolment. In October three Acadia students enlisted, the first of a large number to do so.[16] By the fall of 1915 there was already a serious decline in the number of upperclassmen, as many Acadia men enlisted as soon as they were old enough. Students departed at any time during the school year, leaving Acadia in a very uncertain position both economically and in terms of enrolment.[17]

Beginning in the fall term of 1915 there was a rapid erosion of the student strength at Acadia. From the pre-war high of 244 the numbers dwindled to 231 in 1915, 213 in 1916, and then plunged to 155 in 1917–18.[18] Of the class of 1918, for example, only 4 of the original 29 men remained at graduation time; the rest had enlisted.[19] In addition, the economic hardship imposed by the war made it difficult for other students, especially the females, to return to university.[20]

The serious decline in enrolment led the board to resort to staff reductions:

Resolved that G.B. Waldrop be notified that owing to the uncertainty with regard to attendance next year and necessary adjustments in consequence thereof his services will not be required for the coming year.

Resolved that Dr. Percy H. Houston be notified by Sec'y of the Board that he is not likely to be re-appointed.[21]

In stark contrast to some of the more recently established provincial universities, Acadia was solely dependent for its financial support on student fees, a small endowment, and voluntary giving from Baptists and alumni; no public funding was provided by the government of Nova Scotia.[22] With dwindling income and rapidly escalating prices, Acadia was forced not only to dismiss faculty but to close the men's residence and practise the "strictest economy" just to keep the university functioning.[23] The price of room and board for the females and the remaining males (now housed in the academy residence) had to be increased from $4.50 per week to $4.75 in 1915, to $5.25 per week in 1917, "with the understanding that if the food prices continue to advance there may be a further raise for the second term," and to $5.75 for the spring term of 1918, substantial increases which the students greatly resented.[24] The loss by fire of several buildings in 1914 and 1915 only added to the university's gloomy economic outlook.[25]

Acadia survived the war years, but it was ill prepared to face the new crises and challenges of the post-war era. A 70 per cent jump in enrolment in 1919 left Acadia staggering under the burden of new and returned students, which strained the university's resources to the limits. In the 1920s the university would have to sacrifice new programs merely to stay afloat, and it would lose much of the initiative and drive that had characterized the pre-war years.

The war changed many things for Acadia, not the least of which was its political stance. Whatever the views of presidents and faculty members, past and present, the Baptist denomination and Acadia University had usually attempted to maintain an official neutrality, especially in federal politics. Dr Cutten, however, found himself more and more deeply involved in political controversy as the result of his recruiting job. The use of Nova Scotia volunteers in the Canadian battalions became a public scandal that, Cutten argued forcefully, was undermining and would eventually destroy the provincial recruitment effort. The problem began as early as August 1914, with the breaking up of Nova Scotia battalions to reinforce other provincial battalions before they were shipped overseas. [26] In spite of direct instructions from Prime Minister Borden to Sir Sam Hughes, his minister of Militia, the problem – and the controversy – continued for several years. [27] Hughes seemed determined not to have a Nova Scotia battalion, and Borden, probably because of his friendship with Hughes, was unwilling to force a showdown. [28] The Borden Papers contain dozens of letters of complaint about this "insult" to Nova Scotia and resulting impediment to its war effort. [29] Cutten had to go over Hughes's head to the prime minister himself in an effort to resolve what became a point of honour for Nova Scotians. In the wake of persistent rumours that the recently raised Nova Scotia Highland Brigade was to be broken up to supply drafts for other units, Cutten did all in his power through political channels to resolve the problem. In December 1915 he wired Borden: "Would appreciate final decision regarding integrity of Highland Brigade before enrolling more recruits to reinforce Brigade. Disintegration of Brigade will seriously hinder recruiting in Nova Scotia." [30]

This messy issue, so important to contemporary Nova Scotians, dragged Cutten further and further into the field of politics, and with this the president seemed to have little trouble. Sir Robert Borden was, after all, a good Nova Scotian and a local boy, even if he had not attended Acadia University. He was admired by Cutten and others at Acadia for his "moral leadership" of the country in time of crisis. [31]

Such feelings would only be strengthened by the events of 1917. Conscription and union government, united with the recruiting zeal that permeated Acadia, formed a powerful combination that propelled Cutten and the university into direct political activity of a kind that in another time both would have found abhorrent or at least unwise. The Baptist denomination prided itself on its advocacy of the complete separation of church and state, but now the war crisis seemed to demand a departure from such a stance. Conscription and union government do not seem to have been even debatable subjects at Acadia in the fall of 1917. However, unlike the situation at McMaster University, its sister institution in Ontario, there is no suggestion that anti-French, anti-Catholic sentiment provided an underlying cause of conscription support at Acadia.[32]

Cutten and other members of the Acadia community were at the forefront of the move to have Sir Robert run in the King's constituency, which included both his boyhood home and the university.[33] Acadia faculty and students openly participated in the campaign. Even the Acadia Theological Club, feeling that "the present crisis of the country is one in which great principles are at stake, and, as leaders of the people, ministers must champion these principles bodily and earnestly," passed the following resolution: "We, the Members of Acadia Theological Club, place on record our hearty sympathy and co-operation with a Win-the-War policy, and further, ... we pledge ourselves to support the movement for a Union Government in all ways possible."[34] The concept of "non-partisan" government, committed to total victory, had a powerful appeal to the university community and its supporters. Seldom in its history had Acadia been as openly and avidly political, although those involved saw it not as political but as patriotic. The Baptists at Brandon College in the west would go one better when their president, Dr Howard Whidden (Acadia, class of 1891), ran as the successful Union candidate for Brandon and remained both president and member of Parliament until 1921.[35]

In many ways, therefore, the institution itself was altered by the war experience. Throughout the war Acadia attempted to deal with a drastically changed world, one not of its making. As an institution Acadia emerged from the conflict somewhat scarred but still intact. If the Great War had an obvious and lasting impact on the university, even more did it mould and shape the generation of Acadia students most directly affected. For both those who enlisted and those who remained at university, the war challenged previous assumptions, destroyed old views, and gave birth to new ones.

One of the most obvious impacts of the war was in the area of recruitment. From the very beginning of the conflict, many members of the university – from President Cutten to the students of the Ladies Seminary – encouraged the eligible young men to enlist in defence of their country. Not that many of them needed much encouragement. By the time college opened in early October 1914 there was already an air of expectancy present. Esther Clark reported to her parents: "The Boys think and talk of little else. There was a sing at Dr. Chute's last night and they were as restless as can be."[36] In his diary Milton Gregg reported "there was an undercurrent of uneasiness. Acker, a brother Monitor, and I used to have frequent talks about enlisting for the war."[37] By mid-October the first three Acadia students had signed up. This news certainly caused a stir of excitement on campus, especially since two of them were presidents of their classes. Acadia was a small, tightly knit community, and this was the first such break in the circle. Emotional farewell parties were held to honour the new heroes; before long Acadia would have some of her sons at the front.[38]

The university itself would soon play a role in active recruitment of soldiers from among its ranks. By October 1914 there was general sentiment on campus that an officer training corps ought to be established; within a month it was a reality.[39] As was the case at many other Canadian universities, for most of the rest of the war military drill would be a part of the life of the college.[40]

The student newspaper / magazine, the *Acadia Athenaeum*, began to promote a war consciousness as well. Beginning in November 1914 the paper was filled with poems, stories, and editorials that emphasized valour, courage, manliness, and "right." "Pan-Germanism," "Theirs But to Do and Die," "Private MacLeod's Christmas Present," and many others might have lacked much in literary merit, but they more than made up for it in patriotic fervour.[41] With the same issue the *Athenaeum* began reporting on the enlistment and, eventually, on promotion, wounding, or death of Acadia graduates and students.[42] As the war dragged on this became an ever larger, and increasingly depressing, part of the paper. It did serve, of course, to keep the Acadia community in touch with the university's involvement in the war.

It would not be articles in the student newspaper, or officer training, however, that would provide the spur to campus enlistment. With the Baptist community in general and the Acadia faculty in particular expressing few reservation about total commitment to this just cause, President Cutten could be at one and the same time an ordained Baptist minister and chief recruiting officer for Nova Scotia – and see no contradiction in such activities. He would eventually be dubbed "Fighting George Cutten" by his students, and "Cutten's Song" – "The Son of God Goes Forth to War" – became a favourite at campus gatherings.[43] Cutten's view of total involvement, whatever the cost to the university, stands in sharp contrast to that of Chancellor A.L. McCrimmon of McMaster, who strongly advocated both national conscription *and* exemptions for prospective university students.[44] For Cutten, and many at Acadia, there could be no such half-way measures.

At Acadia, recruitment rallies took on many of the trappings of a revival meeting. They were usually held at the nearby Baptist church on Sunday evenings with a minister or officer (or both) presiding. Hymns, patriotic songs, "testimonies," impassioned pleas, and an invitation to come forward to join in this titanic struggle against the forces of evil – all of this was within the framework of the Maritime evangelical tradition, something the students could readily identify with and respond to. "Recruiting sermons" became a regular part of many of the morning services as well; the blessings, even the admonitions, of the church were being added to the pressures of state and society.[45] It becomes difficult at times to tell the difference between militancy, Christianity, militant Christianity, and Christian militancy. For many at Acadia, it would appear, they were one and the same, or at least all part of the larger whole.

The visit to the Acadia campus of Captain (Rev.) W.A. Cameron in March 1916 underscored the melding of these various themes in the students' minds. As she did through other correspondence, student Esther Clark captured the mood of the campus in a letter to her younger brother:

Say you want to be sure to go and hear Capt. Cameron while he is in Fredericton. He is *some* man. You know he was pastor of Bloor St. Baptist Church in Toronto and enlisted. He said in his first speech here that he was not here to recruit but the boys said his were the best recruiting sermons they'd ever heard. His first address was The Challenge of the War. All classes were excused for the meetings and the body of College Hall was packed each time. The boys were just crazy over him and kept him till all hours of the night at interviews ... He certainly was magnificent and it was a rare privilege to be able to hear him.[46]

The *Athenaeum* reported that

great good resulted, for Acadia today is a place of solemn religious thought, and many have started anew on the Christian life. A deep spiritual change has come over the students as the result of his soul-stirring addresses. Captain Cameron is a man of strong personality and an interesting speaker, whose earnestness fired our souls. The fact of his being in khaki especially appealed to those students who themselves will soon be fighting ... [Cameron argued that] Canada has a great responsibility placed upon her in preparation for the greatest days to come and through it all she must remember that "righteousness exalteth a nation." We must learn from the past, we must let our Savior of mankind become the King of our nation.[47]

Was Cameron on campus to win recruits for the front or souls for Christ? Or had those become almost the same thing?

Clearly these forces were dramatically successful in stirring the young men at Acadia. Recruitment levels were very high by 1916, as more and more of the young men left their studies for the front. Of the class of 1918 already alluded to, 27 of the 29 males who began the program in 1914 enlisted before the end of the conflict – a remarkable 93.1 per cent.[48] Such a high percentage is even more significant when it is noted that almost all of these young men were Canadian born, often at least four or five generations removed from England.

As important as such high levels of enlistment were for the war effort, they were only the outward manifestation of very important changes that were taking place in the students' minds. New ideas permeated the university, influencing profoundly that war generation of students, male and female alike. The war experience, ideas of social and moral reform, and evangelical Christianity would provide a powerful amalgam in shaping their future lives and the Canada they inhabited.

Long before the war began, social and moral reform had become an important theme in some of the university courses, especially sociology and economics, where the social theories of such writers as Rauschenbush were extensively discussed. Within five years of its publication in 1894 Benjamin Kidd's influential book *Social Evolution* had found a place in Acadia's curriculum.[49] With its emphasis on religion as "an 'irrational' motive for altruism and selfless effort," the Baptists had both a sharper focus and a more comprehensive rationale for their traditional, if selective, emphasis on social reform. Although many Maritime Baptists, and certainly Acadia's students, would come to believe that "social regeneration was historically possible,"[50] they would never accept "that personal salvation was won through losing oneself in the social task." Deeply influenced by the social gospel, they were never willing to submerge totally their own individualism in their passion for social reform. The war, however, caused a deepening concern for these social topics as students and faculty grappled with the perplexing problems thrust upon them by the conflict.

Darwin's theory of evolution might not yet be taught at an institution such as Acadia, where it would still be considered anti-Christian; it is clear, however, that Social Darwinism had greatly influenced the institution and Maritime Baptists over the preceding several decades. Belief in the general upward progress of mankind meshed well with their view of their own educational, social, and economic development in the last half of the nineteenth century. The outbreak of war and the causes advanced to explain it had a serious, unsettling effect on the students. They believed, of course, that right was on the British side. They also believed that Germany, in beginning the war, was not only wrong but immoral, that Prussian militarism, with its "might is right" theories, was a reversion to "the ideals of the Hun, the outlook of the savage," as one student commented.[51] The world was threatened, then, not merely with military defeat but with a reversal of the entire upward progress of mankind.

Certainly Germany's defeat would have to be the first step in assuring the future of the world. Then humankind could continue on its upward climb. As one student commented in his spring oration in 1915:

Patriotism is the cohesive principle that operates today but doubtless before this present epoch closes "humanism" will appear to unify elements of human society into a universal brotherhood. Then shall the revolting, the inhuman, the fiendish "Law of the Jungle" be thrown to the limbo of the obsolete. Then shall dawn that great and glorious day when "every man must be at his best," – that day for which Christ prayed; that day at which social reformers have aimed; that day of which poets have sung –
"When the war drum throbs no longer,
and the battle-flags are furled,
In the Parliament of man, the Federation of the world."[52]

Such sentiments would be echoed in pulpit, podium, and student newspaper.

Within a very short time it became increasingly clear to the students that winning the war would only be a means to an end, not an end in itself. Some of the early naïveté had fled from the campus by the spring of 1915. As one *Athenaeum* article commented: "In moments of idealizing [six months ago], we had hoped with many others that this war were the Armageddon which should usher in the Millennium; today, as we face the realities of greed, 'will to power,' long lists of casualties of our own Canadians, the probabilities of a continued struggle, and the sacrifice of thousands and thousands of human lives, in all likelihood we are not so inclined to look upon the affair with the same degree of complacency."[53] Ministers, professors, and visiting lecturers warned that moral and social reform must *accompany* military victory, or military victory would surely be denied them. In February 1916 Esther Clark reported on the Sunday sermon at the Baptist Church: "It was a call to the nation, the church, and to the individual to commit their way unto God and trust in him. He [the minister] has evidently been feeling the general depression concerning the war and he pointed out that the Empire was not yet to be trusted with victory."[54] The guest speaker at the annual YWCA Muskoka Conference in the summer of 1916 sounded the same warning, arguing in fact that the current war was essential, for from it "will come a purging and strengthening of our faith, and a correcting of our point of view. It is to be the beginning, not the end of things."[55] Poverty, alcoholism, economic exploitation, moral decay, military aggression – these and many others, not just Kaiser Wilhelm, were the problems that threatened the future of the world. The later careers and accomplishments of this generation of Canadian university students might constructively be examined in the light of the molding power of these ideas.

The melding of classroom, Christianity, and khaki is perhaps best exemplified by the frequent use of the term "Christianizing the social order," as typified in a Sunday sermon in the spring of 1915: "He took for his text: 'The Kingdom of God is within you.' The sermon was very much like

'Christianizing the Social order' which we have been studying in Sociology."[56] The *Athenaeum*, in printing the usual biographical sketches of graduating students, observed: "Clarence William Cook hails from Guysboro, N.S., and came to Acadia with the intention of learning to 'Christianize the social order,' but changed his mind as to the best means towards this end, and put on the whole armour of khaki."[57] The recruiting officer on the platform, the professor in the classroom and the minister in the pulpit all used the same rhetoric; the student saw all three elements as part of the larger picture. It would seem, then, that it was the desire to implement the ideals learned in classroom and church that was primarily responsible for propelling the Acadia students into European trenches. Germany and her allies were seen as the major blocks to the creation of the brotherhood of man. It was not the call of Mother England but Christian conscience that was loudest at Acadia. In fact the emphasis on British imperialism was somewhat muted. Certainly Acadia faculty and students were proud members of the Empire, but that was not really why they were fighting this war with such intensity. The connection between social reform and imperialism does not seem to have been made as strongly at Acadia as it was in some other parts of Canada, perhaps because of the dissenting traditions of the Baptists.[58] The sense of mission discussed so well by Carl Berger was certainly present in good measure at Acadia and within the Baptist community, but it had remained an individual or denominational rather than a national or imperial commitment.[59] The transformation of evangelicalism to wholly secular objectives had, in large measure, failed to take place.[60]

Such thinking clearly influenced greatly those who enlisted; perhaps more profoundly did it shape the thinking of those who remained at home. With the lengthening list of killed and wounded countrymen and classmates, the female students at Acadia had many hard questions to ask themselves. In the past the role of women in war was "to suffer in silence at home, and to mourn the slain," contributing only "sympathy and prayers," as one student orator expressed it. This no longer seemed sufficient. That same student commented: "As the European crisis is calling forth latent manhood, so also is it arousing true womanhood to duty and responsibility in the solution of world problems. The new social consciousness of women has been sharpened to an eager demand on their part to be of practical use."[61] There was a strong sense that the circumstances of the moment, the crises of the war, were preparing them for a special future. And, of course, they too had sat in classrooms and discussed the goals of the social reformers. In commenting on the role of women, one coed could write confidently in the *Athenaeum* in 1917: "Yes, the nation is depending much on us [women] now and will depend on us more and more as time goes on ... We, who are being trained for leadership, will have a great opportunity in shaping

the moral, political, social and religious ideals of the rising generation ...
Do we realize that we are to be the leaders of to-morrow?"[62]

To accomplish the social, political and moral reforms so obviously needed
in the world, Acadia women would need the education, the dedication, even
the consecration, essential for the task. When one examines the careers of
the female graduates of this period, it is quickly apparent that more than
lip-service was being paid to these ideals. In an abrupt departure from past
experience the women of this period moved quickly into a number of traditionally male areas, all of which could be said to fall loosely into the
"service to humanity" category. Of the nineteen women of the class of 1916,
one became a medical doctor, three university professors (one with a PhD
in economics, one with a PhD in biology), three were licensed to preach
and held pastoral charges, while a forth became an ordained minister and
two were accepted as foreign missionaries, one of them spending fifty years
in India. The class of 1918, numbering ten females, produced two medical
doctors and two university professors, one of whom earned a PhD in biology.[63]

In these activities they were clearly encouraged by the Acadia faculty as
well as by the spirit of the times. President Cutten could summon Acadia's
young men to war and at the same time ask of a young Bessie Lockhart
(class of 1916) that she dedicate her life to foreign missions.[64] Fighting the
Hun in Europe or the heathen in India – they were part of the same gigantic
struggle for the soul of the world.

In their search for a new future the Acadia women of the war years
received practical experience as well as heady idealism from their university.
As Cutten's successful recruiting took its toll, particularly on the junior and
senior classes, the women were left in almost sole possession of the field,
or more accurately the campus. The traditionally male-dominated offices
and honours now passed into the hands of the females. In the 1914 graduating
class the males outnumbered females twenty-five to twelve. By 1918 the
numbers were ten females to four males. Women were now the valedicto-
rians, the orators, the gold medallists. In its forty-five-year history the
Athenaeum had never had a female editor; by 1917 Helen Starr had climbed
to that lofty position.[65] An enthusiastic Esther Clark reported to her parents
in May 1916: "The laws of the Medes & Persians have changed! The names
of eight Seniors are posted to read their Orations before the Faculty Monday
at 4 p.m. and they are *all* girls ... There has *always* been three boys and a
girl."[66]

Another clear sign of the changing times was the following minute of the
Executive of the Board: "[1 May, 1916] Resignations of L.H. Coldwell,
and R.H. Carter, laboratory assistants in Biology and Chemistry, were
accepted. And Miss Hettie Chute appointed to take the place of Mr. Coldwell

and Elizabeth Eaton that of Mr. Carter at the same salary as that paid to
Messrs. Coldwell and Carter, for balance of year."[67] Hettie Chute would
go on to take a PhD in biology.[68]

Many of these gains would be only temporary, swept aside in the flood
of returning males in 1919 and 1920. But women could never again be
relegated to quite the same position at the university, or be dismissed as
incapable of more serious or onerous tasks.

The experience and confidence gained by the women in the 1915–18
period served them well in the years to come. They had run newspapers,
organized meetings, planned social events, walked away with the honours.
They were thus better prepared to face the "new dawn" that they so confidently expected and that some would work so hard to achieve.

For Acadia's men and women the war period provided the idealism, the
ideology, and the practical experience that would mould and direct their
lives. For many of those who enlisted, however, the war served as the brutal
terminator of their educations, sometimes of their lives. It is difficult to
arrive at exact figures, but it would appear that at least 174 students interrupted their studies at Acadia to enlist. Of those who survived the war, only
34, or 19.5 per cent, resumed their studies at Acadia.[69] Although there were
always some who fell by the wayside in normal years, the figures for the
war period are far above the average. While it is impossible to determine
what role the war played in individuals' decisions not to resume their education, it is clear that such figures do represent dislocated lives and shattered
dreams. Of course, some who did not return to the university on the hill
managed to "make good" in spite of a lack of formal education, as did
Milton F. Gregg, ex 1916, later brigadier-general, president of the University
of New Brunswick, and successively federal minister of Fisheries, Veterans'
Affairs, and Labour, and K.C. Irving, ex 1921, later New Brunswick in-
dustrialist.[70]

The war disturbed the lives of those who remained at college as well,
although not to the same extent. The war caused a restlessness among the
students, both male and female, that could be translated at times into dis-
orderly high jinks and at other times into gloomy depression. By the spring
of 1915, with classmates, friends, brothers, and even fiancés at the front,
the normal life of the university was seriously disrupted. As early as January
1915 the brother of one of the girls was killed in battle, casting a pall of
gloom over the small Acadia community.[71] Far worse was to follow. The
diary of Milton Gregg's fiancé records the constant worry, the desperate
waiting for letters, and the always-present fear when she knew that Gregg
was in battle.[72] One student later characterized this period as a time of
"feverish unrest and excitement; nothing seemed stable."[73] It is no wonder
that the reports of the university could not hide a declining level of scholarship at the institution.[74]

Just as serious, to many, was the decline in the standard of "deportment" reported. During the war period and after, student behaviour appears to have sunk to a new low. Public meetings, especially Sunday church and daily chapel, seem to have been times of special unrest. Esther Clark reported to her parents that at church "the boys acted quite disgracefully. The girls were a little restless also. Finally we buried ourselves in hymnbooks."[75] The campus newspaper found it necessary to lecture the student body in an article entitled "Rowdyism," citing recent disturbances at chapel and "the extraordinary noise in the Baptist Church Balcony on Sunday evenings of late." All of this, it was devoutly hoped, was the work of only "the baser sort of students."[76]

More serious were the actions of a coed (or coeds) leading to changes in rules that would last half a century. Before the war the female students at Acadia were remarkably free to move about the town or countryside, virtually at will. There is no sign of the expected Victorian strictness in controlling the actions of "young ladies" – no permission needed to visit friends, even for the weekend, no signing in and out of residence.[77] An incident (or incidents) – the details are unrecorded – led to a complete reversal of this policy. An outraged Esther Clark wrote to her family: "Dr. Cutten added a crazy rule – that we have to have permission from home to go out over night. Please ask Mother to send in her next letter a statement that she is perfectly willing for me to visit any friends ... I think and hope I've got sense enough not to go visiting anywhere Mother wouldn't approve of."[78] Until the late 1960s "permission from home to go out over night" would be an established if hated aspect of the university's attempt to control and "protect" the female students. Interestingly enough, its origins are to be found not in Victorian Nova Scotia but in the climate of unrest and changing standards of the war years.

The war influenced the lives of some Acadia women in another way as well. The conflict siphoned off the majority of the male student population, and women students had to adjust to the absence of male classmates, friends, escorts, and "beaux." One senior student reported to her mother: "Tuesday night we had a class party at Mildred Brown's. The girls were invited and told to bring a boy since there weren't enough class boys to go around. The result was a queer mixture, Engineers and all the classes except Freshmen. We had a good time but still we missed the boys who are in France."[79] Deprived of their male peers, these women increasingly occupied a world without men.

Before the war the relationships between female students were close, and many of the organizations and activities were exclusively female – the Propylaeum Society, YWCA, the annual Muskoka Conference, and many more.[80] These were balanced by mixed classes, sleigh rides, class parties, long walks, sport and debating excursions, and many other mixed college activities. It is clear, however, that the ties that bound the female students were strong and lasting ones, extending to the campus the pattern of female relationships still existing in the late nineteenth, early twentieth-century Maritimes. Certainly there is ample evidence to suggest that, at Acadia at least, what Carroll Smith-Rosenberg has described as the "female world of love and ritual" lasted longer than that author would have us believe.[81]

The outbreak of war coincided with the opening of Acadia's first female residence; both brought the women into closer physical and emotional proximity. Deprived of classmates, friends, brothers, and sometimes fathers, theirs was increasingly a homosocial world. The war thus emphasized the importance of female friendships, making Smith-Rosenberg's description of nineteenth-century American relations equally applicable to Acadia in the war years: "young women's relations with each other were close, often frolicsome, and surprisingly long lasting and devoted ... An undeniably romantic and even sensual note frequently marked female relations."[82] As with Smith-Rosenberg's nineteenth-century American women, this was clearly an accepted, normal part of the female experience, now given prominence by the sudden absence of the male component at college.

The diary of one Acadia student of this period sheds considerable light on this world without men, in which female friendships assumed such major proportions. The writer was already engaged to the soldier she would marry after the war, and the diary is filled with desperate longing and tear-filled nights. But she devotes a considerable part of the diary to an agonized description of her great affection for a fellow coed and the stormy relationship that ensued. When another woman entered the picture the diarist recounted: "I was absurdly jealous, but by that time I cared for her so devotedly that I was incapable of rational judgment where she was concerned ... My love for her was of an intensity that I could not control, and I went home possessed by very stormy emotions ... the change in her was like a knife in my heart. Sleepless nights and a great many tears didn't improve my disposition." The other women in residence became involved, lending great emotional support to the bereaved student. This, as well as the fact that this remarkably frank diary was kept for the next forty years and was left among the writer's papers on her death, would indicate that this intense relationship was not considered unusual or abnormal for the times.[83] It is, of course, impossible to determine the exact role played by the war in the lingering and possible resurgence of these nineteenth-century norms, but the above-cited diary makes the connection rather clear.

In many ways, then, Acadia and the Acadia student were changed and reshaped by the years of war. The university emerged from the conflict considerably weakened, to confront the turbulent post-war period. The students emerged greatly strengthened, or so they believed. Acadia had fought the war on many fronts and had won at least some of her battles. Certainly, as far as the students were concerned, their "war" had been won even before the Germans laid down their arms. Tempered by the heat of conflict in Europe and of intellectual turmoil at home, they confidently faced whatever the future might bring.

In spite of the carnage, the destruction, the dislocation, for many of this generation the war was seen as a positive experience; only intense heat can produce quality steel. In the spring of 1918, as the war neared its conclusion, the valedictorian summed up the feeling of her college generation when she said:

We entered college under the shadow of war, we go out under the same shadow grown darker and more threatening, but always there is the gleam of light that Right will triumph and so we say: –

Now God be thanked who hath matched us with His hour,
And caught our youth and wakened us from sleeping.[84]

NOTES

* The research for this paper was made possible by a Harvey T. Reid Summer Study Award, for which I thank Acadia University.

1 *Acadia Athenaeum* 45, no. 2 (Jan. 1919): 75–6.

2 See ibid., various issues, 1919–20, for good examples.

3 Ibid. 45, no. 6 (June 1919): 264, valedictory address by Vera G. Ogilvie.

4 Ibid. 45, no. 2 (Jan. 1919): 63–4.

5 For a general discussion of this period, see R.S. Longley, *Acadia University, 1838–1938* (Wolfville, NS: Acadia University 1939), 104–5.

6 Office of the President, Acadia University, Board of Governors minutes, spring 1914; Office of the President, Acadia University, minutes of the executive of the board, spring-summer 1914.

7 Board of Governors minutes, 27 May 1914, 120.

8 Executive of the Board minutes, 15 Dec. 1914, 120-1.

9 Ibid., 29 Mar. 1915, 130.

10 Ibid., 3 Nov. 1915 and 24 Dec. 1915.

11 See Michael Bliss, "The Methodist Church and World War I," *Canadian Historical Review* 49, no. 3 (Sept. 1968): 213–33, and John Reid, *Mount Allison University*, vol. 2, *1914–1963* (Toronto: University of Toronto Press 1984) 4.

12 Reid, *Mount Allison*, 2:16.

13 Board of Governors minutes, 24 Feb. 1916, 147–8.

14 Ibid., 13 Oct. 1916, 158; 14 Oct. 1916, 158–9.

15 Ibid., 3 April 1918, 172.

16 Correspondence of Esther I. Clark, 1912–16, in possession of Dr Esther Clark

Wright, Wolfville, NS, Esther Clark to her mother, 16 Oct. 1914; Public Archives of New Brunswick, Fredericton, NB, Gregg Papers, diaries of Dorothy Alward and Milton Gregg.

17 See *Acadia Athenaeum*, various issues 1915 to 1918.

18 See *The United Baptist Year Book of the Maritime Provinces* (Truro, NS, 1914, 1915, 1916, 1917, 1918) for student enrolments.

19 *Acadia Bulletin*, June 1918; *Acadia Record* (Wolfville, NS, 1953), 129–31.

20 Clark correspondence, Esther Clark to her mother, 21 Mar. 1915; Gregg Papers, file 20, Blanche to Duffy [Dorothy Alward], 10 Oct. 1915; file 21, Mother to Dorothy and Amy, 12 Mar., 1916; file 21, Walter to Amy, 6 May 1916.

21 Minutes of the Executive of the Board, 27 Mar. 1916.

22 Possessing as it did the financial guarantees that assured the future of its programs, the University of Alberta actually doubled the size of its faculty during this turbulent time. Walter H. Johns, *A History of the University of Alberta, 1908–1969* (Edmonton: University of Alberta Press 1981), 22.

23 Board of Governors minutes, 18 Oct. 1915, 146; minutes of the Executive of the Board, 21 Sept. 1916.

24 Ibid., 29 Mar. 1915; 17 Mar. 1917; 30 Nov. 1917; Clark Correspondence, E. Clark to her father, 16 Nov. 1917.

25 Reid paints a similarly gloomy financial picture for Mount Allison. Reid, *Mount Allison*, 2:10.

26 National Archives of Canada, Ottawa (henceforth NAC), MG 26 H I(a), vol. 45, p 20219, R.L. Borden Papers, telegram, Struan Robertson to R.L. Borden, Valcartier, 3 Sept. 1914; ibid., p 20217, telegram, Charles Tanner to R.L. Borden, Valcartier, 3 Sept. 1914.

27 Ibid., p 20221, R.L. Borden to Sam Hughes, 7 Sept. 1914.

28 Ibid., pp 20222–8, report on situation at Valcartier, dated 23 Sept. 1914; R. Craig Brown, *Robert Laird Borden: A Biography* (Toronto: University of Toronto Press 1980), 2:14–17.

29 NAC, Borden Papers, vol. 45, numerous letters, see especially pp 20359–61, Lt Col. R. Innes to F.B. McCurdy, 8 Nov. 1916.

30 Ibid., p 20373, G.B. Cutten to R.L. Borden, 6 Dec. 1916.

31 See for example NAC, MG 26 H I(c), vol. 253, Borden Papers, pp 142685–6, J.F. Tufts to R.L. Borden, 5 Oct. 1911; ibid., MG 26 H I(a), vol. 12, p 2023, J.F. Tufts to R.L. Borden, 17 Apr. 1915.

32 Charles M. Johnston, *McMaster University: The Toronto Years* (Toronto: University of Toronto Press 1976), 1:441–3.

33 NAC, Borden Papers, vol. 140, p 74505, G.B. Cutten to R.L. Borden, 13 Nov. 1917; G.E. DeWitt to R.L. Borden, 13 Nov. 1917; J.F. Tufts to R.L. Borden, 13 Nov. 1917.

34 Wolfville *Acadian*, 7 Dec. 1917. See also 14 Dec. 1917, "The Premier's Visit."

35 C.G. Stone and F. Joan Garnett, *Brandon College: A History 1899–1967* (Brandon, Man., 1969), 88.

36 Clark Correspondence, Esther Clark to her mother, nd [late Nov. 1914].

37 Gregg Papers, diary of Milton F. Gregg, p 1.

38 Ibid., 1,2; Clark Correspondence, Esther Clark to her mother, 16 Oct. 1914; *Athenaeum* 41, no. 1 (Nov. 1914): 23.

39 Clark Correspondence, Esther Clark to her brother Alden, n.d. [fall 1914]; ibid., Esther Clark to her mother, 19 Nov. 1914.

40 See, for examples, Reid, *Mount Allison*, 2:4; Stone and Garnett, *Brandon*, 84; Hilda Neatby, *"And Not to Yield": Queen's University, 1841–1917* (Montreal: McGill-Queen's University Press 1978), 297.

41 *Athenaeum* 41, no. 1 (Nov. 1914): 5–6, 15–17; ibid. 41, no. 2 (Dec. 1914): 66–9.

42 Ibid. 41, no. 1 (Nov. 1914): 34, "Acadia and the War."

43 Ibid. 42, no. 8 (June 1916): 496; ibid. 44, no. 1 (Nov. 1917): 30.

44 Johnston, *McMaster*, 1:144.

45 For examples, see Clark Correspondence, Esther Clark to her father, 16 Jan. 1916; Esther Clark to her mother, 20 Feb. 1916; Esther Clark to her mother, 25 Feb. 1916; *Athenaeum* 42, no. 1 (Nov. 1915).

46 Clark Correspondence, Esther Clark to her brother Thurston, 4 Mar. 1916.

47 *Athenaeum* 42, no. 6 (Apr. 1916): 356–8, "Captain Cameron's Message."

48 *Acadia Bulletin*, June 1915; *Acadia Record, 1838–1953* (Wolfville, NS: Acadia University 1953), 129–31. This volume contains brief biographies of all Acadia graduates.

49 *Calendar of Acadia College for the Year 1899* (Halifax 1899), 20.

50 Richard Allen, *The Social Passion: Religion and Social Reform in Canada 1914–28* (Toronto: University of Toronto Press 1971), 18. See also Ramsay Cook, *The Regenerators: Social Criticism in Late Victorian English Canada* (Toronto: University of Toronto Press 1985).

51 *Athenaeum* 43, no. 4 (May 1917): 308, editorial.

52 Ibid. 41, no. 8 (June 1915): 488–93, C.A.S. Howe, "The Law of the Jungle," delivered at Commencement, 26 May 1915.

53 Ibid. 41, no. 7 (May 1915): 427.

54 Clark Correspondence, Esther Clark to her mother, 20 Feb. 1916.

55 *Athenaeum* 43, no. 1 (Dec. 1916): 17.

56 Clark Correspondence, Esther Clark to her father, 25 Apr. 1915.

57 *Athenaeum* 42, no. 8 (June 1916): 546.

58 Carl Berger, *The Sense of Power: Studies in the Ideas of Canadian Imperialism, 1867–1914* (Toronto: University of Toronto Press 1970), 186.

59 Ibid., 219–30.

60 Ibid., 230.

61 *Athenaeum* 41, no. 8 (June 1915): T-482, "Women's Part in the War," by Evelyn Enid Smallman.

62 Ibid. 43, no. 2 (Jan. 1917): 84, "Ways of Serving our Nation," by [Jean R. Goucher].

63 See *Acadia Record*, 124–131; *Acadia Bulletin* 8, no. 6 (July 1919): 3.

64 Clark Correspondence, Esther Clark to her mother, 7 Nov. 1915.

65 *Athenaeum* 44, no. 1 (Nov. 1917).

66 Clark Correspondence, Esther Clark to her father, 14 May 1916.

67 Minutes of the Executive of the Board, 1 May 1916.

68 *Acadia Record*, 124.

69 These figures were compiled from the *Acadia Record*, 127–52, 409–12, and various issues of the *Acadia Bulletin*, 1914–19, and the *Athenaeum*, 1914–19.

70 *Acadia Record*, 410, 413; *Guide to Canadian Ministries since Confederation* (Ottawa 1957), 57, 58, 63.

71 Clark Correspondence, Esther Clark to her mother, 27 Jan. 1915.

72 Gregg Papers, Diary of Dorothy Alward. See also ibid., file 20, Zell to Duff, 8 June 1975, when Gregg was reported missing.

73 *Athenaeum* 45, no. 2 (Jan. 1919): 48, "Reconstruction at Acadia," by C.B.L. [C. Bruce Lumsden].

74 See Board of Governors minutes, 30 May 1917, 165.

75 Clark Correspondence, Esther Clark to her father, 14 Feb. 1915.

76 *Athenaeum* 41, no. 3 (Jan. 1915): 163.

77 See the voluminous correspondence of Esther Clark from 1912 to 1916 for numerous examples of casual visits that unexpectedly turned into weekend jaunts, of easy movement in and out of residence.

78 Clark Correspondence, Esther Clark to her brother Thurston, 6 Dec. 1914.

79 Ibid., Esther Clark to her mother, 20 Apr. 1916.

80 See Clark Correspondence, 1912–16, and the pre-war issues of the *Athenaeum*.

81 Carroll Smith-Rosenberg, "The Female World of Love and Ritual," in Nancy Cott and Elizabeth Pleck, *A Heritage of Her Own: Toward a New Social History of American Women* (New York: Simon and Schuster 1979), 311–42. I thank Dr Margaret Conrad for her help in interpreting the material in this section of the paper.

82 Ibid., 325, 328.

83 Private diary in possession of the author.

84 *Athenaeum* 44, no. 5 (June 1918): 321, valedictory by Beth Addison.

CHAPTER EIGHT

The War Effort and Women Students at the University of Toronto, 1939–45

Nancy Kiefer and Ruth Roach Pierson

During the Second World War the colleges and universities of Canada did not stand aside from the massive mobilization of the home front. Through the liaison agency of the National Conference of Canadian Universities, institutes of higher education across the country were drawn into co-operation with the wartime goals and priorities of the federal government. The policies adopted by universities to assist in Canada's prosecution of the war did not, however, have a uniform effect on student bodies. In accordance with the differing needs of government, industry, and the military for womanpower as distinct from manpower, the war-related programs of universities differentiated sharply between male and female students. Given the greater and more immediate initial demand for manpower and male-identified areas of expertise, policies affecting male students tended early on towards strict regulation and compulsory service, in contrast to the more relaxed and voluntary approach taken towards female students. While the male student set the patriotic standard, the war service of university women was curtailed and circumscribed by enforced beliefs respecting the separate nature and future role of woman as wife and mother. Thus, as a survey of developments at the University of Toronto during the Second World War will show, the war service of female university students did not result in the breakdown of sexual stereotypes or of the sexual division of labour. On the contrary, the emphasis of women's service programs on the value of unpaid voluntary labour and service in the home tended to reinforce notions of female self-subordination that facilitate women's exploitation in both the public and private spheres.

The war brought Canada's universities closer to the federal government, which actively increased its intervention into higher education in order to maximize the war effort. Through such agencies as the National Conference of Canadian Universities, composed of the heads of Canada's institutions of higher learning, and the Departments of National Defence, Labour, and

National War Services, the federal government guided the universities on how best to put their resources, of "manpower" and expertise, at the disposal of the state. "In September of 1939 all [male] students of military age were advised by the Government to remain in school or university until such time as the nation's war effort was sufficiently organized so that they could be utilized to best advantage.[1] In the meantime, on campuses across Canada units of the Canadian Officers' Training Corps (COTC), dormant for the most part since the end of the First World War, were reformed within days of the nation's entry into the second.[2] In 1940, in response to Parliament's passage of the National Resources Mobilization Act, which made all young men of draft age conscriptable for home defence,[3] the heads of Canada's universities decided "to institute a form of military training as mandatory for all male students whe were physically fit."[4] The compulsory-training requirement could be fulfilled by enrolment in the COTC for those with "leadership qualities"; for the rest, auxiliary corps offering general military studies and drill were instituted. "All such [male] students, provided that they performed their military duties satisfactorily and remained in good academic standing in their universities, were to be exempted from military call-up until the end of their undergraduate program."[5]

From as early as 1940, then, male students experienced a war-related pressure to do well academically. As the military's demand for manpower swiftly rose in 1943 and 1944 with the opening of the African and Italian fronts and in anticipation of the Normandy invasion, not only the academic standing of the male student but his course of study came under scrutiny. As of January 1943 new National Selective Service regulations required that all science and engineering students register with the Wartime Bureau of Technical Personnel and on graduation accept assignment to jobs either in war-essential civilian employment or in the military.[6] Also in January 1943 the National Conference of Canadian Universities debated a proposition, put forward by Principal R.C. Wallace of Queen's and supported by F. Cyril James of McGill and Malcolm Wallace of University College at the University of Toronto, that "arts studies should be severely contracted for the remainder of the war."[7] The proposal was motivated by mounting public disapproval of young men taking "non-essential courses" and personal conviction that the contribution of Canadian universities to the war effort should not lag behind that of their British and American counterparts. None the less, the resolution met up with heavy opposition at the National Conference and was in the end rejected.[8] Then in February 1944 National Selective Service issued another in a series of Interpretive Letters concerning the mobilization of male university students. Those in courses of study deemed essential to "the prosecution of the war or in the national interest," such as mathematics, physics, biology, or chemistry,[9] would continue to be exempt from military call-up until completion of their degrees. Men enrolled in arts courses, like language and literature, fine arts, history, and philosophy, however, would only "be spared the recruiting sergeant" if they placed in the top half of their classes.[10]

While male students thus suffered a high degree of state intervention in their academic careers during the war, those engaged in the study of military and war-industrially important fields stood to benefit from state aid. To ensure a sufficient supply of doctors for the armed forces, the ceiling on admissions to medicine was raised and the program of study was accelerated from six years to five or four.[11] To increase the numbers of engineers and scientists coming out of universities, the federal government introduced in 1942 a scheme of student loans for qualified young males who otherwise would not have been able to acquire a post-secondary education.[12]

Like their fellow university administrators throughout Canada, officials at the University of Toronto during the Second World War endeavoured to ensure that all persons associated with the university, but particularly members of the student body, contributed their fair share to the war effort. As elsewhere in Canada, the body of students was sharply differentiated according to gender. Programs to involve male students took priority. The University of Toronto authorities addressed themselves on only a minor scale to the question of the involvement of women students in the war effort. The authorities never became particularly concerned with the academic pursuits of female students during the war, for the coeds were concentrated in faculties and schools traditionally defined as appropriate for women and having, with the exception of the last two on the list, little direct relevance to warfare: arts, household science, the Ontario College of Education, social work, nursing, and occupational and physiotherapy. While the mobilization of male students reached right into their programs of study, it was decided that women's contribution would be best limited to extra-curricular activities. As the needs of the war effort on the home front accelerated, however, the university administration began to take a greater interest in controlling the extra-curricular activities of the female students. It was never a question of whether to intervene in that area, only of when and to what extent. Over time university officials increased the degree to which they sought to regulate the non-academic lives of the female students and channel their efforts into forms of war service that would complement or compensate for any time taken away from their studies.

Three phases can be discerned in the mobilization of the women students. Phase one (1939 to 1940) is characterized by discussion and debate over what women's proper role should be and informal organizational activity in which female students were involved only peripherally. In the second phase (1940 to 1942) steps were taken to establish a University of Toronto Women's Service Training Detachment of the Canadian Red Cross Corps. And in the third phase (1942 to 1945) the administration's role escalated to the point of requiring a form of compulsory war service from women students.

The question of how women at the University of Toronto should serve the war effort surfaced after the start of the war. The patriotic standards to be met by female students were set by the male students on campus, who were performing what was perceived to be the most important university war work through membership in the Canadian Officers' Training Corps.[13] In October 1939 the University College Parliament debated the advisability of forming a female detachment of the COTC. Arguing in favour of the proposition, acting Prime Minister of the student government Paul C. McGillicuddy held that the "entire active and reserve forces of the Cold Cream Guards must be enlisted for service at home and abroad."[14] Despite the facetious reference to his female counterparts, McGillicuddy maintained that the role of women in war was very important, as it was they who were called upon to preserve civilization and culture. A female COTC, he claimed, would serve to "teach women to lead others in work the government might decide to be of maximum benefit to the nation."[15]

Speaking for the University College opposition, Eric Hardy argued that, "with their temperament and emotional instability ..., women would have a serious disrupting effect on the morale of the army."[16] Citing the provision of uniforms as one practical difficulty, the University College Parliament rejected the idea of forming a female COTC. It decided that women's war service could be co-ordinated without resort to such measures. The editor of the student undergraduate newspaper, the *Varsity*, agreed. He argued that regimentation of the women of the University of Toronto was not necessary at the present time and that the greatest demand was for practical courses that might be useful in the future.[17] According to the *Varsity*, the opinions of two "freshies" more than likely reflected those of the majority of the University "fair sex": "The idea of girls merely drilling is ridiculous, but we should follow the example of British women who are really serving in Red Cross work, Ambulance Training Corps, and a thousand other ways."[18]

The *Varsity* reminded the university officials that "it is obvious that the students, except those in their senior years, have not the time to cooperate on a full-time drive to enrol helpful women ... we can expect the initiative to be taken by those who have more time and experience to deal with such matters"[19] – that is, the women's groups on campus who "remembered the confusion and over-lapping of effort which occurred for several years of the last war."[20]

The impetus to organize voluntary war work for the women on campus came from the executive of the Faculty Wives' Association, who passed a resolution in September of 1939 recording their intention to establish a central organization as a working depot for war work.[21] Mrs H.J. Cody, wife of the president, called a general meeting of female alumnae, faculty, wives of faculty, staff, and undergraduates on 3 October, to decide how the women of the university could best prepare themselves for any call made upon them.[22] A central committee, the Women's War Service Committee (WWSC), was formed under the chairwomanship of Mrs Cody to guide the women into immediate and appropriate forms of war service. Each of the women's groups had one representative on the central committee, with the exception of the undergraduate students, who had three.[23]

"The first matter requiring attention was to decide through what channels the Committee would work, and the Red Cross seemed the obvious answer."[24] Invited to address the meeting on behalf of the Red Cross Society, the vice-president (and later national commandant of the Red Cross Women's Voluntary Service Corps), Adelaide M. Plumptre, suggested three types of service that could be rendered by the group: knitting socks, "remembering the emotional as well as the practical value"; addressing women's groups asking for speakers, after being thoroughly instructed as to Red Cross needs and methods; and transporting nurses to classes across the city.[25]

Appointed to "meet with the various needs as they arise,"[26] sub-committees of the Women's War Service Committee were formed to deal with the Red Cross Workroom; Military Service; Press and Public Relations; Courses of Training for War Service and Home Defence; Refugees; British Overseas Children; and Study of Economic Problems Arising out of the War, Public Relations.[27] The sub-committee on Military Services, for example, was responsible for providing for the needs of the male recruits in the COTC. Used clothing was collected or money was raised to buy new winter coats and other apparel for those male students who could not afford them. Female students on the sub-committee volunteered as typists and stenographers, and mimeographed military manuals in short supply for the members of the corps.[28]

From 5 to 7 December 1939 the WWSC held a registration of "woman-power" to give the women members of staff, graduates and undergraduates, "an opportunity to say how they wished to serve or train for service."[29] A total of 485 women registered for the study group on economic problems and the classes in first aid, motor mechanics, home nursing, and Red Cross sewing. Of the classes offered, simplified motor mechanics proved to be the most popular, with a registration of 170 (only 60 could be accommodated). St John's Ambulance followed with 70, and home nursing with 45.[30] Apart from these extracurricular, voluntary classes organized by the sub-committee on Courses of Training for War Service and Home Defence and open to all university women, few attempts were made in this first phase to organize any activity aimed specifically at the female students.[31]

In 1940–41, the sub-committee decided that "emphasis should be placed on training for organized air raid precaution courses."[32] From then on its efforts were directed in the main towards arranging basic civilian defence courses. Enrolment for the air-raid precaution (ARP) classes stood at 151 members in 1940–41. An additional 35 women registered for the course in motor mechanics, 10 for first aid, and 2 each for home nursing and Red Cross sewing.[33]

Other activities, both organized and unorganized, that were open to the female students in 1939–40 and for the duration of the war when they had a few minutes to spare included: knitting and sewing for the Red Cross; the annual War Service Drive tag days to raise money for war materials[34]; book and magazine collections for the troops; and the Panhellenic Canteen, operated by female faculty, staff, and students for men in active service.[35]

In the first phase of their mobilization, the general conclusion was that women students at the University of Toronto, like Canadian women generally, could best serve Canada's prosecution of the war voluntarily. The only war service developed in this phase was the set of training courses organized by the WWSC's sub-committee on Courses of Training for War Service and Home Defence and designed to prepare women for various types of volunteer war work. While female students were invited to attend these classes and many did so, the instruction was offered for the benefit of female faculty, staff, alumnae, and faculty wives more than for coeds.

The unbidden formation of a war service committee by the women of the University of Toronto under the leadership of the president's wife mirrored the spontaneous decision taken in September 1939 by women in existing or newly created organizations across Canada to throw their support behind the nation at war. In the field of volunteer war work it was not the state but women themselves who took the initiative. In June 1940 the federal government created the Department of National War Services to "coordinate, organize and utilize the voluntary efforts of the Canadian people [and] to organize and ... assist organizations engaged in supporting the war effort."[36] Not until the fall of 1941 did the Department of National War Services establish a Women's Voluntary Services Division to orchestrate and prevent duplication of effort among the thousands of women's volunteer organizations that had been actively engaged for two full years in packing parcels for the boys overseas, raising money for war charities through military whist drives and quilt auctions, and making jam and collecting bundles of clothing and bedding for the bombed-out areas of Great Britain.[37]

The shift into the second phase in the development of war service programs for female students was initiated by the Women's Athletic Association (WAA) in the fall of 1940. When the pressures of military training forced the abandonment of intercollegiate athletic competition for men in 1940, the question of women's continued participation also arose. By October both Queen's and the University of Western Ontario had decided to discontinue intercollegiate sports for the female students as well. At the University of

Toronto the WAA had not received any word from President Cody on the matter. At the beginning of the term Cody had announced that because the coeds had "a chief share in maintaining *morale* ... they [would] consider and devise methods of sharing in the various war efforts of the community within the limits of opportunity imposed by their university studies."[38] The members of the WAA decided that they would discuss the issue of war service among themselves and determine their preferences before taking it up with Cody.

Most of the members of the WAA directorate felt that, as nothing had yet been demanded of the coeds, the main reason for stopping intercollegiate sports for men, namely the lack of time due to military training, did not apply to women. They recognized, however, that "the expenditure of time, money and energy necessary for intercollegiate sports might create some criticism," and they believed that the "women would welcome the opportunity to make a sacrifice in this regard so long as some suitable form of service could be found to replace it."[39] The members of the Directorate discussed the possibility of establishing a special unit of the Red Cross Corps at the University of Toronto with the national commandant of the corps, Adelaide M. Plumptre.

The Women's Voluntary Service Corps of the Canadian Red Cross was formed in June of 1940, when the Ontario and Quebec divisions forwarded a joint recommendation to the national executive, asking for the organization of a voluntary service to train women as ambulance drivers for the Red Cross Society and the armed forces. The recommendation was later amended to include auxiliary nursing, office, and food administration sections, and approved. The university detachments were formed "under the careful and capable management and direction"[40] of the Office Administration Section. In April of 1942 they became a section in their own right.[41]

The members of the Women's Athletic Association directorate agreed that the corps would "be inspirational in character and yet would serve to bring students of the whole University together in a cooperative effort, as did the intercollegiate teams."[42] Interfaculty sports would not be affected. The members of the directorate discussed the possibility of making the corps a general student scheme rather than one sponsored by the WAA, but felt that rather than risk public debate on the issue they would be wiser to make it a purely voluntary activity of the athletes. They hoped that the female athletes would get first consideration for enrolment but recognized that the final decision would have to be made by the Red Cross Society.[43]

The formation of an experimental training detachment of the Canadian Red Cross Corps (CRCC) at the University of Toronto, to train female students for voluntary service with the Red Cross, government, and military, was approved by the Red Cross Society and President Cody in November of 1940.[44] While the corps would be under the direct supervision of the national commandant of the Office Administration Section of the Red Cross, it would be financed and have its university connection through the Women's Athletic Association.[45] Mrs Cody and the Women's War Service Committee were also asked, out of courtesy, to approve the plan.[46] The original announcement of the formation of the detachment was made by President Cody, for "the students in particular felt that the prestige of the Training Corps would be greatly increased" thereby.[47]

Membership in the university detachment followed the general requirements of the Red Cross Society. Applicants had to be between eighteen and forty-five years of age and provide two character references and a certificate of physical fitness. The Red Cross reserved the right to select those applicants "best fitted for future service by virtue of their previous training, physical condition, nearness to graduation and general aptitude for the type of work to be undertaken."[48] Although the recruits were not obliged to serve with the Red Cross after graduation, it was expected that they would offer their services along the lines in which they had been trained.[49]

The *Varsity* recorded its approval of the Women's Service Training Detachment (WSTD) of the CRCC, stating that it provided an excellent means of contributing to the war effort, for only three hours per week of training and drill were required of every recruit.[50] None the less, while the time commitment was not extensive, the recruits were reminded of the seriousness of the training and its ultimate goal: "If they are granted permission to take this course, they are being granted a privilege. No-one is expected to apply for admittance unless they are earnestly desirous of making use of the work taught when they are free to do so ... space will be too valuable to be wasted."[51] The student newspaper later repeated this warning to the female students: "It is no mere pass-time or diversion that they are entering into, but a serious course of training that will require a great deal of their time and energy."[52]

Time and financial and physical considerations dictated that membership in the corps be limited to two-hundred upper-year students. As Jean Forster, assistant physical director and lieutenant in the corps, later explained, "We couldn't cope with any more."[53] The members of the Women's Athletic Association directorate had agreed to provide the instructors and assist in defraying the costs of the uniforms for the corps, but their resources, financial and otherwise, were limited. The WAA directorate received only a small proportion of the funds (5 per cent until 1947–48)[54] collected from the compulsory athletic fee of four dollars levied on all female students. The bulk of the revenue from the fee went to the Men's Athletic Association. The athletic needs of the male students were well provided for by Hart House; those of the female students were not. To accommodate the training and sports requirements of the coeds, the members of the WAA directorate were required to rent additional facilities – the Ontario College of Education gymnasium, the Victoria College rink house, the University of Toronto Schools' pool, and so on – to supplement the gymnasium and pool provided for the women in the Household Science building.[55] During the war the WAA directorate was also responsible for booking drill and lecture halls of the University for the Women's Service Training Detachment, and space in the Education or Engineering building, one night a week, for the course in code.[56]

The greatest number of applicants for the WSTD in 1940–41 were from University, Trinity, and Victoria Colleges, although the Ontario College of Education, the Faculty of Household Science and the Department of Occupational and Physiotherapy were also well represented. A total of 170 women signed up for service in the first year.[57] The six platoons of the detachment were organized along college and faculty lines: one each from St Hilda's and Victoria; one from Occupational and Physiotherapy; and three from University College, one made up of graduating students, one of second-year students, and one of non-graduating third-year students.[58]

The athletic secretary, Miss A.E.M. Parkes, was appointed commandant of the corps, and Jean Forster, assistant physical director, was appointed lieutenant. The female students in charge of the platoons were all fourth-year undergraduate members of the WAA directorate. The importance of the relationship between the women's athletics background and their ability to assume leadership positions in the corps was stressed by one University of Toronto graduate: "Nearly all of the officers in the Women's Army Corps at the beginning were women that we knew from the University teams, various team sports – women [generally] didn't have the same opportunity to organize and administer as you did in the sports field. And so you had a little more practise at doing that sort of thing."[59]

A fear that paramilitary service would require a degree of time and initiative detrimental to the physical and academic well-being of the female students was not the only problem addressed by university authorities, who were ultimately responsible, *in loco parentis*, for all aspects of the coeds' training and discipline. They also had to deal with the response of female and male students and the public to the semi-military nature of the corps – the women's fear of military drill and discipline, and the public's objections to women wearing uniforms – issues that would later be faced by recruitment officers for the Canadian Women's Army Corps.[60] But, as one graduate suggested, "the fact that it was Red Cross was somewhat less threatening than if it had been Armed Service uniforms ... the Red Cross is definitely service-oriented rather than militarily oriented."[61]

Financial and moral considerations played an important role in determining the type of uniform ultimately selected. The university recruits were responsible for providing for their own uniforms and wearing them all day on the two days per week scheduled for training. Appearance could not be sacrificed to economics, however, so care had to be taken, it was believed, to insure that the uniform chosen enhanced rather than detracted from the female students' feminine attributes: "The selection of a suitable uniform proved somewhat of a problem as it must be cheap yet durable, attractive yet workmanlike, and could for obvious financial reasons include neither greatcoat or shoes. Finally, a smart dress of slightly military cut was chosen, made of dark grey alpine cloth with service cap of the same material water-proofed. A tie of royal blue, insert in the cap peak of the same colour and a blue arm badge bearing parts of the University crest gave character to the uniform."[62]

In addressing the question of whether or not service in the detachment would affect their femininity, the *Varsity* reassured the coeds that their uniforms "not only look appropriate, but what is better still, they are ex-tremely attractive, and have been gathering more than a few compliments for their wearers ... the girls could scarcely have done better."[63] At the same time, however, the *Varsity* suggested that it was not the uniform but the attitude and example of women who joined the war organizations strictly for appearance's sake that was the primary cause for concern. The amuse-ment and sometimes resentment roused by women in uniform could be explained, according to the *Varsity*, "by the example of those flurrying individuals who feel they ought to do something ... rather than give the matter any thought they plunge into the nearest group which seems to be doing anything which might be considered appropriate, especially if that group happens to be wearing a uniform."[64] In the opinion of some observers, women of that type could not be regarded with confidence or admiration, for they were simply "amusing themselves" and "showing off."

Yet the *Varsity* felt that the university could and should be particularly proud of the WSTD, CRCC, for most of its members realized what they were doing and why. A definite sacrifice of time and effort was required, as well as plans for future service. The national commandant of the corps, Adelaide M. Plumptre, agreed. Membership in the university detachment was not a fad to attract attention but "an outward and visible sign of an inward and spiritual strength."[65] The uniform of the corps stood for "qualifications, training, discipline and service."[66]

The high expectations of the *Varsity* were not initially shared by the supervisors for training in the corps, Sergeant West and Corporal Pursar of the Veteran Guards of Canada. Both doubted that the female students had the necessary aptitude for military service. Corporal Pursar, in particular, believed that the girls lacked the necessary serious attitude, but he hoped that the platoon, squadron, and company drill practised by the "raw recruits" would teach them "a degree of self-control, an essential quality in meeting all emergencies."[67]

In an article written for the Christmas 1940 issue of the *Trinity University Review*, Margaret Duncan, one of the recruits in the corps, described some of the more humorous experiences she had had in the detachment. From her account it would appear that the girls were eager, almost too eager, to follow orders: "I believe the *Varsity* said that 'one guy' in the COTC route march changed step forty-seven times in two hours. This might be said quite justly of most members of the WSTD. Our downfall is that we have a tendency to look at the feet of the person in front of us. Thus every time she changes step the whole platoon changes with her. One afternoon a lieutenant, drilling us, told us to keep our heads up and like true soldiers we obeyed blindly. Blindly, I say, for no-one consequently saw the hole en route and one after another in we went."[68] Able to laugh at herself as she was, Duncan took the business of the WSTD, CRCC, very seriously and was, therefore, offended by the statement of Corporal Pursar that "we are instructing them only in the most elementary drill – it will take them all winter to get that down pat." She felt that the female students "certainly try hard enough even if some of our efforts backfire at times." She recalled the day Pursar said, "You may be blinking coeds but you are in the Army now. I don't care what you do before or after, but you are in the Army now." The corporal may not have cared, Duncan observed, but the female recruits did. "Fun though it may be, yet we have a serious intention – to be trained for voluntary relief work in an efficient military manner."[69]

By the spring of 1941 Commandant Parkes was able to report that the female members of the corps were showing great improvement: "They are mastering new formations and carrying out orders with greater ease, and there has been a general smartening of the whole company. On the command 'halt' every foot stops simultaneously, there is a general clicking of heels that lends a military and more dignified air to the platoons."[70] President Cody seconded that positive assessment, stating that "University girls of a disciplined intelligence are able to master the intricacies of military work, in both drill and lectures."[71]

The recruits were not subject to military discipline, but they were required to heed the rules and regulations governing the behaviour of Red Cross workers and "observe the rules of courtesy, such as saluting when in uniform all their superior officers ... If they are in mufti when [a superior officer] salutes them, they are required to 'at least smile sweetly in acknowledgement.'"[72] The standing orders of the Red Cross Corps stated that "members in uniform should be especially quiet and courteous in public and act in such a way as to avoid unfavorable comment."[73] The coeds in the WSTD, CRCC, were expected to set an example for women all over the university. For instance, Miss Parkes asked that the recruits be more punctual than others in their attendance at classes and university functions generally and that they wear "sockees of a more conservative colour ... rather than the various rainbow colours now in vogue on campus."[74]

It was also believed that service in the WSTD, CRCC, was establishing important precedents for the coed's post-war future. The relationship between military training, voluntary service, the war effort, and the post-war world was outlined by Adelaide M. Plumptre: "Even if today ... your training seems of no use and no-one knows what the future will bring, everything that you can do to train yourself mentally and physically for the trials and bitterness that may come is work well done. There is not one thing that you learn but is of value for public service."[75] The courses of training offered in the corps were designed to prepare the female students for service in wartime and peacetime. All of the members of the detachment were required to take basic training in elementary first aid, civilian defence (ARP), and Red Cross history and organization.[76] Advanced training was provided in each of four sections: transport, nursing auxiliary, office administration, and food administration.[77] Female recruits entering the advanced sections were encouraged to choose the training closest to their academic field of study.

The transport section proved to be the most popular division, possibly because it was the most directly related to the war effort.[78] Corps members were instructed in St John's Ambulance procedure, stretcher drill, first aid, and map reading. Of particular interest was an eight weeks' certificate course in motor mechanics offered by the Ford Motor Company. It included "instruction in running repairs, vehicle maintenance, and tire changing."[79] Upon completion of the advanced training, female students rendered practical assistance to the Red Cross Society, driving ambulances and assisting at the blood-donor clinics.[80]

Female students in the nursing auxiliary section received instruction in stretcher drill and ambulance procedure and took two St John's courses in first aid and home nursing, each of which granted the successful candidate a certificate.[81] Upon graduating from the course, the young women looked after the records in the Red Cross clinics and assisted in the orderly room at corps headquarters.[82]

The office-administration section was made up of "women trained in the various types of office administration, secretarial duties, general executive and organization work."[83] Courses of training included orderly-room procedure, military law, telegraphy, and the use of code. Specialized instruction in the operation of the switchboard and long-distance telephone was given under the auspices of the Bell Telephone Company.[84] It is possible that a large corporation like Bell viewed the provision of free instruction as one means to recruit employees for the future. Members of the office-administration section were able to apply their practical training in the Red Cross clinics, volunteering for telephone and clerical duty.[85]

Enrolment in the food-administration section was restricted to senior students in the Departments of Household Economics and Household Science. Theoretical studies in emergency feeding and wartime nutrition were supplemented by field work in the blood-donor clinics, the kitchens of Hart House and No 1 Manning Depot, RCAF, and the laboratories of the Red Cross mobile clinics.[86]

The corps members who completed all the training requirements of the detachment were qualified upon graduation to enter the regular sections of the Canadian Red Cross Corps or, once the women's corps of the armed services were created, the appropriate divisions of the army, navy, and air force. According to the student yearbook, *Torontonensis*, of 1941, the raison d'être of the WSTD was to

provide a body of young women of superior intelligence with a general background of military knowledge in order that they may be qualified to act as officers and instructors in any women's auxiliaries to the fighting services that many be organized in the future; that those with technical abilities such as Occupational and Physiotherapists and graduates of the Household Economics course may have the requisite knowledge for dealing with military services; and that others may be qualified to act as organizers and supervisors of the staffs of military offices should it become necessary to relieve men of these tasks.[87]

The federal government consistently refused to grant military status to wartime Canada's many unofficial women's paramilitary corps, like the Canadian Red Cross Corps, despite frequent appeals from those groups for official recognition. At the same time, the war departments of government could not afford to ignore the amount of womanpower enrolled in those volunteer corps. When the Departments of National Defence and National War Services finally decided to organize official women's services, they looked to the already existing unofficial corps as a recruiting ground for officers and other ranks. The first of the Armed Services to found its own women's corps was the air force, in July 1941, followed by the Canadian Women's Army Corps in August of the same year and the Women's Royal Canadian Naval Service in July of 1942.[88] Presumably some of the female students active in the University of Toronto Women's Service Training Detachment of the Canadian Red Cross Corps were among the approximately 325 who eventually served with one or the other of the women's services of the Canadian armed forces before their dissolution in 1946 or with the medical corps of one of the three services.[89]

From September 1939 to April 1942 the participation of female students in the activities of the Women's War Service Committee and Women's Service Training Detachment, Canadian Red Cross Corps, at the University of Toronto, was strictly voluntary, for Red Cross principles and regulations would not permit compulsory membership in the national organization.[90] Nevertheless, at Canadian universities across the country where women's contribution to the war effort was made compulsory, enrolment in the Red Cross Corps came to be regarded as the equivalent of compulsory service.

The third phase in the University of Toronto's war-service program for female students was marked by the introduction of compulsory national-service training in the fall of 1942. The move was prompted locally by the establishment of compulsory military service for all male students of draft age on campus, and nationally by labour shortages that had encouraged the federal government in the spring of 1942 to create the Women's Division of National Selective Service, charged with mobilizing Canada's reserves of women workers[91] for employment in war industry and essential services.[92]

Miss Parkes, acting secretrary-treasurer of the Students' Administrative Council, had suggested to President Cody on 4 September 1942 that it was time compulsory service for women was introduced on the University of Toronto campus. She believed that

during the past year a noticeable condition of uncertainty and unrest existed among women students of the upper years ... particularly those in the Pure Arts courses. Should the Selective Service regulations become more stringent, it is very possible that University women who are not enrolled in "essential" courses will have to be drafted for some form of service. It would appear that some specific training while they are still at the university will not only make these women of more value to the country when the call comes but will help solve the problem for the many conscientious students who do not know where they duty lies.[93]

In the fall of 1941 the *Varsity* had addressed the question of whether the university was to take the responsibility for seeing that its women students were actively engaged in some kind of compulsory war service or war training. At that time, its position had been that "every girl is at liberty to choose the type of war service for which she feels she is best suited and to which she can contribute most. It is more desirable than enrolling in comparatively rigid courses, but only on one condition: that every student does choose some kind of work and carry it out faithfully."[94] The *Varsity* later argued that the decision to introduce compulsory training in the 1942–43 term was the result of the wishes of the girls themselves, who felt that they should do everything in their power to assist in the nation's war effort.[95] The paper distinguished between compulsory training and conscription, categorically rejecting the latter on the grounds of its incompatibility with women's cultural relegation to domesticity. Conscription of women, the *Varsity* intoned, "is utterly foreign to our precious ideals of civilization and culture. The strength of our system of government is rooted in the individual family and home, thus in the central figure of that home, the mother ... [women's] best service in the interest of the war effort is to preserve the home."[96]

On 23 September 1942 President Cody announced that the board of governors had decided that all of the female students, except those in first year ("who were considered to have already a sufficient problem of adjustment as well as required physical training")[97] and those in "professional" courses, would be required to register for war service and contribute sixty hours per year of war work. Professional courses were defined as all courses other than pass or honours arts, and so included occupational and physiotherapy, nursing, science and engineering, physical and health education, social work, and courses at the Ontario College of Education.[98]

When the registration had been completed, it was announced that training would have to be provided for nine hundred students in 1942–43 alone.[99] President Cody and the board of governors "welcomed this spontaneous decision on the part of the students, showing, as it did, that our women students are no less conscious of the great duties and responsibilities of the times than are the men."[100] University officials argued that the academic studies of the coeds would continue to hold top priority: their program was "designed to make possible a measure of national service without interfering with the completion of the student's academic course and so impairing her future value to the country as a fully trained University woman."[101] As far as possible the instruction would be given on Tuesdays and Thursdays, from four o'clock to six o'clock in the afternoon, so as not to interfere with the coed's studies or her free time.[102]

The committee appointed to arrange the courses to be offered to the students was chaired by the university registrar, A.B. Fennell. Its members included Miss Parkes, secretary-treasurer of the Students' Administrative Council and commandant of the Red Cross Corps at the university; Miss M.B. Ferguson, Miss J. Macpherson, and Mrs M.M. Kirkwood, deans of Women at University College, Victoria, and Trinity Colleges respectively; and Dr Victoria Mueller, acting dean of Women for St Michael's College.[103] The program that they established was designed to teach the female students skills useful for the war effort and to educate them to apply the skills they had learned and assume their share of responsibility as Canadian citizens in the local community. Once again, organizers justified the training on the grounds that it would also prove valuable after the war[104] for those students who had not previously received any "professional" training for future roles as wives and mothers.

The courses offered replaced those previously given by the Women's War Service Committee, combining instruction with practical and / or field work.[105] They included training as hospital nursing aids (maximum enrolment of 100); training as volunteers for the child-care facilities established under the Dominion-Provincial Wartime Day Nurseries Agreement (50); nutrition (150); training in recreational leadership (150); Red Cross sewing (25); civilian defence and home nursing or first aid (150).[106]

Courses were added in 1943–44 in practical work as dietitians' aids (for fourth-year Home Economics students only); community needs and resources (50); group leadership (50); laboratory technique (third- and fourth-year chemistry students, 30); conservation of textiles and budgeting (no Home Economics students, 145); training as farm service-camp recreation leaders (12); repairing and remodelling of clothes (Home Economics students only); and laboratory war work (for psychiatry and fourth-year physiology students only).[107] The coeds trained as group leaders, for example, would lead discussions, singsongs, and rallies in the war factories, in the community, and in the home, lifting morale on the home front.[108] By the end of the war approximately 500 female students had received the day-nursery training, 400 the hospital nurses' aid, 100 the dietitians' aid, 300 the community needs and resources, and 100 or more the Red Cross sewing.[109]

As membership in the Women's Service Training Detachment of the Canadian Red Cross Corps was included in the list of options for war service, the introduction of compulsory training did not have the impact on enrolment in the corps that many university officials feared. The detachment continued in much the same manner, though with less emphasis on drill.[110] Approximately 75 women were recruited into the corps every year after its creation. An estimated 40 per cent re-enlisted for a second year of training, and a few for a third. By 1945, when the detachment was dissolved, about 540 female students had received paramilitary training.[111]

Of the approximately 9,000 women students who attended the University of Toronto during the Second War, only an estimated 325 enlisted in the armed forces of Canada to serve as a member or officer of the Royal Canadian Air Force, Women's Division, the CWAC, or the WRCNS, or as a nurse, doctor, or occupational or physiotherapist in the medical corps of one of the three services.[112] The largest proportion (118) had studied occupational or physiotherapy, a testimony to the armed forces' increased need for these skills. Given that the majority of the women attending the university during the war years were to be found in the arts colleges, it is not surprising that the second highest proportion of volunteers (106) were arts students, 21 of whom enlisted before completing their studies. A total of 33 women in medicine signed up, only ten of whom were already in possession of an MD degree. The University of Toronto women enlistees who interrupted their studies to serve their nation at war formed part of that tiny female minority of returning veterans in 1945–46 who took advantage of Canada's educational rehabilitation benefits.

As was the case with the vocational training of women for the civilian labour market under the Dominion-Provincial War Emergency Training Program, the nature of war-training programs for female students at the University of Toronto during the Second World War was determined by "social definitions of femininity" and "conceptions of women's social role." "The type of training provided for the women did indeed vary with changes in demands on the labour market, but what was considered 'normal' work for women remained surprisingly constant"[113] throughout the war emergency.

Changes in the university's war-training program for female students were introduced by the president and the board of governors on the recommendation of female staff, women's groups, and student organizations. But the aim of their program remained the same, to train the coeds for voluntary war service and teach them skills that would prepare them for their future careers as wives and mothers in the home and volunteer workers in their local communities.

The Women's War Service Committee of the University of Toronto, which had been established in the fall of 1939 to organize the war work of women on campus, focused on female faculty, staff, and alumnae, and wives of male faculty. Only a limited attempt was made by the committee members at that time to recruit the female students. Most believed that the coeds had neither the time nor the experience necessary to make much of a contribution to the war effort, and that the committee bore no responsibility to ensure that they did. It was left to the individual female student to do all she could for the war effort, and knitting was a popular activity.

When the question was raised whether or not the female students should follow the example set by the male students and establish a women's branch of the Canadian Officers' Training Corps on campus, the real issues at stake for university authorities were clarified. They did not fear the adverse effects that war training might have on the time or studies of the female students so much as they feared the implications that military drill and discipline and the donning of a uniform would have for the "femininity" of the coeds. The decision made in principle by the University College Parliament, not to form a female COTC, established an important precedent for the future. Decisions about how the female students could best serve the war effort would be made by university authorities, within the boundaries of what was considered socially acceptable.

The Women's Athletic Association's proposal to form a Women's Service Training Detachment of the Canadian Red Cross Corps in the fall of 1940 was approved by the president and the board of governors precisely because it was designed as a patriotic endeavour to replace intercollegiate sports for women. It was an activity of the Red Cross Society and was, therefore, voluntary and service oriented. The courses offered in the four sections –

transportation, nursing, and food and office administration – enhanced rather than threatened the femininity of the female students, for they emphasized the value of unpaid labour and service in the home and local community, during the war and for the future. Given the nature of the training and the restrictions placed on enrolment, the example provided by the corps had a limited impact, if it had any impact at all, on popular attitudes towards military training for women.

Compulsory training for female students was not viewed as necessary, at the University of Toronto, until the fall of 1942. Manpower shortages in the armed forces and labour shortages at home prompted the introduction of compulsory military service for all men of draft age and the recruitment of women from every level of the reserve labour force for industrial war work. Only then did compulsory war training for the coeds become acceptable. The initiative had again come from university women themselves, and they agreed to devote their time and energy to training the undergraduates. The courses of training offered were aimed at the female students in the non-professional or arts courses and were designed to make them more valuable to their country during the war while at the same time preparing them for volunteer work and unpaid domestic labour once the war was over. The young women were taught the skills and values necessary to preserve the traditional home and local community, and educated to assume their duties and responsibilities as wives and mothers in the post-war era.

The women of the University of Toronto – faculty, staff, and students – earnestly desired to make a positive contribution to the war effort, and did, no questions asked. The university's programs for war training and service were introduced on suggestions forwarded by the women, and maintained by their time and effort, but the final credit was always assumed by the president and the board of governors. The programs that the women helped to establish worked against them in the end, for those programs reinforced their inferior status and popular conceptions of femininity. When the women tried to obtain proper athletic, social, and cultural facilities during and after the war, their pleas and history of service were both ignored.[114]

NOTES

1 Gwendoline Pilkington, "A History of the National Conference of Canadian Universities 1911–61" (PhD thesis, University of Toronto 1974), 316. According to Pilkington, in her more recent published study of the relationship between the federal government and the Association of Universities and Colleges of Canada, the attitude of the United States government towards the mobilization of male university students and faculty differed markedly from that of the Canadian gov-

ernment. In the American case, university membership brought little or no exemption from the draft except for those enrolled in dentistry and medicine. Gwendoline Evans Pilkington, *Speaking with One Voice: Universities in Dialogue with Government* (Montreal: McGill University 1983), 23–4.

2 The University of Saskatchewan had maintained Canadian Officers' Training Corps throughout the Depression of the 1930s on the strength of President Walter Murray's argument that "Saskatchewan students had suffered such a large number of casualties in 1914–18 because they had not been trained." Michael Hayden, *Seeking a Balance: The University of Saskatchewan 1907–1982* (Vancouver: University of British Columbia Press 1983), 183. In the case of McGill, the outbreak of war brought the overnight expansion of corps enrolment from "125 to more than 1,400 cadets, with fifty instructors." Stanley Brice Frost, *McGill University: For the Advancement of Learning*, vol. 2, *1895–1971* (Montreal: McGill-Queen's University Press 1984), 217. See also Frederick W. Gibson, *"To Service and Yet Be Free": Queen's University, 1917–1961* (Montreal: McGill-Queen's University Press 1983), 181; Charles M. Johnston, *McMaster University*, vol. 2, *The Early Years in Hamilton 1930–1957* (Toronto: University of Toronto Press 1981), 88; Pilkington, *Speaking with One Voice*, 25; and John G. Reid, *Mount Allison University*, vol. 2, *1914–1963* (Toronto: University of Toronto Press 1984), 152.

3 Gibson, *"To Serve,"* 183.

4 Pilkington, "A History of the NCCU," 309.

5 Gibson, *"To Serve"*, 183.

6 Pilkington, "A History of the NCCU," 321, 326; Reid, *Mount Allison*, 2:186; Johnston, *McMaster*, 2:107.

7 Gibson, *"To Serve,"* 209.

8 Ibid., 207–12.

9 *President's Report*, University of Toronto, 1943–44, 1.

10 Johnston, *McMaster*, 2:109.

11 Gibson, "To Serve," 189.

12 Because women were not initially eligible for this program, a special fund from the Kellogg Foundation was established for their use as well as for the use of physically unfit men. *President's Report*, University of Toronto, 1941–42, 21–3.

13 *Torontonensis* 43 (1941): 213.

14 *Varsity*, 19 Oct. 1939, 1, 3.

15 Ibid., 23 Oct. 1939, 4.

16 Ibid.

17 Ibid., 31 Oct. 1939, 2.

18 Ibid., 20 Oct. 1939, 4.

19 Ibid., 31 Oct. 1939, 2.

20 University of Toronto Archives (UTA), Records of the Department of Athletics and Recreation–Women, A83-0045, Women's Athletic Association, file: University Training Detachment of the Red Cross Corps, memo: "Women's War Service at the University of Toronto," 29 Feb. 1944, 1.

21 UTA, Records of the Women's War Service Committee, B68-0002, vol. 1, file: Preliminary Papers (13 Sept.–6 Nov. 1939), Extract from Minutes of Faculty Wives Executive for 13 Sept. 1939.

22 *Varsity*, 29 Sept. 1939, 4.

23 UTA, B68-0002, vol. 1, file: Ontario Legislature Companies Act, Correspondence with WWSC re 1942, re incorporation, constitution and organization, memo: "Constitution of the University of Toronto Women's War Service Committee."

24 UTA, A83-0045, WAA, file: University Training Detachment, RCC, memo: "Women's War Service," 24 Feb. 1944, 1.

25 UTA, B68-0002, vol. 1, file B72-0004/001 (03), Organization and Membership Correspondence 1939–46, memo of 3 Oct. 1939, 2–3.

26 *Varsity*, 24 Nov. 1939, 1.

27 UTA, B68-0002, vol. 1, file: Ontario Legislature Companies Act, Correspondence with WWSC re "Constitution of the University of Toronto WWSC.

28 *Varsity*, 10 Mar. 1943, 3.

29 UTA, A83-0045, WAA, file: University Training Detachment RCC, memo: "Women's War Service," 24 Feb. 1944, 2.

30 *Varsity*, 8 Jan. 1940, 1.

31 UTA, A83-0045, WAA, file: University Training Detachment RRC, memo: "Women's War Service," 24 Feb. 1944, 2.

32 UTA, B68-0002, vol. 4, file: Sub-Committee on Training Courses, reports 1939–42, B72-0004/001 (18), report of 20 Nov. 1941 by Norma Mortimer.

33 *Ibid.*, vol. 1, file: Minutes (17 Oct.–9 Dec. 1940), Minutes of 11 Nov. 1941, 65.

34 Ibid., vol. 4, file: Sub-Committee on Training Courses, B72-0004/001 (20), report of undergraduate work, 5 Dec. 1941, from J. Laing, SAC delegate.

35 UTA, A83-0045, WAA, file: University Training Detachment RCC, memo: "Women's War Service," 24 Feb. 1944, 4.

36 National Archives of Canada (NAC), Records of the Department of National War Services, RG 44, vol. 11, file: History of Voluntary and Auxiliary Services Division, "Purpose and Scope," 1–3.

37 NAC, RG 44, vol. 11, file: History of Voluntary and Auxiliary Services Division, "Purpose and Scope," 1–4; Ruth Roach Pierson, *"They're Still Women After All": The Second World War and Canadian Womanhood* (Toronto: McClelland and Stewart 1986), 33–41.

38 *Varsity*, 26 Sept. 1940, 6.

39 UTA, A83-0045, WAA, Directorate Minutes, 7 Oct. 1940, 1–2.

40 NAC, RG 44, vol. 33, file: WVS (vol. 1) General Correspondence, Davis to Heeney, 8 May 1941.

41 Red Cross Library, box: Canadian Red Cross Service – H & CS Corps, file: CRCC Corps, World War Two, "History of Red Cross Corps."

42 UTA, A83-0045, WAA, file: University Training Detachment RCC, memo: "Women's War Service," 24 Feb. 1944, 3.

43 UTA, ibid., Directorate Minutes, 7 Oct. 1940, 1–2.

44 Red Cross Library, box: CRCS–H & CS Corps, file: CRCC Corps, World War Two, "History of Red Cross Corps."
45 *University of Toronto Monthly* (Apr. 1941).
46 UTA, A83-0045, WAA, Directorate Minutes, 1 Oct. 1940, 2.
47 UTA, Records of the Office of the President – Letters, A68-0006, vol. 38, A.E.M. Parkes to President Cody, 9 Oct. 1940.
48 *Varsity*, 10 Oct. 1940, 1.
49 Ibid., 6 Mar. 1941, 2.
50 Ibid., 21 Sept. 1942, 1.
51 Ibid., 10 Oct. 1940, 2.
52 Ibid., 5 Nov. 1940, 2.
53 Interview with Jean Forster, 11 Jan. 1984.
54 UTA, A68-0006, vol. 137, file: Undergraduate Activities, M.M. Kirkwood and A.E.M. Parkes to Smith, 17 June 1948.
55 UTA, A68-0006, vol. 93, file: Building Program, "A Statement of the Need for a Women's Building," 27 Jan. 1947.
56 UTA, A68-0006, vol. 46, University of Toronto Superintendent's Office, 5 Oct. 1942, 2–3.
57 *Varsity*, 24 and 31 Oct. 1940, 1. An estimated 2,100 women were eligible for training in the corps. Approximately 60 to 70 women participated in intercollegiate sports per year, and many of these women joined the detachment.
58 *University of Toronto Monthly* (Apr. 1941): 186.
59 Interview with Helen Gurney, 16 Nov. 1983.
60 NAC, Records of the Department of Labour, RG27, vol. 1523, file: 21–16 pt 1, "Minutes of Meeting on Recruitment of Women for Armed Forces Held in the office of Mrs. Rex Eaton, 19 Apr. 1943," and "Reasons Applicants Have Given for Not Being Interested in Employment."
61 Interview with Kay Fallis, 17 Jan. 1984.
62 *University of Toronto Monthly* (Apr. 1941): 186.
63 *Varsity*, 21 Jan. 1941, 2.
64 Ibid., 15 Oct. 1941, 2.
65 Ibid.
66 Adelaide M. Plumptre, "Women in Uniform," Canadian Red Cross *Despatch* (July–Aug. 1941): 5.
67 *Varsity*, 15 Nov. 1940, 1.
68 *Trinity University Review* 3, no. 2 (Christmas 1940): 31–2.
69 Ibid.
70 *Varsity*, 12 Feb. 1941, 1.
71 Ibid., 21 Jan. 1941, 1.
72 Ibid., 15 Nov. 1940, 1.
73 UTA, A83-0045, WAA, University Training Detachment RCC, section 3, WVSC Standing Orders, "Deportment," 2.
74 *Varsity*, 12 Feb. 1941, 1.

75 Ibid., 9 Dec. 1941, 1.
76 Ibid., 21 Sept. 1942, 1.
77 Ibid., 10 Oct. 1940, 2.
78 Ibid., 8 Oct. 1941, 1.
79 *Torontonensis* 44 (1942): 222.
80 *Varsity*, 1 Nov. 1943, 1.
81 *Torontonensis* 44 (1942): 222.
82 *Varsity*, 1 Nov. 1943, 4.
83 Ibid., 10 Oct. 1940, 2.
84 Ibid.
85 Ibid., 23 Oct. 1944, 1.
86 Ibid., 1 Nov. 1943, 4.
87 *Torontonensis* 43 (1941): 213.
88 Pierson, *"They're Still Women After All,"* 102–3, 95.
89 See p. 177.
90 *Varsity*, 28 Sept. 1942, 1.
91 Ibid., 1 Oct. 1942, 2.
92 Pierson, *"They're Still Women After All,"* 23–6.
93 UTA, A58-0006, vol. 46, Parkes to Cody, 4 Sept. 1942.
94 *Varsity*, 3 Oct. 1941, 2.
95 Ibid., 1 Oct. 1943, 2.
96 Ibid., 26 Oct. 1943, 2.
97 UTA, A83-0045, WAA, University Training Detachment RCC, file: Women's War
   Service," 24 Feb. 1944, 2.
98 *Varsity*, 28 Sept. 1942, 1.
99 UTA, B68-0002, vol. 1, file: B72-0004/001 (20), "Undergraduates," memo from
   Parkes re "Undergraduate Women's War Service," 1945.
100 *Varsity*, 1 Oct. 1942, 2.
101 Ibid., 21 Sept. 1942, 1.
102 Ibid., 25 Sept. 1942, 1.
103 Ibid.
104 Ibid., 28 Sept. 1942, 2.
105 UTA, B68-0002, vol. 4, file: Sub-Committee on Training Courses, reports B72-0004/
    0001 (18), report of 16 Nov. 1942.
106 *Varsity*, 21 Sept. 1942, 1.
107 Ibid., 25 Sept. 1943, 4.
108 Ibid., 8 Oct. 1943, 1.
109 UTA, B68-0002, vol. 3, file: (2), "Undergraduates," memo: "Undergraduate
    Women's War Service," 1945, 2.
110 *Varsity*, 10 Mar. 1943, 6. As Miss Parkes explained, the courses under the com-
    pulsory program were "attractive in themselves and did not involve the purchase
    of a uniform or compulsory drill." A83-0045, WAA, file: correspondence re WAA,
    1945–47, Annual Report, University of Toronto Detachment CRCC, 16 Nov.
    1942.

111 UTA, B68-0002, vol. 3, file: (2), "Undergraduates," memo: "Undergraduate Women's War Service," 1945, 2.

112 The figures and proportions in this paragraph have been calculated from UTA, University of Toronto, "Honour Roll for World War II," 5 vols., 1939–51.

113 Pierson with Marjorie Cohen, "Government Job-Training Programs for Women, 1937–1947," in Pierson, *"They're Still Women After All,"* 62, 63.

114 Anne Rochon Ford, *A Path Not Strewn with Roses: One Hundred Years of Women at the University of Toronto 1884–1984* (Toronto: University of Toronto Press 1985), 65–75. According to Susan M. Hartmann, "The postwar transformation of higher education [in the United States] enlarged the differences between men and women. As enrollments swelled, as college education spread beyond the exceptional or privileged few and became a key to middle-class status, women lost ground." Hartmann, *The Home Front and Beyond: American Women in the 1940s* (Boston: Twayne Publishers 1982), 107.

PART FOUR

Student Movements and Social Change

CHAPTER NINE

"The Call to Service":
The YWCA and the Canadian College Woman, 1886–1920*

Diana Pedersen

According to a female student reporting in 1909 on "Life among the Women at University College, University of Toronto," "the most popular social life of the girls is that which is solely for girls." The first generations of Canadian college women were avid joiners, and a significant dimension of their experience of higher education was the opportunity to associate with other women in the multitude of religious, literary, athletic, and social clubs and societies within which they created what they liked to call "a 'little sphere' all their own."[1] By seeking religious fellowship in societies such as the Young Women's Christian Association (YWCA), where they affirmed their membership in "a great family of sisters seeking education," the pioneering generations of women students sought to cope with their status as relative newcomers to the male-dominated colleges. By joining the YWCA and identifying herself "with the Christian girls," noted one McGill student in 1902, a new student was "no longer a stranger in a strange land."[2]

Recent studies of Canadian college women suggest the existence of a distinct female student culture that flourished in college classrooms, residences, clubs and societies but whose religious dimension has yet to be explored fully.[3] This paper will argue that through their contacts with the YWCA, Canadian women students were exhorted to heed "the call to service," an invitation to dedicate their lives to Christian social service and the "regeneration" of society. The YWCA's active presence in the majority of Canadian colleges and universities, and its continuing popularity with a substantial portion of the female student population, indicate a need to consider both the place of religion in women's experience of college life and the participation of women in the influential Christian student movement. Within the YWCA evangelical religion served to unite women in bonds of "Christian sisterhood" yet simultaneously divided them as they disagreed over the meaning and implications of the teachings of Jesus both for women and for the larger Canadian society. The YWCA's experience suggests the

immense complexity of the religious question in both the student movement
and the women's movement during the critical turn-of-the-century decades.

Appearing in Canadian cities beginning in the 1870s, following established models in Great Britain and the United States, YWCAs were founded
by middle-class evangelical Protestant women who perceived the existence
of a widespread "girl problem" as the experiences of employment, independent living, and higher education threatened to undermine the traditional
close relationship of young women to family, home, and church. The stated
purpose of the association was to offer protection and supervision to young
women in this formative, and dangerous, period of their lives.[4] The YWCA
gave to the maternal feminism of the contemporary Canadian women's
movement a distinctly evangelical cast. Christianity, from the perspective
of YWCA women, legitimated their rejection of a passive, decorative, and
purely domestic femininity. By requiring of them a commitment to usefulness, sacrifice, and service, it implied that women were central to the
churches' campaign to remake Canadian society "in the image of Christ's
Kingdom on earth." The YWCA defined a redemptive role for young women
as "God's own cornerstones" and the mothers of the future generations, and
linked with "the coming of the kingdom" an improvement in the position
of women and a high valuation of womanly qualities.

During the critical decades of the late nineteenth and early twentieth
centuries, evangelical Protestantism was radically altered under the impact
of higher criticism and the social gospel. The evangelical movement tran-
scended denominational boundaries, emphasizing an individual commitment
to Christianity and a personal relationship with Jesus Christ, an intense
preoccupation with spiritual health, the demonstration of faith through a
commitment to good works and morally upright behaviour, a preference for
public and emotional forms of religious observance, and a belief in the
importance of the experience of conversion as a prelude to salvation. Within
the YWCA, a belief in the special message of the life and teachings of Jesus
for young women coexisted with a spectrum of positions on theological and
social questions ranging from support for biblical literalism to liberal and
even radical views on the institutional church and the divinity of Jesus, and
from an endorsement of conservative moral reforms such as enforced Sabbath
observance to active support for the construction of a new Christian social
order.[5]

More commonly associated with its city branches, which offered boarding
houses, swimming pools, and other programs and services to young single
women in the urban workforce, the YWCA was also, prior to the formation
of the Student Christian Movement of Canada in 1920, one of the principal
societies for women students and, by its own claim, "the only comprehensive
Christian organization among the women students of Canada." During their
college years, when the lives of students were filled with "possibilities for

good" and their minds were most "impressionable and open," the YWCA was provided with an excellent opportunity for bringing to bear upon them "the influence of a movement which stands for the fundamental verities of Christianity."[6] Such efforts were well received by many students who shared a belief widely held among late-nineteenth-century middle-class Protestant women, "that women had a special role to play in the coming struggle for social regeneration." Conscious of their privileged backgrounds and unique opportunities, such students felt themselves to be charged with a great responsibility to the nation, which looked to them "for higher ideals and truer conceptions of life and its purposes [and] to raise the standard for manhood and to regenerate society, cleansing it of its moral impurity."[7] Fully supporting the entry of women into the professions and an enhanced female presence in church and state, the YWCA hoped to forge an alliance with students by undertaking:

1 To win the non-Christian students to become followers of Jesus Christ;
2 To guard them against the temptations common in college, to deepen the spiritual life, and to develop an efficiency in Christian service;
3 To lead the young women to place their lives after graduating in the service that will tell most for the extension of the Kingdom of God.[8]

From the perspective of the YWCA, student work was a small department and only one of several critical components of a larger strategy to transform the nation. In scale and scope its significance paled in comparison with the work undertaken by city YWCAs for working women and immigrants, yet for three decades its importance was judged to be "out of all proportion to its numerical strength, for it is reaching the coming women leaders and is helping to call them into obedience to Christ and into His service."[9]

Nineteenth-century Canadian YWCAs, both student and city branches, developed in the context of a North American movement dominated by the more numerous American associations. From their inception they were united in their commitment to interdenominational co-operation as a means of augmenting the resources available to the churches and enhancing the autonomy of organized churchwomen. At a time when denominational loyalties – and rivalries – were still strong, the success of this policy depended upon deflecting attention from doctrinal questions and indeed from the matter of denominational affiliation itself. It is undoubtedly for this reason that surviving records shed little light on possible denominational influences or tensions within the YWCA.[10] The YWCA's commitment to a Protestantism that was avowedly evangelical as well as interdenominational was considerably more problematic, at least during the nineteenth century. Until the 1890s, Canadian YWCAs were affiliated with either the International Committee of YWCAs, based in Chicago, or the International Board of YWCAs,

based in New York, two bodies that were seriously divided over the issue
of evangelical control of the YWCA. The former favoured the evangelization
of individual young women, while the latter called for a broader platform
of Christian social reform and co-operation with the secular women's movement.[11] As supporters of the evangelical conception of the YWCA's mandate,
student branches enshrined in their constitutions an evangelical membership
basis, which restricted active (voting and office-holding) membership in a
student YWCA to full members of evangelical churches.[12] Unhappy with
what they perceived to be the loose and indefinite mandate and basis of
much of the American movement and its failure to uphold the principles of
"true Christianity," students were an important force in the creation of a
distinctly Canadian national YWCA in 1893, representing both city and student branches and committed to evangelical control.

   Unlike college associations in Britain, where male and female students
united in an autonomous organization, the Canadian college associations
followed a North American pattern that saw the Christian student movement
develop along gender-segregated lines under the auspices of the YWCA and
YMCA. This annexation of the fledgling student movement by the larger
adult-sponsored organizations, as in the creation of Epworth Leagues, Christian Endeavours, and Young People's church groups, reflected the hopes of
religious leaders that the freshness and vitality of youth could be harnessed
in the interests of world evangelization and the preservation of Christian
ideals.[13] Leaders of the city YWCA movement, well established by the end
of the 1870s, increasingly turned to the recent college graduate as the ideal
candidate for volunteer service on the board of directors of a city YWCA or
for employment as a "general secretary," a salaried professional worker
who instituted and administered the numerous programs for working women.
Women students, however, had their own reasons for being interested in
the YWCA. College YWCAs were preceded in both Canada and the United
States by the YMCAs, which had, by the late 1880s, according to the president
of a leading American college, "well nigh the monopoly of the religious
culture of students in our universities and colleges."[14] The increasing numbers of women students frequently turned to the YMCA as their only opportunity for religious fellowship, often playing an active role on the executive.
Objections were soon raised to the presence of women on the grounds that
such a broadening of the YMCA's mandate threatened to make it into another
denomination, competing directly with the churches. At the same time, many
women students were dissatisfied with their place in an organization that
was dominated by men and that provided no means of contact between coeds
and students in women's colleges, leaving them receptive to the overtures
of the city YWCA movement.[15] From the point of view of women students
seeking Christian fellowship, the YWCA, with its established reputation as
a Christian organization specializing in the needs of young women, offered

the advantages of an interdenominationalism that promised to unite rather than fragment all the Protestant students on campus, and membership in an international sisterhood of Christian women.

The interest taken by the YWCA in the welfare of the college student reflected the conviction of its leadership that even within the sheltered confines of Canada's institutions of higher learning, a "girl problem" existed, if in a form very different from that of the workplace, the unsupervised boarding house, and the streets. The YWCA was fundamentally sympathetic to the educated woman, symbol of "the aspirations of generations of her sex." Predictions of societal breakdown and the "unsexing" of women were confidently dismissed with the observation that "college education has *not* eliminated or even marred the modesty, the grace, the tenderness of her nature, and because she is a scholar, she is not less a woman."[16] Yet the female student was believed to require "a safeguard against those dangers which her increased sphere has brought," for college life, YWCA literature explained, was not without its hazards and could come as a great shock to a young woman who had lived a sheltered, protected life. Students experienced an unprecedented degree of religious freedom at college, where there was "no stern parent to march them out to Church, rain or shine, no small sisters or brothers to whom they must act as shining examples, no home minister looking to them to take their part in Church work as the worthy daughters of their parents."[17] During this turbulent period in the history of Christianity, many students underwent a crisis of faith as they attempted to reconcile the religious teachings of their childhood with evolutionary theory and the new humanist and materialist currents labelled "modern thought." Christian students like Ivy Gardiner of Royal Victoria College, McGill, advised new arrivals to join the YWCA and to "take warning from Darwin, who regretted towards the end of his life, that he had become so absorbed in his studies as to neglect his God."[18] Convinced that nine-tenths of those who left college unconverted were never won for Christ, the YWCA attempted to provide "a strong, active, spiritual force in each college" that would aid in the production of "graduates who have grasped and inculcated the principles of true Christian womanhood ... who have learned to know God, and who have their faith firmly based on Jesus Christ."[19]

In explaining the need for Christian work among students, YWCA supporters frequently observed that, contrary to popular belief, it was not only young men who faced temptations at college. According to Professor Scrimger of McGill University, who addressed YWCA convention delegates in 1907, young women had "their own trials and their own difficulties," chief among which was the fact that they had "hardly found themselves" and therefore had "difficulty in knowing to what use they should put their knowledge."[20] YWCA leaders were deeply concerned by what they perceived as a tendency towards "intellectual and social selfishness" prevalent in college life and evident in the failure of students to appreciate "that education, for education's sake alone, is not sufficient, but education for the development of character and the increase of power to use in the service of Christ is the right conception." YWCA writings tried to reconcile traditional conceptions of middle-class womanhood with a notion of Christian character that was "not negative and passive, but positive and active, as the earthly life of Jesus Christ was."[21] One paean to the womanly quality of sympathy, for example, endorsed two powerful models of evangelical womanhood and of an active and public life to which students might legitimately aspire in undertaking the service of Christ. "Do you think anything else could have led Florence Nightingale to undertake the work she did? Was it not sympathy for the suffering and ignorant which prompted Frances Willard to devote her life to temperance reform?"[22] Invested in the YWCA's student work were great hopes that the new generations of college women could be induced to place their unique combination of professional training, high moral standards, and womanly sympathy at the disposal of the causes of Christian social reform, the women's movement, and the YWCA.

The first Canadian student YWCA was organized in 1886 at Albert College, Belleville, Ontario, some fourteen years after the founding of the first student YWCA at Illinois State Normal University. Rooted in a traditional conception of "youth" as a loosely defined, status-related category straddling childhood and adulthood, YWCA student work embraced young women ranging in age from their teen years to their early twenties and attending a variety of institutions. Not until 1916, when the YWCA had embraced the concept of "adolescence," was responsibility for high-school girls turned over to a newly created Girls' Work Department.[23] By the end of the nineteenth century approximately two dozen student YWCAs had been organized at universities, agricultural colleges, nursing schools, normal schools, and ladies' colleges between Brandon and Cape Breton.[24] Many of these early branches resembled prayer circles, meeting for devotions and coaching members in the techniques of "personal work" among fellow students. With the 1901 reorganization of the Dominion Executive into a Dominion Council of YWCAs of Canada, based in Toronto, came the creation of a Student Department headed by a committee of alumnae and faculty wives and employing a national student secretary who regularly toured Canadian colleges to promote the Christian student movement. From 1900 until about 1912, when the task of organizing new branches was largely completed, women students welcomed the assistance of the Dominion Council's Student Department, which provided them with printed constitutions, pamphlets outlining the duties of officers and committees, and advice on methods of recruiting and fund-raising.[25] In 1903 Susie Little reported that she had visited thirty colleges in a single three-month tour, delivering addresses on "The Place and Purpose of the College Association," "The Value of Bible

Study in the Student's Life," "The Prayer Life of Christ," "The Canadian Colleges' Mission," "Personal Work," and "Consecration." By 1915, the Student Department reported, branches had been organized "in every University enrolling women, in most of the Residential and Household Science Colleges, and in many of the Teacher-training institutions throughout Canada."[26]

Within the college the YWCA was a significant presence. Although active membership was limited to full members of evangelical churches, a non-voting and non-office-holding category of associate membership permitted participation by Protestant non-church members and, in theory, by non-Protestants, although the latter could hardly have found the atmosphere congenial. Nor was it congenial to certain conservative evangelical students, who criticized the "flabby" undenominationalism of the YWCA that, in their view, encouraged competition with the churches and disloyalty to the doctrinal teachings of the various denominations.[27] Their two-tiered membership and commitment to interdenominational co-operation, however, allowed YWCAs to view themselves as models of religious toleration and as potential vehicles for uniting the entire population of female students. While in smaller colleges, particularly in the nineteenth century, as the *Dalhousie Gazette* reported in 1896, the membership often comprised "nearly all the lady students," doubts were sometimes expressed about the meaning of the statistics gathered by the Student Department. As one secretary remarked, membership could "indicate anything from the most definite Christian attitude to one of such indifference that it merely means paying an annual fee because the unwilling member cannot very well escape the importunities of the Treasurer."[28] None the less, the figures are suggestive. Shortly after its formation in 1901 the Student Department reported that the twenty-two affiliated colleges had about 1,325 women students, of whom more than 67 per cent were YWCA members (44 per cent active and 23 per cent associate). By 1914 it was reported that the 2,389 YWCA members constituted 61 per cent of registered students in universities, 64 per cent in residential colleges, and 54 per cent in all colleges, universities and normals combined (the latter institutions having a much lower average because of a rapid student turnover). The national student membership peaked in 1916–17 with 2,794 members in 49 regularly organized branches. As Barbara Miller Solomon has noted with respect to the American case, the success of the YWCA in evangelical colleges is hardly surprising, but it is significant that it flourished in public and private secular institutions as well.[29]

The YWCA's presence in Canadian colleges was welcomed by the faculty, whose attitude was reported as "almost universally friendly and sympathetic." Ruth Rouse, touring Canadian universities in 1912 on behalf of the World's Student Christian Federation, observed that "in no country have I had so much sympathy and help from the Faculty in every college, almost without exception. Even in the universities supported by the Government there is a strong Christian atmosphere."[30] While in universities the role of faculty was generally limited to leading an occasional Bible class, the presence of a supportive faculty member was often critical to maintaining continuity in the normal schools and agricultural colleges, where student turnover was much more rapid. It is probable, too, that in the branches organized for younger students in ladies' colleges, teachers played a more direct supervisory role. Ella Gardiner, Lady Principal of Albert College, explained in 1902 how, from her perspective, the YWCA helped "to create the ideal college":

The Faculty value the Y.W.C.A. in that it fosters among the students a true Christian spirit. Girls learn the sacredness of living, learn that an opportunity is an obligation, learn to value their time, realizing that hours of leisure are not well employed when spent in school-girl gossip or mere worldly pleasure. United in purpose, and that purpose to win their fellow-students for Christ, they do not form cliques, which are the bane of college life ... Many objectionable things can be corrected or prevented by Christian girls quietly influencing and restraining thoughtless companions. Thus the Y.W.C.A. becomes an important auxiliary to the Faculty in preserving good discipline and fostering the best interests of the school.[31]

Undoubtedly endearing the YWCA to Gardiner and other administrators was the helpful list of "College 'Do's and Dont's'" provided by the Albert College YWCA in 1903, which exhorted: "Do be loyal to your parents," "Do your Bible study," "Do be womanly," "Do be punctual at Y.W.C.A.," "Don't be irreverent," "Don't be selfish," and "Don't forget – Teachers First."[32] For faculty and teachers, YWCA secretaries and Christian student leaders, the college atmosphere of "intimacy and tender associations" provided "an unparalleled opportunity to the would-be soul-winner." Special committees composed of the most "tactful, sympathetic, enthusiastic, sociable, sincere, persevering, deeply spiritual and prayerful" students were appointed to attend to the welfare of their unconverted sisters.[33]

Reports of college life suggest that the YWCA was not necessarily associated with only the most religious students. In a welcome to the 1903 "freshettes," the editors of the ladies' column in the *Queen's Journal* advised the new arrivals to join the Levana Society, go to church, go skating each season – "but don't slope lectures for the rink – unless you have a headache" – and "attend the Y.W. every Friday afternoon, for all the best girls go to Y.W."[34] Asking "why should the secular societies work harder to win the interest of the new students than that which stands for Jesus Christ?" student YWCAs launched an annual fall recruiting drive even before classes began, when there was a "keen susceptibility to influences." Welcoming committees sent letters of greeting to prospective students, met new arrivals at the train station, helped them find suitable accommodation, placed flowers in their rooms in residence, introduced them to teachers, took them to church, and tried in every way to "be a true friend to them, and in every way make them feel the absence of loneliness."[35] At the annual fall reception sponsored by the YWCA, the Queen's branch reported in 1891, "all the lady students of both Colleges were in attendance, and the sceptical ones who feared the lack of the male element would be seriously felt soon discovered their error, and frankly acknowledged that girls were nicer than boys to talk to anyway."[36] Most YWCAs also sponsored occasional social functions with their male counterparts. The women students at Acadia reported, somewhat ruefully, that the annual joint social "always takes the form of a topic reception, for being a Baptist institution, nothing gayer is permitted." By contrast, Saturday night parties co-sponsored by the YWCA and YMCA at McGill, where students skated "till ten to the tune of a hurdy-gurdy, when all retire again to Strathcona Hall for a good cup of hot coffee, etc.," were reported as "one of the most pleasant memories of the McGill student."[37]

Students frequently testified that the YWCA was "by no means an unimportant factor in the college life of the majority of the ... girls." Like other societies, the YWCA claimed to demand "the best minds, the finest characters, and most cultured students the college possesses" and urged students to join in the interests of strengthening the college "esprit de corps."[38] Unlike most other student societies, however, the YWCA promoted Christianity, as revealed in the teachings of Jesus, as a firm foundation for female friendship and association. In the YWCA, one student wrote, "intellectual superiority is laid aside" and "all are one in Jesus Christ."[39] In identifying religious life with social life in the college, the YWCA hoped to acquaint students with "the blessed union that comes from a common striving after higher, holier things," to draw them "into closer sympathy as sisters in Christ," and to establish "a Christian sisterhood, more dear and permanent than any other tie."[40] Queen's medical students expressed their regret at being so busy with lectures that they were unable to attend meetings. "We cannot help feeling the loss, as our Y.W.C.A. is the chief bond of union between the girls."[41] The annual YWCA summer conference, held in idyllic natural surroundings that were thought to encourage a spirit of religious introspection, was also promoted as "a time of new friendships and new inspirations."[42] Conference organizers fostered the rituals of female friendship, including picnics and athletic competitions, Maypole dances and concerts by "kitchen orchestras," ice cream provided by the National Council of Women, and costumed skits on the subjects of female suffrage and women's education. Queen's students reported in 1910 that "it was certainly surprising how many discovered a talent for singing and giving yells at that conference." The enthusiasm of the participants for the "jolly good times" at Muskoka prompted one national secretary to warn prospective delegates that the conference should not be regarded as "a continuous house party with a few religious meetings sprinkled in."[43]

All student YWCAS held weekly devotional meetings, with scripture readings and hymn singing, as well as discussion of a prescribed topic. A typical topic card distributed at the University of New Brunswick in 1907 listed upcoming talks on "The Call to Service," "Glorifying God in Our Recreations," "What Seekest Thou as a College Girl?" "What is Worth While?" "The Sense of Responsibility," "Prayer as a Means of Accomplishment," "The Power of Personal Influence," and "The Pure Life." A Queen's student testified that the "excellent papers" read at the Friday afternoon meetings of the YWCA were "very helpful in our striving after the best life."[44] Student participation in the weekly meetings was considered highly desirable. The University College YWCA noted in 1903 that while the devotional meetings had frequently been addressed by ministers, missionaries, and professors, the majority were reserved for the students so that they might "serve as a training school for the girls." Student YWCAS stressed the importance of "system," "method," and "business habits" for future society women, philanthropists, and professionals, and provided a supportive female environment for the acquisition of experience in public speaking, fund-raising, and conducting business meetings. Service on a YWCA committee was highly recommended by Adelaide Plumptre, a prominent member of the Board of Managers of the Montreal YWCA, who wrote an open letter to students advising them to take up some "official work" during their college years: "The business of the world must be organized by the few, acting for the many: or in other words, all societies must be 'run' by committees; and the sooner you are trained for this part of the world's work the better."[45]

Many young middle-class women, particularly during the nineteenth century, sought higher education to satisfy a craving for meaningful employment, rejecting domesticity and the social round and sharing the longing of Elizabeth Smith, one of the first Canadian women to graduate as a medical doctor, to become "a woman with a purpose."[46] During her years at college, the woman student was pursued by the question "After College, What?" as she sought ways to reconcile her career ambitions with "the family claim" that was generally expected, in the case of daughters, to take precedence over personal inclinations. Addressing the Queen's YWCA in 1903, Principal Gordon warned students that too often, following graduation, there was "a narrowness and restraint felt with the home life."[47] Yet judging from surviving literature and the titles of topics discussed at the weekly meetings, it appears that, for the most part, YWCAS equated service with paid work and devoted little attention to the theme of college life as preparation for "educated motherhood." One of the principal objectives of the weekly meetings was to provide students with advice and information about choosing and preparing for a life-work that would channel their talents and ambitions into Christian social service. "The truest college woman," YWCA literature exhorted, "does not crave a career in which she shall merely enjoy herself, or earn wealth, or gain a reputation. She hopes to be of the greatest real usefulness to the community, and so to the world."[48] In 1916 Winifred Harvey, national student secretary, reflected on the widening range of career choices available to college women, comparing them with opportunities in the nineteenth century, when "even those with little aptitude and less liking for teaching were induced to take up educational work." Given the changed circumstances, she advised students to avoid "safe work," to consider their talents, and to "choose fearlessly" from secretarial work, library work, social service, business, household science, commercial art, journalism, and the professions of dentistry, medicine, and law. Endorsing expanded options for aspiring professional women and participating in the creation of a distinctive female work ethic, the college YWCAs glorified self-control and discipline and identified the quintessentially feminine virtue of altruism, rather than profit or hedonism, as the principal motivating factor underlying women's quest for work.[49]

To strengthen the faith of Christian women students and thereby influence their preparations for life after college, YWCAs encouraged their members to enrol in a course in Bible study that would promote "the development of Christian character, and training for service in the Association, in the church, or wherever the need is found." The Bible-study movement, launched in the late 1880s, advocated group discussions in preference to the existing system of lectures by professors, who had rarely been successful in influencing students to undertake independent study outside the class hour. Authorized courses requiring "systematic, devotional Bible study" were especially recommended because they provided "an intellectual discipline, a training and developing of the mental powers."[50] YWCA students were particularly influenced by Henry Burton Sharman's *Studies in the Life of Christ*, published in 1896, which inspired several generations of Canadian students to undertake a personal quest for "the historical Jesus" by approaching the synoptic gospels with an open and critical mind and putting aside preconceptions derived from traditional church teachings. Visiting national student secretaries did much to facilitate the organization of group Bible-study classes employing the new historical methods of biblical criticism.

According to Ramsay Cook's recent influential study of social criticism in late Victorian English Canada, many liberal Protestants attempted to resolve the crisis provoked by biblical criticism and Darwinian science by emphasizing the social and practical aspects of Christianity. Students with liberal theological leanings were particularly drawn to the Sharman method of group Bible study because of its emphasis on frank discussion, critical thought, and active participation by students; for some, the effect on their intellectual and spiritual development was profound and lasting. For women, however, it is likely that the study of the life of Christ, who embodied the principles of love, altruism, sacrifice, and service, had a particular significance. The "historical Jesus," as Cook has noted, was a symbol that could be interpreted in different ways and adapted to suit varying requirements.[51] In seeking to become more "Christ-like" in their own lives, YWCA students adopted an unimpeachable role model who helped to legitimate their pursuit of learning and career ambitions in their own eyes and in the eyes of others.

A career in foreign missions, or the evangelization of "our sisters in far-off lands," exemplified the ideal career model for budding professionals in the YWCA, who were told that there was "no service at home or abroad in which a Christian college woman [could] make her life count for more in extending the Kingdom of God."[52] "These are missionary days," declared Professor Scrimger of McGill to the YWCA convention in 1907: "And there never was a time when the doors were so wide open as now for the work of women in other lands – a kind of work that can be done by women only for the sake of their sisters. And it is to our institutions, and especially the members of the Young Women's Christian Association, we must look for those who are to go forth to carry the message of the Gospel to the dark and heathen places of the earth."[53]

The student YWCAs responded enthusiastically to American evangelist John Mott's call for "the evangelization of the world in this generation," participating in the founding of the Student Volunteer Movement for Foreign Missions in 1888.[54] Most branches engaged in fund-raising for the foreign field and devoted one of their weekly topic meetings each month to a missionary subject. Particularly popular were the frequent addresses by missionaries on furlough, providing "word pictures of India, South America, China and even Canada, of miseries that, to most of us college girls at least, were quite horrifying in their suggestive power." Authorities in the churches and colleges who supported the YWCA's provision of missionary education to students when they were highly impressionable and their souls "pliable, open to new claims and ideas, sympathetic towards new obligations," believed that such training was of value to all students, embracing as it did "historical, philosophical, ethnological, geographical and linguistic no less than directly religious elements."[55] For aspiring professionals, a career as a missionary opened up possibilities of independence, travel, and adventure that were otherwise inaccessible to young middle-class women, while still allowing them to appear, both to others and to themselves, appropriately respectable and self-sacrificing. The YWCA at the Ontario Medical College for Women emphasized mission study as of "especial interest to medical students" and reported in 1900 that five of the eight members of the graduating class were preparing to go as foreign missionaries.[56]

By 1910 the Dominion Council of YWCAS, attuned to the new national and international currents of thought that were combining to form the "social gospel," was seriously addressing the question of the role to be played by the YWCA in "the social and industrial awakening" and was encouraging a revaluation of the city YWCAS' traditional moralistic and individualistic stance on issues affecting working women.[57] Until this time the student YWCAS had remained largely indifferent to social conditions, but a dramatic upsurge of interest in the immigration question became evident as, with encouragement from the national leadership, mission-study classes broadened their mandate to include "social study" or "the fearless and uncompromising study of social conditions as they exist in our Dominion." One contributing factor appears to have been the 1912 tour of Canadian colleges by Ruth Rouse of the World's Student Christian Federation, who addressed YWCAS across the country on their obligation to help to assimilate the immigrants and defend "Canada's Goodly Heritage" of Christianity and democracy.[58] More influential, however, was the presence at annual summer conferences of James Shaver Woodsworth, Methodist minister and founder of the All People's Mission in Winnipeg. At the 1915 conference Woodsworth addressed women students on "The Coming of the Kingdom," urging them to provide leadership in resolving the great social questions of the day: "for the first time in our history we are beginning to apply the teachings of Christ to the corporate standards of politics and internationalism and business." Each summer from approximately 1909 to 1916 he led intensive discussions of the immigration question, and his books, *Strangers within Our Gates*, and *My Neighbour*, were rapidly adopted as standard texts for YWCA social study classes.[59] The Dominion Council heartily endorsed and encouraged student interest in this revised understanding of the coming of the kingdom, which required, in addition to the task of world evangelization, a commitment to working for a new Christian social order. Addressing the 1913 convention of Canadian YWCAS meeting in Winnipeg, one speaker "likened Ruskin's awakening of the students at Oxford University to a social consciousness, to the opportunities of the Young Women's Christian Association in the student body to-day."[60]

While some students responded enthusiastically to the appeal of the social gospel, the results of their efforts were somewhat disappointing from the perspective of the Dominion Council and varied from one college to another, perhaps according to denominational affiliation and the views of certain influential professors. Queen's delegates, who reportedly "grew several inches" during the 1910 summer conference, announced that "as a result of the enthusiasm brought back from Muskoka" three classes were being organized on "Japan and its Degeneration," "The Stranger within Our Gates," and "South America."[61] In the most ambitious follow-up to the summer conference, delegates who attended Woodsworth's class on "My

Neighbour" at Muskoka in 1914 established an informal commission of
graduates and undergraduates from across the country to arouse interest in
the questions of emigration, immigration, and social welfare through study
groups and lectures. Members hoped to work with the Canadian Welfare
League and to become the nucleus of "a growing, progressive club."[62]
Some student YWCAs encouraged their members to attend lecture courses
on the principles of social service and to volunteer at local settlement houses.
Victoria College, Toronto, reported in 1912 that "our Association has procured girls to teach sewing in the Evangelia Settlement, gymnasium work
and cooking in the Central Neighbourhood Settlement, and teachers for
Jewish girls in the newly organized women's department of the University
Settlement."[63] Yet enrolment in YWCA social-study classes remained low
in comparison with Bible and mission study, and the liberal theological
views of many students did not necessarily lead them to involvement in
practical efforts at social reform or to the adoption of a "sociological"
perspective on social questions. In fact, many activities undertaken by students in the spirit of social service seemed reminiscent of more traditior.al
Christian charity. The University of Saskatchewan YWCA, for example,
reported in 1915 that "visits were made to the Children's Shelter and the
General Hospital, baskets of provisions were distributed among needy families in Saskatoon, and help was rendered the Home Makers Clubs by
collecting clothing for the poor in country districts." One frustrated national
secretary observed that many students appeared to exhibit a "superficial"
interest in social problems and "a readiness to do philanthropic and palliative
work rather than make a study of courses and constructive work."[64]

By 1914, with the task of organizing new branches largely completed,
national secretaries were reporting "a growing group-consciousness and a
consequent development of student initiative in the Canadian Student Young
Women's Christian Association."[65] This initiative was encouraged by the
secretaries, who saw in it evidence of a growing maturity and sense of
responsibility among the students. Both the secretaries and the Student
Department believed that, as women students mobilized in a stronger and
more autonomous movement under their own leaders, they would align
themselves with the broader objectives of the YWCA, to the advantage of
both the Dominion Council and the city branches. Hopes were expressed
that students would learn, with one 1916 conference delegate, to see the
college YWCA as not merely "a detached organization of purely local origin
and interest" but rather "as part of a magnificent plan for the advancement
of the Kingdom of God among the womanhood of the nations."[66] In 1912
students were granted three elected representatives with full privileges on
the Dominion Council's Student Committee. In 1914 the Dominion Council
responded to "a frequently expressed desire on the part of the students" by
approving a restatement of the purpose of the student movement to encourage

discussion of "the importance and urgency of world-wide evangelization and the Christian solution of social problems and the permeation of public life with Christian ideals."[67] Much encouragement was derived by the national leadership from the activities of the Elgin House Student Committee, formed at the 1914 summer conference to serve as "the voice of the student movement," which regularly recommended to student YWCA executives that both prayer and Bible study be promoted among women students, that every college woman acquire a knowledge of the social conditions in her community, that the principles of Christianity be applied to the social situation at home and to international relationships, and, most encouragingly, "that an effort be made to point out to students the significance of the Woman's Movement in its broader aspects, as an essential part of the establishment of the Kingdom of God."[68]

With the outbreak of the First World War, the Dominion Council confidently expected that the wartime circumstances would cause the majority of women students to rally more strongly than ever before to the support of the Christian ideals of service and self-sacrifice. The YWCA, with the Protestant churches, supported the national war effort as a divine cause and a crusade for Christianity, linking the conflict with Germany to the struggle to establish Christ's kingdom on earth.[69] Yet the Dominion Council strove simultaneously to ensure that women were full participants in that struggle and to prepare the coming generation of Canadian womanhood for their new political responsibilities, new occupational choices, and their obligations to assume the duties of the men killed in battle and to maintain the moral and religious standards of the nation. Every effort was taken to ensure the contribution of the newly enfranchised university woman to the "national awakening" that would inevitably accompany the coming of peace. A McGill student who attended the 1919 Central Student Conference on the theme "A Living Faith for an Age of Rebuilding" reported that "from great fields of service there were brought living, stirring messages that made one's heart leap to hear, and one's desire eager to enter into work that would render less dreadful the sufferings of the ignorant and the oppressed." The Student Department communicated to each member of the 1918 graduating classes of Canadian universities the results of a survey of openings in social service and church work to encourage students "to take a responsible part in the task of social and spiritual reconstruction made evident by the war."[70]

YWCA national secretaries urged women students to support the war effort by thinking of the soldiers, learning to work together, cultivating discipline, making sacrifices, and undertaking their national service "in the spirit of Christ."[71] In the early phase of the conflict students were pointedly reminded that "some of the hours frittered away in idle gossip" could be spent knitting and making Red Cross supplies, that "feeds" much less expensive than those held in the dormitories would be appreciated by the families of the unemployed, and that less elaborate college functions and reduced personal expenditures on "eats," matinees, and extravagances in dress could help to raise funds to support patriotic and relief agencies and the Red Cross.[72] Beginning in 1917 the Dominion Council of YWCAS was actively involved in efforts to recruit, house, and supervise women land workers, or "farmerettes," in Ontario and British Columbia during the summer months. Students were particularly urged to take advantage of this opportunity to experience "something of the daily experience of the millions of wage-earning women" and thereby acquire knowledge that would supplement the lessons of YWCA social-study classes: "Those old economic problems that will come again in the winter's study will now be alive with pictorial interest; social service will be no mere dream of a future life-hobby for it will be really and vitally here now, as the new sense of kinship, with all who labour, makes itself manifest. Some day we hope to welcome as Association workers the graduating students who first began to think of industrial problems on the farms in 1917."[73]

Yet, despite hopes that the war, in combination with "the growing consciousness of the Woman's Movement and the Labor Movement," would all combine to give student leaders a "vision of the things that lie beyond the immediate sky line of the college," national secretaries remained convinced that only a limited number of students were "doing really honest thinking."[74] There were frequent complaints that students were donating their time and money to the Red Cross not by making additional sacrifices, as the YWCA had urged, but by neglecting the cause of foreign missions, which seemed to fall rapidly out of favour with students during the war years. Despite the YWCA's efforts, the majority of Canadian college women appeared to remain indifferent to the Bible, and the religious life of too many colleges to show "a tendency to be tinged with the artificial spirit of the secular element."[75]

YWCA national secretaries did acknowledge that a minority of students had in fact been profoundly affected by the war and had been stimulated to undertake a critical re-examination of the values with which they had been raised. Such critical inquiry, however, frequently led these thinking students in directions that the YWCA had not anticipated. The effect of the war, for many students, was not to deepen their attachment to religious values but rather to leave them "finding it extremely difficult to hold the Christian faith with conviction."[76] For some the result was a deep disillusionment with the churches that had so ardently supported the conflict. Those who a few years earlier might have supported the cause of foreign missions now questioned the wisdom of exporting a religion that had been used to justify such slaughter and destruction among "Christian" nations. Students who responded to the appeal of the social gospel sometimes adopted causes that were unpopular with conservative middle-class congregations and turned away from the churches altogether, as one UBC student reported in 1917: "Organized labour, which is very strong here, is unfortunately alienated from organized religion, and all the young social dreamers in our college, looking towards democracy, are apt to be disgusted by the self-righteousness and blindness to social conditions which they find in some church-going people."[77] At the same time, liberal evangelical and moderate liberal students, influenced by Henry Burton Sharman, whose Bible-study classes had become a regular feature at Muskoka by 1919, had embraced a "scientific" quest for "the Truth" that led many to reject the theological conservatism of the denominational churches. They adopted the position that religion was a deeply personal matter not requiring corporate expression through church membership.[78] This increasing hostility towards organized religion, which one recent study has identified as particularly prevalent among women students,[79] marked the beginning of a serious rift between the Christian student movement and the YWCA, as for the first time students openly and publicly discussed and criticized the larger objectives of the YWCA and its place in college life.

Most of this criticism centred on the restriction of voting and office-holding rights to full members of evangelical churches. Those liberal students who had rejected church membership and were therefore denied the privileges of active membership in the YWCA bitterly resented the implication that they had no right to call themselves good Christians. One sympathetic president, in praising the generosity of a student who volunteered her help despite being denied a vote, noted that "any suffragette" would fail to be appeased by mere gratitude.[80] Student YWCAS were accused of being undemocratic and autocratic unions having "an established point of view and plan of execution which is *ipso facto* the right one and beyond criticism or discussion."[81] In response to student demands, therefore, the Dominion Council gave its sanction in 1916 to an optional "personal" basis of membership that would allow college associations to substitute for the evangelical test a requirement that members sign a pledge of their loyalty to Jesus Christ and support for the goals of the YWCA. This compromise, however, did not put an end to criticism of the YWCA. In 1917 cabinets of college YWCAS across the country reported that "the time has passed when the women students are willing to take even the underlying principles of the Association for granted, and they are no longer willing to accept their religion stated in stock phrases." Pleas for toleration and for "the 'modern mind' to appreciate the position of those to whom all Christian belief is a matter of simple unquestioning faith" indicate a heightening of tensions between students with liberal views on theological questions and those with more conservative views.[82] YWCAS had to defend themselves against charges that they were refuges for the "intellectually slovenly" and attempted to convince liberal critics that they "presented a challenge to the keenest study of which they were capable, a challenge to consider not only their individual lives but beyond that the whole organization of present society in the light of Christianity." Despite the more liberal membership regulations, many students who were "in revolt against orthodox religion" continued to refuse to sign the YWCA pledge card.[83]

Criticisms levelled at the YWCA by the larger population of women students also indicate a substantial degree of alienation caused by the behaviour and attitudes of YWCA members, one of whom observed that "a sort of protective legend has grown up around us, which says, in brief, that Christian Associations are synonymous with 'piousness,' with one-sidedness, with a holier-than-thou attitude."[84] In 1915 Alma Conway, recent president of an unidentified, newly organized college YWCA, undertook a survey "to discover just why so many girls either objected to the new society or were indifferent to its claims." Her frank, highly critical, and extremely revealing report, published in *The Young Women of Canada*, claimed to provide a range of representative responses from students hostile to the YWCA. She noted that some students, who subscribed to the view that religion was not an everyday topic of conversation, resented the tendency of YWCA members to intrude upon the privacy of their religious beliefs. The danger, in Conway's opinion, was that "some girls of another type become such Y.W.C.A. enthusiasts and such inveterate fishers for souls that they defeat their own end, and disgust the reserved ladies by their vehemence and their air of belonging to the elect." One irate victim complained that "the Y.W.C.A. is a body of fanatics, interfering with other people and making of itself a centre of emotional, sanctimonious religiousness. The people who are really good pray by themselves, 'do good by stealth' and don't preach." Conway urged YWCA students to respect the privacy of their companions, to avoid "cant," lack of dignity, and "emotional gush" in conducting their meetings, and especially to avoid overly zealous recruiting by membership committees. "Christ stands at the door and knocks; He never goes inside and nags." She also warned YWCA executives to try to render the administrative and financial aspects of the work invisible as much as possible. A preoccupation with fund-raising and organizing meetings and events sometimes resulted in the "real motive" of the YWCA being "lost sight of, swamped, killed off, and buried ten fathoms deep." This led some students to complain that the YWCA was "all organization" and that its members had no time for "real religion." "If I could see any true religion in your old Y.W.C.A., I'd join, for that's what I'm looking for, but you people just talk money, money, all the time." If YWCAs wished to retain the loyalty of women students, Conway advised, they would have to meet these objections with "honesty and humility" and provide answers that were "neither smug nor self-satisfied."[85]

As college women were beginning to question their allegiance to the YWCA, it was also the case that the Student Department no longer occupied a central place in the Dominion Council's national vision for the young women of Canada. As part of a major expansion of its operations during the war years, made possible by contributions from the National Council of YMCAS' enormously successful Red Triangle campaigns, the Dominion Council greatly increased its allocation of resources to the Student Department. By 1919 four national student secretaries, one solely responsible for the eight college associations in Toronto, were touring the country in an attempt to ensure that each branch was visited at least once or twice a year. A Western Field Committee was established in 1916 to facilitate organization of some of the new colleges springing up in the western provinces. In addition to the annual summer conference at Elgin House, Muskoka, three regional conferences were also launched at Whytecliffe, British Columbia, Lumsden Beach, Saskatchewan, and Deep Brook, Nova Scotia. Yet the fact remained that in the context of its larger efforts on behalf of the entire population of Canadian young women, the Dominion Council was paying less rather than more attention to college students. The larger share of its staff and resources was being devoted to assisting the rapidly expanding city YWCA movement with organizational and building campaigns and with addressing the needs of the burgeoning population of immigrants and industrial workers in Canadian cities. More significantly, however, the Dominion Council, responding to the new adolescent psychology and the growing interest of the Canadian churches in the teenage group, had transferred its hopes for the future from college students to the rapidly expanding, and apparently more malleable, population of high-school girls. With the unexpected failure of the 1919 Red Triangle campaign, the Dominion Council was confronted with severe budgetary constraints, and a decision was reluctantly taken to transfer the responsibility for financial support of the Student Department to the students themselves.

Although the subsequent withdrawal of the college students from the YWCA came as a shock to the Dominion Council, it seems hardly surprising in retrospect that the students should have decided to take full control of a movement that they had to finance themselves. Nor was it surprising that they should have elected to form a partnership with male students from the YMCAS and other Christian student organizations, to whom they had in fact been drawing closer for some time. Stimulated by wartime nationalism and by the problem of lack of Canadian representation on the World's Student Christian Federation, a Council of Canadian Student Movements was formed in 1914. By 1918 YWCAS and YMCAS in some colleges had established joint committees having jurisdiction in all matters affecting both bodies. Both women and men within the YWCAS and YMCAS were becoming convinced of their common interests as Christian students and argued increasingly that having separate organizations within the same institution was inefficient and failed to recognize "the principle of co-education."[86] In the *Canadian Student*, which began publication in 1918, students accused the churches of being hostile to liberal thought and reluctant to confront fundamental economic and social realities. Both women and men were critical of their parent organizations and expressed a desire for more autonomy and a more democratic structure. Male students were particularly hostile to the National Council of YMCAS, both because of widely publicized accusations that it had profited from its wartime services to the troops overseas and because it had refused to abolish the evangelical membership test in favour of the "personal" basis of membership.[87] While the Dominion Council of YWCAS had proven more responsive to liberal and social-gospel currents within Protestant Christianity than had its male counterpart, it was still the case that many city YWCAS, closely tied to the local churches and the business community, were viewed by women students as bastions of social and theological conservatism. Convinced that their "honest expression of opinion" was hampered by their connection with organizations that were forced to rely on the "good will and support of a conservative element – the community,"[88] both women and men hoped to realize their objectives within an autonomous, democratic, and co-operative movement. In January 1921, subsequent to a Canadian caucus in December 1919 at the Student Volunteer Convention at Des Moines, Iowa, a national student assembly was held in Guelph, where representatives from the student YWCAS and the Christian organizations of nearly every Canadian university approved the constitution of the new Student Christian Movement of Canada.[89]

From the founding of the first Canadian student branches, the YWCA had claimed that evangelical Christianity provided the surest basis upon which all women could unite, overcoming their differences by becoming "one in Christ." The ultimate withdrawal of the students from the YWCA exposed a critical weakness in this claim. For some women, at least for those who qualified as "true Christians," it was indeed the case that the YWCA performed an important supportive function. Providing opportunities for social life, intellectual development, the acquisition of organizational skills, vocational guidance, and membership in a Christian sisterhood, the YWCA must be considered an integral component of female student culture in turn-of-the-century Canadian colleges and universities. Yet even within this relatively homogeneous group of women who shared a commitment to advancing Christ's kingdom on earth, significant differences could and did occur. As conservative evangelical, liberal evangelical, moderate liberal and social-gospel interpretations of the teachings of Jesus co-existed, and clashed with a growing frequency, it became clear that "the coming of the kingdom," with all its implications for women, was a vision that could be interpreted in very different ways. The matter of women's special role in the evangelization of the world also became problematic as students, like so many other young women of the war and post-war generations, were drawn to the prospect of association with men and rejected the YWCA's commitment to an organized Christian sisterhood as old-fashioned. As modern young women and aspiring professionals, they were confident that their goals could best be realized in an equal partnership with men, dedicated to achieving the "brotherhood of man."

Yet the influence of the YWCA should not be dismissed. For more than three decades it was a significant presence in Canadian colleges, shaping the religious and social life of a substantial number of women students. Encouraging women to become physicians, missionaries, settlement workers, YWCA secretaries, and social workers, the YWCA promoted among women students an ideal of Christian service to which some, by their own testimony, were very responsive. It remains for future studies to consider the impact of exposure to that ideal in their formative college years on the career choices and later lives of individual women students. Further examination may yet reveal that the evangelical commitment to usefulness, service, and self-sacrifice helped to shape the work experience of the first generations of college women and the character of the emerging female professions.

NOTES

* The writing of this paper was supported by a post-doctoral fellowship from the Social Sciences and Humanities Research Council of Canada. An earlier version was presented to the Canadian Historical Association in Windsor, Ont., June 1988. I am grateful to Patricia Dirks, Chad Gaffield, Deborah Gorham, Don Kirkey, Blair Neatby, and Neil Semple for their helpful comments and suggestions.

1 *Queen's Journal*, 1 Mar. 1909, 341. Editors of the "Ladies' Column" of the *Queen's Journal* commented in 1902 on behalf of Queen's women that "we belong to the general student body ... but we also feel that we have a little sphere all our own." Quoted in Lynne Marks and Chad Gaffield, "Women at Queen's University, 1895–1905: A 'Little Sphere' All Their Own?" *Ontario History* 78, no. 4 (1986): 332. See also Barbara Miller Solomon, *In the Company of Educated Women: A History of Women and Higher Education in America* (New Haven and London: Yale University Press 1985): 94–114.

2 National Archives of Canada, YWCA of Canada Records, MG 28 I 198, v 46, Miss Lena M. Forfar, Queen's College, Kingston, "One in Christ," *Dominion Tie*, Apr. 1902, 22; Miss Ivy Gardiner, Royal Victoria College, "Benefits Reaped from the Y.W.C.A.," *Dominion Tie*, October 1902, 75. From 1900 to 1920 the Dominion Council of YWCAs of Canada published a monthly magazine successively titled the *Young Woman's Gazette*, the *Dominion Tie*, the *Young Women of Canada*, and the *Association Outlook*. All references to this publication throughout this paper are to v 46 of the YWCA of Canada Records.

3 See in particular Marks and Gaffield, "Women at Queen's University, 1895–
  1905," 331–49; Margaret Gillet, *We Walked Very Warily: A History of Women at
  McGill* (Montreal: Eden Press 1981); John G. Reid, "The Education of Women at
  Mount Allison, 1854–1914," *Acadiensis* 12, no. 2 (Spring 1983): 3–33; Lee
  Stewart, "Women on Campus in British Columbia: Strategies for Survival, Years
  of War and Peace, 1906–1920," in Barbara K. Latham and Roberta J. Pazdro,
  eds., *Not Just Pin Money: Selected Essays on the History of Women's Work in
  British Columbia* (Victoria: Camosun College 1984), 184–93; Anne Rochon
  Ford, *A Path Not Strewn with Roses: One Hundred Years of Women at the Uni-
  versity of Toronto, 1884–1984* (Toronto: University of Toronto Press for the
  Women's Centenary Committee 1985); Paul Axelrod, "Moulding the Middle
  Class: Student Life at Dalhousie University in the 1930s," *Acadiensis* 15, no. 1
  (Autumn 1985): 84–122. See also essays by Judith Fingard and Nancy Kiefer and
  Ruth Roach Pierson in this volume.
4 Diana Pedersen, "The Young Women's Christian Association in Canada, 1870–
  1920: 'A Movement to Meet a Spiritual, Civic and National Need'" (PhD thesis,
  Carleton University 1987), chap. 3. See also Diana Pedersen, "'Keeping Our
  Good Girls Good': The YWCA and the 'Girl Problem,' 1870–1930," *Canadian
  Woman Studies / Les Cahiers de la femme* 7, no. 4 (Winter 1986): 20–4;
  "'Building Today for the Womanhood of Tomorrow': Businessmen, Boosters and
  the YWCA, 1890–1930," *Urban History Review* 15, no. 3 (Feb. 1987): 225–42;
  and "The Photographic Record of the Canadian YWCA, 1890–1930: A Visual
  Source for Women's History," *Archivaria* 24 (Summer 1987): 10–35.
5 For an introduction to evangelical Protestantism in nineteenth-century Canada, see
  Goldwin French, "The Evangelical Creed in Canada," in W.L. Morton, ed., *The
  Shield of Achilles: Aspects of Canada in the Victorian Age* (Toronto and Montreal: McClelland and Stewart 1968), 15–35. For a discussion of its special sig-
  nificance to middle-class women, see Pedersen, "The Young Women's Christian
  Association," chap. 1.
6 "The Student Department," *Young Women of Canada*, Mar. 1907, 12.
7 Ramsay Cook alludes to this belief in his discussion of the thought of Agnes
  Maule Machar in *The Regenerators: Social Criticism in Late Victorian English
  Canada* (Toronto: University of Toronto Press 1985), 190. Miss Evelyn Overholt,
  "The College Woman," *Dominion Tie*, May 1904, 77. See also Annie B. Rankin,
  University College, "The College Girl: Her Friendships – Her Life Ambitions,"
  Dominion Tie, Feb. 1904, 29; C.C. Benson, "The College Woman's Character,"
  Young Women of Canada, Mar. 1914, 96–7.
8 National Archives of Canada, Montreal YWCA Records, MG 28 I 240, V 25, Mis-
  cellaneous, "Young Women's Christian Association Work in Canada," Dominion
  Council pamphlet, ca 1902.
9 Una M. Saunders, *The Work of the Young Women's Christian Association in
  Canada* (Toronto 1918), 13.
10 In the YWCA records, neither conference speakers, writers of articles, leaders, secretaries, nor members are ever identified, as individuals or in the aggregate, by

denominational affiliation. Nor are university records especially helpful, for the religious observances of many students while at college consisted of attendance at YWCA meetings and the compulsory "chapel." Thus, tracing the denominational affiliations of YWCA members is nearly impossible. I am grateful to Don Kirkey for his insights into this dilemma, which frustrates the historian but attests to the strength of the interdenominational commitment within the YWCA.

11 Pedersen, "The Young Women's Christian Association," chap. 2. For detailed histories of the North American student YWCAs, see Elizabeth Wilson, *Fifty Years of Association Work among Young Women, 1866–1916: A History of the Young Women's Christian Associations in the United States of America* (New York: National Board of the Young Women's Christian Associations of the United States of America 1916), chaps. 10 and 11; and Clarence P. Shedd, *Two Centuries of Student Christian Movements: Their Origin and Intercollegiate Life* (New York: Association Press 1934), chap. 12.

12 The YWCA employed the following definition of an evangelical church: "We hold those churches to be evangelical which, maintaining the Holy Scriptures to be the only infallible rule of faith and practice, do believe in the Lord Jesus Christ, the only begotten Son of the Father, King of Kings, Lord of Lords, in whom dwelleth the fullness of the godhead bodily, and who was made sin for us, though knowing no sin, bearing our sins in His own body on the tree, as the only name under heaven given among men whereby we must be saved from everlasting punishment." *Constitution of the Young Women's Christian Associations in Universities, Colleges and Seminaries of the Dominion of Canada*, article 3, 1902.

13 Patricia Dirks, "Beyond Family and School: An Analysis of the Changing Place of Protestant Churches in the Lives of Canada's Young, 1900–1918," paper presented to the Canadian Historical Association, Vancouver, June 1983, and "Canada's Sunday Schools: The Shift to Church Control and the Formation of the Religious Education Council of Canada," paper presented to the Conference on the History of Education, Vancouver, October 1983; David MacLeod, "A Live Vaccine: The YMCA and Male Adolescence in the United States and Canada, 1870–1920," *Histoire sociale / Social History* 11 (May 1978): 5–25; Diana Pedersen, "'On the Trail of the Great Quest': The YWCA and the Launching of Canadian Girls in Training, 1909–1921," paper presented to the Canadian Historical Association, Ottawa, June 1982; Margaret Prang, "'The Girl God Would Have Me Be': The Canadian Girls in Training, 1915–1939," *Canadian Historical Review* 66, no. 2 (1985): 154–84; and Neil Semple, "'The Nurture and Admonition of the Lord': Nineteenth-Century Canadian Methodism's Response to 'Childhood,'" *Histoire sociale / Social History* 14, no. 27 (May 1981): 157–75.

14 Quoted in Richard C. Morse, *History of the North American Young Men's Christian Associations* (New York: Association Press 1918), 189. On the early student YMCAs in Canada see Murray G. Ross, *The Y.M.C.A. in Canada: The Chronicle of a Century* (Toronto: Ryerson Press 1951), 114–22. See also Percy C. Leslie, "The Intercollegiate Movement of the Young Men's Christian Association," *McGill Fortnightly*, 24 Nov. 1893, 83–5; and 8 Dec. 1893, 108–10.

15 Shedd, *Two Centuries*, 187–213.

16 Miss Evelyn Overholt, "The College Woman," *Dominion Tie*, May 1904, 76–7.

17 "Y.W.C.A.," *McGill Fortnightly*, 12 Oct. 1893, 8; "The Queen's Girl as a Religious Character," *Queen's Journal*, 6 Dec. 1901, 22.

18 Cook, *The Regenerators*, 7–25; Carl Berger, *Science, God and Nature in Victorian Canada* (Toronto: University of Toronto Press 1983); A.B. McKillop, *Contours of Canadian Thought* (Toronto: University of Toronto Press 1987), 59–77; Miss Ivy Gardiner, Royal Victoria College, "Benefits Reaped from the Y.W.C.A.," *Dominion Tie*, Oct. 1902, 75.

19 "Those Interested in Young Women," *Daily Examiner* (Peterborough), 6 Oct. 1898, 5; Montreal YWCA Records, v 25, Miscellaneous, "Young Women's Christian Association Work in Canada," Dominion Council pamphlet, ca 1902.

20 Professor Scrimger, "Value of the Young Women's Christian Association in the University," *Young Women of Canada*, Mar. 1907, 27. This was probably the John Scrimger, professor of exegesis, Presbyterian College, Montreal, who is mentioned in Cook, *The Regenerators*, 20.

21 YWCA of Canada Records, v 79, *Second Biennial Report of the Young Women's Christian Association of Canada* 1896, 11; "Report of the Executive Committee of the Dominion Council," *Young Women of Canada*, Feb.–Mar. 1911, 31; "Bible Study," *Dominion Tie*, Dec. 1903, 328.

22 Ethel Gould Misener, "A Message for the Holidays", *Dominion Tie*, June 1904, 93. On the promotion of an ideal model of evangelical womanhood by churchwomen's organizations, see Anne M. Boylan, "Evangelical Womanhood in the Nineteenth Century: The Role of Women in Sunday Schools," *Feminist Studies*, 4, no. 3 (1978): 62–80.

23 Pedersen, "The Young Women's Christian Association," 387–404.

24 For a table of dates of organization, see Mary Quayle Innis, *Unfold the Years: A History of the Young Women's Christian Association in Canada* (Toronto: McClelland & Stewart 1949), 228–30.

25 For examples of this literature see YWCA of Canada Records, v 44, Scrapbook A.

26 Susie Little, "Report of the National Secretary of the Student Department of the Young Women's Christian Associations of Canada," *Dominion Tie*, Dec. 1903, 287; YWCA of Canada Records, v 44, Scrapbook B, 4, "Facts of Interest in Association Work," 1915.

27 It is likely that some of these students rejected membership in the YWCA in favour of the more conservative Student Volunteer Movement for Foreign Missions, another important Christian organization in many Canadian colleges. Given that the SVM may have indirectly encouraged the liberal leanings of the YWCAS and YMCAS, and later the Student Christian Movement, by siphoning off more conservative students, its activities merit further investigation.

28 "College Societies," *Dalhousie Gazette*, 7 Dec. 1896, 79; "Student Report," *Young Women of Canada*, Jan. 1914, 27.

29 Montreal YWCA Records, v 25, Miscellaneous, "Young Women's Christian Association Work in Canada," Dominion Council pamphlet, 1902; "Statistical Report

of the College Associations, 1901–02," *Dominion Tie*, June 1902, 43; "Statistical Report of Student Associations 1913–1914," *Young Women of Canada*, Nov. 1914, 218–19; "Student Report," *Young Women of Canada*, Jan. 1914, 28; "Student Committee," *Association Outlook*, Jan. 1917, 22; "Student Department," *Association Outlook*, Jan. 1920, 22; Solomon, *In the Company of Educated Women*, 106.

30 "Student Report," *Young Women of Canada*, Jan. 1914, 29; Miss Ruth Rouse, "Some Impressions of Canadian Student Life," *Young Women of Canada*, Dec. 1912, 337.

31 Miss E. Gardiner, BA, "The Y.W.C.A. Helps to Create the Ideal College," *Dominion Tie*, Oct. 1902, 74. See also Susie Little, "Report of the National Secretary of the Student Department of the Young Women's Christian Associations of Canada," *Dominion Tie*, Dec. 1903, 288.

32 YWCA of Canada Records, v 44, Scrapbook A, 10, topic card, Albert College YWCA, 1903–04.

33 Carrie H. Holman, "Personal Work," *Dominion Tie*, Dec. 1903, 320; Miss E.K. Price, "Fundamentals of Committee Work," *Dominion Tie*, Sept. 1902, 63.

34 16 Oct. 1903, 25.

35 Miss E.K. Price, "Fundamentals of Committee Work," *Dominion Tie*, Sept. 1902, 63.

36 *Queen's Journal*, 8 Nov. 1891, 5.

37 "A College Girl's Life at Acadia University," *Queen's Journal*, 18 Jan. 1909, 218; "A College Girl's Life at the Royal Victoria College," *Queen's Journal*, 15 Feb. 1909, 302.

38 "College Jottings – Queen's College, Kingston," *Dominion Tie*, Feb. 1902, 7; M.E.T. Addison, Victoria College, Toronto, "The Place of the Y.W.C.A. in the College Girl's Life," *Young Women of Canada*, Apr. 1909, 61.

39 Miss Ivy Gardiner, Royal Victoria College, "Benefits Reaped from the Y.W.C.A.," *Dominion Tie*, Oct. 1902, 75.

40 Susie Little, "Report of the National Secretary of the Student Department of the Young Women's Christian Associations of Canada," *Dominion Tie*, Dec. 1903, 288; "College Jottings," *Dominion Tie*, Feb. 1902, 7; Montreal YWCA Records, v 25, Miscellaneous, "Fundamental Principles of the Young Women's Christian Association," American Committee pamphlet, 1902.

41 "Women's Medical College," *Queen's Journal*, 20 Feb. 1892, 108.

42 YWCA of Canada Records, v 44, Scrapbook B, 1, "Y.W.C.A. Student Work in Canada," 1913. The Dominion Council initiated a Canadian summer conference in the Muskoka district of Ontario in 1909. Prior to that date, Canadian delegates attended conferences at Northfield, Massachusetts; Silver Bay, New York; and Lake Geneva, Wisconsin.

43 "First Canadian Y.W.C.A. Summer Conference," *Queen's Journal*, 27 Oct. 1909, 40; "Echoes from Muskoka," *Queen's Journal*, 9 Nov. 1910, 67–70; S. Bedinger, intercollegiate secretary, Toronto, "Why Go to the Summer Conference?" *Young Women of Canada*, Apr. 1909, 62–3. See Solomon, *In the Company of*

Educated Women, for a reference to the significance of eating treats as a ritual of friendship among women students.

44 YWCA of Canada Records, v 44, Scrapbook A, 3, University of New Brunswick Y.W.C.A., "Topics for 1907–08"; "College Jottings," *Dominion Tie*, Feb. 1902, 7.

45 "University College," *Dominion Tie*, Dec. 1903, 295; *Dominion Tie*, Nov. 1904, 141. See also Miss S. Little, "The Selection of New Officers," *Dominion Tie*, Apr. 1902, 21; Miss E.J. Yuill, BA, Acadia University, "The Value of Systematic Work in College Associations," *Dominion Tie*, May 1902, 31–2; Miss E.K. Price, "Fundamentals of Committee Work," *Dominion Tie*, Sept. 1902, 63; Miss A. Allen, BA, Victoria College, "The Finances of the College Association," *Dominion Tie*, Nov. 1902, 91; "The Policy," *Dominion Tie*, Sept. 1903, 220; Mary L. Baird, "The Girl for President," Helen Thompson, "The Choice of a Cabinet," Katharine E. Cullen, "The Selection and Training of Committees," *Young Women of Canada*, Mar. 1909, 46–7.

46 See Elizabeth Smith, *A Woman with a Purpose: The Diaries of Elizabeth Smith, 1872–1884*, ed. Veronica Strong-Boag (Toronto: University of Toronto Press 1980). In her later life, following her marriage to Adam Shortt, she served as president of the Kingston YWCA.

47 Helen Ekin Starrett, *After College, What?* (New York: Thomas Y. Crowell 1896); "After College, What? For Girls," *Queen's Journal*, 18 Mar. 1899; Joyce Antler, "'After College, What?': New Graduates and the Family Claim," *American Quarterly* 32, no. 4 (Fall 1980): 409–34; "The Principal's First Address to the Girls," *Queen's Journal*, 20 Feb. 1903, 32.

48 Montreal YWCA Records, v 25, Miscellaneous, "Of Use to Others and of Value to Herself," Elizabeth Wilson, American Committee pamphlet, 1902.

49 Winifred Harvey, "Occupations Open to College Women," *Young Women of Canada*, Dec. 1916, 184–7. For a discussion of this emerging female work ethic, see Dina M. Copelman, "Masculine Faculty, Women's Temperament: Victorian Women's Quest for Work and Personal Fulfillment," *Feminist Studies* 13, no. 1 (Spring 1987): 185–201.

50 Cook, *The Regenerators*, 4; "Bible Study," *Dominion Tie*, Dec. 1903, 328–9. See also Ella Gardiner, "The Necessity for a Personal, Devotional Bible Study," *Dominion Tie*, Dec. 1903, 330–1. On the Bible-study movement, see YWCA of Canada Records, v 44, Scrapbook A, 5, Clayton S. Cooper, *Brief Historical Sketch of the Voluntary Bible Study Movement among North American Institutions* (New York: Young Men's Christian Association Press 1908); "The Bible Study Movement," *Queen's Journal*, 3 Nov. 1905, 40–3.

51 Cook, *The Regenerators*, 230. On the rise of biblical criticism see Michael Gauvreau, "The Taming of History: Reflections on the Canadian Methodist Encounter with Biblical Criticism, 1830–1900," *Canadian Historical Review* 65, no. 3 (1984): 315–46. On Sharman's career and influence see Donald L. Kirkey, Jr, "'Mediating the Religion of Jesus': Henry Burton Sharman and the Student Christian Movement of Canada," paper presented to the joint meeting of the Canadian

and American Societies of Church History, Hamilton, April 1987, and "The Decline of Radical Liberal Protestantism: The Case of the Student Christian Movement of Canada," paper presented to the Canadian Historical Association, Windsor, Ont., June 1988; *This One Thing: A Tribute to Henry Burton Sharman* (Toronto: Student Christian Movement of Canada 1959); Prang, "The Girl God Would Have Me Be," 165–9.

52 "Y.W.C.A.," *McGill Fortnightly*, 27 Oct. 1893, 35; YWCA of Canada Records, v 44, Scrapbook A, 14, Mrs Lawrence Thurston, *The College Woman's Opportunity* (New York: Student Volunteer Movement for Foreign Missions 1906), 13. See also Scrapbook A, 13, Ruth Rouse, *Women Students and the Foreign Mission Field* (London: Student Volunteer Missionary Union 1907).

53 Professor Scrimger, "Value of the Young Women's Christian Association in the University," *Young Women of Canada*, Mar. 1907, 28.

54 C. Howard Hopkins, *John R. Mott 1865–1955: A Biography* (Grand Rapids, Mich.: William B. Eerdmans 1979), 60–2.

55 T.F.B. 1911, "Echoes from Muskoka," *Queen's Journal*, 9 Nov. 1910, 68; Miss Cartwright, "The Value of Mission Study in the Student Life," *Dominion Tie*, Dec. 1903, 324. See also Joan Jacobs Brumberg, "'Zenanas and Girlless Villages': The Ethnology of American Evangelical Women, 1870–1910," *Journal of American History* 69, no. 2 (1982): 347–71.

56 "College Notes," *Young Woman's Gazette*, Feb. 1900, 9; "Missions at the Ontario Medical College for Women," *Young Woman's Gazette*, May 1900, 7. See also Winifred Heston, *A Bluestocking in India: Her Medical Wards and Messages Home* (New York: Fleming H. Revell 1910); and Barbara Welter, "She Hath Done What She Could: Protestant Women's Missionary Careers in Nineteenth-Century America," *American Quarterly* 30, no. 5 (1978): 624–38.

57 Pedersen, "The Young Women's Christian Association," chap. 5. On the rise and influence of the social gospel in Canada see Richard Allen, *The Social Passion: Religion and Social Reform in Canada, 1914–1928* (Toronto: University of Toronto Press 1973); and Richard Allen, ed., *The Social Gospel in Canada* (Ottawa: National Museums of Canada 1975).

58 *Young Women of Canada*, Sept. 1912; M.S.E. [Mary S. Edgar?], "The Study of Missions, 1912–1913," *Young Women of Canada*, Oct. 1912, 312; "Miss Rouse in the Canadian Universities and Institutions of Higher Learning," *Young Women of Canada*, May 1912, 256–7; Ruth Rouse, "Canada's Goodly Heritage," *Young Women of Canada*, June 1912, 272–7.

59 J.S. Woodsworth, "The Coming of the Kingdom," *Young Women of Canada*, Sept. 1915, 121–3; *Strangers Within Our Gates, or Coming Canadians* (1909), with an introduction by Marilyn Barber (Toronto: University of Toronto Press 1972); and *My Neighbour: A Study of City Conditions, A Plea for Social Service* (1911), with an introduction by Richard Allen (Toronto: University of Toronto Press 1972). For an analysis of Woodsworth's thought at this stage in his development as a social reformer see Cook, *The Regenerators*, 213–23. See also

Young Women of Canada, June 1915, 118, for Woodsworth's review of Malcolm Spencer, *Students and the Regeneration of Society* (London: Student Christian Movement 1914).

60 Miss Jones, Havergal College, Winnipeg, "Relating the Student to the Community," *Young Women of Canada*, Jan. 1914, 6.

61 "Echoes from Muskoka," *Queen's Journal*, 9 Nov. 1910, 68; *Queen's Journal*, 20 Oct. 1910, 32.

62 "Social Service," *Young Women of Canada*, Sept. 1914, 180.

63 "College Notes," *Young Women of Canada*, Jan. 1912, 204.

64 "Student Notes," *Young Women of Canada*, Feb. 1915, 36; YWCA of Canada Records, v 40, "Report of the Canadian Student Young Women's Christian Association, 1914–1915."

65 Mabel C. Jamieson, "Student Initiative in the Canadian Associations," *Young Women of Canada*, Oct. 1914, 195.

66 M.B. Ferguson, "Elgin House – Student Sessions," *Young Women of Canada*, Oct. 1916, 152.

67 *Young Women of Canada*, Dec. 1914, 240; Oct. 1914, 201.

68 "The Recommendations of the Elgin House Student Committee," *Young Women of Canada*, Oct. 1915, 149–50; "Recommendations of the Elgin House Conference Student Committee," *Association Outlook*, Oct. 1917, 174.

69 Michael Bliss, "The Methodist Church and World War I," *Canadian Historical Review* 49, no. 3 (1968): 213–33; Pedersen, "The Young Women's Christian Association," 404–6.

70 Isobel Thomas, University of British Columbia, "The College Woman and the Vote," *Association Outlook*, Feb. 1918, 36; Helen R.H. Nichol, "Ten Days at Couchiching Conference," *Canadian Student*, Oct. 1919, 24; "Student Committee," *Association Outlook*, Mar. 1918, 54.

71 "Student Notes – National Service," *Association Outlook*, Mar. 1917, 61–2.

72 "The War and Students," *Young Women of Canada*, Oct. 1914, 200.

73 "Students as Wage-Earners," *Association Outlook*, Oct. 1917, 153. See also "One Student's Summer School Course," 171–2.

74 Mabel C. Jamieson, "Retrospect and Prospect," *Young Women of Canada*, Oct. 1915, 145–5.

75 "Student Notes – Missions," *Association Outlook*, Mar. 1917, 60; "Editorial Notes," Oct. 1917, 154; "Student Notes – University of British Columbia," *Association Outlook*, May 1917, 106.

76 Mabel C. Jamieson, "Retrospect and Prospect," *Young Women of Canada*, Oct. 1915, 146.

77 A Sophomore, "The Outlook of the Y.W.C.A. in the University of British Columbia," *Association Outlook*, Oct. 1917, 170.

78 Kirkey, "Mediating the Religion of Jesus," 5–9; Professor S.H. Hooke, "Why Should I Join a Church?" *Young Women of Canada*, Dec. 1916, 182–4.

79 Donald L. Kirkey, "'Building the City of God': The Founding of the Student Christian Movement of Canada" (MA thesis, McMaster University, 1983), 50.
80 Alma Conway, "Your Old Y.W.C.A.," *Young Women of Canada*, Dec. 1915, 197.
81 "Findings," *Young Women of Canada*, Feb. 1916, 36.
82 "Student Notes," *Association Outlook*, Nov. 1917, 191; M.B. Ferguson, "Elgin House – Student Sessions," *Young Women of Canada*, Oct. 1916, 151.
83 "Conference of Student Committee," *Association Outlook*, June 1917, 120; Elsinore Macpherson, University College, Toronto, "A Protest," *Association Outlook*, Feb. 1918, 37.
84 "Findings," *Young Women of Canada*, Feb. 1916, 36.
85 Alma Conway, "Your Old Y.W.C.A.," *Young Women of Canada*, Oct. 1915, 158–9; Dec. 1915, 195–8.
86 "The Canadian Student Council," *Young Women of Canada*, June 1914, 163; *Canadian Student*, Jan. 1919, 23; *Canadian Student*, Feb. 1920, 25–6.
87 *Canadian Student*, Dec. 1919, 3. On the accusation of profiteering, see Ross, *The Y.M.C.A. in Canada*, 291–4.
88 *Canadian Student*, Mar. 1920, 31.
89 *Canadian Student*, Jan. 1921, 15. For a full account of the formation of the SCM, see Kirkey, "Building the City of God." 72–131.

CHAPTER TEN

The Student Movement of the 1930s*
Paul Axelrod

University students of the 1960s discovered the phenomenon of radical campus politics, but they did not invent it. Throughout history students have participated fervently in reformist and revolutionary movements. The 1930s provided conditions particularly conducive to students activism in Europe and North America. Collapsed capitalist economies, the rise of fascism, and the imminence of war threatened to deface or destroy the world that youth was preparing to enter. Even privileged, educated youth could not be insulated from these enormous pressures. How would they face the challenge? To what degree did their responses involve collective political action? While historians have examined the student movement of the 1930s in the United States and Europe, virtually nothing has been written of the Canadian experience.[1] This article examines the extent to which Canadian students of that era participated in efforts to transform the political and social order of Canadian society.

In 1930 some thirty-three thousand students attended Canadian universities full time, representing a mere 3 per cent of college-aged youth. Their denominational origins in the still-recent past, most Canadian universities viewed themselves as non-doctrinaire, God-fearing institutions, responsible for graduating middle-class professionals with sound moral values and the qualities of good citizenship. The social crises of the 1930s, in the eyes of university authorities, made such a mission even more important.[2]

Although hardened war veterans and unruly, drunken students had occasionally challenged authority on and off campus, university officials had traditionally succeeded in managing and socializing the youth placed in their custody.[3] The political moderation of university students was reflected in the activities of the National Federation of Canadian University Students, an organization founded at a Montreal conference of student-council representatives from eleven universities in December 1926.[4] Inspired by the encouragement of Ralph Nunn May, a member of the Imperial Debating

Team and a former president of the National Union of Students in England, NFCUS arose in part out of the post-war desire for international harmony and peace among students in Europe and North America. NFCUS resolved to "promote national unity" through campus co-operation and to facilitate the exchange of information on student concerns. It was soon evident that NFCUS perceived itself primarily as an apolitical, service organization for students. It gained some respect for its promotion of inter-university debating competitions, of which it had sponsored some five hundred by 1935, and its university exchange program, in which students from one region of the country would spend a year of university in a different region. NFCUS also sought to obtain reduced transportation rates for students travelling within Canada and abroad.[5]

Only a handful of students actively participated in the affairs of NFCUS on a regular basis, though it generally elicited positive, if perfunctory, editorial comment from the student press. Throughout the Depression, when other student groups promoted peace and social reform, NFCUS stood on the sidelines, studiously avoiding taking controversial positions on issues of the day. As an editorial in the University of Manitoba student newspaper explained, NFCUS "many be compared to a mechanical robot. It carries out its obvious duties, but possesses none of the dynamic quality which can only be obtained with a solid body of student support for its activities and student thought on its problems."[6] University authorities and the Royal Canadian Mounted Police agreed. According to a 1939 RCMP surveillance report, NFCUS, unlike more radical groups, was a "reliable and approved institution."[7]

Somewhat less "reliable," and far more committed to raising the political consciousness of Canadian students, was the Student Christian Movement. Founded in January 1921 when the student departments of the YMCA and YWCA joined forces with a group of young Christian activists, SCM was an outgrowth of the social gospel, a Christian reform movement "seeking to realize the Kingdom of God in the very fabric of society."[8] The SCM was the most important and enduring element of the Canadian student movement of the 1930s. Inspired by the activities and writings of reformist theologians such as Reinhold Niebuhr and J. King Gordon, it convened chapters on most Canadian campuses, sponsored talks by controversial speakers, raised relief funds for war victims in China, and most importantly, campaigned relentlessly for peace and social justice. While there were political differences within the organization, with some students promoting religion over politics and others promoting radical ideology and mass action, the SCM (unlike other student groups) remained unified and reasonably well organized at both national and local campus levels.[9]

With its tradition of mission-oriented Methodism, Victoria College at the University of Toronto was a particularly important centre of SCM activity;

approximately 10 per cent of the college's one thousand students participated in the movement in the mid-thirties.[10] At the University of Alberta twelve SCM study groups met throughout the 1930–31 year, drawing an average of 130 students (some 10 per cent of the student body), while the Universities of Manitoba, Dalhousie, McGill, and Mount Allison had equally active though smaller constituencies.[11] Although SCM's left-wing politics roused periodic concern in more conservative quarters, its righteousness and moderation earned it the support of most university authorities. R.C. Wallace, president of the University of Alberta from 1928 to 1936 and principal of Queen's from 1936 to 1951, was an SCM booster who served as its honorary national president in 1937, and Chancellor E.W. Beatty of McGill, no enthusiast of radical politics, believed that SCM played an important role in helping to shape students' "moral development."[12] Thus, because of its protected niche on Canadian campuses, the SCM provided a "haven of legitimacy" for some student radicals; more importantly, it served as an outlet for the minority of students interested in combining Christian living with social change.[13]

Another national student organization worthy of note was the Canadian Student Assembly, founded in January 1938 following a national student conference in Winnipeg organized by the SCM.[14] Under the leadership of its national secretary Grante Lathe, a graduate medical doctor from McGill, the CSA posed a serious challenge to the politically listless National Federation of Canadian University Students, and the rivalry continued until the CSA broke up in a swirl of controversy over its policy on the war in 1940. Composed of local "student assemblies," which students could join as individuals or club members, the CSA established a presence on most campuses by 1939. It opposed militarism, favoured greater educational opportunity, closer relations between French and English Canada, and the preservation of civil liberties.[15]

The CSA's most important undertaking was a campaign to pressure the federal government to provide a thousand "national scholarships," worth five hundred dollars each, for university students. On 6 March 1939 a CSA delegation of six students, bearing petitions and documentation of the low level of financial support available to Canadian students, met the minister of Labour, Norman Rogers, to press their claims. Their efforts yielded mixed results. Bursaries totalling $225,000, to be distributed to students over three years, were incorporated into the Dominion-Provincial Youth Training Plan in 1939, but because the program required provincial co-operation at a time of considerable federal-provincial conflict, the provinces of Ontario, Quebec, New Brunswick, and Nova Scotia refused to participate in the scheme, thus depriving their students of financial assistance. Students in the west received more benefit.[16]

While the CSA never succeeded in its efforts to build a mass movement, attracting by its own (problably exaggerated) estimate the active involvement of 2 per cent of Canadian students, along with other groups it played some role in making the public more aware of the problems and needs of Canadian youth.[17] Canadian historians of the 1930s have ignored the emergence of a significant youth movement in Canada in the last half of the decade, which attracted wide and generally favourable public attention. At the centre of the movement was the Canadian Youth Congress, of which the CSA and the SCM were member groups. At its peak in the late 1930s the CYC represented every major youth organization in Canada, with a total constituent membership of over four hundred thousand. Beginning in 1936 it held annual national conferences (with up to 730 participants), out of which it issued a Declaration of the Rights of Youth and a program favouring youth employment training, improved health, recreational, and educational facilities, and world peace. It also sent a number of delegates, representing the political spectrum from conservative to communist, to the 1936 World Youth Congress in Geneva. On the whole, middle-class university students were far less involved in the activities of the CYC than volunteer groups representing working-class youth, although a group of students from the University of Toronto played a major role in the events leading to the founding of the CYC and one of its graduates, Kenneth Woodsworth, became the full-time national secretary of the organization.[18]

Communist youth played an important role in the Canadian Youth Congress and took a less influential part in the university-based student movement of the 1930s. While most of the considerable energy of the Young Communist League (the youth branch of the Communist Party of Canada) was channelled to the organization of workers, the unemployed, and the campaign against fascism and war, some of this effort spilled on to university campuses through the CP's united-front and popular-front policy.[19] Where possible, co-operative work was engaged in with groups like the SCM and the CSA, although YCL members rarely declared publicly their major affiliation. The fear of harassment and repression, in part, explains this tactic. Applying draconian municipal laws, the Toronto police force broke up numerous Communist meetings in the late twenties and early thirties, some of which included students.[20] Then, in 1931, under Section 98 of the Criminal Code, which made it illegal simply to "advocate" political change "by the use of force," the Communist Party was declared "an unlawful association" and eight of its leaders were tried, convicted, and jailed. The law lapsed in 1936, allowing Communists to operate more openly, but was reimposed in Quebec in 1937 in the form of the Padlock Law, which made it a criminal offence to circulate literature "tending to propagate communism."[21] RCMP informers infiltrated student meetings where Communists were present and filed reports on others merely suspected of having Communist links. One account contained the names of three McGill professors who where scheduled to attend a scientific conference in Moscow, and others reported on speeches by a (non-Communist) socialist student named David Lewis and a political-science lecturer, Eugene Forsey, both from McGill.[22] When right-wing spokesmen charged that university campuses were filled with communists, an accusation hurled frequently at McGill University, the claims were found to be without substance. In 1931 even an RCMP Inspector, J.W. Phillips, declared "ridiculous" the view that McGill was a "hot bed of communism." Still, most such charges, no matter how suspect the source, were followed up with investigations in the illiberal political climate of the 1930s.[23] The UBC student newspaper perhaps adopted the most appropriate response to these groundless complaints – sarcasm. After a British Columbia cabinet member, R.H. Poole, claimed that some university faculty were teaching communism, the *Ubyssey* titled an editorial "Are Our Faces Red?" and a columnist in the liberal *Vancouver Sun* dismissed Pooley's "communistic hallucinations."[24]

A Communist club was permitted to function openly at the University of Toronto in 1936, an "experiment" that received national attention in student newspapers, though because the membership was small and the majority of students were viewed by the university's president as "level-headed," this was not considered a particularly dangerous initiative.[25] Communists were known to be leading forces in the League against War and Fascism, which, as part of its united-front national campaign, held meetings on various campuses throughout the decade. The *Manitoban* recalled that the league had had a "short and unimpressive existence" at the university.[26]

Inspired by events in the United States, where a Communist-led National Student League was formed in 1932, a Canadian Student League emerged later that year at the University of Toronto and established small groups in other Canadian cities. It held at least two conferences, where it attempted to unite university and high-school students in a common organization favouring scholarships for the poor, freedom of speech and assembly, the abolition of campus officers' training corps, opposition to fascism and fascist propaganda, and the creation of an economic system based on "use, not profit." Its most noteworthy activity was the role it played in a 1934 Montreal campaign against increased high-school tuition fees, which included a student walkout from two schools. It also participated in a 1935 May Day "strike" by a reported three thousand Vancouver (mostly high-school) students who marched in a demonstration with area relief-camp workers. Student League groups operated on several Canadian campuses, where they co-operated with other reform organizations but had a minimal impact on the student body as whole. At its peak the Young Communist League had seventeen hundred members across the country, and while it was most active in Montreal, Toronto, Vancouver, and Winnipeg, where it forged some effective alliances with non-Communist youth groups, only a small proportion of the YCL's members were university students.[27]

If Communist youth sometimes made their presence felt on Canadian campuses, so too did democratic socialists. The organization of the League for Social Reconstruction and the Co-operative Commonwealth Federation led to the formation of like-minded study groups and clubs on a number of campuses. Some of these were affiliated with the Co-operative Commonwealth Youth Movement (CCYM), formed in 1934, which, like the Young Communist League, focused most of its organizing efforts on working-class, not university, youth. In 1938 the CCYM was strongest in Alberta, where it drew upon links with the long-established United Farmers of Alberta. It was active as well in Ontario and Saskatchewan, where its members attracted the attention of some students by delivering speeches and selling newspapers on street-corners.[28] Under the tutelage of professors such as W.H. Alexander at the University of Alberta, Leonard Marsh, Frank Scott, and Eugene Forsey at McGill, Eric Havelock, Frank Underhill, and Harry Cassidy at Toronto, A.W. Carrothers at the University of British Columbia, and J. King Gordon at the United Theological Institute in Montreal, sympathetic students sought to raise the political consciousness of their classmates along socialist lines. A University Society for Social Reconstruction (with the ironic abbreviation of USSR) formed at the United College in Winnipeg, as did similar groups at Mount Allison University in New Brunswick and Queen's University in Kingston. The most energetic and intellectual university socialist group was the McGill Labour Club, whose publication, the *Alarm Clock*, was banned from the campus in 1933 by Arthur Currie, the McGill principal, and whose activities were followed closely by the RCMP.[29]

Off campus, youth associated with the CCF continually battled those tied to the Communist movement (particularly in organizations such as the Canadian Youth Congress), but within universities left-wing students maintained a greater degree of unity in the SCM, the CSA, and various peace-movement activities. Their small numbers made open conflict futile.[30]

No event demonstrates the unity and promise of the student movement more than an unprecedented national student conference held in Winnipeg in December 1937. The idea of the conference originated in discussions between individual members of the SCM and the Canadian Youth Congress who sought to create a "live, all embracing" assembly of students, comparable to the dynamic meetings of the Canadian Youth Congress.[31] The Student Christian Movement, considered the only national body capable of organizing such an event, agreed to do so, and in the fall of 1937 its associate general secretary, Margaret Kinney, toured campuses generating interest among student councils, the politically active student groups, and the press. Open meetings were held on many campuses, where agenda topics were discussed and delegates chosen. In the ebullient view of the *Manitoban*, the three hundred plus delegates from some twenty universities were treated to "the greatest student intellectual marathon" ever organized.[32] Speeches by the internationally known Reinhold Niebuhr, and by T.Z. Koo (the secretary of the World Student Christian Federation) attracted considerable attention, but what made the conference particularly lively were the open debates among students themselves on issues ranging from educational reform to Canadian foreign policy. French Canadians participated actively, explaining to bemused but engrossed English Canadians their support for the repressive Padlock Law, their opposition to free speech for Communists, and the importance of Catholicism in their lives. The conservative views of Quebec students were offset by resolutions calling for labour's right to bargain collectively, political equality for Canadian-born Orientals in British Columbia, and an independent foreign policy for Canada (supported by French Canadians). The conference ended in idealistic high spirits, leading to its one concrete accomplishment, the founding of the Canadian Student Assembly. The conference's largely left-of-centre policies drew less public attention than the favourable contribution it was perceived to have made to national unity. Returning to their campuses, the politically active Christian, socialist, communist, and pacifist students re-encountered the reality that building and sustaining a reform movement was easier said than done.[33]

Despite the abundance of concerns that might have inspired it, there was no mass political movement of university students during the 1930s. At best perhaps 5 per cent of students joined or participated regularly in reform-oriented organizations, though the last half of the decade involved more students than the first.[34] Socialist students and others moved by the plight of workers and the unemployed joined marchers in the "On-to-Ottawa Trek" in 1935 and supported coal miners in a New Brunswick strike in 1937.[35] But they were a distinct minority. In 1937 an Indian student visiting Canada was "appalled by the lack of political movements amongst the Canadian youth. They are far behind the youths of other countries in this respect."[36] Student activists and non-activists alike agreed that the bleak economic climate did not rouse much protest among university students. If anything it had the reverse effect. According to University of Manitoba student Earle Beattie, "the students doing political things were just a minority. The bulk of students didn't give a damn." Gertrude Rutherford, an SCM organizer from the University of Alberta, observed in her tour of western campuses in 1931 that "nowhere had the social life of the universities been affected by economic conditions. There were the same number of dinners, dances, teas, and other events." While the outbreak of the Depression deepened the political commitments of those already inclined to activism, it made most students more cautious. Indeed, prior to the 1935 federal election the student newspaper at Western advised students to be wary of political movements and new ideas: "In time of crisis, we cannot afford to gamble on any new political system which is as yet largely theoretical and not proved by experience ... radicalism is a luxury of stability." An earlier editorial claimed that capitalism was "the only system for Anglo Saxons."[37]

Canadian students were not necessarily as conservative as the *Gazette* editorial implied, but they were far less politically conscious than activists thought appropriate for the times. Why? Students were privileged to be at university, but apart from an extremely well-heeled minority, they were not wealthy. The typical student was the child of a merchant or a teacher for whom university was first and foremost a stepping-stone to a more secure professional career.[38] The Depression removed any guarantee of such employment, but as many observed, it made students work harder in the hope of enduring and surviving the difficult times.[39] Radical ideas were discussed and debated, but their advocates were perceived as well-intentioned dreamers out of step with reality. At best, recalled Kenneth Bradford, a University of Toronto student in the early thirties, the typical student attitude towards politics was one of "pure inquiry without passion." "We were political observers," echoed Marjorie Bowker of the University of Alberta, "not participants." Though they might challenge authority in other ways, students tended to support the political choices of their parents. When Prime Minister Bennett visited a number of Canadian universities in 1933, he was treated with near reverence by most student newspapers, one of which commented on the "inspirational qualities and sound common sense" of his platitudinous speech.[40] Two years later a student poll at the University of Saskatchewan gave 45 per cent support to the Liberals, 25 per cent to the CCF, 21 per cent to (Bennett's) Conservatives, and 8 per cent to the Communists, results consistent with those of the province of Saskatchewan in the imminent federal election. A similar survey of four thousand students at the University of Toronto gave the electoral edge to the Conservatives over the Liberals (35 per cent to 30 per cent), with the CCF receiving 13 per cent, the Reconstruction Party 9.8 per cent, and the Communists 3.2 per cent of the vote. The polls signified, first, that student opinion followed the shift toward Liberalism in the country as a whole (though University of Toronto students proved *more* conservative than voters in Ontario generally, where the Liberals won handily), and secondly, that the Canadian university was, in the words of the *Sheaf*, "no hotbed of radicalism."[41]

Students did, however, pour enormous energy into the social life of the campus, including dances, sports, fraternities, and clubs. These activities, most of which radical students also joined, were cherished experiences through which social relationships were forged, youthful vitality expended, and Depression cruelties escaped. University officials, too, believed that a healthy extra-curricular life (free of extreme vices) was a necessary part of youthful maturation. Students treasured the good times their universities offered, while radicals unhappily reminded them of the social misery they sought to escape.[42]

The campus culture of conformity was reinforced by university officials, who occasionally used repressive measures in order to discredit heretical ideas. Universities normally permitted students to express themselves freely – particularly in organized debates on topics ranging from the evils of Hollywood to the benefits of communism – but there were many notable and remarkable exceptions to the liberal approach. University authorities did not consider students fully formed adults, and they did their best to shape the students environment in ways that fit the dominant cultural and political values of the community. Such paternalism was expressed by the University of Western Ontario in its reasons for allowing students to run their own student council. The "educative effect of self-government upon students ... during the days when their minds are yet plastic cannot but be the best preparation for the duties of citizenship, notably the duty of sharing in the responsibilities of governing their country."[43] When students badly overstepped the bounds of propriety and good taste and brought public criticism to bear on the university, this was considered unacceptable, even dangerous. Acknowledging publicly the existence of petting and atheism at the University of Toronto cost two *Varsity* editors their jobs, and forced in the latter instance the suspension of the paper's publication. Because of its irreverent, cynical, and off-colour quality, Arthur Currie, principal of McGill, banned a publication called the *Black Sheep*, and on another occasion warned the *McGill Daily* that if it did not "improve in tone and in character the articles it contains, it should be suppressed." In 1938 the university forced the McGill Social Problems Club to rescind an invitation to Tim Buck, the leader of the Communist Party, for fear of being charged under the Quebec Padlock Law. Notably, Adrien Arcand, the leader of the fascist movement in Canada, had spoken earlier at the university without interference. In 1931 the editor of the *Ubyssey* was suspended by the University of British Columbia board of governors after the paper denounced the educational spending policies of the provincial government. And at the University of Saskatchewan in 1938 a Remembrance Day article claiming that soldiers killed in the First World War "were fools and dupes" who fought to "make the rich richer" caused the resignation of the editor. Less believable, perhaps, was the University of Toronto's cancelling of the library subscription to the *New Republic* because of its alleged slur on the king of England. It referred to his "dull and negative personality."[44]

A number of Canadian universities – particularly in western Canada, where, paradoxically, authorities were generally more liberal than in the east – did not permit students to form "partisan" political clubs on campus. While concerned students (and some professors) denounced these limitations on their freedom to assemble, the universities in question rationalized their actions by invoking liberal argument. They claimed that if students formed partisan clubs that antagonized the parties in office, then the university as a corporate entity might well be threatened, thereby jeopardizing everyone's ability to teach, learn, and pursue knowledge. Keeping political parties at bay preserved the independence of the university. As Walter Murray, president of the University of Saskatchewan explained, "when this University was projected in 1903, a dominating idea was to prevent it from becoming subservient to political parties." The policy also prevented professors from these institutions from running for political office.[45] Where such clubs could operate freely, Conservative and Liberal students formed groups alongside the socialists and communists.

Such limits on the freedom of expression reduced further the outlets through which student political activism might be channelled and encouraged, and helped to reinforce a political culture that marginalized radical thought.[46] As the University of Alberta *Gateway* conceded, "It is unwise for us ... to tread on religious or ideological corns ... to antagonize the powers that be – those on whom the University must rely for its very existence – would be to harm our public, the students."[47] Yet censorship could, and sometimes did, have the reverse effect, by angering and, at least temporarily, mobilizing the normally apolitical. Student editors from one part of the country almost always came to the defence of their besieged colleagues elsewhere,[48] and students also rallied round professors victimized by university, government, or public censure.[49] For fear of aggravating campus tensions University of Saskatchewan President Walter Murray found "friendly discussions" a more effective method than censorship in moderating student opinion.[50]

While students generally kept the campus peace, avoided joining political organizations, and provided university authorities with few headaches, there were other occasions when they behaved far less passively. Incidents that roused their passion could turn them into a formidable force. Universities often incited student protests when dances were restricted or banned.[51] In 1931 students in residence at the University of Alberta organized a successful petition campaign demanding a reduction in the price of room and board.[52] Perhaps the most remarkable collective action based on local concerns was a massive student protest in Vancouver in 1932 against drastic provincial spending cuts and a proposal to close the University of British Columbia. An intensive organizing effort culminated in a petition campaign in which a reported two thousand students "tramped the streets of Greater Vancouver" and collected sixty-five thousand signatures opposing the frightening financial recommendations of the "Kidd" Report.[53] And in 1939 students from the University of Western Ontario conducted a similar campaign against a funding reduction of twenty-five thousand dollars imposed on the university by the Ontario government. Students marched to Labatt's

Park, raised local support, and sent a petition with over twenty thousand signatures to the premier's office.[54]

Such impressive protests reflected less the politicization of the students than the spirited commitment they felt to their universities. The type of institutional loyalty that UBC and Western students expressed was common in the 1930s. Because their universities played such a significant role in their social lives and professional development, students happily sought to protect them from external challenges, a sentiment that was usually directed at rival football and debating teams and less frequently at threatening governments imposing punishing financial policies. As small, fairly intimate institutions offering a temporary haven from a gloomier world, universities successfully elicited the fidelity of their students. As the president of the student council said of the events at Western in 1939, "the student body has become self conscious and conscious of its own power ... We can develop a school spirit, not for its own sake but for the sake of the school."[55] Such school spirit could spontaneously erupt, but it contributed little to the sustenance of a politicized student movement committed to changing the social order. And unlike student radicals of the 1960s, who made the university itself a target of their antipathy, those of the 1930s focused almost all their critical attention on those governing the world, not the schools. Activists, too, were fond of their future alma maters.[56]

One external concern – the fear of world war – did touch the souls of otherwise politically quiescent students of the 1930s. While students quietly endured a Depression economy, hoping to use their education as an instrument of survival, the prospect of renewed war evoked active concern because it brought the very ability to survive into question. Students were not obsessed with the issue on a daily basis, but it occupied a permanent place in the recesses of their minds, and even before 1939 it was periodically pushed to the forefront by activists in the student movement.

Several petition campaigns, usually initiated by international organizations such as the World Student Christian Federation or the International Student Service, were carried on to Canadian campuses by national groups such as the Student Christian Movement, the League of Nations Society, or the Student Peace Movement. Almost ten thousand Canadian students signed a petition in late 1931 encouraging Prime Minister Bennett, in somewhat vague terms, to push for peace at the upcoming Geneva disarmament talks.[57]

The infamous Oxford Pledge in February 1933, in which students at the Oxford Union voted 275–153 in favour of the resolution that "this House will in no circumstances fight for King and Country," received wide international attention, in the United States. Nothing as sensational as the annual American "student strikes for peace" occurred in Canada, owing in part to a national culture that still stressed loyalty to Britain, but there were significant anti-war statements and events north of the border.[58]

In the fall of 1934 the *McGill Daily* circulated a questionnaire on war similar to those being distributed internationally, the results of which were to be collected in Geneva by the International Student Service. Most Canadian campuses participated in the exercise, though the response rate averaged only about 20 per cent, and the opinions of students were difficult to define clearly. The results at the University of Alberta were representative. While students feared the prospect of war, 70 per cent would fight if Canada were invaded, and 55 per cent if Britain were attacked. If Britain declared war under other circumstances, only 10 per cent said they would fight. War was never justified in the opinion of 20 per cent of students, and an equivalent proportion would refuse war service of any kind.[59]

In the period after 1935, as international tensions increased, student activists held peace vigils, sponsored anti-war "counter" services on Rememberance Day, circulated new questionnaires and petitions, and protested military training in campus Canadian Officers' Training Corps. The fear of war was real and widespread, though it scarcely interrupted the normal campus routine. And, like other Canadians, students were uncertain of the best strategy to be followed to prevent war. Following a 1936 national survey the *McGill Daily* was asked to produce a summary of campus opinion, based on reports from the campus press. It found a somewhat strained effort to reconcile a mood of isolationism with a belief in the value of collective security. "Campus papers showed a 50-50 stand on the question of increased defence," with students on the west coast and the Maritimes somewhat less isolationist than those elsewhere. As the *Dalhousie Gazette* had observed earlier, students "want to punish Italy [for invading Ethiopia], but they don't want to have any part in the punishing." Canadian students do not, echoed the *McGill Daily*, "speak with one voice." Uncompromisingly clear, however, was the universal opposition of students to conscription for wartime service. The *Daily* concluded, "It is agreed with scarce a dissenting voice, that there is much less prospect of Canadian youth supporting the government to the extent that they did in 1914 if war came."[60]

Growing concern among students about the rise of European fascism was reflected in the student press, and kept alive throughout the thirties by the periodic appearance on campus of spokesmen for such organizations as the League against War and Fascism. Communists and others among the politically committed were especially active in the campaign on behalf of the besieged Loyalists in the Spanish Civil War. On a number of occasions student editors raised their voices on behalf of Jews persecuted by the Nazis, and an admirable effort by Mount Allison students in 1938 to sponsor the emigration of refugee Jewish students to Canada was spurned by the university president and federal immigration authorities.[61]

Yet until war actually erupted, student opinion, like that in the country as a whole, could be benign, even favourably disposed, towards the rulers

of Italy and Germany. Occasional commentary in the campus papers described the sense of purpose, idealism, and nationalism that the Nazis and
Italian Fascists seemed to be generating. According to an article in the
Dalhousie Gazette in 1933, Hitler had succeeded in bringing the "German
people out of their slough of despondency by a system of organization and
national thought." An extremely sympathetic article in Laval's student newspaper, *l'Hebdo Laval*, claimed that Mussolini "is above all a patriot."[62]
Seeking to exploit and promote such sentiment, the Italian government
sponsored a 1934 Canadian speaking tour, which included lectures at several
universities by apologists for the Italian regime. Denying the existence of
a dictatorship and defending the country's economic and social reforms, the
speakers elicited wide, uncritical coverage, both on and off campus. No-
torious Canadian fascist Adrien Arcand also found an occasional platform
at Canadian universities.[63]

Sympathy for fascism was notably stronger in French-speaking Quebec
than in English Canada, and this led to an ugly political confrontation among
Montreal students in 1936. During the last week of October three delegates
from the anti-facist, Loyalist government of Spain were invited to Montreal
and, having been denied the right to speak at city hall, were asked by the
McGill Social Problems Club to lecture at the university. A group of students
from Université de Montréal gathered outside the McGill Union, where the
event was to occur, and threw rocks at those on the steps of the building.
Later a mob of some 250, consisting mostly of Université de Montréal
students, marched through the city streets shouting anti-communist and
anti-Jewish slogans. They proceeded to the Mount Royal Hotel, where the
Spanish delegates were staying and, apparently unprovoked, assaulted a
McGill professor. The turbulent weekend ended with an anti-communist,
pro-Catholic demonstration of an estimated hundred thousand people at
Champs de Mars.[64]

Termed a "riot" by the press, these confrontations seemed to symbolize
deep political and cultural cleavages between students from the two universities. Certainly, student political attitudes at the French Canadian universities (Montréal and Laval) were shaped by an official ideology stressing
Catholicism, conservatism, and violent anti-communism. The 1928 Annuaire Général of Université de Montréal promised to protect its students
from the forces of "materialism, liberalism and modernism."[65] The small
Université de Montréal – based Les Jeunes-Canada (founded in 1932) promoted the rights of youth in a populist, reformist, and nationalist program,
but combined this with a powerful expression of anti-Semitism.[66] Left-wing
students in Quebec could be found, but in minuscule numbers.[67] The opposition of socialists and communists to the church and to the pervasive
nationalism of the province contributed to their ostracization from university
campuses.[68] Université Ouvrière, a French Canadian adult-education facility

serving workers, where "anti-clerical and radical economic views" were taught, offered critical political education but remained well outside the mainstream of French Canadian education and was subject to considerable harassment, including an assault on its premises by a "band of students" from Université de Montréal in 1930.[69] A somewhat more respectable outlet for reform thinking was the school of social science founded by Father Georges-Henri Lévesque at Laval University in 1938.[70]

Despite the obvious contrasts it is possible to exaggerate both the depth of conservative activism among Quebec students and the differences between student life in the "two solitudes." In their interests, extra-curricular activities, and professional aspirations English Canadian and French Canadian students shared a great deal.[71] Politically, too, rapprochement appeared possible. The good feelings generated at the 1937 national student conference in Winnipeg were one indication of this spirit. And in the wake of the 1936 October "riot," which the Montreal *Gazette* attributed to "schoolboys and adults looking for excitement," the student councils of McGill and Montréal "agreed to patch up their differences" by publicly shaking hands and symbolically "burying the beret." To encourage better communication, the editors of the *McGill Daily* and the *Quartier Latin* agreed to write columns in each other's papers.[72]

What inferences can be drawn from such events? An energetic minority of English Canadian student activists leaned left politically, while a minority of French Canadian students campaigned with enthusiasm on the (far) right. The ideological and educational environment of English Canadian universities was less conservative than that of French Canada, where the church still wielded enormous authority. But the majority of students in both cultural groups were not preoccupied with politics and did not join political movements of the left or right. Thus, the political differences between students in the two cultures should neither be overlooked nor overstated.

The coming of the Second World War mobilized the student movement into one climactic assault on conventional values, only to leave it enfeebled and in disarray. The Canadian Student Assembly called its third national conference over Christmas in 1939 in the hope, once again, of stirring student activism on a wide range of issues, from curriculum reform to national unity. But as it had throughout the decade, the question of war dominated the students' political discussions, only now under very different conditions. In September war had actually been declared. The War Measures Act now made it a crime to issue statements that could be seen to undermine the war effort of Canada and Britain. Openly opposing Canada's participation in the war itself was therefore out of the question. For students promoting the cause of peace, the discussions were no longer academic.[73]

Situated at Ste Anne de Bellevue, Quebec, the conference elicited strong participation from francophone students, whose views on the meeting's most

controversial issue – conscription – were unmistakable. Against the background of militant nationalism in a province with deep, bitter memories,
French Canadian students gave powerful and unanimous support to a resolution opposing compulsory wartime service. Their position reflected the
policies of the Bloc universitaire, a movement of students from the
Universities of Ottawa, Laval, and Montréal created earlier in 1939 and
devoted to a nationalist "plan" that opposed massive immigration of European exiles to Canada, "completely and very vigorously all war measures
presently adopted, and any developments which would render more onerous
our participation in the war."[74] On the latter issue francophone students
were not alone. With the additional backing of a block of English Canadian
delegates the CSA passed a resolution that "opposed conscription for the
duration of the war, and ... military commitments such as a large expedi-
tionary force which would prepare the way for conscription."[75]

This resolution would be the death-knell of the Canadian Student Assembly. The statement was opposed strongly by a significant section of the
anglophone delegates, which was acknowledged in the conference report
from the CSA executive. "It appeared that in the West large numbers of
students are opposed to conscription; in Ontario fewer members are opposed
but their opposition is more active; in the Maritimes there is no opposition,
while French Canada is solidly opposed to conscription."[76] Debate climaxed
with a widely publicized walk-out led by the Mount Allison delegation,
whose spokesman, dean of men C.A. Krug, claimed that the conference
was being manipulated by those who where "anti-British, anti-war, and anti
all those principles which form the basis of our ties with the British Empire."[77] In light of the tension the conference undertook to distribute
a questionnaire at university campuses following the meeting "to ascertain the opinion of youth in this matter" and to publish the results.[78] Co-
sponsored by the Canadian Youth Congress and Bloc Universitaire, the
questionnaire surveyed youth opinion on conscription, civil liberties,
war profiteering, and youth employment.[79]

The enemies of the CSA used the anti-conscription resolution and the
controversy generated by the questionnaire to mobilize withdrawals from
the organization. By the end of January member groups from seven universities had seceded from the CSA, and more desertions followed. A particularly tense confrontation erupted at McGill University, where five
hundred students reportedly "smashed a CSA rally in a riotous session."[80]
According to the president of the student council, the CSA was suspended
at the University of British Columbia "on the grounds that the national
conference had brought adverse publicity to the university by its reported
anti-war atmosphere."[81] Many English Canadian campuses voted not to
distribute the CSA questionnaire, though at Laval and Montréal students were
polled and almost unanimously favoured the CSA position on conscription.[82]

Pockets of support for the CSA could still be found in English Canada, but the organization's influence and effectiveness, far from massive at the best of times, were quickly slipping away.[83]

The problems and demise of the CSA came as a great relief to the RCMP, which followed closely the activities of the organization and particularly those individuals who remained sympathetic to it. Convinced in January that the CSA was "permeated thoroughly by the YCL and CPC [Communist Party of Canada]," the superintendent commanding "O" Division included among his list of those "regarded in University life as being men of extreme thought, if not definitely Communist," five faculty resource leaders who participated in the CSA conference: Frank Underhill (Toronto), Father St Denis (Montréal), F.R. Scott (McGill), Professor Roy (Laval), and Arthur Lower (United College).[84] By March, however, Kemp concluded, "It is impossible to establish any tie-in between the Communist Party and the Canadian Student Assembly at the present time."[85] One RCMP report found it worth noting that the "amount of Jews in the CSA, mostly from the West and McGill, was remarkable."[86] The RCMP was equally concerned about the potential dangers flowing from the conscription survey of youth opinion: "It is considered that some form of education to combat this subversive activity and to instill into the minds of young Canadians the patriotic aspect of War Service in the present struggle is essential."[87] It is not clear what additional role the RCMP played in educating the student body "to think along patriotic lines," apart from monitoring CSA activities and the fate of the conscription questionnaire on every campus, but by April it could report that the CSA in Ontario, and elsewhere, was a "dead issue." Despite attempts by the CSA to confront its opposition and save its reputation, "a small number of radical thinkers," wrote one RCMP informant, "are becoming somewhat discouraged at their lack of progress."[88]

The extreme concern in the RCMP raised by the CSA position on conscription was ironic in the Canadian political climate of early 1940. Public opposition to conscription had been expressed by none other than Mackenzie King, prime minister of Canada, yet students who promoted the same position were considered potentially subversive, suspected of being communist, and subject to intensive surveillance. In any event, serious opposition to the war effort, with an active peace movement to lead it, all but disappeared from campuses in English Canada and was muted in Quebec. Across the country voluntary recruitments in campus Canadian Officers' Training Corps rose dramatically in the fall of 1939, doubling at Mount Allison, more than doubling to 600 at the University of Alberta, quadrupling to 700 at the University of Manitoba, and rising sixfold to 500 at the University of British Columbia.[89] Once compulsory military training was imposed upon male students over eighteen in 1940, the number of conscientious objectors refusing COTC training appeared quite small. At the University of Saskatchewan

15 students, most of whom were Mennonites or Doukhobors, declared themselves, as did "fewer than half a dozen" at McMaster.[90] A detailed report concerning the University of Alberta's 1,700 students revealed the COTC exemptions were granted to 47 students for medical reasons, 20 to married men over age twenty-four, 23 to final-year medical students, 3 to clergymen, and only 1 to a (Mennonite) conscientious objector. One other student refused training but was not exempted.[91] A 1941 "Discipline" report at the University of Manitoba noted that the expulsion of two students refusing military duty was "being considered."[92] Across Canada students joined "parade," curtailed much of their frivolous activity, and supported the war effort in other ways. A campus mood that so recently had combined elements of cynicism, isolationism, and even pacifism had by 1940 yielded to one of vigorous, public-spirited patriotism. As the *McGill Daily* observed, students appeared to be "against war until war arrives."[93]

Was there a student movement in Canada during the 1930s? Like campus activists elsewhere, small groups of Canadian undertook a vigorous campaign to raise students' awareness of social and political problems.[94] They successfully provoked discussion and debate but largely failed to elicit the active involvement of the vast majority of students in reform, let alone revolutionary causes. How can this be explained? The social-class background of university youth is one factor. Students were privileged, but they were not, for the most part, bathed in opulence. University provided these middle-class youth with the potential of surviving the Depression and achieving long-term security. Hard times made them more individualistic on the one hand and determined to participate fully in campus social life on the other. In this apolitical atmosphere, grim, erudite radicals promoting untried, collectivist ideologies could get a hearing, but not a large following.

The role of religion in shaping the direction and fate of the student movement cannot be overlooked. In Quebec, Catholic students had no time for atheistic communists and Protestant social democrats. While English Canada had become increasingly secular by the 1930s, the association of Christianity with higher education still lingered, particularly at universities like McMaster and Acadia, which maintained direct denominational links. This helped to preserve a campus environment of stability, piety, and paternalism. At the same time, reformers such as those in the Student Christian Movement derived their political inspiration from religious conviction, thereby gaining a secure place on university campuses and usually carrying out their activities in an unthreatening manner that university authorities could tolerate and oversee. Thus, in a subtle way, religion both fuelled and restrained an important element of the student movement.

Of course, campus authorities sometimes used more direct means, including censorship, to temper opinion considered not only radical but inappropriate and distasteful. From their parents and teachers students had learned to be deferential, respectable, and patriotic. Universities did their best to reinforce these values, which students as a whole were disinclined to defy on an ongoing basis. Being occasionally drunk or rowdy was condemned but expected; being a student activist could involve more risks, particularly for those linked, by accusation or fact, to communist or other "subversive" activities.

However, students were not mere putty in the hands of university authorities. We have seen how they could sometimes be moved to protest arbitrary or punitive actions by those in control. Because the university was the centre of their existence at a critical time in their development, students resented actions that unfairly restricted their freedom of expression (such as bans on dancing) or threatened the survival of the institutions (including excessive funding cutbacks). But these were single-issue events, in which student activists participated but which they could not sustain and direct to other causes. Students wanted to benefit from being at university and did not want to devote much energy to changing the world. Activists could not convince them, even during the Depression, that these causes were linked. As the straw polls indicated, students followed the political mood in the country as a whole, which was far from radical.

The apparent exception to the rule of campus apathy was the alarm generated by the prospect of world war. The peace movement, with its mix of isolationists, pacifists, anti-fascists, and proponents of collective security found its way on to Canadian campuses. Widespread involvement in the movement was intermittent and usually confined to the signing of petitions, but the anxiety was genuine. Haunted by the memory of war, students feared its renewal and the threat that it posed to everything they cherished. For most, however, this was not an overly controversial position. It was hard to find anyone in Canada who favoured war, and university presidents sometimes talked admiringly of the students who were part of the peace movement. At the same time, it was equally hard to find many students who believed, along with the highly political League against War and Fascism, that war and fascism were the products of capitalism, which should be abolished. Their concern about war, though heartfelt and instrumental in keeping the campus student movement alive, was not ideologically based.

If the fear of war inspired the student movement, the reality of war ended it. The Canadian Student Assembly, the Canadian Youth Congress, and even the National Federation of Canadian University Students were all its victims. The Student Christian Movement survived, but was riven by division over its policy on Canada's participation in the war. When the Communist Party reversed its position in 1941 to one of support for the war effort, the politics of opposition it had previously brought to the student and youth movement also dissipated.[95] In the face of increased Nazi aggression, the clamouring for peace, in vague and often contradictory terms, seemed to university students and Canadians as a whole an inadequate national response.

Despite their small numbers, and however limited their achievements, the student activists of the 1930s made campus life more vital, engaged, and interesting than it otherwise would have been. Like other "radicals" they were ahead of their time in the fight for civil liberties, minority rights, student assistance, and youth employment policies. They left an important but largely unknown legacy.

NOTES

* Research funding for this article was provided by the Social Sciences and Humanities Research Council of Canada.

1 See Alexander DeConde, ed., *Student Activism: Town and Gown in Historical Perspective* (New York: Charles Scribner's Sons 1971); Lewis S. Feuer, *The Conflict of Generations: The Character and Significance of Student Movements* (New York: Basic Books 1960); Herbert Moller, "Youth as a Force in the Modern World," *Comparative Studies in Society and History* 10, no. 3 (Apr. 1968): 237–60; Aline Coutrot, "Youth Movements in France in the 1930s," *Journal of Contemporary History* 5, no. 1 (1970): 22–35; Arthur Marwick, "Youth in Britain, 1920–1960: Detachment and Commitment," in ibid., 37–51; Brian Simon, "The Student Movement in England and Wales during the 1930s," *History of Education* 13, no. 3 (Sept. 1987): 189–203; Seymour Martin Liptset, *Rebellion in the University: A History of Student Activitism in America* (London: Routledge and Kegan Paul 1972); Philip Altbach, *Student Politics in America: A Historical Analysis* (New York: McGraw Hill 1974); Eileen Eagan, *Class, Culture and the Classroom: The Student Peace Movement of the 1930s* (Philadelphia: Temple University Press 1981); Ralph Brax, *The First Student Movement: Student Activism in the United States during the 1930s* (London: National University 1981); R.L. Schnell, *National Activist Student Organizations in American Higher Education, 1905–1944* (Ann Arbor: University of Michigan 1976); Eric W. Riser, "Red Menaces and Drinking Buddies: Student Activism at the University of Florida, 1936–1939," *Historian* 48, no. 4 (1986): 559–71. On Canada, there are scattered references to student politics in some of the institutional histories cited throughout this paper.

2 Robert Falconer, "Do Our Graduates Make Worthy Citizens?" President's Address, University of Toronto, 30 Sept. 1931; "Life is Enriched by Universities," report of a speech by H.J. Cody, president of the University of Toronto, *Globe*, 3 June 1936, 9; R.C. Wallace (principal, Queen's University), "Inaugural Address," *Queen's Journal*, 14 Oct. 1936; C.G. Stone and F. John Garnett, *Brandon College: A History, 1899–1967* (Brandon: Brandon University 1969), 127

(views of President R.J. Evans); statistics from Dominion Bureau of Statistics, *Annual Survey of Education in Canada* (Ottawa 1933), xv.

3 Michael Hayden, *Seeking a Balance: The University of Saskatchewan, 1907–1982* (Vancouver: University of British Columbia Press 1983), 139–46; James Pitsula, "Student Life at Regina College in the 1920s," in this volume; Frederick W. Gibson, *"To Serve and Yet Be Free": Queen's University, 1917–1961* (Montreal: McGill-Queen's University Press 1983), 66–82.

4 Reports, Findings and Minutes of a Conference of Representatives from Canadian Universities Held at McGill University, Montreal, 28–31 December 1926, Canadian Union of Students Collection, McMaster University Archives.

5 History of the National Federation of Canadian University Students, 1926–48, NFCUS Publicity Committee, McMaster University, M.J. Diakowsky, editor, ca 1948, Students: SAC General, History of NFCUS, University Historian's Collection, A-83-0036/031, University of Toronto Archives.

6 *Manitoban*, 22 Feb. 1935.

7 Memo prepared by H.A.R. Gagnon, Supt Commanding "C" Division, 24 Mar. 1939, Canadian Security Intelligence Service (CSIS) Files. The CSIS material cited in this article was obtained following application through the Access to Information Act. Much useful information on the surveillance of student organizations was retrieved, though it was heavily edited, with names of individuals usually blacked out.

8 Richard Allen, *The Social Passion: Religion and Social Reform in Canada, 1914–1928* (Toronto: University of Toronto Press 1973), 219–23; Margaret Beattie, *SCM: A Short History of the Student Christian Movement in Canada* (Toronto: Student Christian Movement 1975); Ernest A. Dale, *Twenty-one Years a-Building: A Short Account of the Student Christian Movement in Canada, 1920–41* (Toronto: SCM, nd); Donald L. Kirkey, Jr, "The Decline of Radical Liberal Protestantism: The Case of the Student Christian Movement of Canada," paper presented to the Canadian Historical Association, Windsor, Ont., 1988.

9 See Beattie, SCM, 38, 87–8; internal political debate reviewed in Jean J. Hunter to A.E. Morgan, 24 Mar. 1936, Student Christian Movement File, Principal's Papers, RG C52, McGill University Archives: "Should the Movement, as an organization, adopt definite stands and take united social action on live issues, or should it be primarily concerned with developing religious people, in the best sense, by a sound modern educational method? We discovered that as a group we were divided on this question so basic to our work." See also Kirkey, "Decline," 26–7.

10 Interviews with W.E. Mann, 17 Dec. 1985; Jean Woodsworth, 30 Dec. 1985; Jean Burnett, 19 Dec. 1985, and Kenneth Woodsworth, 7 Mar. 1986.

11 "The Student Christian Movement of the University of Alberta, Annual Report, 1930–31," President's Papers, 1928–36, Student and Alumni Affairs, SCM: Correspondence 3286-3, University of Alberta Archives; *Managra* (student publication of the University of Manitoba Agricultural College) 24, no. 1 (Nov. 1930); Harry Avison Papers, MG 30 D 102, vol. 13, file 71, National Archives of Can-

ada; "Annual Report of the Student Christian Movement, 1933–34," President's Office Papers, Student Christian Movement File, Dalhousie University Archives.

12 R.C. Wallace to J.H. Woods, 21 Nov. 1939, President's Papers, 1928–36, University of Alberta, Student and Alumni Affairs, SCM: Correspondence 3286, University of Alberta Archives; Gibson, "To Serve," 147, though Wallace did note his concern about SCM's increasingly political orientation; E.W. Beatty to Chas. H. Hale, 30 June 1934, Student Christian Movement RG2 C52, McGill University Archives; see also positive comments of J.S. Thomson, president of the University of Saskatchewan, to Rev. Beverly L. Outen, 1 Sept. 1937, Presidential Papers, II B-175 (1), University of Saskatchewan Archives.

13 Quotation from correspondence with David Woodsworth, 21 Jan. 1986; also interview with John Webster Grant, 19 June 1985.

14 For information on the founding of the CSA, see Canadian Youth Congress Collection, box 8, file 5, McMaster University Archives.

15 Briefs and conference resolutions from the CSA for 1939–40 are found in the CSIS files, in possession of the author. Reports of CSA activities also found in student newspapers from 1938 to 1940. The events leading to the breakup of the CSA will be discussed below. Neil Morrison, a CSA proponent, explained the difference between NFCUS and the more "democratic" CSA in a talk at the University of Alberta, Gateway, 24 Nov. 1939.

16 "State Scholarships for Canada: A Brief to the Royal Commission on Dominion Provincial Relations from the Canadian Student Assembly," June 1938, Student Christian Movement Collection, 84-2-9, United Church Archives; Jack Chernick, "National Scholarships," Manitoba Arts Review 1, no. 2 (Fall 1938); information in CSA "News Letter," no. 2, 27 Feb. 1940, CSIS Files; Varsity, 7 Mar. 1939; Ubyssey, 22 Sept. 1939; "Report of Commission on the Extension of University Education," Summary of Conference Resolutions, Third National Conference of the Canadian Student Assembly, December 1939, CSIS Files.

17 Canadian Student Assembly, "A Brief on National Student Life," 6 Dec. 1939, CSIS Files.

18 Kenneth Woodsworth, "The Canadian Youth Congress" (history and background, ca 1943), box 1, file 1, Canadian Youth Congress Collection, McMaster University Archives. It includes favourable comments cabled to the 1938 congress conference from Prime Minister Mackenzie King. See Toronto Star, 26 May 1936; interview with Kenneth Woodsworth, national secretary of CYC, and with Jean Woodsworth, 30 Dec. 1985; material also in the Frank and Libby Park Papers, MG 31 K9, vol. 7, file 128A, National Archives of Canada; and in CYC magazine publication called The Youth Forum, National Library of Canada; also interview with Peter Hunter, 17 Dec. 1985, an organizer for the Young Communist League who was active in the CYC. The latest and most comprehensive historical accounts of the 1930s, by John H. Thompson with Allen Seager, Canada, 1922–1939: Decades of Discord (Toronto: McClelland and Stewart 1985), and Robert Both-

well, Ian Drummond, and John English, *Canada 1900–1945* (Toronto: University of Toronto Press 1987), do not mention the Canadian Youth Congress and do not discuss the youth movement.

19 This policy was followed internationally. See Richard Cornell, *Youth and Communism: An Historical Analysis of International Communist Youth Movements* (New York: Walker and Co. 1965), 59–71; *Canada's Party of Socialism: History of the Communist Party of Canada, 1921–1976* (Toronto: Progress Books 1982), 108–18. The latter, the official history of the Canadian Communist Party, claimed that "the Young Communist League played a key role in establishing the Canadian Youth Congress" (117), a claim that YCL's enemies did not dispute. See also Norman Penner, *Canadian Communism: The Stalin Years and Beyond* (Toronto: Methuen 1987), 146–8.

20 Lita-Rose Betcherman, *The Little Band: The Clashes between the Communists and the Political and Legal Establishment in Canada, 1926–1932* (Ottawa: Deneau 1982). The University of Western Ontario *Gazette*, 20 Feb. 1934, reports on members of the Student League being ejected from a meeting where Communist A.E. Smith was speaking on behalf of the Canadian Labour Defence League.

21 Thompson and Seager, *Canada, 1922–1939*, 223–9, 285.

22 On professors attending scientific conference, F.J. Meade, Supt Commanding "C" Division to the Commissioner, 6 June 1935; report of Forsey speech delivered on 14 Jan. 1932, file no. 175/6540; on David Lewis, J.W. Phillips to Cortlandt Starnes, 19 May 1931, CSIS Files.

23 J.W. Phillips to Commissioner Cortlandt Starnes, 9 May 1931, CSIS Files; Cortlandt Starnes to Arthur Currie, 13 May 1931. A charge in 1935 by Mr J.F. Pouliot, Liberal MP for Temiscouta, that McGill was filled with Communists, was denied by the university (*Ottawa Journal*, 3 Mar. 1935, clipping in CSIS Files); and again in 1937 Montreal surgeon Henry Gray claimed there were Communists at McGill, an accusation denied by Principal A.E. Morgan (*Montreal Gazette*, 9 Apr. 1937, clipping in CSIS Files).

24 *Ubyssey*, 20 Nov. 1934; *Vancouver Sun*, 22 Nov. 1934.

25 *Varsity*, 5 Dec. 1935; *Mail and Empire*, 6 Dec. 1935; *Gateway*, 10 Dec. 1935.

26 *Manitoban*, 5 Feb. 1937; *Manifesto of the Canadian Congress against War and Facism* (Toronto 1934), Special Collections, York University Library.

27 For material on the Student League, see *Manitoban*, 13 Jan. 1933, 1 Feb. 1934; University of Western Ontario *Gazette*, 20 Feb. 1934; *Ubyssey*, 23 Nov. 1934; report from C.D. LaNauze, Supt. Cmdg. "O" Division, 21 Feb. 1935, CSIS Files. The Student League's activities were covered in the *Young Worker*, the publication of the Young Communist League. See R.S., "The Canadian Student Movement," 17 Apr., 13 May, and 30 June 1933, and other articles on 7 May, 16 July, 13 Aug. 1934, and 24 Aug. 1935. On the YCL, see Ivan Avakumovic, *The Communist Party of Canada* (Toronto: McClelland and Stewart 1975), 122–4, and interview with Peter Hunter, 17 Dec. 1985, a YCL organizer in southwestern

Ontario. Communist youth acted in political plays through the Progressive Arts Club at the University of Toronto and elsewhere in the country: Dorothy Livesay, *Right Hand Left Hand: A True Life of the Thirties* (Erin, Ont.: Press Porcepic 1977), 73–86; Gregory S. Kealey, "Stanley Brehault Ryerson. Revolutionary Intellectual," *Studies in Political Economy* 9 (Fall 1982): 105–6.

28 "Minutes of Third Annual CCYM Convention, Edmonton, July 26, 27, 1938," CCF Records, CCYM, General 1935–39, MG 28 IV-I, vol. 344, Public Archives of Canada. This was confirmed by Ben Swankey in an article in *League Life* (October 1938), a publication of the Young Communist League: "The healthiest section of the CCYM, as regards size, influence and activity, is undoubtedly in Alberta." The CCYM was weakest in French Canada, the Maritimes, Manitoba, and British Columbia. It was somewhat more active in Ontario and Saskatchewan. See also Ernest Shulman, "The Cooperative Commonwealth Federation and Its Youth Movement in Ontario" (MA thesis, University of Wisconsin, ca 1955), 39–40. Carney Morris, a University of Toronto student from 1932 to 1934, who joined the CCF, recalled listening to street-corner speeches by CCF members such as Morden Lazarus; interview, 20 Sept. 1985.

29 See the following sources: A.G. Bedford, *The University of Winnipeg: A History of the Founding Colleges* (Toronto: University of Toronto Press 1976), 197; the *Alarm Clock* reports on socialist activity around the country, Feb., Mar. 1933, Student Activities, 1927–33, *Alarm Clock* magazine, RG2 C52, Principal's Papers, McGill University Archives; David Lewis, *The Good Fight: Political Memoirs, 1909–1958* (Toronto: Macmillan 1981), 28–9; John G. Reid, *Mount Allison University*, vol. 2 *1914–1963* (Toronto: University of Toronto Press 1984), 150; Michiel Horn, *The League for Social Reconstruction: Intellectual Origins of the Democratic Left in Canada, 1930–1942* (Toronto: University of Toronto Press 1980); Arthur Currie to J.H.B. MacBrien, Commissioner of the RCMP, 11 Feb. 1933, and file no. 175/6540, CSIS Files; *McGill Daily*, 7 Dec. 1933.

30 Interviews with Kenneth Woodsworth, 7 Mar. 1986, and W.E. Mann, 17 Dec. 1985. David Lewis, national secretary of the CCF, believed that the Canadian Youth Congress was dominated by Communists, and recommended that the CCYM consider withdrawing in 1938. Lewis to Eamon Park, 18 May 1938, CCF Records, CCYM, General, 1935–58, MG-28, IV.I, vol. 344, National Archives of Canada. Officially, the Young Communist League policy involved criticism of but cooperation with reform groups like the CCYM. See *Young Worker*, 30 June 1933.

31 Kenneth Woodsworth to Don Sutherland, 10 Dec. 1936, and Sutherland to Woodsworth, 3 Dec. 1936, Canadian Youth Congress Collection, file 4, box 8, McMaster University Archives.

32 *Manitoban*, 7 Jan. 1938.

33 For a vivid description of the conference, see Armour McKay, "Canadian Students Draw Together at Winnipeg," *Saturday Night*, 15 Jan. 1938. See also *Gateway*, 7 Jan. 1938; *Ubyssey*, 7 Jan. 1938. See also Student Christian Movement Records, 84-2-6, United Church Archives, and the *Montreal Star*, 5 Jan. 1938;

interview with a Dalhousie delegate to the conference, Gene (Morison) Hicks, 12 Aug. 1983.

34 No precise figures are available, but my own rough estimate and one by a study for the Canadian Youth Commission are close. According to the latter, during the 1930s "perhaps not more than five per cent of the student body took part in discussions ... about the position their own nation should take in the coming world crisis." *Youth Speaks out on Citizenship* (Toronto: Ryerson Press 1948), 5.

35 Interview with Douglas Cherry, 11 July 1984; correspondence with Frank W. Park, 26 May 1986.

36 Dashan Singh was cited in *Ubyssey*, 8 Oct. 1937; similar message in a *Sheaf* editorial, 22 Oct. 1937.

37 Interview with Earle Beattie, 19 Dec. 1985; Gertrude Rutherford to Graduate Members and Friends, 14 Apr. 1931, University of Alberta, President's Papers, 1928–36, Student and Alumni Affairs, SCM: Correspondence, 3286-3, University of Alberta Archives; UWO *Gazette*, 11 Oct. 1935, 6 Mar. 1934. There are many other examples pointing to the political quiescence of most students, including the recollections of some 40 ex-students interviewed by the author. Interviews with Marjorie (Montgomery) Bowker (an ex–University of Alberta student), 7 July 1984, Gene (Morison) Hicks (Dalhousie), 12 Aug. 1983, and interview with Olga Volkhoff, transcript, University of British Columbia Archives.

38 See Paul Axelrod, "Moulding the Middle Class: Student Life at Dalhousie University in the 1930s," *Acadiensis* 15, no. 1 (Fall 1985): 86–94, which contains statistics on class backgrounds of students and interviews. Statistical analyses of the University of British Columbia, the University of Alberta, and the University of Toronto confirm these perceptions.

39 According to H.C. Cody, president of the University of Toronto, "At present the hard times are impelling students to work harder than ever at their regular studies, so that there seems to be little inclination to go into sporadic journalism": Cody to Arthur Currie, 17 Feb. 1933, Student Activities – *Alarm Clock*, 1927–33, RG2 c52, Principal's Papers, McGill University Archives. Carleton Stanley, president of Dalhousie, notes the same phenomenon: Axelrod, "Moulding the Middle Class," 99.

40 Correspondence with J. Kenneth Bradford, 10 Jan. 1986; interview with Marjorie Montgomery Bowker, 7 July 1984; *Manitoban*, 19 Oct. 1933. See also *Sheaf*, 12 Oct. 1933.

41 *Sheaf*, 21 Mar. 1935; *Varsity*, 11 Oct. 1935. On the shift towards Liberalism, see Thompson and Seager, *Canada, 1922–1939*, 331. There were complaints from students studying away from home who were eligible to vote about the lack of absentee voting rights.

42 *Manitoban*, 5 Oct. 1934, defends students against complaint by Professor W.H. Alexander, of the University of Alberta, that there was not enough radical thinking on campus. Everywhere, the social life of the campus predominated. See various institutional histories.

43 University of Western Ontario, *President's Report, 1930–31*, 22 (W. Sherwood Fox was the president).

44 *Globe*, 12, 19 Feb. 1929; *Varsity*, 3 Mar. 1931; Arthur Currie to Alec Edminson, 5 Jan. 1932, Principal's Papers, RG2 C52, Student Activities, McGill University Archives; Stanley B. Frost, *McGill University: For the Advancement of Learning*, vol. 2, 1895–1971 (Montreal: McGill-Queen's University Press 1984), 195; Principal's Papers RG2 C44, Fascism and Communism (February 1938), McGill University Archives; *McGill Daily*, 22 Feb. 1938 and subsequent issues; *Ubyssey*, 13, 18, 20 Feb. 1931; *Sheaf*, 10, 17 Nov. 1938; and Hayden, *Seeking a Balance: University of Saskatchewan*, 182–3; *New Republic* incident in *Globe and Mail*, 25 Jan. 1937, 4. The *Oasis* of the Ontario Agricultural College in Guelph was suspended in 1932 because of its "critical attitude" towards the college's faculty: University of Western Ontario *Gazette*, 4 Feb. 1932.

45 *Sheaf*, 3 Dec. 1937; *Manitoban*, 18 Jan. 1937; *Gateway*, 10 Feb. 1932, 10 Feb. 1933; *Vancouver Daily Province*, 16 Nov. 1937. One way around these bans was the formation of social-problems or political-science clubs, where students could discuss political ideas, supposedly free of partisan affiliation. See AMS Records, Clubs: Social Problems Club, 1938, folder no. 15-32, University of British Columbia Archives.

46 On the limits to academic freedom for Canadian professors, see a prevealing address by Sir Edward Beatty, "Freedom and the University," *Queen's Quarterly* 44, no. 4 (1937): 463–71. See also Michiel Horn, "Academic Freedom and the Canadian Professor," *CAUT Bulletin*, December 1982; and Frank Abbott, "Academic Freedom and Social Criticism in the 1930s," *Interchange* 15 no. 1 (1983–84): 107–23.

47 *Gateway*, 18 Nov. 1938; it also noted that there is "absolutely no such thing as complete freedom of the press. And perhaps, after all, it is just as well."

48 There are many examples of this, particularly related to the incidents described above. Student newspapers carried stories of censorship elsewhere in the country, usually defending the right of free speech. An amusing example was the *McGill Daily's* comment on the "atheism" controversy at the University of Toronto. It claimed that no one could charge that atheism was rampant at McGill because the university was a "theocracy" – the chancellor and vice-chancellor were "gods." *McGill Daily*, 1931, undated copy in Principal's Papers, RG2 C43, Socialism: Professors and the CCF, McGill University Archives.

49 In 1931 sixty-eight University of Toronto professors were widely criticized for publishing an open letter objecting to Toronto police harassment of "allegedly" communist meetings. Victoria College students purchased an advertisement in the student newspaper defending the right of professors to free speech: *Globe*, 22 Jan. 1931. See also Michiel Horn, "Free Speech within the Law: The Letter of Sixty-Eight Toronto Professors, 1931," *Ontario History* 72, no. 1 (March 1980): 35. In 1938 Carlyle King, a University of Saskatchewan professor, was defended by students after he was publicly attacked for making "anti-war" statements:

Hayden, *Seeking a Balance*, 183. In 1939 a group University of Toronto students supported Professor Frank Underhill following similarly critical comments: R. Douglas Francis, *Frank Underhill: Intellectual Provocateur* (Toronto: University of Toronto Press 1986), 113. The University of Toronto and McGill appear to have had the largest number of such incidents among Canadian universities.

50 Murray to P.J. Philpott, president, Saskatoon Branch of Canadian Legion of the BESC, 1 Nov. 1935, Presidential Papers: ser. 1, B.109, *Sheaf*, University of Saskatchewan Archives.

51 *McGill Daily*, 9 Nov. 1939, reports on such an event at the University of Alberta; *Dalhousie Gazette*, "Student Government History, #54," 6 Nov. 1975; Charles Johnston and John Weaver, "Founding a Collegiate Atmosphere; Traditions at the Crossroads: 1930–1939," in *Student Days*, (Hamilton: McMaster University Alumni Association 1986).

52 "Petition to the Board of Governors of the University, 2 March 1931," President's Papers, University of Alberta, 1928–36, General: Correspondence – Reports 3285-1, University of Alberta Archives; also interview with ex-student, John W. Chalmers, 4 July 1984. Boarding costs were rolled back from $30 to $27 a month.

53 *Ubyssey*, 16 Feb. 1932; *The Totem*, 1932, 85; interview with Volga Volkhoff, transcript in UBC Archives, who describes the publicity campaign as "extraordinary"; see also David C. Jones and Timothy A. Dunn, "All of Us Common People and Education in the Depression," *Canadian Journal of Education* 5, no. 4 (1980): 41–56.

54 University of Western Ontario, *Gazette*, 31 Mar., 6 Apr., 14 Apr. 1939.

55 Ibid., 14 Apr. 1939.

56 Interview with Douglas Cherry (left-wing student at the University of Saskatchewan), 11 July 1984, and with W.E. Mann, (University of Toronto), 17 Dec. 1985.

57 The Student Peace Movement was formed in 1931, then appeared to lapse, and was revived in 1935. On the 1931 petition, see the *Dalhousie Gazette*, 24, 31 Oct. 1931, and *Manitoban*, 5, 12 Jan. 1932. On the Student Peace Movement, see Canadian Youth Congress Collection, box 9, file 3, McMaster University Archives; interview with Kenneth Woodsworth, who recalled a strong YCL presence in the organization; *Manitoban*, 18 Feb. 1936; Charles M. Johnston, *McMaster University*, vol. 2, *The Early Years in Hamilton, 1930–1957* (Toronto: University of Toronto Press 1981), 75. For an overview of peace-movement activities that includes some reference to student involvement, see Thomas P. Socknat, *Witness against War: Pacifism in Canada 1900–1945* (Toronto: University of Toronto Press 1987), espec. 153–7.

58 Cited in Eagan, *Class, Culture and the Classroom*, 58–9. The first "strike" occurred on 13 Apr. 1934, when thousands of students walked out of class for an hour. Possibly the largest was in 1936, when up to five hundred thousand students joined peace demonstrations. Historical estimates of the sizes vary. See

Eagen, *Class, Culture and the Classroom*, 135; James Weschler, *Revolt on Campus* (Washington: University of Washington Press 1973), 171; Brax, *The First Student Movement*, 40; Hal Draper, "The Student Movement of the Thirties: A Political History," in Rita James Simon, ed., *As We Saw the Thirties: Essays on Social and Political Movements of a Decade* (Chicago: University of Illinois Press 1967), 169–71.

59 *Gateway*, 7 Dec. 1934. See also *Ubyssey*, 4 Dec. 1934; UWO *Gazette*, 23 Nov. 1934; *Sheaf*, 30 Nov. 1934.

60 *McGill Daily*, 15 Dec. 1936; *Dalhousie Gazette*, 10, 17 Oct. 1935. Other peace activities included a conference sponsored by the Quebec Student Peace Movement in November 1935: Principal's Papers, RG2 C52, Student Activities: General, McGill University Archives; and a "peace hour" on a number of campuses in March 1936: *Manitoban*, 4 Mar. 1936. A "counter" Remembrance Day demonstration was planned by the Student Christian Movement at the University of Toronto in 1935: *Varsity*, 14 Oct. 1935.

61 Reid, *Mount Allison University*, 2: 151–2; *Dalhousie Gazette*, 2 Oct. 1936; *Sheaf*, 25 Nov. 1938.

62 *Dalhousie Gazette*, 2 Nov. 1933; *L'Hebdo Laval*, 6 Mar. 1936 (trans. P. Axelrod).

63 *Vancouver Sun*, 16 Feb. 1934; *Gateway*, 9 Feb. 1934; on Arcand, *McGill Daily*, 11 Feb. 1937. Arcand, who headed the National Social Christian Party, seemed to temper his comments when he spoke at McGill, giving "a polished and well delivered speech," according to the *Daily*. For material on fascism in Canada, in which there is very little discussion of the role played by university students in these organizations, see Lita-Rose Betcherman, *The Swastika and the Maple Leaf: Fascist Movements in Canada in the Thirties* (Toronto: Fitzhenry and Whiteside 1975); Jonathan Wagner, *Brothers Beyond: National Socialism in Canada* (Waterloo, Ont.: Wilfrid Laurier University Press 1981); Fred Rose, *Fascism over Canada: An Exposé* (Toronto: New Era Publications 1938).

64 Montreal *Gazette*, 23, 24, 26, 27 Oct. 1936; *McGill Daily*, 23, 26 Oct. 1936; University of Western Ontario *Gazette*, 26 Oct. 1936. There were also reports of a demonstration several days earlier, consisting of some four hundred people, most of whom where thought to be Université de Montréal students, who marched through the streets and attacked the offices of a building housing a Communist bookstore. *McGill Daily*, 15 Oct. 1936.

65 Cited in Frank Scott, "The Nineteen Thirties in the United States and Canada," in Victor Hoar, ed., *The Great Depression: Essays and Memoirs from Canada and the United States* (Toronto: Copp Clark 1969), 184–5.

66 McGill University, the University of Manitoba, and the University of Alberta all put restrictions on the numbers of Jews they would admit, particularly to professional programs. Jewish (and non-white) students were excluded from many campus fraternities. See Axelrod, "Moulding the Middle Class," 109–10. Vicious anti-Semitic slogans are found on a poster reprinted in a pamphlet called "Com-

munauté juive," 18 Oct. 1932, fonds D35 107, Archives, Université de Montréal. For other examples of anti-Semitism in Quebec and elsewhere, see David Rome, *Clouds in the Thirties: On Anti-Semitism in Canada, 1929–1939*; section 7 (Montreal: Canadian Jewish Congress, 1979), 36–55.

67 Betcherman, *The Swastika and the Maple Leaf*, 34–7; Andrée Lévesque, *Virage à gauche interdit: les communistes, les socialistes et leurs ennemis au Québec, 1929–1939* (Montréal: Boréal Express 1984), 127–30; Lucienne Fortin, "Les Jeunes-Canada," in F. Dumont, J. Hamelin, J.P. Montminy, eds., *Idéologies au Canada français, 1930–1939* (Québec: Les Presses de l'Université Laval 1978), 215–33; Denis Chouinard, "Des contestataires pragmatiques: les Jeune-Canada, 1932–1938", *Revue d'histoire de l'amérique française* 40, no. 1 (été 1986): 5–28; Mason Wade, *The French Canadians: 1760–1967*, vol. 2 (Toronto: Macmillan 1968), 901–3.

68 The Young Communist League published *l'Ouvrier canadien* and had a small following among French Canadians. See Lévesque, *Virage à gauche interdit*, for a detailed discussion of Communist and socialist activity in Quebec during the 1930s. See also Norman Penner, *The Canadian Left: A Critical Analysis* (Toronto: Prentice-Hall 1977), 108–13.

69 F.R. Scott, "Freedom of Speech in Canada," offprint of paper from the Papers and Proceedings of the Canadian Political Science Association, V (1933): 187.

70 Michael Behiels, "Le père Georges-Henri Lévesque et l'établissement des sciences sociales à Laval, 1938–1955," *Revue de l'Université d'Ottawa* 52, no. 3 (1982): 355–76, and translation of this article in this volume.

71 An examination of student newspapers and archival records at Laval, Université de Montréal, and a variety of English Canadian universities cited in this article shows great similarities in the extra-curricular and social activities of students throughout Canada.

72 Montreal *Gazette*, 24 Oct. 1936; *McGill Daily*, 3 Nov. 1936.

73 According to the Dominion censor's "Regulations", "any adverse or unfavourable statements, report or opinion likely to prejudice the defence of Canada or the efficient prosecution of the war ... or to interfere with the success of His Majesty's forces" was prohibited; cited in *Sheaf*, 29 Sept. 1939.

74 The program of Le Bloc Universitaire is published in *l'Hebdo Laval*, 10 Nov. 1939 (trans. P. Axelrod). See also *Le Quartier Latin*, "Nous voulons la paix," 28 Apr. 1939. According to a report in the *Ubyssey* (12 Jan. 1940), 35 of the 185 students attending the CSA conference were French Canadians.

75 Canadian Student Assembly, conference report to delegates, 9 Jan. 1940, CSIS Files. By contrast, NFCUS, which held a conference at the same time as the CSA, "pledged student support to the Canadian government during the present period of national emergency." *Ubyssey*, 16 Jan. 1940.

76 CSA, conference report to delegates, 9 Jan. 1940, CSIS Files.

77 Cited in *Ubyssey*, 16 Jan. 1940. See also Reid, *Mount Allison*, 2: 153–4. Faculty members were involved in the conference as resource leaders.

78 CSA, conference report to delegates, 9 Jan. 1940, CSIS Files.
79 The following questions were included: "Should compulsory service of manpower be introduced?"; "Indicate where you believe freedom of speech, press, pulpit, radio, assembly and association should be restricted as at present under the Defence of Canada Regulations"; "Do you believe that Government measures such as the Excess Profits Tax and the Price Control Board have prevented profiteering?"; "Do you believe that it is fair that youth with army rejection slips should be given preference for jobs in industry and for relief?" *Queen's Journal*, 9 Feb. 1940, cited in Gibson, *"To Serve,"* 455.
80 *Montreal Gazette*, 7 Feb. 1940. The CSA attempted to put the events in a less dramatic light in its newsletter, no. 2, 27 Feb. 1940. The McGill episode was followed closely by the RCMP: C.W. Harrison to the Commissioner, 21 Feb. 1940, CSIS Files.
81 *Ubyssey*, 9 Feb. 1940. Dalhousie, Mount Allison, the University of British Columbia, the University of Saskatchewan, the University of Alberta, and Queen's all withdrew, though small groups of students attempted to carry on with "independent assemblies" on some of these campuses. See CSA Newsletter, no. 2, 27 Feb. 1940, CSIS Files.
82 Laval students opposed conscription 2,673 to 8, as did Université de Montréal students, 935 to 35: *Le Quartier Latin*, 15 Mar. 1940.
83 The University of Manitoba voted on the questionnaire and solidly opposed conscription, 773 to 227: *Winnipeg Free Press*, 2 Mar. 1940, cited in CSIS Files. The University of Toronto also held the survey, CSA Newsletter, no. 2, 27 Feb. 1940. Among others, the University of British Columbia, Alberta, Queen's, and Mount Allison did not distribute it: various CSIS Files.
84 V.A.M. Kemp, Supt Comgd "O" Division, to the Commissioner, RCMP, 26 Jan. 1940, CSIS Files.
85 V.A.M. Kemp to the Commisioner, RCMP, 8 Mar. 1940, CSIS Files.
86 H.A.R. Gagnon to the Commissioner, 15 Feb. 1940, CSIS Files.
87 Kemp to the Commissioner, 26 Jan. 1940, CSIS Files.
88 Kemp to the Commissioner, 8 Apr. 1940; E.F. Kush to Sgt Leopold, 12 Apr. 1940, CSIS Files. The CSA issued defensive public statements that included supportive comments from several faculty resource leaders present at the 1939 conference, including Arthur Lower, who criticized C.A. Krug from Mount Allison for his "colonial sentiment" and whom he accused of taking refuge "in the weakest of all defenses, name calling, [dragging] out a singularly weather-beaten bogey to frighten people with, to wit, communism"; cited in the *Manitoban*, 9 Feb. 1940. The Canadian Youth Congress was declared an "unlawful organization" during the war. See Reg Whitaker, "Official Repression of Communism During World War II," *Labour / Le Travail*, 17 (Spring 1986): 143.
89 Reid, *Mount Allison*, 2: 153; W.A. Kerr to Norman Rogers, minister of National Defence, 5 Oct. 1939, President's Papers, 1936–42, 3388-1, Military: General Correspondence, University of Alberta Archives; University of Manitoba, *Brown*

and Gold 1940, 60; *Report of the President of the University of British Columbia for the year ending 31 Aug. 1940*, 56–62, University of British Columbia Archives; University of Western Ontario *Gazette*, 13 Oct. 1939, cited increased COTC enlistments around the country, including a total of 1,500 at the University of Toronto. See also in Gibson, *"To Serve,"* where some 842 students had joined the COTC by November 1939 (181); for McGill situation, see Frost, *McGill University*, 2: 218–19.

90 Such students posed special problems for university authorities because males exempted from war service because of their status as students were not officially entitled to refuse COTC training as conscientious objectors; see Hayden, *Seeking a Balance*, 184; Johnston, *McMaster University*, 2: 90.

91 C.P. Tracy to Dr Kerr, 8 Nov. 1940, President's Papers, 1936–42, University of Alberta, 3388-1, Military: General Correspondence, University of Alberta Archives.

92 Discipline folder, UA 20, President's Papers, box 25, fd. 11, ca Mar. 1941, University of Manitoba Archives.

93 *McGill Daily*, 2 Nov. 1939. For accounts of patriotic campus activities see Frost, *McGill University*, 2: 216–29; Gibson, *"To Serve,"* chap. 8; Reid, *Mount Allison*, 2: 152–9; Johnston, *McMaster University*, 2: chap. 3.

94 While there has been a tendency to overstate the degree of student activism in Britain and the United States, it is likely that a larger proportion of students in those countries participated in the student movement than in Canada. The proximity of British universities to European hostilities, including the martyrdom of a Cambridge student in the Spanish Civil War, gave a particular urgency to student politics there. In the United States student activism was especially evident in universities such as City College of New York, which drew its students from poor, immigrant, and working-class families, less hostile to socialist or communist ideology than middle-class Anglo-Saxon Protestant Canadian or French Canadian Catholic families. Canadian universities enrolled both a narrower range of students with respect to class origins and a smaller proportion of college-aged youth in total. In addition, the Communist Party was at the centre instead of on the fringes of the American student movement. From 1932 to 1935 the Communist-led National Student League and the socialist League for Industrial Democracy were the most important national student organizations. In 1935 they united in the American Student Union, in which Communist influence was especially strong. For reasons that have not been adequately explained, the ASU, with a maximum of twenty thousand student members, was able to organize the massive student "strikes" for peace in the mid-thirties. Still, the mood on American campuses was far from militant. Two contemporary studies – Maxine Davis, *The Lost Generation: A Portrait of American Youth Today* (New York: Macmillan 1936), and "Youth in College," *Fortune Magazine*, June 1936 – concluded that the degree of political awareness and activism on American campuses had been widely exaggerated by the media. In addition to the sources cited in nn 1 and 58, see Victor

Kiernan, "Herbert Norman's Cambridge," in Roger W. Bowen, ed., *E.H. Norman: His Life and Scholarship* (Toronto: University of Toronto Press 1984), 27–45; H.S. Ferns, *Reading from Left to Right: One Man's Political History* (Toronto: University of Toronto Press 1983), chap. 2–5; and Irving Howe, *A Margin of Hope: An Intellectual Biography* (New York: Harcourt Brace Jovanovich 1982), 63–73.

95 On the SCM, see Beattie, *SCM*, 23–5; NFCUS suspended activities in 1940 but was revived in 1944. It became the Canadian Union of Students in 1963 and played a leading role in the student movement of that decade, but dissolved in 1969. On the Communist Party, see *Canada's Party of Socialism*, 140–1.

CHAPTER ELEVEN

"In Pursuit of Human Values (or Laugh When You Say That)": The Student Critique of the Arts Curriculum in the 1960s

Patricia Jasen

The first part of this essay's title is taken from a collection of epigrams that are sprinkled, McLuhan style, through a book about student protest published in Canada in 1968.[1] The juxtaposition of academic cliché and flippant dismissal expressed the student activists' conviction that a deep gulf separated the rhetoric and the reality of liberal-arts education in the universities of English Canada. For decades, administrators and professors had spoken of the importance of the arts curriculum in making society more humane. This was accomplished, they said, by passing on, to greater and greater numbers of students, the cherished "values" of the Western cultural tradition. Graduates of arts courses should possess heightened powers of imagination, reason, moral sensitivity, and good taste, and be ready to assume the practical duties of citizenship as leaders in government and the business world.[2] Such claims concerning the spiritual and financial rewards of an arts education became more insistent than ever during the period of feverish fund-raising and university expansion in the 1950s and 1960s, but when the advantages of a sojourn in the overcrowded multiversities failed to correspond to this ideal, many students felt betrayed. One of their main grievances was that the arts curriculum seemed to have little to do with human values and ignored the most fundamental questions about the quality of life in the Western world. From the point of view of activists on the left, the university merely contributed to society's problems by suppressing, rather than encouraging, free inquiry and genuine social change.

The analysis that follows is based upon two premises. First, it assumes that the radical student critique of the arts faculties, despite its excesses, developed in response to circumstances that were real and that discontent among ordinary students was pervasive and in many cases legitimate. Some of the problems, such as the mass-teaching techniques that facilitated expansion, were new, but others, including the confusion of educational aims that beset arts faculties, were decades old. Even though the movement itself engaged only a minority, a much larger proportion of students – less aggressive perhaps, or ambivalent about the style or ideology of activist politics – were deeply dissatisfied with the university but did not engage in student protest. Whatever the reason for the outward passivity of the average student, enough of them sympathized with at least some of the movement's complaints to vote radicals into power on many campuses.[3]

Secondly, this essay treats curricular issues as a major area of student discontent. So far, university histories have downplayed the significance of the classroom experience in arousing student disaffection, as have histories of the movement itself. For example, Cyril Levitt's recent study of student activism, entitled *Children of Privilege*, virtually ignores the content and method of instruction as a target of radical criticism, although his work illuminates other important aspects of the Canadian movement.[4] Evidence from the period itself shows that this neglect is unwarranted. Canadian Union of Students leader Steven Langdon acknowledged in 1968 that course content "may be the crucial issue" and that one of the most important goals of "student power" was to achieve "a more humane, critical, and socially responsible curriculum."[5] Students found fault with many characteristics of the arts curriculum, including the rigidity of the boundaries between the disciplines, the preoccupation with "value-free" empiricism in the social sciences, the prevalence of American course content and the lack of Canadian material, and the omission of major areas of human experience, including working-class history. As the New Left Caucus of the Toronto Student Movement put it, "The smorgasbord of irrelevances that constitute the staples of the general arts course is at the heart of student discontent."[6]

A study of the radical critique of the arts curriculum helps to illuminate the underlying conservatism of the student movement. In many instances students were reacting against the intellectual chaos that years of unregulated curricular expansion had produced. Their protest was as much a call for order, albeit a new order, as it was a demand for greater freedom or "power" in curricular decision-making. An educational policy of laissez-faire was, according to their ideological position and their experience as students, the source of much of what was wrong with the modern university.

During the 1950s far more Canadians came to believe in the importance of higher learning than ever had before. This was partly because of an intensive public-relations campaign conducted by the universities and government to justify the enormous expansion in the university system, which was intended to accommodate the post-war "baby-boom" generation of students. All industrialized nations experienced a similar trend, and the notion that higher education was essential to a nation's prosperity and well-being became the accepted wisdom. The 1950s and 1960s was the era of the "human-capital theory," according to which a high monetary value should be placed on the skills and knowledge possessed by well-educated persons.[7] Both government and the private sector assumed that the gross national product would increase in proportion to the country's investment in higher learning. This theory did not apply only to vocational training, for, as Paul Axelrod has shown, employers in business and industry saw the arts degree as the ideal preparation for life in the corporate world. They had become convinced that graduates who possessed a broad understanding of society and who could "think," solve problems imaginatively, and communicate effectively would have the greatest potential as employees.[8]

Faith in the value of study of the arts owed something to the Cold War atmosphere of the period as well. Since the Second World War advocates of liberal education had put forward the theory that the arts curriculum – conceived as an immersion in the values embodied in the Western tradition – was a powerful agent in the protection of our way of life against communism. As the Massey Commissioners (who recommended the first federal operating grants to universities and the creation of a Canada Council) warned, "Our military defences must be made secure, but our cultural defences equally demand attention; the two cannot be separated."[9] Initially, some Canadian educators spoke as if liberal education existed only in the free world, claiming that the Russians were interested merely in the technical expertise through which they could achieve world domination.[10] But it soon became apparent that the enemy did, in fact, place a good deal of emphasis on cultural studies, and North American universities in the Sputnik era felt obliged to compete with Russia in this as in every other area of education. By the end of the 1950s knowledge of all kinds was equated, quite simply, with power.[11]

Liberal education was not only associated with holding our own against communism but with the more idealistic search for a means to end the Cold War and the arms race. "A new weapon will not bring peaceful relations," wrote President MacKenzie of the University of British Columbia in 1957; "a new philosophy or a new understanding of past conflicts may."[12] There were several reasons why the liberal arts were said to be the arts of peace. The use of the atomic bomb and the subsequent obsession with making bigger and deadlier weapons suggested to many that our "technical progress has outstripped mankind's moral and political development," and they hoped that the traditional "values" found in literature, philosophy, and history, combined with the grasp of contemporary problems offered by the social sciences, would guide people to a wiser use of scientific knowledge.[13] The liberal arts also offered the means to a more sensitive and accurate understanding of people in distant places, and could show the way to more fruitful diplomatic relations. And, most importantly, the arts graduate was widely believed to possess the qualities required for sound leadership in a divided world, such as empathy, integrity, a sense of perspective, and the ability "to see life steadily and see it whole."[14]

Throughout this period the notion that higher education was, by definition, financially and spiritually rewarding for both the individual and society at large was popularized by government, the press, the universities, and high-school counselling services; and if many students entering faculties of arts in the early to mid-1960s had at least a vague sense of being special people embarking on a special mission, they can be forgiven a certain naïveté. The irony was that there were tens of thousands of young people heading in the same direction, for as long as minimal requirements were met, all high-school graduates could find a place in the rapidly expanding university system. For middle-class youth in particular a degree was increasingly re-garded as both a prerequisite for future success and a guarantee that a selection of well-paying and responsible jobs would be waiting upon grad-uation.[15] If, for some individuals, the security of a job mattered less than the non-material rewards of higher learning, they could at least look forward to a three- or four-year retreat to a "community of scholars" devoted, they had been told, to free intellectual inquiry, self-discovery, and the search for ways to make "human values" manifest in a troubled world.

The expectations were high, and the universities were not prepared to deliver. Much of that story has been told elsewhere. Levitt describes the shock experienced by students who found themselves adrift in huge mul-tiversities that bore little resemblance to the intimate scholarly communities they had expected to find. Universities had grown and multiplied to meet the educational needs of the baby-boom generation *and* the dictates of the human-capital theory. But in the process they had been transformed from elite (in the sense of serving a small minority of the population, who would be distinguished by their degrees) to mass institutions. Anonymity and as-sembly-line educational techniques, including huge classes; the novice lec-turer, teaching assistant, or closed-circuit television screen as instructor; computerized testing and the bell curve – all were now the regular fare of undergraduates in arts. "Students who had been expecting a first-class pas-sage on a luxury-liner," says Levitt, "soon discovered that they were second-class passengers on a tramp steamer."[16] He believes that students mainly experienced "anticipatory alienation"; that is, they realized that the imper-sonal university was merely a prototype of the huge firms or government bureaucracies in which they would eventually find themselves employed – not as leaders, for there were far too many of them, but as members of a huge "new working class" of intellectual labourers.[17] Levitt may overplay this point; although there are student writings from the period that bear out the idea that some arts students rebelled against their own diminished job expectations, there is ample evidence to show that the alienation was not primarily anticipatory but was experienced with immediacy and a genuine sense of frustration directed at the kind of education they were receiving.

Throughout the years of unrest students complained constantly of dull teaching, as students will, but also of poorly prepared instructors, of lectures that "emerge almost completely from a text book," and of professors with no time to treat students as individuals. "We ... protest the impersonality of the university to a point where the statement seems trite," wrote a political-science student at the University of British Columbia in 1968,[18] but given the confusion that reigned on many burgeoning campuses, the charge was frequently justified. A large proportion of arts professors were freshly hired, many with dissertations still to be written,[19] and they were suddenly faced with new courses to teach to classes of two hundred or more. Some established scholars also neglected students because far more emphasis than ever was being placed on the maxim that "teaching is not enough," and many professors were taking advantage of generous new research funds to finance the scholarly work that would build their professional reputations.[20] The paradox, of course, was that while research would eventually lead to better teaching in the various disciplines, as one observer put it, "the strategies of scholarship" were not necessarily "the same as those of education."[21] Many arts students found that professors seemed to avoid contact with them and suspected that it was partly because they took up "time needed for learned articles and books."[22] Some of them realized that, although their own success depended solely on achievement within the university, their professors' careers were built on reputations made nationally or internationally within their specific disciplines. Thus it was relatively easy for the undergraduate to conclude, as Sol Stern said of Berkeley, that "of all the functions of the Great University his own education is perhaps the least important."[23]

Another characteristic of the modern university that drew criticism from students was its service-station role – in other words, its willingness to let the short-term economic and social goals of governments and private enterprise influence both the content and the atmosphere of higher learning. "We are confused by the inconsistencies of principles in our universities which degrade them and their position in society," wrote a student at the University of Victoria. "We are told that the pursuit of knowledge should be free, yet in practice we are given the opportunity to learn only certain things. We are told that the pursuit of knowledge and the betterment of men are our prime goals, yet our education is determined to a large extent by demands of the economy and job expectations."[24] This issue too had antecedents deep in the past. Ever since the late nineteenth century, when universities began to undertake professional training and applied research on a large scale, critics had protested that they had forsaken their role of intellectual leadership and – in exchange for public and corporate funding – had become tools of government and industry.[25] University administrators, meanwhile, had exalted public service as their highest duty, while still trying to maintain their commitment to disinterested scholarship.[26] Also controversial was the fact that their obligations to business and the state motivated universities to restrict freedom of political expression among students and faculty, a policy that helped to precipitate a student strike in the 1890s at Toronto and led to some highly publicized abuses of "academic freedom" during the 1930s.[27] Widespread student condemnation of the universities' complex service role did not surface until the 1960s, however, when a "New Left" interpretation of the issue gained currency.

The international movement known as the New Left began in the 1950s as a reaction against the corruption of socialist ideals manifest in the "old left" (especially in Soviet-style communism) and against the conservatism of post-war policies in the West. Marxism, existentialism, and anarchism were among the "isms" which contributed to the ideological eclecticism of the New Left. It was essentially a youth movement, although it gained much of its inspiration from such aging intellectuals as Herbert Marcuse. It embraced many causes and passed through several phases. In Canada, it originated with the peace movement but was deeply affected by the American civil-rights cause, so that by the 1960s the plight of minorities and the poor was a primary concern. The war in Vietnam, though not "our" war, fuelled the movement's growth in the second half of the decade and contributed to a complex vision of Canada as both a partner in and a victim of American imperialism.[28]

Canadian students had participated in left-wing movements before, most notably in the 1930s, but had neither focused their criticism upon the university itself nor developed a Marxist critique of the relationship between the university and society.[29] During the 1960s, however, the accumulating sense of unease that had previously been expressed by only a small minority of intellectuals burst forth in a massive assault from the left upon the university's role as a servant of government and industry. Like everyone else, the radicals believed that knowledge was power, and from their point of view the university had become a co-conspirator in its misuse. Known instances of co-operation in policies opposed by the left, such as the military's use of academics or the universities' investments in South Africa, were used to discredit these institutions as a whole, as were the many ways in which the universities seemed to be merely "servicing the capitalist system" while failing to speak out against its injustices. Poverty, pollution, the Vietnam war, American domination of the Canadian economy – all these sources of discontent now seemed to implicate the university, which was described as a mere arm of a huge "military industrial complex." As the student movement saw it, by selling out to the class that controlled society for its own self-interest, the universities made a mockery of their much-advertised commitment to human values. The movement was divided, and many students were divided in their own minds, over whether the university was capable of being reformed before society itself underwent some form of revolutionary change. "The class which has the means of material production at its disposal," a writer called "D" reminded readers of the *Canadian Forum*, "has control at the same time over the means of mental production."[30]

Marxist terminology was readily applied by student radicals in their interpretation of the mass teaching techniques and methods of administration they encountered in the multiversities. Institutions of higher learning were seen as "extensions of the marketplace" – as factories that produced graduates moulded to the specifications of the job market.[31] The metaphor frequently took another form, and the student was described not as the product but as the worker producing a commodity, namely, knowledge. The point remained, however, as Jon Bordo said, that "it is the outside society which defines the ends of the University and its uses of knowledge production."[32] Another critic wrote that "the learning environment, the acquisition of skills, the setting of the curriculum are not determined by the university. The price the university has paid for becoming attached is that on all these life and death matters it stands in much the same relationship to market liberalism as does the student: both are subordinate and passive parts of the whole."[33]

Activists felt that they had a duty to try to make the university uphold the ideals and values that their elders had praised but were unwilling to put into practice. They accused the older generation of hypocrisy and were profoundly distrustful of adult and institutional authority per se, preferring to trust their own impulses rather than the accumulated wisdom of those who had, in their view, made a vast mess of the world in the name of progress and human betterment. The attack upon adult authority often reeked of piety, but given the tenor of the rhetoric that had been used to exalt higher education during the fifties and sixties, the criticism was sometimes unanswerable. As a veteran of the American movement put it: "You have given us our visions and then asked us to curb them. You have offered us dreams and then urged us to abandon them ... We have been asking for no more than what you have taught us is right. We can't understand why you have been so offended."[34] By nurturing the idea that the university was the single most important institution in securing the welfare of the nation, the earlier generation had fostered a conviction that the university must be forced to live up to its proclaimed humanistic ideals. It had also encouraged among students an exaggerated perception of their own political influence. If the university possessed so much power, a *Canadian Forum* writer suggested, it followed that students who could capture control of such institutions would "possess a lever that can move society. The megalomania that creates the multiversity also creates those who seek to destroy it."[35]

All the issues discussed above had a direct bearing on the students' critique of the arts curriculum. They argued that the course of study had little to do with human values and was geared instead to training them for jobs they did not want, that it prepared them to be passive workers and consumers instead of politically active citizens, that it reflected the research interests of professors rather than the educational needs of students, and that its content was distorted by the assumptions of the capitalist system. A sympathetic *Toronto Star* editorial observed that "Our children are growing up in a world where there are thousands of atom bombs, where our lakes and rivers are polluted, where the rich get richer and the poor get poorer, where there is a massive population explosion, and we're not saying anything about it in our courses."[36] An umbrella term used to encompass all such alleged defects in the arts curriculum was "irrelevance." The demand for a relevant course of study did not begin with the student movement,[37] but it was such an important aspect of the student activists' platform that its several meanings and implications deserve a close examination.

Relevance, of course, is in the eye of the beholder, and there was an element of self-contradiction in the arguments of both the proponents and the critics of the concept of relevance. For their part students became impatient with their opponents, who insisted upon seeing the university as a place of disinterested scholarship ("in this world but not of it," as the saying went) and who felt that a socially or politically active role for such institutions was a violation of principle. Activists held that the university's long commitment to public service had already contradicted that ideal.[38] Furthermore, the university had proclaimed throughout the fifties and sixties that its mission was to create leaders who would change the world for the better, and the activists demanded that it live up to that ideal. As things stood, the arts curriculum seemed to fall far short of equipping students for a life of effective social action. That goal could only be achieved, they said, if the student were taught how society *really* worked, so that he could "come to grips with his environment" and transform it.[39]

But while student activists objected to courses that appeared to have been designed to meet the needs of outside agencies, some of them insisted that the curriculum must be responsive to the problems they considered important. This caused academics and others who believed in that vague but very useful notion of the "liberal university," in which the interests of scholarship are supposed to determine the course of study, to fear that students merely wanted to replace traditional subjects and approaches with their own, politically oriented topics of interest, which would be taught from a left-wing point of view. "On every Canadian campus the issue of the curriculum has been raised," George Woodcock told readers of *Saturday Night*, "and the authoritarian activists – like Nazi student activists – have demanded that courses be relevant to contemporary issues, i.e., shaped to fit their own socio-political views. They are in practice hostile to academic freedom, brothers-under-the-skin of the John Birchers who demand that nothing radical should be taught."[40] While Woodcock used the model of fascism to explain the excesses of the student movement, Northrop Frye compared the activists to nineteenth-century anarchists because of their rejection of established authority and order – both on the part of the university itself and within the disciplines they studied. He observed that student demands for relevance "tend to minimize continuity ... in learning, and to emphasize the discontinuous experience of teach-in, sit-in, confrontation and conversation."[41] It was not, in Frye's view, the students' right to disturb the order and hierarchy of knowledge that was handed down to them in the arts curriculum through their insistence that simplistic criteria of relevance be applied.

The student movement was, in fact, often interpreted as an assault upon the past. Frye and other critics feared that the student movement, by equating the contemporary with the relevant, wished to sever the present from the past and thus disrupt the continuity that was the essence of "the Western cultural experience." It was true that many activists rejected the notion that traditional Western values had created the best of all possible worlds. (These values were seldom defined in the institutional rhetoric of higher education, but radicals tended to associate "the West" with the Protestant work ethic, a preoccupation with economic growth and territorial expansion, assumptions about racial superiority, and so on.) Judging the past by the world it had produced, some students questioned the quality of their cultural inheritance. The Canadian Union of Students in 1969 recognized that a main function of the university was to pass on "to the young the wisdom, culture, myths, values, and the technical skills of the parent society," but added that "it is our view that the present social system in Canada is economically and socially irrational and inhuman."[42]

And yet, as far as the arts curriculum was concerned, it was frequently not the value of the past but the uses to which the past was put that were really being disputed. A common complaint was that students were exposed to a carefully edited version of Western history and culture so that they would be imbued with a standard vision of human progress. Such an attitude on the part of students foreshadowed a future change in outlook in the academic world itself, where many scholars would eventually decide that the study of "Western civilization" had, in fact, long been used as "a rite of initiation for freshmen into a civic religion of the Western world."[43] A portion of the literature of the student movement was devoted to the discussion of those aspects of historical reality that arts courses tended to overlook; in addition, student polemics often used a historical approach to expose the roots of current social and economic problems.[44]

For some students, however, relevance had less to do with drawing connections between education and "the real world" than with the creation of courses that would allow them to explore private worlds of their own. "The primary concern of students today is establishing self-identity," wrote Bruce Campbell in the University of Toronto *Varsity*, and, as Lawrence Veysey says, the tendency during the sixties to see arts courses as "therapy" could lead to the assumption that "the aim of education is to study oneself more than anything else."[45] Again, several influences and factors were involved. This outlook derived in part from the movement's links with the counterculture philosophy of personal liberation or "doing your own thing," and also from the vogue for Eastern religious practices such as transcendental meditation. In addition, the belief that "one's own views are necessarily valid," as one irritated professor of English put it,[46] reflected the students' mistrust of university authority and their feeling that prescribed course material was automatically suspect because it was the product of someone else's vested interests.

But one also needs to recognize that there were fewer institutionalized ways of "studying oneself" or pursuing areas of deep personal concern than are available in many universities today. There were virtually no independent-study courses, little in the curriculum that dealt with such topics as third-world problems, non-Western religions, radical political movements, or working-class and aboriginal peoples; there were no women's-studies programs; scant attention was paid to Canadian literature; and there was a shortage of Canadian courses generally. Critics of the movement were capable of seizing upon the less substantial of student complaints about the curriculum while overlooking the fact that the call for relevance arose in the first place because a liberal education seemed to overlook so much that was central to human experience.

A closer look at a few of the disciplines that came under fire from the student movement may shed more light on the complex relationship among the call for relevance, New Left politics, and the nature of the arts curriculum in the 1960s. The teaching of Canadian history, for example, drew criticism because it ignored the study of those groups with traditionally low status in Canadian society, including the working classes, women, native Indians, and minority ethnic groups. There could be no doubt that social and cultural history as a whole had been neglected for decades while historians concentrated instead on the study of political, imperial, and economic policies.[47] During the late 1960s the profession itself was just beginning to acknowledge its deficiencies. Ramsay Cook told the Royal Society of Canada in 1967 that "the overriding emphasis on nation and national unity has obscured the ways in which Canada is divided into section, class and ethnic group ...

Our history has been very much the history of the 'ruling classes,' while labour history has been almost totally ignored ... As for ethnic history, it is in its infancy in Canada."[48]

To Marxists in the student movement such omissions had great political significance. Student leader Bob Baldwin charged that the way history was taught gave students "a false consciousness" by concentrating on the study of "kings and princes, of glorified wars, of capitalist entrepreneurs, imperialist exploiters and murderers."[49] Students remained ignorant of the experiences of ordinary people because, as Danny Drache wrote, "the Canadian proletariat is a faceless entity" in the mind of the "bourgeois historian." In his view this neglect had implications for the progress of the movement itself, for until there was a comprehensive analysis of the evolution of social class in this country, Marxism would be "without a foundation." He and his colleagues believed that the uncovering of "that part of Canadian history and the national consciousness which has been submerged is a political act of enormous consequence."[50]

In the subject of history, nevertheless, the study of Canada occupied a healthy share of the curriculum. In other disciplines the quest for relevance was motivated in part by the students' frustration at how little they learned about their own country and culture. Canadian literature, for example, had been taught on a regular basis by only a few departments of English before the 1960s, and offerings were still scant, even in comparison to the number of American literature courses that were available.[51] Similarly, at almost all English-speaking universities French was studied solely as a European language,[52] which provided students with little incentive even to attempt to understand or appreciate the culture of Quebec, which was undergoing a renaissance during that decade. In the social sciences the neglect of Canadian topics was pervasive. Sociology and anthropology, and, to a large extent, economics and political science, were dominated by American theory and content, and Canadian systems, institutions, and problems received little attention.[53]

The reasons why Canadian liberal-arts students were unable to study their own culture and society were numerous. The humanities had long been dominated by the idea that their mission was to expose students to "the best that has been thought and said" – according to British or American standards – and Canadian works seldom gained admission to that canon. A.S.P. Woodhouse, head of the English Department at Toronto for many years, had expressed a common sentiment when he observed that "it is not easy to have first-class criticism of a literature which is, with a few honorable exceptions, unmistakably second-rate."[54] Universities in this country had also traditionally preferred to hire Englishmen to teach English and Frenchmen to teach French,[55] and most of these newcomers had little interest in the literature of their adopted land. In the social sciences, course content was strongly influenced by the more rapid development of these disciplines in the United States. Throughout the twentieth century Americans had conducted research, developed bodies of theory, written texts, and trained graduate students, while Canada, with more limited resources, lagged far behind.[56] When the universities entered their period of expansion in the late 1950s, Canada had to import the vast majority of its new social scientists, along with large numbers of professors in virtually every other arts discipline. It was estimated that in 1968 over 80 per cent of new appointments went to non-Canadians, and it was not unheard of for Canadians to constitute less than 10 per cent of the staff of a social-science department, especially in a newer university.[57]

The effect of such trends on the discipline of sociology was particularly striking and drew much criticism from the student movement. Because a majority of American-born professors had at that time no intention of remaining in Canada or becoming Canadian citizens, their choice of research topics was guided by the American academic market.[58] The content of their lectures was similarly foreign in emphasis, and the use of American textbooks was taken for granted. Campus radicals could support their claim that students were encouraged to think like Americans and learned little about their own society by citing evidence supplied by faculty themselves. A sociology professor in Vancouver, for example, reportedly devised a course on mass society and protest movements for which the reading list was to be entirely American, although he felt that he saw these phenomena in universal terms. "I just didn't conceive the issue along national lines," he explained, but then he added that there was "a kind of built-in selectivity."[59] In his recent study of sociology and nationalism Donald Whyte confirms that as "departments were established or expanded, the character of sociology undergraduate programs came to resemble the American standard package."[60]

Even though a large number of professors came from Britain and other countries, it was the massive American migration that aroused the antagonism of the student movement and caused the greatest general controversy in the universities as a whole. During the 1960s, when nationalism was becoming a stronger force in Canadian society – spurred by concern over foreign ownership, growing criticism of American foreign policy, the celebration of the Centennial, and other factors – the hiring of thousands of American academics struck many as a backward step. There were others, however, who argued that Canada was fortunate to receive these scholars, and some faculties were bitterly divided over the issue of whether hiring quotas should be introduced. The campaign for such restrictions, led by two Carleton English professors, had the active sympathy of the student movement.[61]

Some student leaders did not, however, see such provisions as adequate weapons against "intellectual imperialism" because many Canadian-born professors showed little concern over the autonomy of their own country and viewed Canadian culture and scholarship as poor substitutes for what the United States had to offer. "The implementation of a quota system would obfuscate the real social, cultural and economic roots of Americanization," declared the CUS in 1969.[62] They saw Americanization not as an isolated issue but as part of the whole problem of capitalism in Canada and its hold on the universities, which they viewed as merely another sector of the "branch-plant economy."[63] Such institutions must be freed from American control before educational reform could seriously begin. "Much of the conflict in the universities today is student reaction not just to American professors," wrote John Warnock, "but against a Canadian educational system which is totally oriented towards preserving the status quo."[64]

The question of whether the curriculum was geared towards protecting the capitalist order focused particularly on the social sciences. These disciplines (far more than the humanities) were influenced by the priorities of outside agencies and, from a radical perspective, were devoted to the perpetuation of the present structure of power.[65] This kind of criticism had surfaced before; in the 1930s, for example, Frank Underhill had denounced his colleagues in political economy for serving as "the garage mechanics of Canadian capitalism."[66] But during the 1960s the social sciences came under a much more concerted attack when many students became convinced that their main function was to stifle social reform and provide the strategies and techniques of social control. The authors of *Social Science and the Ideology of the Status Quo* explained to their readers that social scientists conduct their work "within the tightly drawn parameter of Capital ... The psychologist and sociologist in cooperation with the economist provide the technique for the manipulation of the consumer and worker. Applied anthropology supplies a vital part of the technique for neo-colonialism. The voting studies of the political scientist serve the political party in the manipulation of the electorate. Modern advertising in all its excesses is a direct product of the most sophisticated social science technique."[67]

A relevant social science, in the view of such critics, would turn the tables and "study the bosses and give the information to the people"[68] instead of the other way around. They believed that the social scientist's proper task was to act as a critic rather than a servant of those in power, and many felt that Marxism – an ideology that was sometimes studied but seldom applied in Canadian university classrooms – would provide the necessary tools of analysis. Student radicals held that the American influence in Canadian social science was at least partly responsible for the fact that Marxism had gained little recognition in Canadian universities as a legitimate academic approach. Warnock quoted pioneer Canadian sociologist S.D. Clark's observation that "the American professor is dedicated to proving Marx wrong: American sociology denies the existence of class."[69]

Opponents of the movement saw it as an assault upon the scientific objectivity of these disciplines, which, in a sense, it was. Activists believed that the status of the social-science "expert" rested on claims to complete objectivity that served to mask the biases that necessarily governed all social research. The debate over this issue was as old as the disciplines themselves; in the past the idea of a "value-free" social science had been attacked – on both intellectual and moral grounds – from both the left and the right.[70] In the 1960s the student movement found an ally in conservative philosopher George Grant, who declared that the "controlling role" of the "quantification-oriented behavioral sciences" required that they should be interpreted by the public as completely unbiased, or "value-free."[71] Drache drew upon Grant's ideas when he associated the cult of objectivity with the academics' refusal to become involved in social change. "In the name of the scientific method the student is repeatedly told to be 'objective,' which he soon realizes is the intellectuals' version of academic laissez-faire," wrote Drache. "The tradition of value-free learning creates an ideology out of professionalism, a praxis of passivity and a deep fear of acting on social and political questions ... The point which Grant repeatedly makes is that learning accentuates the feeling of powerlessness."[72] Radicals asserted that value judgments must, in fact, be seen as integral to academic activity in the social sciences if these subjects were to serve morally defensible ends. As Thompson and Brown observed, "the attempt to eradicate values must of necessity also eradicate much of the meaning of the work. If, in fact, a 'value-free' social science could be constructed it would be irrelevant to human needs."[73]

The debate over relevance and the tensions between so-called objective analysis and a more subjective attitude were not confined to the social sciences but permeated the radical critique of the humanities as well.[74] In departments of English, for example, students and faculty clashed over the content, method, and general atmosphere of classroom teaching. Student activists stressed the validity of an intuitive and personal approach to literary interpretation and expressed their distaste for professorial authority and the competitive style of learning, which, they felt, discouraged creative thinking. In a CUS publication called "Literature and Learning" Bob Bossin explained that "poetry demands, as living does, that we thrust, conjecture, think for ourselves; our courses demand that we learn writ, follow others' authority, decisions and schedules. To learn we must create; yet the pattern of relationships, of playing it safe, makes this impossible for almost all of us. Understanding literature is a co-operative effort; in the class we are trained to compete."[75]

Part of the problem was that students' expectations with respect to their literature courses were at odds with current trends within the discipline itself. There was a strong tendency, dating back to the advent of the "New Criticism" earlier in the century, to divorce literary works from their historical or social context and actively to discourage questions concerning the relevance of a literary work to the period that produced it. Literature was seen as existing in a realm outside of history – as a separate system, a great tradition – with its own claims to a non-evaluative, scientific methodology. And, as was the case in the sciences and social sciences, the status of the literary critic (or professor of English) was associated with the notion of the "expert."[76] Northrop Frye, for example, preached the necessity of *informed* criticism and taught that "a public that attempts to do without criticism and asserts that it knows what it likes, brutalizes the arts."[77]

In the English classroom there was a corresponding tendency to downplay the importance of both the student's intuitive or "uncritical" responses to literature and the search for the author's own intentions in writing: each work was part of a unified literary canon, and the critic-professor was its legitimate interpreter. Literature was taught through the technique of "close reading," whereby an elaborate structure of meaning (frequently not open to debate in the undergraduate classroom) billowed from each stanza of poetry or selected pages of fiction. This method might have challenged the anti-intellectualism of restless students who preferred merely to "get the feeling" of a work rather than "take it apart," but for the already disaffected a course in English literature tended to reinforce the suspicion that most professors did not seek relevance in their teaching but actively avoided it. Most student radicals did not reject the study of literature itself but rather its apparent isolation from life and from the rest of the curriculum. "The problems of literature," as Bossin rather obscurely observed, "are the problems of our lives. Coriolanus may be archetypal, but he is also alive and hung up as Hell in the UC Refectory."[78]

Finally, student dissatisfaction with the various subjects in the arts curriculum coalesced into an ongoing critique of the disciplinary structure itself. Like far more traditionally minded critics in previous decades, student activists deplored the proliferation of disciplines and sub-disciplines that had turned the arts curriculum (in the words of a University of Manitoba president some twenty years earlier) into "an undigested pot-pourri of segmented studies."[79] As Dennis Lee wrote, liberal education in the modern university "does not consist of apprehending the order of all knowledge ... it consists of apprehending the order of a discipline."[80] The campaign for relevance was inspired, in good part, by the discontinuity between course offerings and the self-absorbed, increasingly specialized, and sometimes arcane nature of academic activity within the individual knowledge industries. Anticipating the preoccupation with interdisciplinarity that surfaced in Canada during the 1970s, student activists of the sixties had already decided that "the administration of knowledge is not an innocent affair ... A disciplinary division of knowledge is power masquerading as reason."[81]

In their view, the disciplines that made up the arts curriculum served the interests of professors and the agencies for which they performed their research but did not meet the needs of the students themselves or society as a whole. Don Ray observed that the "neat and abstract compartmentalization of knowledge does not correspond to life,"[82] and David Tocoll declared that, in this artificial framework, "thought is divorced from practice," by which he meant that it was difficult to use one's knowledge to take a critical, comprehensive, or confident look at any aspect of how the world worked. The new society that the movement envisaged, "where control over production and intellectual development is exercised by and for the entire society rather than in the interest of profit for the few," depended on "a critical analysis of social institutions," which was not, he believed, possible within the present system.[83] The CUS resolved that the social sciences had to be recognized as a collection of "false categories," and Thompson and Brown argued that it "is impossible for a social science committed to the betterment of man to develop without its being an integrated social science, rather than the social science of isolated disciplines we see today."[84]

Student activists realized that the universities' power to dictate what they should learn was dependent to a large extent on the authority vested in the established disciplines. "There is no real thought outside such disciplines," Frye had said, and he also maintained that liberal education depended on "the surrender of the ego to the laws and conditions of the discipline being studied."[85] Such obedience to authority was the antithesis of the radicals' philosophy, and they saw interdisciplinarity as a means of removing those "discrete limitations ... on what is to be learned or thought on a certain matter."[86] They were especially critical of introductory courses in the social sciences, seeing them as initiations into the specialized methodologies, organizing principles, and jargon of the various subjects, which taught students to distrust their own assumptions and values and to accept each discipline's jurisdiction over its own particular area of human experience.[87] Activists thus linked the fragmentation of knowledge with the universities' passivity in the face of social problems, and believed that, in all areas of the arts curriculum, an interdisciplinary approach would be an essential feature of a truly relevant program of study.

The radical assault upon the arts curriculum was an important episode in the history of higher education in Canada. Some of its concerns were ephemeral and some of its demands were naïve; yet it gave expression to fears about the quality of arts education that had been building up for decades, and it forced both scholars and administrators to open their minds to fresh ideas.

The weaknesses of the student critique are painfully obvious. It was beset by the contradictions inherent in New Left thinking, which demanded allegiance to an ideology of social change while proclaiming the necessity of individual freedom. The campaign for relevance was thus undermined by the conflict between political and personal considerations – between the vision of a curriculum that was designed to bring about the new society and one that was sensitive to the personal needs of each student. The movement over-simplified the issue of relevance in another sense, by ignoring the overwhelming intellectual difficulties that beset any attempt to decide what knowledge is important and what is not. The critique of the university's service role was weakened by the same kind of problems because the activists argued for the university's independence from society at the same time as they pressed for an arts curriculum committed to social change. The students were over-confident and sometimes unfair, and they tended to assume that the complex questions of the university's relation to society, the professors' relation to their students, and the proper content and structure of the arts curriculum would find ready solutions in their hands.

But even if the student movement often seemed to demand the impossible, one can cite many examples of change and experiment in the 1970s and 1980s that vindicate much of the protest. Just as the activists condemned a war that has since been discredited and demanded disinvestment in South Africa twenty years before such sanctions became fashionable, their critique of the arts curriculum also anticipated numerous reforms in the content of the course of study that are now taken for granted. The lack of Canadian material and the predominance of foreign faculty became the subject of major inquiries in the 1970s, and there have since been significant improvements in the status of Canadian scholarship. Other sins of omission in the arts curriculum have also been at least partially rectified: the working classes, the poor, natives and other Canadian ethnic groups, women, radical political movements, popular culture, the Canadian "power structure," and many more topics that were previously ignored are now the subjects of university courses and programs. Interdisciplinarity has become an accepted curricular principle, even if its results tend to fall short of expectations because the boundaries between the disciplines remain as rigid as ever. In contrast to the 1950s and 1960s, Marxist theory has become an honoured mode of inquiry in disciplines ranging from sociology to English. Experimental programs, such as Arts I at the University of British Columbia, have acknowledged and tried to tackle, on a small scale, the students' sense of isolation and of disconnectedness in their course of study, while pressing home, to all concerned, the difficulty of achieving true coherence and relevance in the arts curriculum.

Some of the most important curricular problems raised by the student movement, in fact, are those that remain unsolved. Radicals in the sixties became caught up in the fundamental contradictions of liberal-arts education, which had been developing for decades: the conflict between job training and general culture, between research and teaching, between the inculcation of values and the quest for objectivity, and between curricular pluralism and curricular order.[88] The radical critique of the arts curriculum was a response both to old problems and to new conditions – among them, the students' immersion in an institution that had become so obsessed with self-glorification and the necessity of its own growth that it was unwilling to acknowledge that these problems existed, or to admit that they mattered. Only a generation raised on very high expectations of what the university *should* be able to do for society could have nurtured a student movement inspired by such idealism and indignation, and the activists' self-confident, abrasive, yet perceptive campaign for curricular reform was the product of a unique era in the history of Canadian youth.

NOTES

1 Gerald F. McGuigan, ed., *Student Protest* (Toronto: Methuen 1968), inside cover.
2 For example, see E.W. Nichols, "The Arts Course, Its Purpose and Essential Elements," *Proceedings of the National Conference of Canadian Universities* (1925): 20–7; W.H. Alexander, "The Classics in a Liberal Education," ibid. (1930): 47–56; George Wilson, "Why Teach History?" *Queen's Quarterly* 40 (1933): 406–13; Desmond Pacey, "The Humanities in Canada," *Queen's Quarterly* 53 (1943): 354–60; W.R. Taylor, "The Philosophy of Higher Education," *University of Toronto Quarterly* 16 (1946–47): 420–4; Watson Kirkconnell, *Liberal Education in the Canadian Democracy* (Hamilton: McMaster University 1948); David A. Stewart, "Aims of a University Education," *Dalhousie Review* 30 (1950): 81–9.
3 McGuigan wrote, "There is no doubt that a majority of students are dissatisfied, uneasy, and even anxious about their place in society and in the university. However, the uneasiness among most students remains nameless." McGuigan, *Student Protest*, 9.
4 Cyril Levitt, *Children of Privilege: Student Revolt in the Sixties* (Toronto: University of Toronto Press 1984).
5 *Varsity* (15 Nov. 1968), quoted in Jack Quarter, *The Student Movement of the Sixties* (Toronto: OISE Press 1972), 24.
6 New Left Caucus (Toronto Student Movement), "A Draft Manifesto," mimeo., nd, 2. On the importance of the curriculum also see Barbara Cameron and Alison Black, "Trends in the Development and Curriculum and Governing Bodies of Canadian Universities," CUS mimeo., Ottawa, nd, 21; George Grant, "The Univer-

sity Curriculum," in Howard Adelman and Dennis Lee, *The University Game* (Toronto: Anansi 1968), 47–68. All of the CUS publications used in this article are in Paul Axelrod's collection, and I am indebted to him for their use.

7 Levitt, *Children of Privilege*, 20–1. For a discussion of this theory's impact on higher education in Canada, see M.J. Bowman, "The Human Investment Revolution in Economic Thought," *Sociology of Education* 39, no. 2 (1966): 111–37, cited in Levitt, 20. Also see Paul Axelrod, *Scholars and Dollars: Economics and the Universities of Ontario, 1945–1980* (Toronto: University of Toronto Press 1982), 23–33.

8 Axelrod, *Scholars and Dollars*, 106–10. And see Cyril James, "Education: A National Problem," *Proceedings of the N.C.C.U.* 1950, 10–14; G.P. Gilmour, ed., *Canada's Tomorrow: Papers and Discussion* (Toronto: Macmillan 1954); V.W. Bladen, "The Role of the University," *UTQ* 26 (1956–57): 483–95.

9 Canada, Royal Commission on National Development in the Arts, Letters, and Sciences, 1949–51, *Report*, pt 2 (Ottawa 1951), 274–5.

10 See Watson Kirkconnell, *Liberal Education*, 15; Kirkconnell, "Totalitarian Education," *Dalhousie Review* 32 (Summer 1952): 61–77; P.J. Nicholson, "The Universities as the Custodians of Western Civilization," *Proceedings of the N.C.C.U.* 1951, 10–13.

11 See N.A.M. MacKenzie, "Education in a Satellite World," *University of British Columbia President's Report* 1956–57, 1–11; J.F. Leddy, "The Humanities in an Age of Science," in *Three Lectures at St. Dunstan's University* (Charlottetown 1961), 29–37; J.A. Corry, "The University and the Canadian Community," in *Farewell the Ivory Tower* (Montreal: McGill-Queen's University Press 1970), 30; C.T. Bissell, "Sputnik and the Humanities," in Gerald McCaughey and Maurice Legris, eds., *Of Several Branches* (Toronto: University of Toronto Press 1969), 37–49; Bissell, *Halfway Up Parnassus: A Personal Account of the University of Toronto* (Toronto: University of Toronto Press 1974), 47–50.

12 MacKenzie, "Education in a Satellite World," 9.

13 N.A.M. MacKenzie, "Government Support of Canadian Universities," in C.T. Bissell, ed., *Canada's Crisis in Higher Education* (Toronto: University of Toronto Press 1957), 190. And see Sidney Smith, "Let Knowledge to Wisdom Grow," in Richard Saunders, ed., *Education for Tomorrow* (Toronto: University of Toronto Press 1946), 24; John Irving, *Science and Values: Explorations in Philosophy and Social Science* (Toronto: Ryerson Press 1952), 88, 109.

14 See Watson Kirkconnell and A.S.P. Woodhouse, *The Humanities in Canada* (Ottawa: Humanities Research Council of Canada 1947), preface; Malcolm Wallace, "The Humanities," in Royal Commission on National Development, *Special Studies* (Ottawa 1951), 99–118; Donald Creighton, "Education for Government," *Queen's Quarterly* 61 (1954): 25–33; Maurice Lebel, "National Conference on the Humanities," *Culture* 16 (June 1955): 162–88.

15 Levitt, *Children of Privilege*, 29–30.

16 Ibid., 34. And see 25–8, 41–2, 81.

17 Ibid., 33.

18 David Zirnhelt, "A Student Manifesto: In Search of a Real and Human Educational Alternative," in McGuigan, *Student Protest*, 59. And see Cameron and Black, "Trends in the Development ... of Canadian Universities," 21; Lee and Adelman, "A Note on the Multiversity," *The University Game*, 173-4.

19 According to figures quoted in the *Canadian Forum*, only 27 per cent of the 2,642 new appointees in 1968-69 held doctorates. Joanne Patricia Burgess, "Canadianizing the University," CF (July 1969): 77.

20 Before the Second World War Canadian arts professors had generally been less productive than their American counterparts, partly because they received very little financial support for research or publication. Funding became far easier to obtain after the creation of the Canada Council in 1957, and during the late 1950s and the 1960s the pressure to publish was increasing. For example, see David Corbett, "The Social Sciences in Canada: An Appraisal," *Queen's Quarterly* 66 (1959): 56-73; V. Basmajian, "Double Standards and the University Professor," *QQ* 68 (1961): 249-55.

21 James Jarrett, "Interchapter," in W.R. Niblett, ed., *Higher Education: Demand and Response* (London: Tavistock 1969), 58.

22 Robin Matthews, "The New University: An Old Role," (May 1963): 35-6. Principal John Deutsch of Queen's openly acknowledged the problem and quoted William Arrowsmith's comment that "the scholar has disowned the student ... and the student has reasonably retaliated by abandoning the scholar." Deutsch, "The Best of Times, the Worst of Times," in Arthur Koestler et al., *The Ethics of Change: A Symposium* (Toronto: Canadian Broadcasting Corporation 1969), 74. Northrop Frye showed little sympathy with the student movement in his writings but admitted that "this movement began with the impatience of students with instructors who regarded their teaching as a second-rate activity and an obstacle to research." See Frye, "The University and Personal Life: Student Anarchism and the Educational Contract," in Niblett, ed., *Higher Education*, 49. Also see Harold Taylor, *Students Without Teachers* (New York: Avon 1969).

23 Sol Stern, "The Berkeley Model," *Canadian Dimension* (Sept. 1966): 10.

24 Frank Frketich, "We see the university as a servant of industry and government," from part 1 of "The Need for Change," a document submitted to the president of the University of Victoria by the president of the university's alumni association, reprinted in *University Affairs* (Oct. 1968): 11. And see Jon Bordo, "Parallel Structures and Student Power," CUS mimeo., Ottawa 1968, 1; Cy Gonick, "Self Government in the Multiversity," in *The University Game*, 39-43; Julyan Reid, "Some Canadian Issues," in Tim and Julyan Reid, eds., *Student Power and the Canadian Campus* (Toronto: Peter Martin 1969), 1-2; Zirnhelt, "A Student Manifesto," 56.

25 See James Cappon, "Is Ontario to Abandon Classical Education?" *QQ* 12 (Oct. 1904): 190-206; E.F. Scott, "The Effects of War on Literature and Learning,"

QQ 27 (Oct. 1919): 147–58; J.M. Macdonnell, "The Decline of the Arts Faculty," *QQ* 30 (Jan. 1923): 311–18; W.H. Alexander, "The Higher Learning: Twenty-five Years of Conflict," in W.H. Alexander et al., eds., *These Twenty-Five Years: A Symposium* (Toronto: Macmillan 1933), 1–26; H.A. Innis, "A Plea for the University Tradition," *DR* 24 (1944–5): 298–305; George Grant, "The Minds of Men in the Atomic Age," in *Texts and Addresses Delivered at the 24th Annual Couchiching Conference* (1955), 39–45.

26 The difficulty of combining "pure" scholarship and an ethic of public service is a major theme in the history of higher education in the twentieth century and is even reflected in the titles chosen for university histories: for example, F.W. Gibson, *"To Serve and Yet Be Free": Queen's University, 1917–1961* (Montreal: McGill-Queen's 1983); Michael Hayden, *Seeking A Balance: The University of Saskatchewan 1907–1982* (Vancouver: University of British Columbia Press 1983).

27 On restrictions of political expression at the University of Toronto in the late nineteenth century see *Varsity* editorials between 1880 and 1886 on the university's refusal to hire a political scientist; see also Ian Drummond, *Political Economy at the University of Toronto* (Toronto: University of Toronto Governing Council 1983), 21, on the provincial government's involvement in hiring the first political scientist; and H.S. Ferns and B. Ostry, *The Age of Mackenzie King: The Rise of the Leader* (Toronto: Heinemann 1955), 21–5, on James Mavor's refusal to allow students to invite a socialist as a guest speaker in 1895. On the 1930s, see Michiel Horn's chapter "Professors in the Public Eye" in *The League for Social Reconstruction: Origins of the Democratic Left in Canada 1930–42* (Toronto: University of Toronto Press 1980).

28 On the New Left in Canada, see Levitt, *Children of Privilege*, 158–63, 170, 176, 188.

29 See Paul Axelrod, "The Student Movement of the 1930s," in this volume.

30 "D," "We Have Come to Quit," *CF* (April 1969): 7.

31 Ibid. And see New Left Caucus, "A Draft Manifesto," 1; Cameron and Black, "Trends in the Development ... of Canadian Universities," 21; Cy Gonick, "Self-Government in the Multiversity," in Adelman and Lee, *The University Game*, 41.

32 Bordo, "Parallel Structures," 1.

33 Danny Drache, "Canadian Student: Revolt and Apathy," *CD* 5–7 (Dec. 1968–Jan. 1969): 25. Drache quoted Harold Innis's remark that "the descent of the university into the market place reflects the lie in the soul of modern society."

34 "Committees ... 'a device to buy time rather than make changes'?" *University Affairs* (Oct. 1969): 12. The article was a reprint of a speech by Meldon Levine that had appeared in the Halifax *Chronicle Herald* (9 July 1969).

35 Paul E. Gottfield, "Notes on Academic Unrest: 1," *CF* (Aug. 1969): 116.

36 "Their care is truth, not ideology," Toronto *Star*, 12 Nov. 1968, quoted in Reid, "Some Canadian Issues," 5.

37 For example, see Murray Ross's very frequent use of the word in his book outlining his plans for York's curriculum in Ross, *The New University* (Toronto: University of Toronto Press 1961).

38 See Howard Adelman, "In Search of the New University," in Adelman and Lee, *The University Game*, 157; David Tocoll, "Society and the University: Draft for Final Report of the Tripartite Commission on the Nature of the University," CUS mimeo., Ottawa, nd, 3–10; Cameron and Black, "Trends in the Development ... of Canadian Universities."

39 Don I. Ray, "Political Thought of CUS," CUS mimeo., Ottawa, nd, 6.

40 George Woodcock, "A Radical Dilemma," *Saturday Night*, July 1969, reprinted in Reid and Reid, *Student Power*, 62.

41 Frye, "The University and Personal Life," 35–51. And see Frye, "The Ethics of Change: The Role of the University," in *The Ethics of Change*, 44–55.

42 CUS, Policy Proposals 1969, 2.

43 Gilbert Allardyce, "The Teaching of History," *CHA Newsletter* (Summer 1986): 12.

44 For example, see Tocoll, "Society and the University"; Cameron and Black, "Trends in the Development ... of Canadian Universities"; W.F.P. Pringle, "Political Oppression in Canadian History," CUS mimeo., Ottawa, nd; Peter Warrian, "Staples, Structures and the State: Notes on Canadian Economic History up to the Depression," CUS mimeo., Ottawa, nd; Tony Hyde, "Economics: Large Questions, Short Answers," CUS mimeo., Ottawa, nd; Jim Russell, "Education and Society: British Columbia," CUS mimeo., Ottawa, nd. R. Thompson and H.R. Brown, in *Social Science and the Ideology of the Status Quo*, Hogtown Press pub. no. 4 (Toronto, nd), criticized the social sciences for being ahistorical and "failing to understand man in terms of his past."

45 Bruce Campbell, "Macpherson's superficial report: how better to program students?" *Varsity* (8 Nov. 1967): 5. And see *Varsity* (6 Nov. 1967): 5; (13 Nov. 1967): 7. Lawrence Veysey, "Stability and Experiment in the Undergraduate Curriculum," in Carl Kaysen, ed., *Content and Context: Essays on College Education* (New York: McGraw-Hill 1973), 20.

46 Michael Hornyansky, "Rubbing souls together in 'learning situation' is not education," UA 10, no. 7 (Sept. 1969).

47 See Carl Berger, *The Writing of Canadian History* (Toronto: Oxford University Press 1976), 263–4.

48 Ramsay Cook, "Canadian Historical Writing," in R.H. Hubbard, ed., *Scholarship in Canada 1967: Achievement and Outlook* (Toronto: University of Toronto Press 1968), 80. And see S.R. Mealing, "The Concept of Social Class in the Interpretation of Canadian History," *Canadian Historical Review* 46 (Sept. 1965): 201–18.

49 Bob Baldwin, quoted in Ray, *Political Thought*, 9.

50 Danny Drache, "A Strategy for Research: The National Consciousness and Marxism," CUS mimeo., Ottawa, nd, 4–8.

51 The bias against Canadian literature is evident in the offerings listed in university calendars throughout the period.

52 A.G., "French departments mostly ignore French Canadian Studies survey shows," *UA* (Dec. 1972): 9.

53 The influence of American scholarship is discussed in the various essays in Hubbard, *Scholarship in Canada*, and in T.N. Guinsburg and G.L. Reuber, eds., *Perspectives on the Social Sciences in Canada* (Toronto: University of Toronto Press 1974).

54 A.S.P. Woodhouse, "Research in the Humanities," *Humanities Research Council Report* 2 (1947–49): 20.

55 J.A.S. Evans, "For if Canadian academics are inferior ... it is because our universities have made them that way," *UA* (July 1976): 16–17; Robin Mathews, "The Americanization of Canadian Universities," *Canadian Dimension* 5 (Feb. 1969): 53.

56 See B.S. Keirstead and S.D. Clark, "Social Sciences," in Royal Commission on National Development, *Special Studies*; B.S. Keirstead, "The Social Sciences," in Bissell, *Canada's Crisis*; C.B. MacPherson, "The Social Sciences," in Julian Park, ed., *The Culture of Contemporary Canada* (New York: Cornell University Press 1957); Corbett, "The Social Sciences in Canada."

57 For statistics and other evidence, see Robin Mathews and James Steele, eds., *The Struggle for Canadian Universities: A Dossier* (Toronto 1969); Mathews, "The Americanization of Canadian Universities"; K. Jean Cottam, *Canadian Universities: American Takeover of the Mind?* (Toronto: Gall Publications 1974).

58 "A Look at the Universities," *CD* 7 (Oct.–Nov. 1970): 4.

59 Ibid., 44. And see the cases cited in Mathews and Steele.

60 Donald Whyte, "Sociology and the Nationalist Challenge in Canada," *Journal of Canadian Studies* 19, no. 4 (1984–85): 113.

61 See Burgess, "Canadianizing the University," 77–9; "Universities must develop a sense of Canada," from a brief submitted to the Commission on University Government by the University of Toronto Graduate Students' Union, reprinted in *UA* (Oct. 1969): 9.

62 CUS Policy Proposals 1969, 7–8.

63 Melville Watkins, "Education in the Branch Plant Economy," *CD* 6 (Oct.–Nov. 1969): 37, 39; New Left Caucus, "A Draft Manifesto," 9; Peter Warrian, "The State of the Union," excerpts from his presidential address to the CUS in 1968, *CD* 5 (June–July 1968): 10; Ray, "Political Thought of CUS," 6–10.

64 John Warnock, "The Americanization of Canadian Universities," *CD* 7 (Oct.–Nov. 1970): 38.

65 For two very influential works concerning the uses to which knowledge was put, see Theodore Roszak, ed., *The Dissenting Academy* (New York: Vintage Books 1968); and Robin Blackburn, ed., *Ideology in Social Science* (London: Fontana Books 1972).

66 Underhill is quoted by Danny Drache in "A Strategy for Research," 6. Also see

Underhill, "On Professors and Politics," *CF* 15 (Mar. 1936): 6–7; W.H. Alexander, "Noli Episcopari (Letter to a Young Man Contemplating an Academic Career), *CF* 19 (Oct. 1939): 220–3.

67 Thompson and Brown, *Social Science and the Status Quo*, 16. On anthropology, see Kathleen Gough Aberle, "Anthropology and Imperialism," CUS mimeo., Ottawa, nd. Gough was a contributor to *The Dissenting Academy* and was one of those dismissed in the purge of Simon Fraser's Department of Political Science, Sociology and Anthropology following its confrontation with the administration. See M. Briemberg, *A Taste of Better Things*, Hogtown Press pub. no. 9 (Toronto, nd). The dismissals were censured by the CAUT. See *CF* 54 (Mar. 1975): 4.

68 University of Alberta *Gateway* (19 Sept. 1969), quoted in Myrna Kostash, *Long Way from Home: The Story of the Sixties Generation in Canada* (Toronto: Lorimer 1980), 71.

69 Warnock, "The Americanization of Canadian Universities," 39.

70 See, for example, the efforts of early Canadian sociologists to establish their scientific claims, in C.A. Dawson, "Sociology as a Specialized Discipline," and C.W.M. Hart, "Some Obstacles to a Scientific Sociology," both in Hart, ed., *Essays in Sociology* (Toronto: University of Toronto Press 1940).

71 George Grant, "The University Curriculum," in Adelman and Lee, *The University Game*, 52–3.

72 Danny Drache, "Canadian Student: Revolt and Apathy," *CD* 5 (Dec. 1968–Jan. 1969): 25.

73 Thompson and Brown, *Social Science and the Status Quo*, 1–4. And see MacPherson, "Politics: Post-Liberal Democracy," in Blackburn, ed., *Ideology in Social Science*. MacPherson writes that "empirical, value-free analysis" in political science assumes the rightness of "liberal democracy," and that "political values have become more, not less, in need of central attention." The New Left was, of course, indebted to "mainline" social science – especially sociology – for much of its theory and terminology. This issue is explored by Levitt, *Children of Privilege*, 142–8.

74 Adelman remarked on how the humanities had been fragmented by their conversion into "scientific" disciplines, and Grant criticized his fellow humanists – including Frye – for trying to turn the humanities into "non-evaluative sciences"; see Adelman and Lee, *The University Game*, 164; 58–9. Frye himself maintained that the humanities "have their laws and disciplines like the sciences, despite their emotional and aesthetic connections." See "The Critical Discipline," in George Stanley and Guy Sylvestre, eds., *Canadian Universities Today* (Toronto: University of Toronto Press 1961), 36.

75 Bob Bossin, "Literature and Learning," CUS mimeo., Ottawa, nd, 4. And see Lee, "Getting to Rochdale," 69–70.

76 On the rise of the professional critic, see Chris Baldick, *The Social Mission of English Criticism* (London: Oxford 1983).

77 Northrop Frye, "The Function of Criticism at the Present Time," *UTQ* 19 (Oct. 1949): 1. Frye's major theoretical work was *The Anatomy of Criticism* (Princeton: Princeton University Press 1957).

78 Bossin, "Literature and Learning," 2. Bossin probably meant that literary figures have significance not only in Frye's world of archetypes (that is, as images that occur repeatedly in the world of literature) but because they can help us to understand our own society.

79 Sidney Smith, "The Liberal Arts: An Experiment," *QQ* 51, no. 1 (Spring 1944): 7. There was widespread criticism of the "fragmentation" of the arts curriculum throughout the first half of the century. Thompson and Brown's critique of the disciplinary structure was influenced by Robert Lynd's *Knowledge for What?* (New York 1939).

80 Lee, "Getting to Rochdale," 86.

81 Arthur Kroker, "Migration from the Disciplines," *JCS* 15, no. 3 (Fall 1980): 5–6.

82 Ray, "Political Thought," 8.

83 Tocoll, "Society and the University," 10–11.

84 CUS Policy Proposals 1969, 6; Thompson and Brown, *Social Science and the Status Quo*, 2.

85 Frye, "The Critical Discipline," 35–6. Historian Frederick Gibson made a similar point in his defence of the specialized honours course: "There is no thought outside the framework of the great subjects of human knowledge." "University and the Student in a Changing Society," *QQ* 70 (Summer 1963): 278.

86 Ray, "Political Thought," 8.

87 Thompson and Brown, *Social Science and the Status Quo*, 13–14. On the problem of the special uses of language in the social sciences, see also Calvin Woodward, "Diogenes in the Tower of Babel: The Generation Gap and the Role of the University," *Journal of Educational Thought* 12, no. 3 (1978): 190–6.

88 On the history of these and other problems associated with the arts curriculum, see P. Jasen, "The English-Canadian Liberal Arts Curriculum: An Intellectual History from 1800 to 1950" (PhD thesis, University of Manitoba 1987).

PART FIVE

The Learning Environment

Beyond the Democratic Intellect: The Scottish Example and University Reform in Canada's Maritime Provinces, 1870–1933*

John G. Reid

On 1 November 1870 Dalhousie College's newly appointed professor of mathematics, Charles Macdonald, gave his inaugural address at a convocation held in the Assembly chamber of Province House in Halifax. Although he opened with the conventional speech of welcome to new and returning students, he soon moved beyond such platitudes to deliver a vigorous attack on the shortcomings of denominational colleges in Nova Scotia. Macdonald advocated the creation of a single university for the province, and he went on to defend himself against any suggestion that he was being unrealistic. "I am not," he insisted, "spinning a cobweb hypothesis out of my own consciousness. I proceed not only upon the abstract reasonableness of the scheme, but on the ground of realized fact. The four Scottish Universities are in all respects National Institutions, and supply ... College Education sufficient for the wants of the three millions of Scotchmen." The Scottish example contrasted, in Macdonald's opinion, with the existing situation in Nova Scotia, where "the number of our young men that are liberally educated ... is very small."[1] More than sixty years later, on 2 January 1933, a Halifax newspaper carried an article by a Maritime academic of a later generation, President George J. Trueman of Mount Allison University, which apparently indicated that Macdonald's advice had been heeded. "In the Maritime provinces," Trueman declared, "we have tried to maintain the Scottish tradition, to bring higher education within the reach of any brilliant and ambitious boy, regardless of the income of the family."[2]

In reality the two statements had little in common, beyond the fact that each was drawing upon the Scottish example to substantiate an interpretation of the proper ways in which higher education should serve students and regional society as a whole. Macdonald was initiating a debate on university reform that would last eleven years. Trueman was pronouncing an epitaph on another debate, on similar issues, that had begun in 1921. Macdonald believed that the virtues of the Scottish universities could best be replicated by centralization, whereas Trueman was an avowed advocate of the scattered denominational institutions of the Maritimes. The differences between their respective visions illustrate the changing significance of the Scottish example in perceptions of higher education in the region. The openness of Scottish universities to students of varied social and religious backgrounds – the "democratic intellect"[3] – had been frequently cited in the Maritimes since the early nineteenth century as a tool of argument in the struggle to mitigate the exclusiveness of the earliest colleges. Macdonald's speech represented, in part, a late attempt to argue in this way. By the mid-1870s, however, it was becoming clear that the Scottish example had lost its force as an instrument of reform and that the intellectual roots of movements for radical change would henceforth lie elsewhere. As a mythology the Scottish tradition remained strong. By the interwar years, as exemplified in Trueman's remark, it had come to represent a conservative and essentially rural conception of the role of higher education. The purpose of this essay will be to explore the way in which this transition had taken place, as an element of the relationship between universities, students, and society in an era of rapid socio-economic and intellectual change.

The university-reform debates of the 1870s and the 1920s, and the changing role of the Scottish example, must be seen in both historiographical and historical contexts. The Scottish tradition in Maritime and Canadian higher education has been extensively studied. In the early decades of the nineteenth century, as numerous historians have pointed out, Scottish individuals had been closely involved in the foundation and early development of many institutions. Thomas McCulloch, founder of Pictou Academy in 1805 and appointed as the first president of Dalhousie in 1838, is a case in point. In recent studies by such authors as D.C. Masters, W.B. Hamilton, Gordon Haliburton, and R.A. MacLean, as well as in older works, including those of D.C. Harvey and Sir Robert Falconer, McCulloch is portrayed as a Scot who may even have had, as MacLean argues, "a greater impact than any other upon the educational progress of Nova Scotia."[4] Other examples of influential Scots are abundant. G.M. Grant and Sir William Dawson, Nova Scotia–born but Scottish-trained, were active in educational fields in their native province – and, in the case of Dawson, in New Brunswick – before departing for later careers at, respectively, Queen's University and McGill.[5] Scots from religious denominations other than Presbyterianism can also be cited: the Roman Catholic Scots of eastern Nova Scotia who founded St Francis Xavier University in 1853, and notably Bishop Colin Francis MacKinnon, or the two long-serving Scottish colleagues on the faculty of King's College, the Church of England institution in Frederiction, and later of the University of New Brunswick, William Brydone Jack and James Robb.[6]

The imprint of such individuals on Maritime higher education in the early and middle decades of the nineteenth century was clear. It was seen partly in matters of curriculum and philosophical outlook. The export of the "Common Sense" school of philosophy from Scotland to North America has had many historians, and in the Canadian context has found persuasive exposition in the recent work of A.B. McKillop.[7] With its ability to reconcile reason with revelation, empirically known truths with eternal realities, the Common Sense school provided an especially workable basis for education in denominational colleges. Closely associated, and also drawn directly from Scotland, was the pre-eminence of moral philosophy in curriculum. In the Maritime provinces the clearest examples of Scottish-inspired curricula can be found at Pictou Academy and then at Dalhousie, first under the presidency of McCulloch and then, when the institution was revived in 1863 from a period of dormancy, under a predominantly Scottish-trained faculty.[8] Nor was the influence of moral philosophy on the Scottish pattern confined to institutions staffed by Scots. Mental and moral philosophy assumed prominence also at academies and colleges such as the Wesleyan Academy at Sackville, and subsequently at the Mount Allison Wesleyan College opened there in 1862 and at the Baptist Acadia College in Wolfville.[9] Curriculum analysis by R.S. Harris has shown that throughout the English-language colleges of British North America in the mid-nineteenth century, "the philosophic system propounded ... was that which had been developed by the Scottish common sense school; the texts prescribed everywhere were by such authors as Reid, Stewart, McIntosh, and Sir William Hamilton."[10] In this respect Scottish influence was pervasive, and was even represented to some degree at institutions such as King's College, Windsor, where the dominant influence on curriculum was the English classical model, and at St Francis Xavier, which although founded by Scots was heavily influenced by the classical patterns of other Roman Catholic institutions in Quebec and in Rome.[11]

The legacy of early Scottish influence on higher education in the Maritime provinces, as elsewhere in Canada, has been seen by historians to lie also in the values of the democratic intellect: in the popular demand for education in communities composed of Scottish immigrants and their descendants, and in the willingness of institutions to offer their services widely. W.B. Hamilton, for example, has maintained that "the democratic outlook characteristic of Scotland's entire system of education was destined to flourish in the frontier environment," while D. Campbell and R.A. MacLean have similarly argued with regard to Nova Scotia that "the attitudes of the Scots in the homeland towards education were carried with them and congealed in this new society; the bright lad of the crofter or tradesman was not turned away from Edinburgh University nor was he kept out of institutions of higher learning in Nova Scotia because of class distinctions." [12] For A.B. McKillop, "a general appreciation of the necessity for popular education" was an important element of the Scottish influence in Canada, and J.M. Bumsted has illustrated the point by the example of Andrew MacPhail's community school at Orwell, Prince Edward Island, which sent nearly two hundred of its pupils to university during the nineteenth century. [13] The democratic character of Scottish-influenced higher education was identified not only by later historians. It was frequently proclaimed by the institutions themselves in the early nineteenth century. In laying the cornerstone of Dalhousie College in 1820, the Earl of Dalhousie declared that "this College of Halifax is ... formed in imitation of the University of Edinburgh; its doors will be open to all who profess the Christian religion ... to all, in short, who may be disposed to devote a small part of their time to study." [14] Similarly, Thomas McCulloch's Pictou Academy publicly described itself in 1824 as "formed upon the model of the Scottish Universities; and, like them ... open, in its scientific privileges, to Students of all classes in the community." [15]

How far, though, was this an accurate portrayal of Scottish higher education? No serious historian would argue that Scottish universities, in the nineteenth century or previously, were open to all regardless of social class or of gender. Nevertheless, there is a substantial Scottish historiography that argues that male students of proven ability enjoyed exceptional opportunities; as one author, James Scotland, put it, "there were many lads of parts, and they did attain eminence, and it was easier for a Scottish boy to reach a university than for his brothers in most countries of the western world." [16] Modern analysis of the possible origins of this trait of Scottish higher education began with the works of two earlier historians, L.J. Saunders and George Elder Davie. Saunders, in his *Scottish Democracy, 1815–1840: The Social and Intellectual Background*, published in 1950, explicitly linked developments in education with socio-economic change. Scotland in the early nineteenth century was, for him, to be seen as "a small country with as self-conscious and intense a tradition as Switzerland or the Netherlands or New England, a country which ... was now increasingly caught up in that wider movement of economic and intellectual change which formed early industrial society." [17] Into this period Scottish educational institutions at all levels brought characteristics that could justifiably be described as democratic in two senses. First, they offered to all who could afford their fees – which were low enough, Saunders argued, that few would be deterred – the prospect of education as a means of moral and intellectual self-improvement independent of social class. A rural student, for example, might come directly to one of the universities from a parish school at the age of fourteen or fifteen and attend lectures for the winter with no intention of graduating, before returning to farm work in the summer. [18] Secondly, however, educational institutions also functioned as instruments of social mobility. Even at parish-school level, with the fostering of the talents of such "lads of parts" as were identified by local teachers, the process was begun by which academic, clerical, and professional elites were replenished with recruits from other social classes. The universities contributed also, not only in the obvious sense of providing training for able young men but also in their accessibility to young students whose previous educational opportunities had been limited and who therefore could not have hoped to pass entrance examinations on the English model. Others were too poor to attend university continuously for intensive study but were able to complete their studies through accumulated attendance at lecture courses.[19] In these senses, Saunders suggested, the Scottish universities were indeed democratic. Yet, in the early decades of the nineteenth century debate was already beginning as to whether such characteristics as the attendance of young students, the lack of entrance examinations, and the unsystematic character of the academic structures were not in fact severely handicapping Scottish graduates in an industrializing age.

It was this debate that was examined by George Elder Davie in his influential 1961 study, *The Democratic Intellect: Scotland and her Universities in the Nineteenth Century*. In the course of a "dour struggle" lasting virtually throughout the nineteenth century, he argued, Scotland surrendered the most important distinctive features of its traditional approach to higher education: wide accessibility, opposition to overspecialization, and the preeminence of philosophy.[20] Increasingly, advocates of specialized study on the English pattern and of higher research schools along the lines of those developed in Germany called into question the excessive sacrifices of intellectual quality that they believed were demanded by the tradition of the democratic intellect. That the Scottish universities finally capitulated before these pressures was attributed by Davie partly to the inevitable "educational preponderance of England in the United Kingdom" and in part to "a failure of intellectual nerve among the Scots."[21] The Scottish Universities Act of 1858, preceded by a bitter debate between traditionalists and anglicizers, introduced only an unstable compromise. While stopping short of imposing radical measures such as the amalgamation of the four universities into a federal University of Scotland, as proposed in Parliament by the young W.E. Gladstone, the act gave no countenance either to Scottish proposals to revitalize the traditional pattern of Scottish higher education by superimposing German-style research schools on the existing structure.[22] Instead, relatively minor changes were prescribed, and the universities were thus deprived of a way of meeting changed circumstances without sacrificing their traditional character. By 1889, when a new royal commission was created to inquire into the state of the Scottish universities, the anglicizing forces had gathered strength, and, Davie argued, the resulting reforms of 1892 swept away the

traditional qualities of Scottish higher education in the interests of a reform
of the curriculum along rigidly specialized lines.[23] What had taken place,
he concluded, was a "tortuous, dark revolution whereby a nation noted
educationally both for social mobility and for fixity of first principle gradually reconciled itself to an alien system in which principles traditionally
did not matter and a rigid social immobilism was the accepted thing." The
"continuing adventure of the democratic intellect" had come to an end.[24]

Davie's provocative thesis, as in the case of any bold interpretation painted
on a broad canvas, was controversial from the first. Asa Briggs, for example,
praised Davie in the *English Historical Review* for the important questions
he had raised but reproved him for attaching "an absurdly monolithic quality
to 'Southern values' in an age when there was rapid change both in Oxford
and Cambridge as well as Scotland" and questioned the adequacy of his
explanation of the evolution of events towards the reforms of 1892. "For
historians," commented Briggs, "the book is perhaps best regarded as an
invitation to further scholarship."[25] Yet in certain important respects Davie's
thesis has fared well at the hands of subsequent researchers. The criticism
that there are limits to the validity of a clear-drawn contrast between English
and Scottish educational values, at a time of change in institutions on both
sides of the border, has persisted.[26] On the democratic character of the
universities – democratic, that is, in the limited senses propounded by Saunders and Davie – further research has given some credence to the notion of
a distinctive Scottish pattern. Writing in *Past and Present* in 1966, for
example, W.M. Mathew constructed a detailed study of the origins and later
occupations of students of that university from 1740 to 1839. The picture
presented was of an institution serving a wider range of social classes than
its English counterparts and responding to industrialization by admitting
students from working-class families. That students were young – some
entering as early as the age of thirteen – and that they may have left the
university lacking in specialized knowledge in any field were, for Mathew,
characteristics that "were in some measure the price which Scotland paid
for maintaining a democratic ideal."[27]

Most recently debate has focused on the mythical elements of the democratic tradition in Scottish education: mythical, that is, not in the sense
necessarily of denoting untruth but rather because the concept itself has been
as important in some respects as the reality it has been supposed to represent.
The major study of *Education and Opportunity in Victorian Scotland* published in 1983 by R.D. Anderson has made this distinction especially clear.
Disavowing any intention to "demolish the myth of educational democracy,"
Anderson argues that "there can be no doubt that throughout our period the
recruitment of the Scottish elite was from a very wide social range."[28]
Through detailed quantitative analysis of university enrolments and exam-
ination of the relationship between schools and universities, this contention

is buttressed by a more sophisticated portrayal than was possible before. The late nineteenth century and early twentieth century, for example, were a time of increasing representation of working-class and lower-middle-class students, which suggests a less dramatic interpretation than the stark betrayal of democratic values presented by Davie.[29] Yet in examining the mythology of the tradition – in the book and in a subsequent article, "In Search of the 'Lad of Parts': The Mythical History of Scottish Education" – Anderson is able convincingly to show the influence of the social pressures arising from industrialization. The democratic ideal, he argues, was originally based on a rural experience, in which the parish schools succeeded in creating high literacy rates in small Lowland communities and thus in providing considerable opportunity for individuals to pursue further education. As adapted in the course of nineteenth-century industrialization, however, the myth attained a power of its own. It could still be used to promote the development of rural education, as in the movement to extend the availability of secondary education in rural counties during the 1890s, but it also could form the basis of an ideology of meritocratic selection in which "a limited equality of opportunity was held to justify the reinforcing of structural inequalities."[30] The Scottish historiography of the democratic intellect suggests, therefore, that the concept retains validity as a representation of important real characteristics of Scottish education and as a myth significant in its own right, but also that the relative importance of myth and reality were shifting under the influence of late nineteenth-century socio-economic change.

In the Maritime provinces it was natural that the Scottish democratic influence should have been strongly felt in the early and middle decades of the nineteenth century, though it should be re-emphasized that democracy in this sense did not imply egalitarianism but rather the opportunity for moral and intellectual self-improvement as an end in itself, and the possibility of social mobility through educational achievement. The Scottish influence was securely based on the large proportion of Scots in the overall population. The first Canadian census showed in 1871 that some 131,000 Nova Scotians (33.7 per cent of the population) and 41,000 New Brunswickers (14.3 per cent) claimed Scottish origins, as compared with a national proportion of 15.8 per cent. The population of Prince Edward Island in 1881 – the year of the first federal census after the island's entry into Confederation – included almost 49,000 Scots, or 44.9 per cent. Of the total Maritime population of some 871,000 in that year, 28.1 per cent claimed Scottish origins. Even by 1931 the regional proportion of Scottish origin had dropped only to 22.7 per cent. It remained substantially higher in Nova Scotia (27.3 per cent) and Prince Edward Island (36.9 per cent).[31] Clustered in northeastern Nova Scotia, Cape Breton, and Prince Edward Island, and with substantial numbers spread throughout other parts of the region, the Scots – although heterogeneous, as between Highland and Lowland, Protestant and Catholic – represented one of the region's most numerous ethnic groups throughout the 1870–1933 period. By 1870, however, the major Scottish immigrations to the Maritimes were over. Later arrivals, like other immigrant groups of the post-Confederation era, were more likely to settle in central and western Canada. Even in the 1881 census only 2.1 per cent of the Maritime population was Scottish-born, and by 1931 the proportion had fallen to a negligible 0.7 per cent.[32] In the same period the number of Scottish-born and Scottish-trained faculty members and administrators also declined, even in most Scottish-influenced universities of the region.

Prior to this decline, and especially in the earlier part of the nineteenth century, the Scottish example had been frequently evoked in the interests of university reform. In the hands of an individual such as Thomas Mc-Culloch, and the supporters of Pictou Academy, the principle of the democratic intellect was a powerful weapon. In attacking the social and religious exclusiveness of King's College, Windsor – where, until 1829, students were required to subscribe to the Thirty-Nine Articles of the Church of England before receiving their degrees – McCulloch frequently appealed to the more open character of the Scottish universities.[33] By the late 1820s the controversy had fused with the wider question of political reform, and debate over legislative financial aid to Pictou provoked acrimonious disputes between the Nova Scotia assembly and council in the late 1820s and early 1830s. Ultimately the hostility to Pictou that prevailed both in the council and in the Church of Scotland – McCulloch was a minister of the rival Secessionist branch of Presbyterianism – was enough to ensure the demise of the academy. Similar forces combined to frustrate McCulloch's later ambition to make Dalhousie College a genuinely non-denominational institution.[34]

Historically, therefore, the democratic intellect was early recognized as a characteristic of Scottish-influenced education in the Maritime colonies. Associated primarily with Presbyterian communities and institutions, and used by McCulloch to challenge the religious exclusiveness of Church of England higher education, the concept was also used as an argument against social elitism. The power of the Scottish example was ensured by the large, though declining, representation of Scots in society at large. Historiographically, the phenomenology of the democratic intellect has been explored with regard to both Scotland and the Maritime provinces. Scottish historians have gone on to consider also the effects of nineteenth-century intellectual and social change, which put severe pressures on the older tradition of university accessibility. Maritime higher-educational historiography has not hitherto gone this far. Yet an examination of the university-reform debates of the 1870s and of the 1920s can offer clear evidence of the transition that was taking place.

By the time Charles Macdonald initiated the university-reform debate of the 1870s, Dalhousie had come closer to the ideal of Thomas McCulloch, at least in principle. The college had been reorganized in 1863 along lines that permitted representation of all religious denominations on the board of governors – even though in practice Presbyterians remained pre-eminent in the ranks of governors, professors, and students – and it was this non-denominational constitution that provided Macdonald with his starting-point in calling for the establishment of a central, non-denominational, teaching university for Nova Scotia. Dalhousie, he implied, would be the natural basis for this united institution, which would supersede the work of the existing denominational colleges. Macdonald rightly pointed out that these institutions had proliferated in the middle decades of the century, but his condemnation of their "sectarian" character provoked predictably angry reactions from the colleges and their parent religious denominations. For two years arguments arose continually in Halifax newspapers as to the relative merits of denominational colleges that did not restrict their student intake according to religious tests, and of Dalhousie with its non-denominational constitution but essentially Presbyterian character.[35]

Debate was resumed in earnest in 1874. In January of that year the Dalhousie board of governors formally proposed a consolidation scheme to the other colleges. Having been quickly and decisively rebuffed, the Dalhousie board – led in this instance by G.M. Grant – successfully proposed to the provincial government of P.C. Hill that the existing government grant to Dalhousie should be enlarged, that the size of its board should be increased, and that Dalhousie be given power to affiliate to itself any other colleges that might so desire.[36] Once again the reaction from other colleges was antagonistic, and the intensity of the response prompted Hill to resolve the matter for the time being by a measure that combined compromise with temporization. On 4 April 1876 two related bills gained passage through the provincial legislature. The first provided for the continuation of grants to all the colleges – Dalhousie, King's, Acadia, Mount Allison, St Francis Xavier, and St Mary's – and reduced the previously wide differential between the sums awarded to Dalhousie and to the others.[37] The second act created a federated, non-teaching University of Halifax, modelled explicitly on the University of London. The colleges would be members of the new university but would not surrender their own powers and privileges. The university, however, would have the power to prescribe curricula and examine candidates for degrees: thus, students from the various colleges and others who prepared themselves by private study would have equal opportunity to graduate from the federated university.[38]

It was envisaged by the framers of the act creating the University of Halifax, which was to have effect for an initial period of five years, that debate could take place at the end of that time over whether the experiment should be continued or the concept of a central teaching university should be revived. In the event the university failed to win enthusiastic support from any of the colleges save Mount Allison, and yet support could not be gathered for the central teaching body. As a result, in 1881 the University of Halifax effectively lapsed, as did government grants to the colleges, and this entire attempt at reform came to an end.[39] What is revealing for the present purpose, however, is not the circumstances of the scheme's demise but rather the terms in which its merits were debated. The Scottish example, prominent at the beginning, steadily lost importance as debate continued. Macdonald, following McCulloch's precedent, contended in 1870 that the Scottish universities were "in all respects National Institutions," in contrast with the petty denominational colleges of the Maritimes. "Nova Scotia being a country so like Scotland in many respects," he continued, "it is the more susceptible of benefit from Scottish precedent."[40] Yet on closer scrutiny any such argument carried considerable dangers for the advocates of the central teaching university. Their case rested essentially on two grounds. The first was the narrowly sectarian character of the denominational colleges. As their opponents pointed out with relish, however, the Scottish universities could not strictly be said to differ significantly in this respect from, say, Mount Allison, Acadia, or St Francis Xavier. All these institutions, like the Scottish universities, had faculties of theology; none of them restricted student intake on denominational grounds. Thus, at every stage of the debate, any attempt to address the Scottish example in the interests of this argument drew swift refutation. A Methodist critic of Macdonald's lecture commented in late 1870, for example, that "accepting the Professor's own description of the Scotch universities, we are irresistibly driven to the conclusion that they resemble, so far as regards the intermingling of religion and education, far more nearly the objects of the Professor's censure than the objects of his praise."[41] Similarly, at a meeting of college representatives in Halifax in March 1876 the only mention of the Scottish universities was a brusque dismissal of their relevance to the debate by the Church of England bishop of Nova Scotia: "The Scottish Universities," he remarked as reported in a newspaper account, "had chairs of theology."[42] The Scottish example, as it related to religious exclusiveness, had been much more serviceable as an argument for reform in the earlier era, when King's, Windsor, had provided an easy target, than it was in the changed circumstances of the 1870s.

The other essential argument for proponents of the central teaching university was also a dangerous one in which to evoke the Scottish example: it was the need for unification of the colleges in order to achieve a greater concentration of specialized expertise. "This," declared G.M. Grant in a lecture reported in the Halifax *Herald* in March 1876, "is an age of specialty. We can no longer have admirable Crichtons who are able to dispute at a moment's notice *de omnium scibili*. If a man is master of one little department of science, he has conquered all the world that is within the reach of one man." In the same lecture Grant referred in passing to the Scottish universities as national institutions and recalled fondly his own fellow-students at Glasgow, now scattered throughout the British Empire; but the fact remained that specialization of the kind he envisaged was not in the Scottish tradition.[43]

The proponents of the University of Halifax, on the other hand, adduced no Scottish examples but rather concentrated on a single model, albeit one that could be regarded as having been heavily influenced originally by Scots: the University of London. Again, there were two essential arguments. One was that the non-teaching university would allow, as in the case of the University of London, for denominational colleges to continue to exert a beneficial moral influence upon their students, while at the same time having their academic standards guaranteed by central examinations.[44] The other was the greater democratization to be expected from such a structure, where students from localities remote from Halifax could continue to attend their local institutions without having the expense of removal to Halifax, and where even an individual who could not attend one of the colleges on a full-time basis would have the right to take examinations on the strength of part-time or private study. The principle was enshrined in no lesser place than the act creating the university, the tasks of which were to be those of "raising the standard of higher education in the Province, and of enabling all denominations and classes, including those persons whose circumstances preclude them from following a regular course of study in any of the existing colleges and universities, to obtain academical degrees."[45]

This aim would not have been controverted, of course, by the proponents of the central teaching university: G.M. Grant, with rhetorical flair, evoked in 1876 Joseph Howe's dream of "an institution where young Nova Scotians, without distinction of class or creed, should contend in that literary contest where defeat is no dishonour, and where victory ensures modesty," while some five years later the Dalhousie professor of natural philosophy J.G. MacGregor – a graduate of Dalhousie and subsequently trained at Edinburgh – would publicly reject the claim of the University of Halifax genuinely to promote popular education.[46] Yet the fact was that for those who argued as did MacGregor, Grant, and Macdonald – all trained at Scottish universities and all closely associated with Dalhousie – the principle of democracy in education turned out on close inspection not to be central to their case, and those arguments that were essential to them could not be advanced by the use of the Scottish example. Reformers they were, but their appeals to the Scottish tradition were misleading. In reality they had more in common with those in Scotland who were advocating change in the Scottish universities than they did with the traditionalists.

The failure of the University of Halifax did not entirely close off debate on university reform in the Maritimes.[47] The question was not seriously reopened, however, until the early 1920s, when a new federation scheme was proposed by commissioners of the Carnegie Corporation of New York. The commissioners, W.S. Learned and K.C.M. Sills, had carried out an inspection tour of the region in late 1921, charged with providing recommendations as to how the Carnegie Corporation could best respond to the many requests for financial support that had recently come to it from Maritime institutions. The recommendations that emerged in 1922 were far-reaching. The Maritime colleges, Learned and Sills reported, suffered generally from underfunding, poor physical plant, and above all questionable academic standards. Only Dalhousie, and perhaps St Francis Xavier, could properly be described in their view as "genuine colleges." The close association of other colleges with secondary schools – such as the Mount Allison Academy, the Mount Allison Ladies' College, and the Acadia Ladies' Seminary – meant that they were "embedded in secondary organizations that divide the attention and interest."[48] The commissioners identified three possible solutions and rejected two of them. It would be impracticable, they believed, to institute a system by which each college would specialize in particular subject areas. To develop Dalhousie to the exclusion of all the others would be academically feasible but would never be accepted by public opinion outside Halifax, let alone outside Nova Scotia. The remaining solution was the only one strongly recommended by Learned and Sills: that Acadia, Dalhousie, King's, Mount Allison, the University of New Brunswick, and St Francis Xavier should join together in Halifax to form a federated University of the Maritime Provinces modelled upon the University of Toronto and the University of Oxford.[49]

Unlike the measures taken with regard to Dalhousie College by the Nova Scotia government some forty-seven years before, the proposals of Learned and Sills met with a generally cordial response from the higher educational institutions of the Maritimes. On 7 July 1922 a conference in Halifax attended by delegates from King's, Mount Allison, Acadia, and Dalhousie – one of three held in that year – unanimously passed a resolution "that we consider some form of Confederation of the existing higher institutions of learning in these Maritime Provinces is necessary for the proper progress of our people, and we undertake to do all in our power to bring this about."[50] Nevertheless, the scheme met with little more success than had those of the 1870s. One solid result was the federation in Halifax of Dalhousie and King's, assisted by grants from the Carnegie Corporation and speeded by the fact that the Windsor campus of King's had been virtually destroyed by a disastrous fire in 1920. Acadia and the University of New Brunswick quickly indicated, however, that they were not willing to compromise their own independence in favour of the scheme. The board of governors of St Francis Xavier, influenced by the Roman Catholic hierarchy of the province and by discouragement from Rome, voted similarly despite evidence of support for the federation proposals among the faculty. Mount Allison took longer to decide but by 1928 had effectively withdrawn from participation. The willingness of the Carnegie Corporation to underwrite the scheme to the amount of three million dollars expired on 1 July 1929, and the proposals were thereupon allowed to lapse.[51]

The question of democratization of university education was argued on both sides of the debate, which continued intermittently from 1922 until 1929. As early as in the Halifax conferences of 1922 the issue was raised and discussed, as by the Methodist minister and Mount Allison delegate H.E. Thomas, who asked on 24 October "[if] education in the Maritime Provinces would be democratized by this federation. Will we fling the door open, giving the poor girl or boy the privilege of education that will determine the course he hopes to pursue. If I so thought, I would sacrifice a great many things to bring it about. There is a fear in the background of my mind that perhaps it will not do that."[52] The point was taken up by the Reverend Gregory McLellan, rector of St Dunstan's, the Roman Catholic college in Prince Edward Island. McLellan was willing to see professional and post-graduate schools centralized in Halifax but maintained that the existing colleges had "opened their doors and made it possible for a great many young men and women to receive an Arts course. Now, can we be assured that, by federating all these Colleges at Halifax these opportunities would be enlarged – we fear rather that they would be curtailed."[53]

A later speaker, Principal Clarence MacKinnon of the Presbyterian theological college in Halifax, neatly turned this argument on its head. "It seems to me," he argued, "that this Federation of the Universities will democratise education. At the present moment it is only the rich man who can get specialized education for his boy, because he has to send him abroad, and as I understand the point, this is to bring facilities which are to be found in the United States and elsewhere, and to place them at the disposal of what the Carnegie people were pleased to say was the best stock they could find in the Dominion of Canada."[54] MacKinnon had thus given an answer to Thomas's original question, and yet it was an answer that confirmed that the essential goal of the federation was not to democratize per se. The president of Dalhousie, A. Stanley Mackenzie, had already contrasted the slim resources of the Maritime colleges with the wealth of their New England counterparts and had asked what chance a Maritime student had of receiving "the best instruction in the advanced work."[55] As perceived by Learned and Sills, and by those who supported their proposals at the Halifax conferences, the real issue was not the democratic intellect but rather the need for a thoroughly professionalized university and for the introduction of specialized academic and professional standards both to undergraduate work and to more advanced study.[56]

This emphasis accounts, in part, for the virtually total absence of references to the Scottish universities in debates over the Carnegie scheme, in 1922 and in later years. The lack can also be accounted for by the fact that Maritime academics of the 1920s, even at institutions with such clearly Scottish roots as Dalhousie and St Francis Xavier, were considerably further removed from those roots than had been their counterparts of the 1870s. Yet in the debates of the 1920s many examples were used: from elsewhere in Canada the federated universities of Toronto and Manitoba, and from England the universities of Oxford and Cambridge, were often cited as examples of what could be achieved by the proposed federation in Halifax. The colleges of New England were also frequently mentioned by both sides, either as representing institutions of established wealth with which the Maritime colleges could compare only by pooling their resources in the federation, or as examples of small, rural colleges that had high standards without being part of a centralized university.[57] An observer from the United States – Wallace Buttrick, chairman of the Rockefeller General Education Board – cited English examples to substantiate his doubts as to the merits of the Learned-Sills scheme. "I believe," wrote Buttrick to a correspondent in 1923, "that three or four small colleges in a province or a state will do more for education than any centralized institution. Oxford and Cambridge have done mighty little to democratize England. The so-called provincial universities at Leeds, Birmingham, and Liverpool have been the great democratizing force in Great Britain."[58] Of the Scottish universities, nothing was said. In some quarters mistrust of the motives of the still predominantly Presbyterian Dalhousie University was translated into ethnic mistrust of what one Methodist observer described as "these wily Scotchmen."[59] Any more serious invocation of a Scottish tradition was forestalled by the fact that Dalhousie, of all the Protestant institutions of the region still the one most closely associated with the Scots, was arguing solidly for more specialized education and for the federation principle, with democratization a peripheral issue. The example of the Scottish universities was not a good one for that purpose.

Yet there was another quite different strain of support for the Carnegie scheme that also originated from a university with strong Scottish roots, that did emphasize the democratic principle, and that was to lead to a further reform movement that bore fruit during the 1930s. For J.J. Tompkins, vice-president of St Francis Xavier University – whose active support for the Learned-Sills proposals, in the face of the opposition of his religious superiors, led to his being relieved of his university duties in late 1922 to be sent as parish priest to the remote coastal village of Canso – popular education was a prime concern. In early 1921 he had initiated a "People's School" in connection with St Francis Xavier, in which fifty-two students had enrolled for a two-month intensive course in subjects as diverse as economics, English language and literature, mathematics, commerce, and agriculture. The majority, thirty, were farmers, with the balance coming from a variety of industrial and craft occupations. Ages ranged from seventeen to fifty-seven years, the average being twenty-three, and all but ten had less than a grade-ten education. In April 1921 Tompkins reported enthusiastically to F.J. Ney of the National Council of Education that "the movement that we have started here is taking a wonderful hold on the people. Next year I hope to be able to take in forty or fifty young men – and old too – Labor leaders – actual and prospective. Of course, we shall give the school also a strong *farmer* tinge as we did this year. To the Labor men we hope to give Ethics, Industrial History, Economics and some instruction on Labor problems."[60]

Tompkins saw in the Learned-Sills proposals a chance to extend these principles. As quoted in a *Canadian Forum* article in 1923, he had hopes that through the federation St Francis Xavier would be "turned into a people's college and a people's school on a large scale."[61] His vigorous advocacy of the scheme consistently sounded this theme. To Learned in 1922, for example, he wrote, "If we judge that the best way to begin here is to put an educational pack on our backs and go to the people then that is what your new institution must do. We don't want a little Yale or a second edition of Chicago University but a university for the *Maritime Provinces*, a fair land that has become covered with mildew by reason of its whole system of education."[62] Among Tompkins's aspirations for the federated university was the hope that it would include a "Labour College," and he corresponded in the fall of 1922 with J.B. McLachlan, Cape Breton–based secretary–treasurer of District 26 of the United Mine Workers of America, with a view to making the existing Workers' Educational Club in Glace Bay the basis for such a college.[63]

Tompkins's efforts to turn the university-federation scheme into a more radical measure of reform had limited effects. The labour-college proposal was short lived. Although the Glace Bay educational club passed a favourable resolution in October 1922 and McLachlan was subsequently invited to attend the conference of colleges in Halifax later that month, he did not do so and the proposal played no part in subsequent discussions.[64] Tompkins's own forced withdrawal to Canso, and the more general problems that led ultimately to the Carnegie scheme's failure, further reduced the effectiveness of the attempt to use federation as a means of popularizing higher education in the region. It was questionable furthermore whether Tompkins could have mobilized popular support to the degree that he believed likely, even to the extent of reconciling his own concept of popular education with the kind of labour college that might have emerged from the Workers' Educational Club:

Tompkins's non-Marxist approach might well have clashed with that of the Marxist McLachlan.[65]

These speculations notwithstanding, Tompkins's advocacy deserves recognition as a distinct reform movement, even though closely linked with the Carnegie scheme. It had begun with the people's schools at St Francis Xavier and would be a forerunner of the adult-education and co-operative ventures – also closely associated with St Francis Xavier, and involving Tompkins as well as his kinsman M.M. Coady and other members of the university's extension department – that would become known in the 1930s as the Antigonish movement. Even during the phase when Tompkins's advocacy of popular education was combined with support for the Carnegie scheme, he distanced himself from its Halifax supporters. Of the Halifax newspapers, for example, he wrote in early 1922 that they were "doing a lot of harm by publishing foolish things in which Dalhousie figures as the great light around which other little stars are to revolve," and he was contemptuous of the way in which the Dalhousie supporters of the scheme preferred to proceed by covert political machination rather than working openly for genuine reform.[66] Reform for Tompkins, and reform for the Halifax advocates of the scheme, had different meanings.

Yet in one respect they shared a similarity. Neither at Dalhousie nor at St Francis Xavier, despite the strong Scottish roots of both institutions, were the Scottish universities regarded as the desirable example for higher education in the Maritime provinces. Tompkins, it was true, was well aware of the mythology of the democratic intellect, and subscribed to it sufficiently to declare in a pamphlet published in 1921 that "the democratic idea of 'college training within the reach of all people' is more completely realized in Scotland than in any other country." The conclusion of this paragraph, however, was that even in Scotland a new wave of reform was needed in order better to reach "the working population."[67] Respectful as Tompkins was towards Scottish education, the real intellectual roots of the democratization he advocated lay elsewhere. In part they originated from the values characteristic of the small, classically educated Roman Catholic elite in eastern Nova Scotia. As Daniel W. MacInnes has argued, "the educational basis of the Scots Catholic elite had been classical rather than commercial and hence their vocational aptitude tended more to such professional activities as religious ministry, law, medicine, and teaching. While such activities (excepting law) did not predispose them to engage in industrial capitalism, they did prompt a critique and evaluation of such activity."[68] In the mind of Tompkins, whose rejection of unrestrained capitalism was matched by an equal disapproval of the historical materialism of Marx and Engels, popular education was a means of asserting a moral and ultimately a religious view of the purposes of society while also enabling the population at large to gain a greater understanding of economic principles and thereby a greater measure of economic self-reliance. At the same time, he was not hesitant to forge alliances with socialist leaders – even McLachlan, whom he considered "a very clever fellow and very *red*."[69]

Nor was Tompkins unaware of other non-Marxist reform movements of the 1920s, and he was briefly attracted, for example, by Italian corporatism. "How long," he asked of his former student (and future Nova Scotia premier) Angus L. Macdonald in late 1922, "are the *young men* of this Country going to permit the state of affairs to last that has kept us as we are for the past 30 years? We need a league of youth and a few Mussolini's. Can't you start an organization through the colleges? We are all ready. This part of the Country would go *en masse* if we had a few young vigorous leaders."[70] More mundane was the close affinity of Tompkins's people's schools with the popular but non-Marxist educational principles of Ruskin College, Oxford. Henry Somerville of Ruskin, for example, who was also an official of the Catholic Social Guild at Oxford, lectured in sociology at the people's school in 1922, giving a course designed especially for "the men who come to us from the industrial centres."[71] Democracy in education, for Tompkins, was directly and inextricably bound up with the effects of social and economic change, and while this concept had points of contact with the "democratic intellect" of the Scottish universities, it clearly departed from the notion of democratic education purely for individual self-improvement and as an instrument of social mobility. That Tompkins did not find the example of the Scottish universities to be the appropriate one for his purposes was hardly surprising.

Thus, in each of the major Maritime university-reform movements examined, and in efforts through them to achieve democratization of education, the Scottish example was either absent or ineffective. Without denying the early influence on Maritime institutions of Scottish individuals and Scottish precepts, it would seem that any conscious affinity with the Scottish universities had been erased with remarkable completeness. Yet not completely, for all that. That Trueman of Mount Allison should have chosen the Scottish example in 1933, to define the tasks undertaken by small-town universities of the region in the wake of the failure of the Carnegie scheme, was one indication of continuing significance.[72] Nor was it unprecedented at Mount Allison: as early as 1896 the *Wesleyan* newspaper had described the institution as "a poor man's college," open like the Scottish universities to "the lad o' pairts."[73] Mount Allison was not a directly Scottish-influenced institution in any significant sense, and yet it had found in the concept of the democratic intellect a way of articulating its professed social role. The Scottish example also survived as a popular tradition in Scottish Presbyterian communities of the region. For the late nineteenth century, it was documented most clearly in Sir Andrew MacPhail's autobiographical account of rural Scottish life in Prince Edward Island, *The Master's Wife*. Combined in the book were family memories of MacPhail's Aberdeen-trained grandfather, who had immigrated in 1833, and the common understanding of the community that for the able student learning was the key to upward social mobility.[74] Interviews with students of Scottish origin who attended Maritime universities in the early decades of the twentieth century provide further confirmation of the vitality of the tradition. One who went to Mount Allison in 1930 from rural Cape Breton credited "the old Scotch instinct" for the high level of university attendance among his contemporaries.[75] A Dalhousie student of the same era recalled that "my father and mother were both of Presbyterian-Scottish background, and these people put a great emphasis on education. The idea of furthering your education was not strange at all in our family."[76]

What had occurred by the 1930s was the transmutation of the Scottish example into a mythology. In part it was a popular tradition, capable of influencing individuals in their decisions to seek higher education. It could also be turned to account, as by Trueman, to justify in the name of opportunity for poor and rural students the maintenance of existing institutions despite the diverse reform impulses that had been generated by the Learned-Sills report. The mythologization of the democratic intellect in the Maritimes indicates parallels with the Scottish experience. Both Scotland and the Maritimes had small populations compared with those of neighbouring areas that tended to attract migrants: in the case of Scotland the neighbour was England, although Scotland had also historically experienced out-migration to continental Europe and to various parts of the British Empire; migrants from the Maritime provinces went chiefly to the New England states and to central and western Canada. Both Scotland and the Maritimes had, by the 1930s, experienced partial industrialization and deindustrialization, with the social and economic dislocations associated with these processes. Yet both still had extensive rural areas with significant, although scattered, populations. Both, in terms of education, offered uneven opportunities for secondary schooling but traditionally had also a number of higher educational institutions that would accept students at a young age and would permit them – if academically able – to make up previous deficiencies through a continuation of general arts education. Specialized or professional education, if any, could be undertaken later on. The late nineteenth century, however, raised new questions for higher education in both Scotland and the Maritimes. New developments in science and social science cast doubt on the notion of general education. Socio-economic changes raised hard questions as to whether the old concept of the democratic intellect was any longer adequate to meet the needs of industrial or rural working classes or, conversely, to meet the perceived need of society as a whole for expansion and renewal of the professional elite.

In Scotland these developments took place over a longer time. The Scottish universities were longer-established than those of the Maritimes, and Scotland began its industrial revolution a century before industrialization had a

significant effect upon the Maritime region. Yet as higher educational institutions struggled to meet the new demands, similar approaches emerged
in both countries.

One possible solution was to maintain the traditional system and its ac-
companying mythology, by continuing to have faith in its ability to locate
and serve academically able individuals in all social classes, while superimposing more specialized institutions of research and professional training.
This was the approach strongly supported in Scotland prior to the inconclusive legislation of 1858, and also advocated in the Maritimes in the 1870s
and 1920s. In the 1870s the proponents of the University of Halifax endeavoured to preserve the rural character of most Nova Scotia colleges while
admitting that professional schools were best located in Halifax. During the
1920s the same approach was taken by opponents of the Carnegie federation
scheme, who argued that to require students to move to Halifax for their
university education would in effect deprive many rural young people of
opportunity. Argued by speakers from St Dunstan's and Mount Allison at
the 1922 Halifax conferences, this contention was strongly endorsed in the
same year by the Acadia University student magazine, the *Acadia Athenaeum*: "The expense of the larger institution together with city life and
increased travelling expenses would place a college education beyond the
means of many of our cleverest people who today can obtain it, and through
it be started well on the road to Success." To mark Acadia's rejection of
the federation, the *Athenaeum* further celebrated in 1923 "the democratic
spirit which [at Acadia] is an almost universal thing."[77] In this view, the
democratic intellect was still alive and well despite the new academic and
professionalizing forces. The Scottish tradition was a mythology that offered
a powerful expression of this belief. It was one that in both countries could
be wielded in favour of genuine enhancement of rural education, although
it also carried the danger of making individual cases of social mobility
amount to an apology for entrenched societal inequalities.

A second possible solution was to give academic professionalization prime
importance, on the ground that anything less than a rigorous training in the
academic disciplines as they now existed was unworthy to be called higher
education, no matter how democratic it might be in the traditional sense. It
was this approach that steadily gained ground in Scotland during the second
half of the nineteenth century and that was embodied especially in the
provision for a compulsory entrance examination as part of the reforms of
1892. It was this approach that was championed by the proponents of the
central teaching university in the Maritimes in the 1870s and then was advocated once again by Learned and Sills and by many of those who supported
their university-federation scheme of the 1920s. Whether or not the new
federated university would be more or less accessible to poor or to rural
students was not, for them, the central issue. Like the Scottish commentator

who in 1882 described the Scottish university graduate as "the hand-loom weaver of the intellectual world," Learned and Sills presented a stark portrayal of the existing situation as one that allowed for little real choice: "To seek to perpetuate present arrangements ... is foregone defeat."[78] For President Mackenzie of Dalhousie and for the student editors of the *Dalhousie Gazette*, who endorsed his speech at the start of construction of a new Carnegie- and Rockefeller-funded clinic at the university's medical school in November 1922, the way of progress was clear: "Quotations from the reports of the representatives of these donors," the *Gazette* maintained, "are evidence of the esteem in which Dalhousie is held by them and it is to be hoped that our University will warrant even greater tributes before many years."[79]

Also represented in the ranks of those who supported the Learned-Sills proposal, however, were those who took a third approach to the problem of university reform. Efforts to include a "people's college" and a labour college in the federation scheme, while philosophically ambivalent in their origins, having been conceived according to both Marxist and non-Marxist principles, represented a belief that new techniques must be employed in order genuinely to democratize the university system. As matters existed, according to J.J. Tompkins, "it is true our young men and women may go to college if they wish, but it is equally true that this privilege pertains to the favoured few." What was needed was to fashion institutions that could actively carry education to "the submerged 70 or 80 per cent of our population" who had been effectively deprived of educational opportunity through social and economic circumstances.[80] Working-class education in Scotland was, by the eve of the First World War, partly a function of the universities: growth in student numbers had brought increasing enrolments from applicants of working-class origins, especially at the University of Glasgow. There was also a strong tradition of independent working-class education outside the universities. Glasgow as a city, for example, was the major Scottish and British centre of Marxist education, through organizations such as the Scottish Labour College, established in Glasgow in 1916 and claiming attendance of some fifteen hundred students throughout industrial Scotland a year later.[81] Marxism, not surprisingly, was not evident in a series of reflections of students of the People's School published in Antigonish in 1921. What does emerge clearly from these comments is a belief in the school as a vehicle of non-revolutionary social change, as in the case of the Fredericton farmer who regarded the school as the force that would finally bring to an end "the willingness of the mass of the people to let others think for them and direct them for their own selfish gain."[82]

Each of the three approaches was a possible response to the dilemmas that had arisen to complicate the relationship between universities and their students, and between universities and society in general, in the late nineteenth and early twentieth centuries. In the Maritimes as in Scotland the question of how institutions should respond to the forces of academic specialization and professionalization had to be resolved in the uneasily co-existing contexts of rapid socio-economic change and of the existence of longstanding popular traditions in higher education. The Scottish tradition in Maritime higher education was real. It had its origins in the direct Scottish influence of the early nineteenth century, and it had been carried on in the ethnic culture of Maritime communities of Scottish origin. As a guide to the charting of future development in higher education, the Scottish example was already losing its force at the outset of the reform debates of the 1870s. Following the reform debates of the 1920s, the democratic intellect was still recognized in the region as a Scottish concept. Its main function, however, was not to promote reform but rather to provide a mythology that would define and justify the existing availability of Maritime universities to academically talented individuals from varied geographical and social backgrounds. As portrayed by George Trueman in 1933, the democratic intellect was a serviceable concept for hard-pressed universities and their students during the Depression. To a reformer, such as Charles Macdonald had been in 1870, it would have seemed that the Scottish example had been thoroughly tamed.

NOTES

* The research for this essay has been funded in part by grants from the Research Committee of Mount Allison University and from the Senate Research Committee of Saint Mary's University. An earlier version was presented at the Tenth Anniversary Conference of the British Association for Canadian Studies in Edinburgh in April 1985, with the assistance of a travel award from the Social Sciences and Humanities Research Council of Canada. The author wishes to thank Judith Fingard and Barry Moody for valuable comments and advice while the essay was being revised for publication.

1 Charles Macdonald, *Inaugural Address, Delivered in Convocation, at the Opening of the Eighth Session of Dalhousie College and University, Halifax, 1st November, 1870* (Halifax: Dalhousie University 1870), 10, 17.
2 *Halifax Chronicle*, 2 Jan. 1933. Although both Macdonald and Trueman used exclusive language in stressing the importance of educating male students, the apparent anti-female bias of Trueman's remark was the more ironic as Mount Allison frequently vaunted – with some justification – its achievements in women's education. See John G. Reid, "The Education of Women at Mount Allison, 1854–1914," *Acadiensis* 12 (Spring 1983): 3–33.
3 On the concept of the "democratic intellect" see George Elder Davie, *The Democratic Intellect: Scotland and Her Universities in the Nineteenth Century* (Edinburgh: University of Edinburgh Press 1961).

4 [R.A. MacLean], "Scottish Influence on Higher Education in Nova Scotia," *Scottish Tradition* 3–4 (1973–4): 41. See also D.C. Masters, "The Scottish Tradition in Higher Education," in W. Stanford Reid, ed., *The Scottish Tradition in Canada* (Toronto: McClelland and Stewart 1976), 252–67; William B. Hamilton, "Education, Politics and Reform in Nova Scotia, 1800–1848" (PhD thesis, University of Western Ontario 1970), 316–33; Hamilton, "Society and Schools in Nova Scotia," in J. Donald Wilson, Robert M. Stamp, and Louis-Philippe Audet, eds., *Canadian Education: A History* (Toronto: Prentice-Hall 1970), 95–8; Gordon Haliburton, *"For Their God" – Education, Religion, and the Scots of Nova Scotia* (Halifax: International Education Centre, nd.), 18, 20–7; D.C. Harvey, *An Introduction to the History of Dalhousie University* (Halifax: privately published, 1938), 40–63; Sir Robert Falconer, "Scottish Influence in the Higher Education of Canada," *Proceedings and Transactions of the Royal Society of Canada*, 3rd ser., 21 (1927): sec. 2, 8–9.

5 Masters, "Scottish Tradition in Higher Education," 258–9. On Dawson's participation in the 1854 commission of inquiry on the future of King's College, Fredericton, see Frances A. Firth, "King's College, Fredericton, 1829–1859," in Alfred G. Bailey, ed., *The University of New Brunswick Memorial Volume* (Fredericton: University of New Brunswick 1950), 30–1.

6 Angus Anthony Johnston, *A History of the Catholic Church in Eastern Nova Scotia*, 2 vols. (Antigonish: St Francis Xavier University Press 1960–71), 2:293–337; Firth, "King's College," 25–7. See also Alfred Goldsworthy Bailey, ed., *The Letters of James and Ellen Robb: Portrait of a Fredericton Family in Early Victorian Times* (Fredericton: Acadiensis Press 1983). Although both Jack and Robb grew up as Presbyterians, both identified themselves with the Church of England while in Fredericton; Jack re-entered the Presbyterian church later in life.

7 A.B. McKillop, *A Disciplined Intelligence: Critical Inquiry and Canadian Thought in the Victorian Era* (Montreal: McGill-Queen's University Press 1979), 24–58.

8 Harvey, *Introduction to Dalhousie*, 47–63; MacLean, "Scottish Influence on Higher Education," 44–5.

9 McKillop, *Disciplined Intelligence*, 33–4; John G. Reid, *Mount Allison University*, vol. 1, *1843–1914* (Toronto: University of Toronto Press 1984), 32–3, 92–3.

10 Robin S. Harris, *A History of Higher Education in Canada, 1663–1960* (Toronto: University of Toronto Press 1976), 52; see also J.M. Bumsted, *The Scots in Canada* (Ottawa: Canadian Historical Association 1982), 12.

11 Harris, *History of Higher Education*, 40–1; MacLean, "Scottish Influence on Higher Education," 47.

12 Hamilton, "The British Heritage," in Wilson, Stamp, and Audet, *Canadian Education*, 39; D. Campbell and R.A. MacLean, *Beyond the Atlantic Roar: A Study of the Nova Scotia Scots* (Toronto: McClelland and Stewart 1974), 156.

13 McKillop, *Disciplined Intelligence*, 24; Bumsted, *The Scots in Canada*, 12.

14 Quoted in Harvey, *Introduction to Dalhousie*, 19.
15 Memorial on Behalf of the Literary and Philosophical Institution at Pictou, Nova Scotia, [1815], Public Archives of Nova Scotia, RG14, vol. 53, 2.
16 James Scotland, *The History of Scottish Education*, 2 vols. (London: University of London Press 1969), 2: 275.
17 L.J. Saunders, *Scottish Democracy, 1815–1840: The Social and Intellectual Background* (Edinburgh: Oliver and Boyd 1950), 1–2.
18 Ibid., 2, 307–8.
19 Ibid., 2, 330–1, 360–2.
20 Davie, *Democratic Intellect*, 5.
21 Ibid., 3, 337.
22 Gladstone's proposal was embodied in the act in a permissive clause that was not implemented. See the comments of Robert Anderson, quoted in Sheldon Rothblatt, "Historical and Comparative Remarks on the Federal Principle in Higher Education," *History of Education* 16 (1987): 178.
23 Davie, *Democratic Intellect*, 41–102.
24 Ibid., 106, 337.
25 Asa Briggs, review of Davie, *Democratic Intellect*, in *English Historical Review* 8′, 1963): 568–9.
26 See C.J. Wright, "Academies and Their Aims: English and Scottish Approaches to University Education in the Nineteenth Century," *History of Education* 8 (1979): 91–7; also R.D. Anderson, *Education and Opportunity in Victorian Scotland: Schools and Universities* (Oxford: Oxford University Press 1983), 24–6, 358–61.
27 W.M. Mathew, "The Origins and Occupations of Glasgow Students, 1740–1839," *Past and Present* 33 (April 1966): 74–94. See also Bonnie Bullough and Vern Bullough, "Intellectual Achievers: A Study of Eighteenth-Century Scotland," *American Journal of Sociology* 76 (1970–71): 1048–63. While cautioning that many Scottish "achievers" came from elite backgrounds, Bullough and Bullough stress the value of education as a tool of social mobility for those of lower and lower-middle-class origins.
28 Anderson, *Education and Opportunity*, 336, 339.
29 Ibid., 209, 318.
30 Robert Anderson, "In Search of the 'Lad of Parts': The Mythical History of Scottish Education," *History Workshop Journal* 19 (Spring 1985): 84. See also Anderson, *Education and Opportunity*, 215–16, 344. For other recent discussions of the mythology of Scottish education, see J. Gray, A.F. McPherson, and D. Raffe, *Reconstructions of Secondary Education: Theory, Myth and Practice since the War* (London: Routledge and Kegan Paul 1983), 36–46, 309–15; and Andrew McPherson, "An Angle on the Geist: Persistence and Change in the Scottish Educational Tradition," in Walter M. Humes and Hamish M. Patterson, eds., *Scottish Culture and Scottish Education, 1800–1980* (Edinburgh: John Donald 1983), 216–43.

31 *Census, 1870–71* (Ottawa 1873), 1:323, 333; *Census, 1881* (Ottawa 1882), 1:301; *Census, 1931* (Ottawa 1936), 1:711–14.

32 See Bumsted, *The Scots in Canada*, 6–18; *Census, 1881*, 1:398; *Census, 1931*, 1:540–4.

33 Judith Fingard, *The Anglican Design in Loyalist Nova Scotia, 1783–1816* (London: S.P.C.K. 1972), 149–58. Between 1803 and 1807 subscription to the Thirty-Nine Articles was required for admission to King's, and from 1807 to 1829 only for graduation.

34 See William B. Hamilton, "The Linkage between Political and Education Reform in Early Nineteenth Century Nova Scotia," and B. Anne Wood, "'The Petty Feuds of Pictou': New Evidence on the 1838 Demise of Pictou Academy as Nova Scotia's Second Institution of Higher Education," papers presented to Canadian History of Education Association, Fourth Conference, Halifax, NS, October 1986; also Harvey, *Introduction to Dalhousie*, 55–6.

35 For example, see *Provincial Wesleyan* (Halifax, NS), 14, 21, 28 Dec. 1870, 11 Oct., 27 Dec. 1871, 10 Jan., 14 Feb. 1872.

36 Harvey, *Introduction to Dalhousie*, 95–6; see also Reid, *Mount Allison*, 1:130–1.

37 Dalhousie would now receive an annual grant of $3,000. King's, Acadia, and Mount Allison would have $2,400 each; Mount Allison, although located in New Brunswick, had traditionally been supported by the Nova Scotia government in recognition of its substantial number of Nova Scotia students. The two Roman Catholic colleges, St Francis Xavier and St Mary's, would receive $1,500 each. NS *Statutes*, 39 Victoria c27.

38 NS *Statutes*, 39 Victoria c28.

39 For detailed discussion of the University of Halifax scheme and its demise, see Denis Healy, "The University of Halifax, 1875–1881," *Dalhousie Review* 53 (1973–74), 39–56; and Reid, *Mount Allison*, 1:131–3, 148–52.

40 Macdonald, *Inaugural Address*, 17–18.

41 *Provincial Wesleyan*, 28 Dec. 1870. On the limitations on the openness of the Scottish universities in terms of religious affiliation, see the comments of R.D. Anderson on the virtual absence of students from Roman Catholic schools: Anderson, *Education and Opportunity*, 305.

42 *Morning Chronicle* (Halifax, NS), 15 Mar. 1876; *Wesleyan* (Halifax, NS), 18 Mar. 1876. A speech at the meeting by Allan Pollok, Glasgow-educated Presbyterian clergyman and professor of Church History at the Presbyterian College in Halifax, apparently referred only in general terms to Scotland "as a land that was developed through the education of its people." *Morning Chronicle*, 15 Mar. 1876.

43 *Morning Herald* (Halifax, NS), 9 Mar. 1876.

44 *Provincial Wesleyan*, 28 Dec. 1870.

45 NS *Statutes*, 39 Victoria c28. On the wider nineteenth-century use of the London model, see Rothblatt, "Remarks on the Federal Principle," 159–61.

46 *Morning Herald*, 9 Mar. 1876; 13, 14, 15, 17, 18 Jan. 1881.

47 See, for example, Reid, *Mount Allison*, 1:165–7, 238.

48 William S. Learned and Kenneth C.M. Sills, *Education in the Maritime Provinces of Canada* (New York: Carnegie Foundation for the Advancement of Teaching 1922), 31.

49 Ibid., 33–43.

50 *Minutes of a Conference of Representatives of Maritime Provinces Universities and Colleges* (Halifax: privately published, 1922), 44.

51 For a general interpretation of the Carnegie scheme, see Reid, *Mount Allison*, vol. 2, *1914–1963*, 64–97.

52 *Conference of Representatives of Maritime Universities*, 54.

53 Ibid., 58.

54 Ibid., 64.

55 Ibid., 55.

56 See Donald W. Light, "The Development of Professional Schools in America," in Konrad H. Jarausch, ed., *The Transformation of Higher Learning, 1860–1930: Expansion, Diversification, Social Opening, and Professionalization in England, Germany, Russia, and the United States* (Chicago: University of Chicago Press 1983), 354–5.

57 For instances of the New England example used by advocates of the continuation of existing colleges, see the arguments advanced by J.A. Faulkner in *Maritime Baptist* (Saint John, NB), 31 Jan. 1923, and by George J. Trueman in *Mount Allison Record* (Sackville, NB), Feb. 1928, 53.

58 Wallace Buttrick to W.S. Richardson, 16 Aug. 1923, J.D. Rockefeller Jr. Papers, RG2, Education Interests, Acadia University, folder 123, Rockefeller Archive Center, North Tarrytown, NY. The Rockefeller agencies had become peripherally involved in the debates over the Carnegie scheme through receiving requests for aid from Acadia University.

59 W.G. Watson to G.J. Trueman, 10 Nov. 1921, Methodist Education Papers, box 24, United Church Archives, Toronto, Ontario.

60 J. Tompkins to F.J. Ney, 11 Apr. 1921, J.J. Tompkins Papers, MG10-2, 5 (a), Beaton Institute, Sydney, NS. On the details of student attendance, see Calendar of St Francis Xavier University, 1921, 67.

61 E. Brown, "The People's School," *Canadian Forum* 3, no. 36 (Sept. 1923): 362–3.

62 Tompkins to Learned, 3 Feb. 1922, Maritime Provinces Educational Federation Files, Carnegie Corporation Archives (hereafter CCA), New York, NY.

63 J.B. McLachlan to Tompkins, 6 Oct. 1922 (copy), Maritime Provinces Educational Federation Files, CCA.

64 *Conference of Representatives of Maritime Universities*, 48.

65 On McLachlan and on concurrent class conflicts in Cape Breton, see David A. Frank, "The Cape Breton Coal Miners, 1917–1926" (PhD thesis, Dalhousie University 1979), passim.

66 Tompkins to Learned, 9 Jan. 1922, Maritime Provinces Educational Federation Files, CCA.

67 [J.J. Tompkins], *Knowledge for the People: A Call to St Francis Xavier College* (Antigonish: privately published, 1921), 9–10. The authorship of this pamphlet, which was distributed by the People's School, is established by a letter of Tompkins to R.F. Phalen, 22 Nov. 1920, St Francis Xavier University Archives, Tompkins Papers, RG30-2/110/71.

68 Daniel W. MacInnes, "Clerics, Fishermen, and Workers: The Antigonish Movement and Identity in Eastern Nova Scotia, 1928–39" (PhD thesis McMaster University 1978), 112.

69 Tompkins to Learned, 5 Oct. 1922, Maritime Provinces Educational Federation Files, CCA.

70 Tompkins to Angus L., Macdonald, 23 Nov. 1922. MG2, Angus L. Macdonald Papers, cabinet 5, folder 1348, Public Archives of Nova Scotia, Halifax, NS.

71 Tompkins to Henry Somerville, 25 Feb. 1921, Tompkins Papers, MG10-2, 5(a), Beaton Institute; Brown, "The People's School," 363. On Ruskin College and its troubled relationship with the Marxist stream of the labour movement, see Brian Simon, *Education and the Labour Movement, 1870–1920* (London: Lawrence and Wishart 1965), 311–26.

72 *Halifax Chronicle*, 2 Jan. 1933.

73 *Wesleyan*, 26 Aug. 1896.

74 Sir Andrew MacPhail, *The Master's Wife* (Toronto: McClelland and Stewart, New Canadian Library, 1977), 19, 112–24; see also Ian Robertson's introduction, xi.

75 Interview with David M. MacAulay, 7 Feb. 1977, Mount Allison University Archives.

76 Gene Hicks, 12 Aug. 1983, quoted in Paul Axelrod, "Moulding the Middle Class: Student Life at Dalhousie University in the 1930s," *Acadiensis* 15 (Autumn 1985): 89. See also Judith Fingard, "College, Career, and Community: Dalhousie Coeds, 1881–1921," in this volume, 34–5.

77 *Acadia Athenaeum* (Wolfville, NS), May 1922, 72; Mar. 1923, 44.

78 Learned and Sills, *Education in the Maritime Provinces*, 32; James Donaldson, in *Contemporary Review* 41 (1882): 150, quoted in Anderson, *Education and Opportunity*, 269.

79 *Dalhousie Gazette* (Halifax, NS), 15 Nov. 1922.

80 Brown, "The People's School," 363.

81 Anderson, *Education and Opportunity*, 308–9; Simon, *Education and the Labour Movement*, 248–9, 337–9.

82 *The People's School, Antigonish, N.S.* ([Antigonish]: The People's School [1921]), 22.

CHAPTER THIRTEEN

Financial Support for Post-graduate Students and the Development of Scientific Research in Canada*

Yves Gingras

According to the historian Hugh Hawkins, "the fellowship as an award to attract graduate students ... was probably the crucial institutional invention that brought success to the early Johns Hopkins."[1] The importance of financial-aid programs for students in the development of graduate studies, and thus in the development of university scientific research, is beyond doubt. However, the organic connection between the generation of knowledge and the training of professors willing to specialize in research, rather than in teaching, is of relatively recent origin in Canada. Before the First World War young Canadians who wished to pursue graduate study in science so as to qualify themselves as researchers were forced either to become exiles at their own expense or to try to secure awards offered by foreign universities seeking to attract outstanding students. Moreover, once they had obtained their doctorates, these researchers had no assurance of being able to return and pursue their scientific inquiries, for in the early part of the twentieth century research was not a central concern of Canadian universities.

In order to understand the circumstances that made possible the development of scientific research in the universities of Canada, this essay will trace the origins of what can be regarded as the first thoroughgoing attempt to promote scientific research in Canada: the system instituted in 1916 and 1917 by the newly created National Research Council (NRC).[2] Although there was already a certain amount of research in progress at major Canadian universities earlier in the twentieth century, the secure integration of this activity into the institutions would depend upon the establishment of a financial-aid program for post-graduate study that would be able to attract and retain a sufficient clientele of potential research professionals. Doctoral programs had appeared in 1897 at the University of Toronto and in 1906 at McGill, but the output of graduates at either master's or doctoral levels did not increase significantly until after the First World War. When it came, the increase owed much to the financial aid of the NRC.

Before examining in detail the ways in which the intervention of the NRC stimulated the growth of university scientific research, it is necessary to examine the major sources of financial support available to Canadian students before 1916. These programs enabled some young Canadians to obtain research training outside Canada, and this equipped them to bring to Canadian universities a new concept of the role of the professor. The professor, they would argue, should not be limited to teaching but should be budgeting time and resources for research.[3] Also, since the existence of research-based post-graduate degree programs was a further stimulus to systematic research, it is necessary also to consider the circumstances that prompted the University of Toronto and McGill University to introduce such programs.

THE GILCHRIST SCHOLARSHIP: AN INDIRECT APPROACH TO GRADUATE STUDY

The Gilchrist Scholarship, inaugurated in 1868 and applicable to any discipline, was awarded annually to a Canadian who wished to study for a BA degree at either the University of London or the University of Edinburgh.[4] In practice, however, most holders of the scholarship had already received their first degrees in Canada and saw little benefit in further undergraduate study. Most would use the scholarship to study at the post-graduate level. This practice implied that candidates would study simultaneously for their graduate research and for their BA finals, and this eventually led to criticism of the program. In 1886 a Dalhousie University statement called for elimination of "the provision that the student has to become a candidate for a degree because of loss of time."[5] Nine years later a report prepared by former holders of the scholarship suggested that the strain of preparation had undermined the health of some candidates.[6] In 1897 the program was abandoned. Nevertheless, it had provided support for eighteen students, of whom seven would go on to be professors in Canadian universities. Among the seven who specialized in science, three would pursue their careers in Canada: S.W. Hunton taught mathematics at Mount Allison, W.L. Goodwin chemistry at Queen's, and J.G. MacGregor physics at Dalhousie.[7]

Because it was awarded to only one student per year, the Gilchrist scholarship could not have any major overall effect on the development of post-graduate studies in Canada, except perhaps indirectly, as illustrated by the career of MacGregor, who was able to pass on to his post-graduate students the benefit of the training in research that he had received in Edinburgh. Oddly enough, the opening of Johns Hopkins University in 1876 would have more effect on the development of graduate study in Canada than did the scholarship offered by the "mother country."

THE BEGINNINGS OF DOCTORAL PROGRAMS AT
THE UNIVERSITY OF TORONTO AND MCGILL

In order to widen the clientele of their new, research-based doctoral programs, universities in the United States offered scholarships to their most able students regardless of nationality. Johns Hopkins began this trend, followed by Cornell, Harvard, and Chicago. Canadian students, just as aware as their American counterparts of the advantages to be derived from studying in these programs, did not hesitate to cross the border in large numbers. During the last quarter of the nineteenth century the four universities mentioned had an enrolment of almost three hundred Canadians, and more than one-third of these received financial support.[8] Of the total number close to one-third came from Toronto, and these students accounted for half of the bursaries received. The University of Toronto, especially hard hit by this exodus of students to the United States, was not surprisingly the first to react.[9]

In 1883 the administrators of the University of Toronto offered nine post-graduate scholarships of five hundred dollars, equal in value to those available at Johns Hopkins.[10] However, whereas at Johns Hopkins the recipients devoted all their time to the preparation of a doctoral thesis, at Toronto they had to assist their professors in teaching duties. Because the university was in a precarious financial situation, departments rapidly came to use these funds simply to hire instructors and demonstrators. At universities in the United States the award of scholarships was tied to a well-defined course of study leading to the doctoral degree. At Toronto, by contrast, the awards represented a hasty effort to ward off the dangers of competition from the south, and there was no genuine structure of post-graduate instruction. Because the work of the scholarship-holders did not lead towards a doctoral diploma, the net result was to intensify the trend towards study in the United States. There, the same work would result in the acquisition of the PhD degree, which was increasingly a necessity for anyone aspiring to a university career.

The first step towards a real solution of the problem of student emigration was not taken until 1897, when the University of Toronto introduced its doctoral program.[11] In July of that year, in the first issue of the *University of Toronto Monthly*, university president James Loudon stated clearly the argument that he had been pressing within the university community for twenty years: "The old ideal of a University as merely an institution for the transmission of knowledge is passing away. This ideal is that of the College as contrasted with the University proper which has the additional function of adding to the sum total of knowledge by original research."[12] In the same year the university calendar announced that "the degree of Doctor of Philosophy has been established for the purpose of encouraging research in the

University." Correspondingly, the *University of Toronto Series* was launched as a means of publishing theses and other works arising from the research of the professors.

This first doctoral program, which initially had no formal structure of courses, evolved under American influence to take its final form during the 1910s. In 1904 the master's program was modified to include the presentation of a paper embodying the results of original research.[13] According to A.B. Macallum, first director of the university's board of graduate studies, these changes were long overdue; if implemented fifteen years earlier, he believed, they would have given direction to the work of the earlier scholarship-holders, to the great benefit of the development of graduate studies at the university. Macallum was well placed to make this judgment, since he had proceeded after graduation from the University of Toronto to obtain a PhD at Johns Hopkins in 1888.[14]

At McGill the first modifications to the master's program were made in 1899, and the PhD degree was not adopted until 1906.[15] Even this institution, which had always enjoyed a privileged relationship with the major British universities and had recruited most of its professoriate in Great Britain, had no alternative but to adapt to North American trends. The McGill doctoral program, like that of the University of Toronto, was heavily influenced by the United States model, and led in 1922 to the creation of a Faculty of Graduate Studies.[16] In the same year the University of Toronto adopted a similar structure under the title of School of Graduate Studies.[17] When, in 1926, the two institutions became members of the Association of American Universities – founded in 1900 in order to co-ordinate the post-graduate offerings of American universities – this was a logical culmination of their increasing assimilation into a North American pattern.[18]

Yet in practical terms post-graduate studies in the sciences, whether at Toronto or McGill, received their real stimulus in the launching in 1917 of the National Research Council's program of fellowships for master's and doctoral students. Before that date McGill had awarded only one doctorate a year on average, all disciplines included.[19] The average at the University of Toronto was the same during the period from 1896 to 1907, and rose to two per year during the ensuing decade.[20] Until the end of the Second World War these two were the only institutions offering the doctoral degree in most disciplines.[21]

THE ADVANTAGES OF COLONIALISM:
THE ROLE OF THE 1851 EXHIBITION SCHOLARSHIP
IN THE TRAINING OF CANADIAN SCIENTISTS

Before the establishment of the National Research Council students interested in a scientific career could expect no significant financial aid from Canadian universities. Fortunately for them, developments in England did enable them to benefit from a program of scholarships designed specifically for young scientific graduates aspiring to training in research. In the mid-nineteenth century a movement in favour of the development of industrial research emerged in England. First taking shape in the report of the 1850 commission of inquiry on the Universities of Oxford and Cambridge, the movement gathered force with the appointment of the Devonshire Commission on technical education, and resulted in 1890 in the creation of a system of scholarships intended to encourage the training of scientists who would contribute to the industrial development of the British Empire.[22]

In 1890 the Royal Commission for the Exhibition of 1851 announced the creation of a new program of scholarships. Charged with the management of the accumulated profits of the Great Exhibition, the commission had already given assistance to such national institutions as the South Kensington Museum and the Royal College of Arts and Science. Now a study committee was quickly established. Following wide consultation its chairman, John Playfair, recommended the launching of a scholarship program similar to that already developed by Jean-Baptiste Dumas at the École pratique des hautes études in Paris. The scholarships proposed by Playfair would amount to £150 a year and would be open to British subjects under thirty years old who had demonstrated during their university studies a special aptitude for, and interest in, research in pure or applied science. Applicants were free to pursue their studies for two or three years in Great Britain or elsewhere in the world.[23] Of the twenty scholarships to be offered each year from 1891, six were to be awarded to parts of the empire outside of Britain, and two of these were reserved for Canada.

The scholarships were further designed exclusively for the scientific disciplines: biology, chemistry, geology, physics, and engineering. From 1891 to 1917 they played an important role in the training of Canadian scientists. R.T. Glazebrook, the director of the program, summed up in 1930 the significance of the 1851 Exhibition Scholarships, in the preface to a report that analysed the career patterns of those who had received the awards:

Established at a time when the field was still untouched by any system that carried training beyond the limits of ordinary degree curricula, these scholarships have undoubtedly given a great and much needed impetus to postgraduate study. They certainly played an important part in raising the standard of teaching in the younger Universities and Colleges of the Empire, and the hope, originally entertained, that in the yearly allocation within the Empire of some eighteen scholarships, a body of well-trained men of science who would be able to extend the bounds of natural knowledge, has since been abundantly realized.[24]

This judgment is borne out by the case of Canada and by the evidence from the four universities that participated in the program: McGill and the University of Toronto shared one scholarship, each university awarding it in alternate years, as did Queen's and Dalhousie. Although McGill and Toronto were already relatively well equipped in the sciences, Queen's and Dalhousie (integrated into the program in 1893 and 1894 respectively) were much less so. Especially at Dalhousie, science teaching benefited greatly from participation in the scholarship program. A committee appointed by the Dalhousie board of governors to study the implications of the new initiative reported that scientists at the university "have never been authorized by the Board of Governors to make a greater annual expenditure on ... [physics and chemistry laboratories] than is necessary for conducting the ordinary university classes ... and that while at present some facilities for research in a few very narrow departments can be afforded ... it will in two or three years be impossible not only to provide these meager facilities but even to provide practical instruction of any kind."[25] The committee estimated that an annual investment of $100 in each laboratory would be enough to halt the deterioration, but that any major improvement would be produced only with new annual expenditures of $300 to $400. It went on to conclude that the offer of an 1851 Exhibition Scholarship could be accepted by Dalhousie for the years 1894 and 1896 if $100 per year was spent on each laboratory, but that "the periodical repetition of the Commissioners' offer cannot be expected unless an additional annual expenditure of about $100 or $150 on each laboratory can be provided for."[26]

As a result the governors authorized the university senate, from 1894, to disburse up to $400 annually for laboratory improvements. The new expenditures allowed the physicist J.G. MacGregor, for example, to buy new apparatus that he had been denied for some years, and thus to "afford greater facilities for original research."[27] MacGregor was put in a position not only to carry out more research himself but also to give effective training to students. He gave his own evaluation in 1901, in a letter of application for the position of professor of natural philosophy at the University of Edinburgh: "Following the traditions of the Edinburgh Laboratory, I have endeavoured to stimulate my students to engage in research. My Advanced Practical Class was organized for this purpose eight years ago, and during this time a number of investigations have been made which have given results worthy of publication."[28] MacGregor was successful in his application, and later in 1901 he succeeded his mentor, Peter Guthrie Tait, to the chair at Edinburgh. During his time at Dalhousie he had trained at least eight students in research; their work had given rise to seventeen publications, all dealing with the physical-chemical properties of aqueous solutions. All of these students had enjoyed 1851 Exhibition Scholarships, and the majority of them used the scholarship to obtain doctoral degrees in physics or chemistry from universities in the United States before finding scientific employment either there or in Canada.[29]

By contrast with Dalhousie, McGill and the University of Toronto were able to meet the requirements of the scholarship program without difficulties.

Table 1

Destinations of 1851 Exhibition Scholars, by institution of origin, 1891–1914,
all disciplines included

University of origin	United States	Great Britain	Germany	Other countries	Total
McGill	4	7	3	0	14
Toronto	1	4	7	0	12
Queen's	6	2	4	0	12
Dalhousie	10	1	1	0	12
Total	21	14	15	0	50[1]
% of Canadian recipients	42	28	30	0	100
% of colonial recipients[2]	20	52	20	8	100

Sources: Record of the Science Research Scholarship of the Exhibition of 1851 (London 1930); R.M. MacLeod and E.K. Andrews, "Scientific Careers of 1851 Exhibition Scholars," Nature 218 (15 June 1968): 1013–14.

1 The total is larger than the total number of recipients (47) because some visited two countries on the same scholarship.

2 The colonies included were Australia, Canada, New Zealand, and South Africa.

McGill nominated its first 1851 Exhibition Scholar in 1891, and Toronto did the same the following year. From 1893 onwards McGill and Queen's named scholars in the odd-numbered years while Toronto and Dalhousie did so the even-numbered years. From 1891 to 1914, because of this financial aid from Great Britain, forty-seven Canadian students were able to acquire scientific training in the leading research laboratories of the world.

Analysis of these recipients (see Table 1) shows that by no means were all of them attracted to study in Britain. Scholars from Toronto and McGill frequently did go there, but those from Queen's and Dalhousie tended to go to the United States. Overall, the Canadians were drawn much more to the United States and Germany than were recipients from other parts of the empire, who overwhelmingly opted for Britain. There was also variation according to discipline. A large majority of students in chemistry went to Germany and used the scholarship to study at the famous laboratory of Wilhelm Oswald in Leipzig. Physicists from McGill and Toronto normally went to Britain, but Dalhousie physicists most often studied at the major American universities. These two different directions reflected to some extent the histories of the various departments and the varying networks or relationships that they had built over the years. The evidence also indicates that, contrary to conventional interpretations, the colonial relationship between Britain and Canada did not prompt Canadian science students to

Table 2
Area of specialization of 1851 Exhibition Scholars, by institution of origin,
1891–1914

University of Origin	Physics	Chemistry	Biology	Geology	Engineering
McGill	6	4	1	0	2
Toronto	6	5	1	0	0
Queen's	2	2	1	6	0
Dalhousie	4	7	0	0	0
Total	18	18	3	6	2
% of Canadian recipients	38	38	6	13	4
% of colonial recipients	49	24	10	9	8
% of British recipients	31	54	7	3	5

Sources: as Table 1.

gravitate inevitably towards Cambridge.[30] A significant factor was the shortage of doctoral programs: those students who studied in the laboratories of British universities would attain only a BA or MA degree, while those who chose universities in the United States or Germany would return with a doctorate. This discrepancy was often noted with disapproval by Canadian university presidents.[31]

As regards the choice of disciplines, Canadians conformed to the general pattern. Physics and chemistry (see Table 2) were far ahead of the rest. The British, perhaps responding to industrial needs, awarded almost twice as many scholarships to chemists as to physicists. Among the imperial recipients that proportion was reversed. Within Canada the universities of Toronto and McGill – with the large endowments – had well-established departments in several of the disciplines, and this was reflected in the choices of their candidates. At Queen's the majority opted for geology; since the opening of the School of Mining in 1893 this had been the university's chief area of scientific specialization.

Even if only half the scholarship recipients subsequently carried on their scientific careers in Canada and if the others found employment in Britain or the United States, it is not justifiable to conclude, with Robin Harris, that the 1851 Exhibition Scholarship program either did not advance or may have retarded the development of graduate studies in Canada.[32] In physics, for example, eleven of the eighteen award-holders returned to Canada, and ten continued to be active in research, nine in the universities and one at the meteorological office of the federal government. Seven of them became members of the Royal Society of Canada and can be regarded as having played an active role in the development of the discipline of physics in the country. To be sure, the limited number of scholarships available – two each year – and the fact that they were used for study at universities outside Canada combined to ensure that the program could never supply a comprehensive, long-term solution to the problem of how to stimulate scientific research at Canadian universities. Nevertheless, it is fair to conclude that, between 1891 and 1917, the 1851 Exhibition Scholarships did play a significant part in the formation of the first nucleus of Canadian scientific researchers and that these early scientists were then instrumental in generating research activity at Canadian universities.

THE FIRST WORLD WAR:
A FAVOURABLE CONJUNCTURE FOR THE GROWTH
OF RESEARCH

"In 1906," remarked H.J. Cody to the Royal Society of Canada forty years later, "research did not occupy its present position in the thought and practice of our Canadian Universities."[33] For a variety of reasons, however, that early twentieth-century situation was about to change. Part of the explanation, as already discussed, lay in the increasing presence in Canadian universities of professors who had been trained in research and who intended to continue as active scientists. Even more important was the influence of the First World War. The conjuncture of wartime circumstances brought about the discussion of scientific research as a matter of national importance that should no longer be the sole responsibility of a handful of scientists at a few universities. During the decade of the 1910s the movement for industrial research gathered strength in Canada. The movement was prompted by the industrial establishment, working through the Canadian Manufacturers' Association and with the Royal Canadian Institute acting as a bridge between industry and the universities. The war made it clear how completely Canadian industry had depended on equipment and technologies imported from Europe.[34]

The pressures exerted by industrial leaders, with the support of the presidents of the major universities, led eventually to the creation, in November 1916, of the Honorary Advisory Council for Scientific and Industrial Research, which soon came to be known as the National Research Council of Canada (NRC).[35] Made up of eleven government-appointed members, the NRC was dominated from the start by university scientists.[36] This university predominance stemmed from the fact that industrial research was virtually non-existent in Canada and that it had been the universities – working through the Canadian Institute of Toronto, and with the support of the Canadian Manufacturers' Association – that had ultimately taken the most active role in pressing the government for action. Throughout the first three decades of the twentieth century, in fact, the promotion of scientific research in Canada was effectively the preserve of a small number of individuals who met frequently – not only at meetings of the NRC, where their regular attendance ensured in itself that they would have a powerful voice, but also at meetings of the Royal Society of Canada and of the National Conference of Canadian Universities (NCCU).

A NATIONAL PROGRAM OF POST-GRADUATE FELLOWSHIPS IN THE SCIENCES

Although the administrators of the major universities had already recognized increasingly the importance of scientific research and of training scientists, the institutions' financial difficulties had hindered the translation of this support into tangible form. At Toronto, for example, the introduction of the PhD program did not lead until 1916 to the establishment of an adequate structure of financial assistance for post-graduate students. The introduction of postgraduate fellowships at that time was, according to J.C. McLennan, the head of the Physics Department, a crucial development. McLennan had been arguing for such a scheme for many years in the interests of securing a healthy future for research in his department, and in 1916 he wrote to the university president, R.A. Falconer, that "it looks as if a new era is opening for the University and I look forward for happier days now."[37] There was reason for McLennan's optimism, all the more so because the NRC would also be instituting a scheme of post-graduate financial support just a few months later. Ultimately, the University of Toronto fellowships would be directed to the disciplines not covered by the NRC awards.

A leading role in the development of the NRC fellowship scheme was taken by A.B. Macallum, former director of the University of Toronto's board of graduate studies and now the first chairman of NRC. Several months before his appointment Macallum had argued at a meeting of the NCCU that "the two great needs of Canadian Graduate Schools were scholarships and increased library facilities, because it was through these that the American Universities were able to attract so many of our Canadian Graduates."[38]

Accordingly, action was taken at the first meeting of the NRC, in December 1916. The university-based members formed themselves into a committee to study the operating principles of the 1851 Exhibition Scholarship and to make recommendations on Canada's particular needs.[39] Two types of assistance were eventually established. "Studentships," valued at $600 for the first year and $750 for the second, were to be awarded to applicants entering on their scientific studies, normally at master's level. "Fellowships," valued at $1,000 the first year and $1,200 the second, were directed to doctoral students.[40] As was true of the 1851 Exhibition Scholarships, the awards were to be confined to students who had already shown "high promise of capacity of advancing science or its applications by original research."[41] Both pure and applied sciences were covered by the programs. The first awards were made in September 1917, less than a year after the creation of the NRC.[42] Although seventy awards had been anticipated, wartime conditions limited the number to seven. Not until 1923, in fact, did the NRC reach the point of spending its entire annual budget of $120,000.

The NRC studentships and fellowships undoubtedly met the requirements of universities such as McGill and Toronto, which were already capable of introducing undergraduate students to research methods, thereby enabling them to qualify for studentships. At a profound disadvantage, however, were those institutions that were less well equipped. There, students had little opportunity to participate in research as undergraduates and so could not demonstrate their "high promise of capacity for advancing science." The result was a circular situation, where a student had to have had experience in research before being considered qualified for training. To break the cycle the NRC instituted in 1919 a system of bursaries. Worth $500, a bursary was intended to give encouragement to able students to begin postgraduate study. Any students who showed, in the first year, "distinct evidence of capacity for original research" would then qualify for a studentship.[43]

Analysis of the distribution of these different types of award shows that, had the bursaries not been offered, universities such as Dalhousie, Queen's, and those in the west would have been unable to benefit from any of the NRC awards. Even as it was, studentships and fellowships were virtually the preserve of McGill and the University of Toronto. Of the 78 studentships and fellowships awarded in physics from 1917 to 1939, for example, 3 went to Queen's students and 1 to the University of Manitoba. The University of Toronto, meanwhile, received 56 and McGill 28. Of the 100 bursaries awarded in physics from 1920 to 1939, 37 went to the smaller universities; even so, Toronto received 31 and McGill 32.[44] Despite variations among disciplines, reflecting the unequal strength of activities among the various scientific departments, the overall predominance of these two universities (see Table 3) was overwhelming. This was inevitable not only because of their large endowments but also in view of the expressed opinion of A.B. Macallum, as NRC chairman, that these two universities should be made centres of post-graduate study for the graduates of all Canadian institutions. As early as June 1918 Macallum put this argument in a letter to his sometime Toronto colleague J.C. McLennan:

One of our great difficulties, in connection with studentships and fellowships, is going to be the places of tenure of these positions. Already three of our fellows

Table 3

Number of National Research Council post-graduate awards, by year and university, 1917–39

University	Year beginning 19–																						Total
	17	18	19	20	21	22	23	24	25	26	27	28	29	30	31	32	33	34	35	36	37	38	
Toronto	3	2	9	13	21	18	16	12	17	14	16	14	11	19	15	7	6	4	4	3	9	nd*	233
McGill	3	5	5	6	11	14	16	18	14	18	22	22	28	32	26	nd	8	16	20	17	24	nd	325
Queen's	—	—	2	1	2	1	5	3	3	2	3	4	1	4	4	5	1	3	2	3	3	nd	52
Alberta	1	—	—	1	—	—	2	1	1	1	1	1	1	—	—	nd	—	—	—	—	—	nd	10
Manitoba	—	—	—	2	1	1	3	3	1	1	1	—	—	—	—	nd	—	1	—	—	—	nd	14
Saskatchewan	2	—	1	—	3	—	1	1	2	2	—	6	4	2	2	nd	1	—	1	1	1	nd	33
British Columbia	—	—	—	—	2	3	4	1	—	—	—	—	—	1	—	nd	—	—	—	1	—	nd	12
Dalhousie	—	—	1	2	1	—	—	—	1	2	3	—	1	1	1	nd	—	—	1	1	1	nd	15
Montreal	—	—	—	—	—	—	—	3	2	1	—	—	1	1	—	nd	—	—	—	1	1	nd	10
Laval	—	—	—	—	—	—	—	—	—	—	—	—	—	—	1	nd	1	1	1	2	1	nd	7

Source: annual reports of National Research Council.
* nd = no data.

have expressed a request to go to the American Universities, which the Council did not think wise to grant. When immediately after the war the number of studentships and fellowships may be increased to fifty, and, ultimately, to one hundred, the problem will become an acute one, and, in view of this, I am proposing that the universities of Toronto and McGill should establish Science Research Faculties, composed of staffs specially selected for research work and the guidance of graduates desirous of entering a scientific career.[45]

In the previous year, during the fourth meeting of the NCCU – held in Ottawa immediately following a meeting of the Royal Society of Canada – Macallum had joined with F.D. Adams, C.J. Mackenzie, and the future president H.M. Tory to prompt the passage of a resolution setting up a special committee chaired by Adams, "to take up with the authorities of the larger Canadian universities the question of organizing jointly graduate work leading to the Ph.D. degree, and that it reports the result at the next meeting of this conference."[46] Later meetings of the NCCU took the proposal so far as to discuss the creation of a national post-graduate university. This scheme had no chance of succeeding, however, because of the fierce competitiveness of the existing universities in their efforts to attract students and in view of the constitutional principle by which education came within provincial jurisdiction.[47] In effect, while the discussions went on, Toronto and McGill were steadily consolidating their ability to attract the majority of aspiring Canadian post-graduate students who did not wish to move to the United States. Their firm grasp on the NRC financial awards was both cause and effect of this consolidation. Because the recipients were obliged to undertake their research work at an institution "where the conditions are thoroughly suitable, and the accommodation ample, for such researchers," the two largest universities enjoyed a clear advantage.[48] Their output of science graduates, at both master's and doctoral levels, increased greatly from the early 1920s onwards.[49]

Obviously, the decision of the NRC to concentrate its financial aid at universities that were already well equipped for research work was not welcomed by all. Queen's University, spurred by the physicist A.L. Clark, was quick to respond by creating an inter-department committee on scientific research. In its first report, appended to the university principal's report for 1916–17, the committee stated its guiding principle forcefully: "It is essential, if Queen's is to maintain her rank among Canadian universities and is to contribute her proper share to the advancement of knowledge and to the development of our national resources, that increased attention and support be given to the world of research."[50] "Very little help is to be expected [from the NRC]," the committee continued, "to establish research work." It recommended that the university establish its own research council, charged with distributing grants to researchers and paying for the hiring of research assistants. The support of summer research was to be emphasized, in view of the problems encountered by professors trying to combine research with their teaching commitments during the regular academic year. The committee further suggested that Queen's offer its own $600 scholarships and $1,200 fellowships.[51] Yet its plans were to prove unrealistic. Full implementation would have required an annual expenditure of $25,000 to $30,000. In its first year the university could provide only $10,000, and there was no guarantee of renewal. As a result, no financial awards were made. Queen's did receive, between 1917 and 1927, nineteen awards from NRC. In terms of numbers of awards it was thus placed immediately behind McGill and Toronto and ahead of the eleven granted to the University of Saskatchewan. Queen's would retain this third-place status throughout the interwar years.

For A.L. Clark, the creation of the Queen's committee on scientific research was only the beginning. Appointed dean of Applied Science in 1919, Clark immediately suggested to G.Y. Chown, retiring as registrar and treasurer of the university, the endowment of a research professorship.[52] Chown agreed, and the Chown Research Professorship was created for the fields of chemistry or physics. The first incumbent was an English physicist, A.L. Hughes, who departed four years after his 1919 appointment to take up a position in the United States. He was succeeded by another physicist, the Australian J.A. Gray, who held the position until retirement in 1951. The establishment of this position had a marked effect on the expansion of research work in physics at Queen's. Between 1923 and 1939 the department's students gained fourteen NRC awards, three times as many as any other physics department except for those of McGill and Toronto. At the same time, the awards themselves were essential to the healthy development of research in the department.[53] Gray himself was quick to feel the absence of fellow-researchers, and in 1926 he confided to his mentor Ernest Rutherford that "I have only one research student at present. I have three x-ray outfits with a fourth one nearly complete and no one but myself to work them."[54] Happily for Gray, two of his students gained NRC awards in the following year, and by 1928 he was supervising three such award-holders.

For the members of the NRC the award of financial support to post-graduate students constituted only a first step towards the establishment of a systematic research capacity in Canada. With post-graduate awards to encourage students to enter on research, it was equally essential that professors should also be in a position to devote themselves to research activities. Therefore, as soon as the regulations for the post-graduate awards had been defined, the council set about designing a scheme for subventions to researchers.[55] The grants, made initially for a single year but renewable on reapplication, would "as a general rule, only be made to persons who are conducting investigation in established laboratories which possess the fundamental ap-

paratus and facilities necessary for research of the nature proposed, and ...
will not be made for the purchase of standard apparatus which a well
equipped laboratory should possess."[56] Naturally, this gave a further advantage to institutions already well equipped – notably McGill and Toronto
– and gave further cause for grievance on the part of the universities that
thought they would be effectively excluded from the scheme.

CONCLUSION

Ten years after the inauguration of the programs providing financial awards
to post-graduate students and grants to researchers, the NRC felt able to claim
that "an active and efficient research organization has been built in Canada,
through which the investigation of any problem of national importance can
be undertaken." A total of 344 postgraduate awards had been made to 199
individuals, distributed among twelve universities. Although "the main purpose of scholarships ... [was] to train men in research work," the council
cited 456 scientific publications by the recipients, which it regarded as a
sign of the high quality of work accomplished. In the context of the old
problem of emigration of scientists to the United States, the council reported
with satisfaction that of 155 award-holders who had completed their studies,
no fewer than 123 had remained in Canada.[57]

Most of these awards had gone to aspiring physicists and chemists. In
physics Canadian universities had graduated, on average, only 1 PhD every
three years between 1900 and 1919. From 1920 to 1930, with the help of
the NRC awards, the rate increased to 2.5 per year, and to 6 per year in the
ensuing decade. The rate of increase was just as rapid at the master's level:
from 2 per year between 1900 and 1919 to 9 in the years from 1920 to 1930
and 12 between 1930 and 1940. Also in physics – though the pattern was
similar in the other disciplines – the doctorates were granted by Toronto
and McGill only. At the master's level, however, those universities accounted only for some 65 per cent of the total, a sign that other institutions,
notably Dalhousie, Queen's, and the prairie universities, had also developed
their research capacities.

The production of scientific publications had also been stimulated by the
NRC programs, with chemistry and physics again the leading disciplines.
The increase in research activity was reflected clearly in the meetings of the
Royal Society of Canada. The number of papers presented to Section III
(comprising physicists, chemists, astronomers, and mathematicians) had
averaged nine per year from 1900 to 1915. Between 1923 and 1930 the
average rose to almost one hundred, with physicists and chemists sharing
equally in some 90 per cent of the total number of presentations.[58]

In summary, the programs of the National Research Council played a
fundamental role in the development of scientific research at Canadian uni-

versities and prompted the growth of distinct research communities in the various disciplines. The existence of a systematized research capability was a necessary precondition for the creation of a national scientific community, which needs well-defined institutional structures in order to reproduce itself. Just as the Gilchrist awards and the 1851 Exhibition Scholarships facilitated the *emergence* of research as a new function of the universities, so the initiatives of the NRC provided for the *institutionalization* of this research capacity. Thus, the generation of professors who, at the turn of the century, had received their scientific training at universities in Europe and the United States was afforded the opportunity and the right to pursue research activities at Canadian institutions that had been devoted hitherto only to teaching.[59]

NOTES

* Translated from the French by John G. Reid.
1 Hugh Hawkins, "University Identity: The Teaching and Research Functions," in Alexandra Oleson and John Voss, *The Organization of Knowledge in North America, 1860–1920* (Baltimore: Johns Hopkins 1979), 25.
2 The council will be referred to as the National Research Council even though this title was not officially adopted until 1924. Before that time it was officially known as the Honorary Advisory Council for Scientific and Industrial Research, though commonly referred to simply as the Research Council. See M.L. Thistle, *The Inner Ring: The Early History of the National Research Council* (Toronto: University of Toronto Press 1966), 131.
3 On the emergence of scientific research in Canada, see Yves Gingras, "De l'enseignement à la recherche: l'émergence d'une nouvelle pratique de la physique dans les universités canadiennes," *Histoire sociale / Social History* 37 (May 1986): 73–91.
4 Robert A. Falconer, "The Gilchrist Scholarship: An Episode in the Higher Education of Canada," *Proceedings and Transactions of the Royal Society of Canada* (hereafter *PTRSC*), 3 rd ser., vol. 27 (1933): sec. II, 5–13.
5 Dalhousie University Archives, Minutes of the Faculty of Arts, 10 Dec. 1886.
6 Falconer, "The Gilchrist Scholarship," 10.
7 "William Lawton Goodwin (1856–1914)," *PTRSC*, 3 rd ser., vol. 39 (1945): 87–8; "James Gordon MacGregor, 1852–1913," *Proceedings of the Royal Society*, ser. A, vol. 89 (1913): xxvi–xxviii; on S.W. Hunton, see John G. Reid, *Mount Allison University*, vol. 1, *1843–1914* (Toronto: University of Toronto Press 1984), 185–6.
8 Figures from P.N. Ross, "The Development of the Ph.D. at the University of Toronto, 1871–1932" (Ed.D. thesis, University of Toronto 1972), 181. For the 1890s Robin Harris gives the following statistics: more than 30 at Johns Hopkins,

more than 60 at Harvard, more than 50 at Cornell, and more than 80 at Chicago. R.S. Harris, *A History of Higher Education in Canada* (Toronto: University of Toronto Press 1976), 191–2.

9 Ross, "Development of the Ph.D.," 199; Harris, *History of Higher Education*, 188.

10 Ross, "Development of the Ph.D.," 89.

11 P.N. Ross, "The Establishment of the Ph.D. at Toronto: A Case of American Influence," in M.B. Katz and P.H. Mattingly, *Education and Social Change* (New York: New York University Press 1973), 193–214.

12 J. Loudon, "Changes and Progress," *University of Toronto Monthly* 1 (July 1897): 6–9; cited in Ross, "Development of the Ph.D.," 118.

13 Ross, "Development of the Ph.D.," 118–96.

14 A.B. Macallum, "The Foundation of the Board of Graduate Studies," *University of Toronto Monthly* 16 (1916): 220. On Macallum, see *Dictionary of Scientific Biography* (New York: Scribner 1973), vol. 8, 583–4; also *PTRSC*, 3 rd ser., vol. 28 (1934): xix–xxi.

15 Stanley B. Frost, *McGill University: For the Advancement of Learning*, vol. 2, *1895–1971* (Montreal: McGill-Queen's University Press 1984), 80–2.

16 Ibid., 177.

17 Ross, "Development of the Ph.D.," 292.

18 Ibid., 245. For further discussion of the AAU, see L. Veysey, *The Emergence of the American University* (Chicago: University of Chicago Press 1965), 175–7.

19 Frost, *McGill University*, 2:177.

20 Ross, "Development of the Ph.D.," 195.

21 W.P. Thomson, *Graduate Education in the Sciences in Canada* (Toronto: University of Toronto Press 1963).

22 Roy MacLeod, "The Endowment of Research Movement in Great Britain, 1868–1900," *Minerva* 9 (1971): 197–230.

23 Roy M. MacLeod and E. Kay Andrews, "Scientific Careers of 1851 Exhibition Scholars," *Nature* 218 (15 June 1968): 1012. On the financial aid program of the École pratique, see Craig Zwerling, "The Emergence of the École Normale Supérieure as a Center of Scientific Education in the Nineteenth Century," in R. Fox and G. Weisz, ed., *The Organization of Science and Technology in France, 1808–1914* (Cambridge: Cambridge University Press 1980), 45.

24 *Record of the Science Research Scholars of the Exhibition of 1851* (London 1930), 1.

25 Dalhousie University Archives, MS IS 4, Minutes of the Board of Governors, vol. 4, 8 Nov. 1892, p 226.

26 Ibid., 227.

27 Ibid.

28 Public Archives of Nova Scotia, MG 100, 182, no. 37, Application of James Gordon MacGregor for the Professorship of Natural Philosophy in the Edinburgh University, 1901, 4–5.

29 For further details of the career patterns of these students, see Y. Gingras, "Les Physiciens canadiens: généalogie d'un groupe social, 1850–1950" (Thèse de doctorat, Université de Montréal 1984), 93–6.

30 See also Y. Gingras, "Le Développement du marché de la physique au Canada, 1879–1928," in R.A. Jarrell and A. Roos, *Critical Issues in the History of Canadian Science, Technology and Medicine* (Thornhill: HSTC Publications 1983), 16–30.

31 The fourth conference of Canadian universities, in 1917, resolved to send a circular letter to the major British universities arguing that "[only with] the establishment of doctorates that may be obtained within a reasonable time ... can we hope that the stream of students which of late has set towards the United States, will be directed to the Universities of Britain." See "Fourth Conference of Canadian Universities, May 24–25, 1917," in *National Conference of Canadian Universities*, 63.

32 Harris, *History of Higher Education*, 315.

33 H.J. Cody, "A Chapter in the Organization of Higher Education in Canada, 1905–1906," *PTRSC*, 3 rd ser., vol. 40 (1946): sec. II, 98.

34 For further details of the evolution of the movement for industrial research, see Philip Enros, "The University of Toronto and Industrial Research in the Early Twentieth Century," in Jarrell and Roos, *Critical Issues*, 155–66; and Enros, "The Bureau of Scientific and Industrial Research and School of Specific Industries: The Royal Canadian Institute Attempt at Organizing Industrial Research in Toronto, 1914–1918," *HSTC Bulletin* 7, no. 1 (Jan. 1983): 14–26.

35 The events surrounding the establishment of the NRC are well discussed in Thistle, *The Inner Ring*.

36 Ibid., 9–12.

37 J.C. McLennan to R.A. Falconer, 9 Aug. 1916, cited in Ross, "Development of the Ph.D.," 274.

38 "Third Conference of Canadian Universities: McGill University, May 22 and 23, 1916," in *National Conference of Canadian Universities*, 23–4.

39 NRC Archives, Minutes of the First Meeting, December 4–6, 1916, Minute no. 21.

40 Thistle, *The Inner Ring*, 27.

41 *Annual Report of the NRC, 1917–18*, 38.

42 Ibid., 37.

43 Ibid., *1918–19*, 42.

44 These figures are compiled from annual reports of NRC, which include each year a list of award recipients, their research fields, and the universities where they worked.

45 A.B. Macallum to J.C. McLennan, 22 June 1918, cited in Thistle, *The Inner Ring*, 36.

46 "Fourth Conference of Canadian Universities," 52–9.

47 Ibid., 53. See also "Fifth Conference, 1918," 11; and "Eighth Conference, 1922," 52–9.

48 A.B. Macallum to Sir George Foster, 25 Aug. 1917, quoted in Thistle, *The Inner Ring*, 27.

49 On the situation at McGill, see Frost, *McGill University*, 2:177–81; and Thomson, *Graduate Education in the Sciences*, chap. 4.

50 Report of the Committee on Scientific Research, in *Annual Report of the Principal of Queen's University, 1916–17*, 30.

51 Ibid., 35.

52 Queen's University Archives, coll. 2400, box 2, A.L. Clark to G.Y. Chown, 23 March 1919.

53 See the remarks of Clark in Report of the Committee on Scientific Research, in *Annual Report of the Principal of Queen's University, 1926–27*, 47.

54 Queen's University Archives, Gray Papers, box 4, J.A. Gray to E. Rutherford, 27 Oct. 1926.

55 NRC, Minutes of the Fifth Meeting, May 12–21, 1917, 4.

56 Regulations Governing the Award for Grants for Research, *Annual Report of the NRC, 1917–18*, 30.

57 *Annual Report of the NRC, 1926–27*.

58 Y. Gingras, "Croissance de la recherche scientifique et transformation de la Section III de la Société royale du Canada," *Scientia Canadensis* 10, no. 1 (Spring 1986): 53–71.

59 See Gingras, "De l'enseignement à la recherche"; and Gingras, "The Institutionalization of Scientific Research at Canadian Universities: The Case of Physics," *Canadian Historical Review* 67 (1986): 181–94.

CHAPTER FOURTEEN

Father Georges-Henri Lévesque and the Introduction of Social Sciences at Laval, 1938–55*

Michael Behiels

If we do not allow scholars, at their own best speed and in full academic freedom, to carry on their research aimed at extending human knowledge and ultimately improving the quality of human life, the result will be to make science sterile and to dry up the main source of human progress.[1]

Georges-Henri Lévesque

The teaching of the social sciences took root in the francophone universities of Quebec at the beginning of a crucial period of socio-economic change stimulated by the Second World War. This process of change would contribute to the renewal of conflict between clerico-nationalist and liberal ideologies. Before the 1940s the Catholic church in Quebec – and the great majority of its clerics – supported the clerico-nationalist ideology, which had as its principal goal the "sacralization" of the institutions, customs, and values associated with the new industrialized urban society. The creation of the School of Social, Economic, and Political Sciences at Laval University in 1938 under the direction of Father Georges-Henri Lévesque would permit the preaching of liberal principles by a small minority of clerics and lay people. Ultimately, a new definition of the collective character of Quebec society would emerge, pervaded by secular values, by individualism and rationalism. Thus the liberal values and beliefs that were long established in Quebec society at a more popular level, as the work of Yves Roby has shown, would receive the open encouragement of a new elite trained in the social sciences.[2] Also, a wider and deeper understanding of the problems facing French Canada would prompt Father Lévesque and his early colleagues to abandon French Canadian nationalism in favour of "clear-sighted integration into a new Canadian federation." The professors of the next generation, however, would reject what they considered to be a false set of options and instead would gradually develop a new nationalism, reflecting the beliefs and aspirations of a new technocratic and bureaucratic class.

At Laval the introduction of the social sciences was not accomplished without difficulty. For fifteen years, there was strong and tenacious opposition both inside and outside the university. The sociologist Marcel Fournier, in his study of the institutionalization of social science in Quebec, argues that the essential cause of these problems can be found in the efforts of social-science professors to obtain social recognition for and institutionalization of their new disciplines. Teaching and research in social science represented, at that time, a threat to established elites and to the power base of the Duplessis government. If the Laval Faculty of Social Sciences wished to preserve and extend its autonomy, it had no choice but to oppose the Union Nationale and the complex of interest groups that kept the party in power. Had it not been for this vigorous resistance, the Duplessis government would have continued its policy of reducing the faculty's subsidies and would have refused to employ social-science graduates of Laval. According to Marcel Fournier,

[Their professors and their dean] could not hope, in view of all the evidence, to gain recognition in society or a higher status in the university except by contributing to the defeat of the government. This implied an alliance, on the one hand, with the trade union and co-operative movements and, on the other hand, with the Liberal party. That party drew inspiration from the faculty's research and reflections, and committed itself to administer affairs of the state "with expertise," that is, by making use of whatever expertise was available. In effect, it was by supplying expertise to these diverse opposition movements and in return receiving their support that the social-science professors were able to redefine their mission outside the university and to take advantage of opportunities for accomplishing their internal goals of building up an accumulation of specialized knowledge, forming an integrated "scientific community," and providing coherent and well-focused education.[3]

There is no doubt that the pressures associated with institutionalization, and conflicts between the interests of social classes, formed part of the explanation for this opposition to the established order both outside and inside Laval. However, an ideological dimension must also be considered in order to explain fully and satisfactorily the social and political action of the dean and his colleagues between 1938 and 1954. It was largely thanks to the skill, determination, and ingenuity of Father Lévesque that the young Faculty of Social Sciences was able to survive this difficult period. Under the aegis of Catholic social doctrine, which they interpreted liberally, the dean and the professors advocated a dualistic concept of the social sciences. The faculty's program of studies reflected this duality: "normative" courses on the social doctrine of the church were accompanied by "positive" courses on the methodologies and scientific theories of the various social sciences. In a society still officially Catholic, with its universities church-controlled, this dualistic approach was absolutely necessary if teaching of the social sciences was to be introduced in Quebec. Had the dean not been a cleric, preaching this dualism with evident conviction, the attacks on the new faculty might well have been successful.

The dualist approach had been inspired by the liberal and socially oriented Catholicism preached by Lévesque and his colleagues. Their ideological convictions had led them to adopt a policy of social action. Imbued with social passion, this first generation of social-science professors intended to turn their new forms of knowledge to the cause of reforming the *mentalité* and the institutions of Quebec society. Thereby, they believed, the Catholic Church could remain as a vital and dynamic force in the daily lives of all French-Canadians. This social movement within Catholicism arrived too late, however, to be successfully established in Quebec. The secularizing process had attained such momentum by the 1950s that this second attempt at "sacralization" – this time involving a more liberal form of Catholicism – was destined for virtually inevitable failure. It is this reality that explains why, when the future of the faculty finally became secure during the decade, it became possible for a second generation of professors, all lay people, to abandon dualism and dedicate themselves solely to teaching the methods and secular theories of social-science fields that were constantly becoming more specialized.

THE ADVENT OF THE SOCIAL SCIENCES AT LAVAL

An essential precondition for the renewal of liberal ideology in Quebec and for its successful confrontation with clerico-nationalism was a profound transformation of francophone university education. The ground had been well prepared by the conjuncture of socio-economic forces in the interwar period. The economic growth of the 1920s, largely based on exploitation of natural resources, had accelerated the urbanization and the secularization of Quebec. After the Depression of the 1930s the double process of urbanization and economic growth began again and eventually destroyed the foundations and the frameworks of traditional society. The number of French Canadians living on farms fell from 41 per cent in 1941 to 13 per cent in 1961. At the same time the number of francophone males working in the tertiary sector of the economy rose from 28 per cent in 1941 to 45 per cent in 1961. These changes, and many others in the same period, contributed to the changing of the occupational structure and – little by little – to the secularization of the customs and values, the *mentalité*, of francophone Quebec.[4] Francophone elites no longer formed a solid bloc, and their socio-political discourses ceased to present a unified image of society. Increasingly, new members of the elites, trained in the social or the natural sciences, preached a liberal ideology and defined a new identity for the Québécois collectivity, one that was rationalistic, individualistic, and secularized.

With the creation in 1920 of the Faculty of Science at the University of Montreal and of the School of Chemistry at Laval, the process of transformation was implanted. It was symbolized in 1923 in the foundation of the *Association canadienne-française pour l'avancement des sciences* (ACFAS), which prompted a vigorous debate on the need to introduce the teaching of natural and physical sciences into the classical colleges.[5] Most professors were opposed to this, for, as Jean-Charles Falardeau has shown, the transformation amounted to nothing less than a radical reorientation of the entire character of university and secondary education by redefining some of the fundamental goals. The classical college, traditionally the cornerstone of Quebec education, had justifiably based its curriculum on the Greek and Latin humanities but for historical reasons had limited its role to directing students towards the liberal professions and in its teaching had emphasized the abstract and other-worldliness.[6]

The introduction of the natural sciences having provoked a major debate, that of the social sciences – involving the study of human beings, and infused with value judgments – generated a second one. It would be longer and more agitated than the first, because the ascendancy of the traditional elites in Quebec society would be called into serious question.[7]

The systematic teaching of the social sciences at Laval began in the fall of 1938. Cardinal J.-M. Rodrigue Villeneuve, eminent theologian and sociologist, archbishop of Quebec (1931–47), and apostolic chancellor of Laval, announced on 1 April 1938 the establishment of a School of Social, Economic, and Political Sciences at Laval, leading to the baccalaureate and to the *licence ès lettres*.[8] Part-time instruction in social science had been available since 1920 at the University of Montreal and since 1932 at Laval. Most of the students had been clerics; the courses had led to no diploma and offered no prospect of professional employment. The purpose of these programs, according to the church hierarchy, had been to provide academic facilities for teaching and propagating the social doctrine of the church, as embodied in the relevant papal encyclicals. The economic crisis that enveloped Canada and the rest of the industrialized world after 1929 made the hierarchy, along with the professional elites and the politicians, extremely nervous. Cardinal Villeneuve believed that if the church were to survive and prosper in Quebec it would need a more elaborate strategy, and a structure, for teaching social doctrine. Moreover, the church also needed more lay workers to assist in such areas as in teaching, in social work, and in the Catholic trade unions.[9] Thus, the creation of the School of Social Sciences at Laval in 1938 represented in part a further step towards the "sacralization" of society, a strategy pursued by the Quebec episcopate since the early twentieth century. Villeneuve and his advisers hoped that Catholic education in the social sciences would dissuade the Québécois from adopting the relativistic philosophy of the "objective" social sciences or the atheistic collectivism of Marxism.[10]

To meet this challenge, Villeneuve chose Father Georges-Henri Lévesque as director. A member of the Dominican order, Lévesque had been a professor of economic philosophy in the Faculty of Philosophy at Laval since 1936. With previous experience teaching at the Dominican College in Ottawa from 1933 to 1935 and at the School of Social Sciences at the University of Montreal in 1935, Lévesque was well qualified for his new position. He also showed himself to be a skilled administrator as the new school grew in its number of personnel. Born at Roberval in 1903, Lévesque had his earliest education from the Marist brothers. He obtained his baccalaureate from the seminary at Chicoutimi, where he decided to become a Dominican. After spending a year of his noviciate at St-Hyacinthe, he attended the Dominican College in Ottawa to complete his studies in philosophy and theology. With the general economic crisis fully evident, his superiors sent him to Europe to specialize in the social sciences at the Catholic University of Lille. Between 1931 and 1933 Lévesque made a number of research trips to Geneva, where he studied the League of Nations and the International Labour Organization. He also visited Belgium to meet with the renowed Father Ceslas Rutten, a militant advocate of Catholic social action who had taken a leading role in the creation of trade unions, co-operatives, and youth movements for Catholic action in his country. Lévesque returned to Canada even more convinced than heretofore that Catholic social doctrine could be successfully applied to the social and economic problems of a crisis-ridden Quebec society.

In February 1933 J.S. Woodsworth rose in the House of Commons to announce the impending establishment of a new political party, the Co-operative Commonwealth Federation (CCF). The CCF advocated democratic socialism for Canada, and fear of socialism prompted the Catholic church in Quebec to oppose it. Father Lévesque, as a teacher of Catholic social doctrine who also sought to put that doctrine into effect, was chosen as one of a team made up of clerics and lay people and charged with drafting the church's response to the menace of the CCF. He was one of thirteen ecclesiastics who were convened in Montreal on 9 March 1933 under the auspices of the École sociale populaire to study the CCF program from the perspective of church social doctrine. Lévesque himself wrote the critique of the new party.[11] He concluded that the CCF had espoused "the three great vices which characterize the pure socialism condemned by the church: violent class struggle, suppression of private property through excessive socialization of assets, and finally a materialistic concept of society."[12] Following the directives in the encyclical *Quadragesimo anno* of Pope Pius XI, Lévesque believed that it was impossible at the same time to be a loyal Catholic and a thoroughgoing socialist. Only if the CCF were to abandon the three "great vices" would it be open to Catholics to support the party.[13]

Gradually, however, Lévesque realized that the socialism of the CCF had virtually nothing in common with the anti-Catholic and materialistic so-

cialism of continental Europe. He began to understand the social and intellectual context of the CCF program, which drew its inspiration from British
Fabian socialism. It had been adapted to Canadian needs by the League for
Social Reconstruction, led by F.R. Scott, Frank Underhill, and other professors of McGill University and the University of Toronto. Lévesque also
came to accept that the CCF had a spiritual and moral dimension that sprang
from the social-gospel movement in the Protestant denominations. In 1939
he changed his opinion of the CCF and began to teach in his courses that,
given a liberal interpretation of Catholic social doctrines, church censure of
the party was neither necessary nor useful. It was Lévesque, in fact, who
persuaded Cardinal Villeneuve to join in October 1943 in the signing of a
declaration of Canadian bishops giving permission to Catholics to vote for
the CCF. Nevertheless, in spite of the efforts of Lévesque, Archbishop Charbonneau of Montreal, and a small group of other priests and lay people to
set forth the affinities between Catholic social doctrines and the democratic
socialism of the CCF, most ecclesiastical leaders in Quebec continued to
adhere to a narrow interpretation of doctrine and rejected socialism in any
form.[14] This majority attitude largely explains the conflict between the
church and Lévesque's new Faculty of Social Sciences.

At first the progress of the School of Social Sciences was slow. It continued to be affiliated with the Faculty of Philosophy, and its mandate was
"to give a higher education on social questions based on Christian principles
and adapted to the particular conditions and needs of our country," with a
view to the training of "the teachers, proselytizers, and leaders without
whom it would be hopeless to aspire to a Christian social order."[15] According to Father Gonzalve Poulin, then a member of the school, the program
of study was strongly oriented towards the teaching of social and political
philosophy, and gave "an over-riding importance to the social doctrine of
the papal encyclicals."[16] As director of the school Father Lévesque firmly
maintained this Catholic approach to the social sciences, and as a priest it
was natural that he should regard "God as the greatest of all sociologists."[17]
Yet his experiences since 1933 had brought him to recognize that modern
scientific methodology could not properly be taught solely through a didactic
consideration of the encyclicals. In 1974, he wrote: "Nevertheless, all my
diverse experiences, all the courses, all the meetings, all the travel, had
brought me to see clearly that we had an enormous and urgent need for
sociologists, economists, political scientists, and industrial relations experts,
and that all the evidence showed that to train these specialists we absolutely
needed to organize genuine teaching of the social sciences in Quebec."[18]

Lévesque declared in 1940 that the school must be upgraded to become
a faculty, with autonomous departments of economics, sociology and social
ethics, industrial relations, and social service, along with an institute of
social research. This transformation was accomplished in 1943 and inaugurated a new era for the social sciences in Quebec. Even if it is true, as

put by Jean-Charles Falardeau, that "it was only little by little that new wine was poured into the old bottle," nobody else could have accomplished the modernization of social science at Laval with the same skill, diplomacy, and tenacity as did Lévesque.[19]

His first challenge was to deal with the near-total lack of French Canadian specialists in social science. In 1943 most professors of the school were clerics with degrees in philosophy and theology. The dean of the faculty dealt with this problem in two ways. First, he recruited well-qualified professors from diverse backgrounds, such as Father I. Eschmann, of German origin (1940–42), Father J. Thomas Delos of France (1940–44), and the renowned University of Chicago sociologist Everett C. Hughes (1942–45). Secondly, he encouraged – often with financial aid – a number of the faculty's most gifted graduates to go to the United States, and after the war to Europe, to undertake doctoral study in sociology, political science, and economics.[20]

This strategy soon bore fruit. Within a few years the new faculty had at its disposal young Québécois who were specialists in the various social-science disciplines. Jean-Charles Falardeau, at the suggestion of Everett Hughes, went to Chicago in 1941 for doctoral work in sociology. He returned to Laval as a professor in 1943 and became director of the Sociology Department ten years later.[21] Maurice Lamontagne and Maurice Tremblay obtained doctorates at Harvard, in economics and political science respectively, and were then employed by Laval. Roger Marier chose the Catholic University in Washington and returned to establish at Laval a school of social service.[22]

Following the end of the war other graduates of the Faculty of Social Sciences were free to pursue their studies in Europe. Léon Dion taught sociology in the faculty before attending the London School of Economics and eventually obtaining in Germany a doctorate in political science. His colleague Gérard Bergeron, with a professional interest in international affairs and the role of the United Nations, spent the year 1947 at the Institut universitaire des Hautes Études internationales in Geneva; he later enrolled for two years at the Faculty of Law of the University of Paris, where in the late 1950s he gained a doctorate for his study of the role of the state in the modern world.[23] Dion and Bergeron returned to Laval to teach in the Faculty of Social Sciences, and made the Department of Political Science a dynamic and progressive centre of study. Two other graduates of the faculty, Guy Rocher and Fernand Dumont, completed their post-graduate studies at Harvard and at Paris respectively. They also returned to Laval and were largely responsible for the complete secularization of the methodology and the curriculum of the faculty.[24]

Most of these candidates were personally selected by Lévesque, and the majority came from similar social and regional backgrounds. Lamontagne, Tremblay, and Dion came from the economically underdeveloped regions of Lac Saint-Jean and the lower St Lawrence Valley, and they had received their classical education at the seminaries of Chicoutimi and Rimouski. Furthermore, this first generation of true social scientists shared common goals: the development of a methodology for objective research, ideological pluralism, dynamic social action, and the political and social modernization of Quebec society.[25]

THE FACULTY AND ITS ADVERSARIES

The first decade of the new Faculty of Social Sciences was a turbulent and demanding time for Father Lévesque and his colleagues. The faculty encountered stiff opposition, as interpreted by Léon Dion, from "groups, including the provincial political leadership and certain ecclesiastics, who – whether through self-interest or through sincere conviction – wanted the faculty to commit itself firmly to the defence of the traditional social order, which is to say that the human sciences would be turned to the service of national mythology and the interests of the wealthy."[26] Apart from the national and Catholic trade unions, it was the Faculty of Social Sciences at Laval that was in the 1940s the main centre of opposition to the policies of the Duplessis regime, to traditional French-Canadian nationalism, and to the supremacy of the church in education and social services.[27] During the 1950s several members of the faculty identified themselves with other opposition groups, such as the *Cité libre* group led by Pierre-Elliott Trudeau and Gérard Pelletier, or the Institut canadien des affaires publiques, through which those on the left developed and publicized a systematic critique of Quebec society and especially of the traditional nationalist ideology.[28]

At first the opposition to Father Lévesque and the faculty came from ecclesiastics, both inside and outside the university. The dean had to deal with the accusation that, simply put, the faculty was producing specialists with radical ideas who would do no more than swell the ranks of the unemployed. The critics argued that the faculty's program of study was too empirical, too positivistic, too secular, too much on the left, that the original function of the social sciences was being neglected – namely, to teach the social doctrine of the church.[29] Much time and energy had to be expended in rebutting these accusations and in asserting the practical importance of the social sciences for Quebec.

Foreseeing in 1938 the allegation that social-science graduates would end up unemployed, Lévesque moved to associate the Faculty of Social Sciences with certain practical programs that he saw as a means of putting Catholic social doctrine into practice. The dean was convinced that the extreme individualism and the pre-eminence of personal gain, which he saw as characteristic of North American capitalism, could induce Quebec workers to leave the church, which they would see as incapable of serving the needs of an industrial society.[30] To forestall this possibility, Quebec must develop an extended co-operative network and must have dynamic Catholic trade unions, fully able to respond to the needs of the workers. To this end, Lévesque founded in 1939 the Conseil supérieur de la coopération, and also established a co-operative journal, *Ensemble*. Until 1944 he was president of the council and editor of *Ensemble*. The council functioned as a federated body, encompassing the Coopérative fédérée, the Alliance des Coopératives de consommation, the Pêcheurs unis, the caisses populaires, the Union catholique des cultivateurs, and the Confédération des travailleurs catholiques du Canada (CTCC). *Ensemble* supported and publicized the socio-economic and cultural advantages of the co-operative movement. It campaigned for the improvement of legislation affecting co-operatives at both federal and provincial levels.[31]

The Department of Industrial Relations and the School of Social Service stressed the study of both practical and theoretical problems. Professors and students took part in programs of outreach to urban and rural communities. The Department of Industrial Relations published a bilingual journal, *Relations industrielles / Industrial Relations*, and from 1946 onwards it organized annual conferences for all those in the province who were interested in this field. The school of social work was responsible for the establishment of the Service familial de Québec, a centre of social rehabilitation for delinquents and former prison inmates, of several recreation centres, and of a Social Service Council to co-ordinate the activities of these organizations.[32] In effect the School of Social Service was successful in creating employment for its students. Father Lévesque made many further efforts to offset the public image of the university as an ivory tower. The Faculty of Social Sciences published a series of *cahiers* on major current issues, established a Centre de culture populaire to provide community education on social subjects and especially to offer courses on family life, urban development, economic problems, and the co-operative movement.[33] The principal goal of the Centre de culture populaire was to democratize higher education by widening the participation of Québécois in the programs of the faculty.[34]

Paradoxically, it was the very success of the new faculty that precipitated a stormy debate that embroiled the faculty with the École sociale populaire, with the Jesuits, and with two-thirds of the Quebec bishops, mainly those from rural dioceses. Lévesque had to offer a public justification of the need for the School of Social Work and for the Department of Industrial Relations. Critics were proclaiming that the social-work specialists and the new centres of social services would soon replace the traditional charitable agencies; Lévesque's response was that modern social services simply represented a rational and systematic way of organizing charitable work. They were, in short, the modern version of "our ancient forms of bodily and spiritual mercy," new techniques put at the service of charity. The methods, but not the goals, had been modernized for the benefit of society in Quebec.[35] These remarks may have helped to turn aside criticism. Nevertheless, the modernization of social services was going to have much more dramatic effect than the dean was willing to admit. Over time the School of Social Work and its graduates would be responsible for the complete secularization of the traditional system of church-administered charities.

Many priests and politicians felt deep anxiety when faced by the challenge of the trade unions during and after the Second World War and were especially disturbed by increased militancy in the Catholic unions. Some among them held that a Catholic university such as Laval should not be encouraging the radicalization of the union movement by establishing a Department of Industrial Relations and organizing annual conferences to discuss labour-management problems. Father Lévesque and Gérard Dion, professor in the Department of Industrial Relations, believed that a society such as Quebec – in the grip of profound changes arising from industrialization and urbanization – desperately needed an institution independent of church, state, business, or unions, where specialized researchers could probe the difficulties created by the new socio-economic structures and try to find solutions. Furthermore, a department of industrial relations could train experts with the leadership qualities and sense of social responsibility needed to administer trade unions, employers' organizations, and government departments. These specialists would play an essential part in ensuring economic progress and continuing social stability in Quebec.[36] Lévesque put up a convincing defence of the need for the social sciences, but for all that his critics were not likely to be persuaded only by theoretical arguments.

In 1946 several Jesuits associated with the École sociale populaire and several bishops, encouraged by Archbishop Georges Courchesnes of Rimouski, tried to discredit Lévesque and his faculty. They forwarded to the Vatican a report accusing Lévesque of writing an article in *Ensemble* in December 1945 arguing that the co-operative movement wished to become officially non-confessional. In 1940 Cardinal Villeneuve and Bishop Charbonneau, by approving the Manifeste du Conseil supérieur de la coopération, approved this policy of deconfessionalization. Lévesque had convinced them that only through this strategy could co-operation be assured between francophone and anglophone co-operative associations in Quebec and throughout Canada. The co-operatives, Lévesque maintained, were essentially economic, not religious, organizations, and the church had no right to insist on a confessional structure. If it did so, it would only destroy the unity of the co-operative movement and risk compromising the church's integrity in certain cases.[37]

The accusation against Lévesque was serious. The combined power and influence of the Jesuits and the bishops was sufficient to ensure that a canonical trial would be held before the Congregation of the Holy Office in Rome. Fortunately for the dean, he was strongly supported by Father

Gaudrault, superior of the Dominicans in Canada, and by Father Suarez, director of the order in Rome. Lévesque's adversaries were unable to convince the Congregation of the Holy Office that he had advocated secularization, and the Congregation in fact gave its approval to the policy of deconfessionalization of the co-operative movement in Quebec.[38] Whether thanks to Lévesque or not, this decision would have the effect of encouraging the secularization of the co-operative movement and of the CTCC. The old strategy of the church, to "sacralize" wordly institutions, simply would not work any more. Seen from this perspective, the concerns of Lévesque's detractors were well justified, though also anachronistic.

Shortly afterwards, a group of priests from Laval, and some others, sent a critical report on the Faculty of Social Sciences to the Congregation on Seminaries and Universities in Rome. They alleged that the faculty was teaching socialist and Marxist theories that were heretical at a Catholic university. Even more pointedly, they accused the dean of hiring too many lay professors who – in their teaching and in their research – neglected almost entirely the social doctrine of the church in favour of propagating socialist theories of class conflict and a methodology based on materialism.[39] This time Lévesque responded directly and aggressively. At the Learned Societies meeting in Quebec in May 1947, and before the general council of Laval University in December, he expounded his dualistic concept of the role of the social sciences.[40]

Lévesque postulated a subtle – perhaps a "jesuitical" – explanation for the importance and necessity of the social sciences. The human being, by nature a social animal, needed knowledge of the various forms of social interaction and of the related pre-conditions and demands. There was, he argued, "a science of life in society, and human progress is contingent on its laws being known and its imperatives heeded." Because life in society could be studied in two essential ways, both of them scientifically valid, two distinct methodologies were needed:

1 The *positive* element: this involves life in society as lived in the past and the present, in other words, the *social facts*.
2 The *normative* element: this is concerned with life in society in the future, which men must necessarily carry on and which, because they are rational beings, they must organize rationally according to rules of conduct that we call *social duties*.[41]

Thus, human progress would require that the human being have a rational and scientific understanding of the laws governing modern society. The role of the social sciences was to discover and clarify those laws. When the laws of human behaviour were made known, it would then be up to the value-loaded normative sciences – philosophy and theology – to determine the proper norms and the goals of social activity. This dualistic approach was not only good strategy in Lévesque's efforts to turn aside criticism; it was also an accurate exposition of the outlook of the first generation of social scientists at Laval.[42] It was a view that could not be acceptable to traditionalists who believed that social-science methodology should be solely determined by Catholic values and by the social doctrine of the church.[43] Nevertheless, it was essential for the Laval social scientists that they be able to specialize in their discipline without rejecting the role of their religious faith in guiding the uses to which their research would be put. Lévesque put the point concisely:

This double approach to knowledge is very important to us, for everyday experience of society shows us that to have scholars without social principles is hardly more desirable than to have philosophers with no knowledge of facts; the narrow authoritarianism of theoreticians who cultivate principles in isolation from factual knowledge is just as unrealistic, and just as harmful to the human spirit, as the excessive relativism of the positivists who wish only to consider the facts without considering the guiding principles of life in society.[44]

In reality, the conflict over the social sciences at Laval was a power struggle between socially oriented Catholics and traditional Catholics, the prize being to determine which of the two groups would dominate the development of the new human sciences in the modern university.

The outcome of this fight would affect the evolution in Quebec both of higher education and of Catholicism in society. At Laval the conservatives were in the majority. Lévesque knew that one mistake could cost him his position. Nevertheless, he took a firm stand in declaring that his faculty would continue to be a faculty of social sciences, not a faculty of philosophy and theology. He took precautions to ensure that his professors would enjoy full academic freedom in their research, so that their scholarly inquiries would always take priority over value-judgments. It was essential, the dean believed, that sociology and economics graduates of Laval should be able to compete effectively with their counterparts throughout the world. At the same time, aware of the power of the critics, Lévesque continued to offer reassurance that the social doctrines of the church had a secure place in the courses and programs of the faculty. Speaking to the general council at Laval, he identified ten "normative" courses in which social problems were studied from the perspective of the social doctrine of the church as embodied in the *Summa theologia* of Aquinas and in papal encyclicals.[45] Finally, he appealed to the faculty's detractors to be tolerant and to understand the pressures under which his professors were working:

Is it not too often forgotten that the faculty is working in one of the most difficult and delicate fields of service: that of human relations, where the danger of making mistakes is surely greater than in other fields, where one works on inert

material such as statistics or literary tests? Is enough consideration given to the
entrenched prejudices and easily offended interest groups that the faculty must
inevitably encounter, which will accuse it of being pro-capitalist, pro-socialist,
anti-worker, anti-business, nationalistic, internationalistic, secularizing, cleri-
calizing and so forth? Is thought given, finally, to the strange predicament of
the faculty in working in a Province where it is considered normal (and rightly
so) to consider as lawyers only those who have completed legal studies, and as
doctors only those who have graduated from medical school, but where so many
improvisers may instantly be declared "eminent sociologists" and thereby claim
the right to make authoritative judgments on those who have specialized in the
field?[46]

Once again, precise arguments, along with Lévesque's firmness and his
influential friends in Rome, prevailed with the church authorities. In a
decision that represented a major victory for the faculty and for socially
oriented Catholicism, the Congregation on Seminaries and Universities determined that there was nothing heretical in the teaching of the social sciences
at Laval.[47] Although, unfortunately, the conflict was not yet over, the critics
could no longer claim that Lévesque and his faculty were suspected of heresy.
The decision marked an important transition in Quebec society, towards an
intellectual climate that was more democratic, pluralistic, and secular than
before. Jean-Charles Falardeau described in 1959 the exhilarating and challenging experience that the faculty's first generation of students and graduates had enjoyed:

In our metings together, we were learning to say exactly what we thought and
to say it well. We were learning to allow others to speak, to respect their opinions,
and to have unrestrained discussions. We were learning how to use cogent
reasoning on a given question, and that social life – any more than human life
itself – was not marked out by a definite line that could never be cut. Little by
little, we formed *a new intellectual attitude*, which was also a moral position.
We learned to accord principles their proper place, but also to realize that it
was easier to enunciate them than to apply them to the realities of a human
society that had its own laws and logic.[48]

This new attitude had an immediate effect on the research interests of
members of the faculty. At the Centre for Social Research, founded in 1943,
the professors undertook a systematic analysis of French Canadian society.
This endeavour was made possible, according to Falardeau, by "a disengagement from the kind of thinking which had hitherto been bound up with
moral and ideological interpretations."[49] The description was not quite accurate, for in reality the first generation of social scientists had its own
moral perspective – social Catholicism – and its own, liberal, ideology. It

was exactly this novel approach to social-economic questions that brought about a new battle with the traditional elites, this time at the level of politics.

THE SOCIAL PASSION

The dualistic approach to the social sciences, like a double-edged sword, could cut both ways. It had been useful for soothing conservative opposition inside and outside the university. Ironically, though, it was the same approach that drove the dean and his faculty on to formulate a philosophy of social and political action. "The process of gaining knowledge about society," wrote Falardeau later, "must not be allowed to prevent the opening up of a practical approach: to know society and to wish to transform it are two faces of the same mountain."[50] Any systematic analysis of socioeconomic and political structures, or of the values and norms of Quebec society, was bound to place the faculty and its professors, in the words of Léon Dion, "outside of the hallowed conventions of nationalism, outside of the traditional ideology of the church, and outside of the prevailing political and electoral mythologies."[51]

In June 1951 Lévesque addressed a joint session of the Canadian Historical Association and the Canadian Political Science Association on the relationship between humanism and social science. Modern humanism, he declared, demanded much more of social scientists than mere scholarly competence: "It demands that they put the results of their research at the disposal of the people and that, whenever possible, they carry their scientific knowledge forward into social action, by entering into conflicts over questions of truth and justice and by bringing their intellect and judgment to bear on the practical issues of the moment. For these days, sciences that do not put themselves at the service of humanity are inevitably turning themselves against it."[52]

Lévesque and his colleagues thus saw themselves as social reformers faced with the great challenge of redefining the traditional values and institutions of Quebec society. Using the weapons of knowledge and methodology of the social sciences, they would be in the forefront of social change.[53] In a sense, they were the social gospellers of French Canada. They had a "social passion," and they were convinced that the Catholic universities had a duty to produce a new elite consisting of social engineers who would become leaders of government, unions, and business. The church would thereby contribute to the development of a more just and democratic society, of the true *cité libre*. For Lévesque, the eventual goal was to create "among men driven by fear and frequently oppressed by injustice, but nevertheless capable of hope and brotherly love, a renewed society bearing on its body and soul the imprint of man regenerated by love, which can only be achieved through a political humanism attaining its true nobility through thought and action."[54] Only through a social Catholicism dedicated to solving the practical problems of the working class, the dean and his professors believed, could the church remain a vital force in the everyday life of French Canadians.

Many members of the traditional francophone elites feared this combination of two new ideological forces, liberal social Catholicism and the social sciences. The political elites of the Union Nationale were apprehensive at the prospect of more militant social and political action by union leaders, social workers, and by the co-operative movement. With the encouragement of some of the bishops, the Duplessis government sent a report to Rome alleging that Lévesque and his faculty were exercising "undue political influence." The report went on to assert that the dean, professors, and graduates of the faculty were creating a political movement aimed at destroying the only Roman Catholic government in North America! Monsignor Montini, however, church Secretary of State for Internal Affairs, rejected the accusations for lack of evidence.[55] If the Duplessis regime had intervened in 1945, it would have had a much better chance of success. By 1952 Lévesque and the faculty enjoyed a high reputation and growing public support. This support existed at all levels of the church, as well as among lay intellectuals associated with *Le Devoir* and *Cité libre* and in the co-operative and trade-union movements. Had Lévesque been forced to resign, in the climate of suspicion recently created by the transfer of Bishop Charbonneau out of Quebec following his intervention in the Asbestos strike, many Catholic Québécois would have concluded that the church in Quebec was under government control. The hierarchy wished to avoid giving any such impression, and this accounted in part for the decision to defend Father Lévesque, at least in the corridors of power in Rome.[56]

THE DECLINE OF THE DUALISTIC APPROACH TO SOCIAL SCIENCE

The hostility between the Duplessis government and the Faculty of Social Sciences was enough to convince Lévesque and his colleagues that Laval must find an alternative source of funding. They believed that they could find a patron in the federal government. In 1949 Prime Minister St Laurent had named Lévesque a member of the Massey Commission on national development in the arts, letters, and sciences. Influenced by the arguments of his colleague the economist Maurice Lamontagne, Lévesque believed that Quebec must pursue "a clear-sighted integration into a new Canadian federalism" so as to ensure survival and the modernization of the traditional and obsolete institutions of French Canadian society.[57] Lévesque convinced his fellow-commissioners that francophone universities in Quebec would support a system of federal subsidies to universities, and the commission recommended accordingly in its report in 1951. In July of that year the St

Laurent government decided to put $7.1 million at the disposal of the universities.[58] Quebec nationalists were furious. Gérard Filion, editor of *Le Devoir*, and the neo-nationalist historian Michel Brunet denounced the scheme and portrayed Lévesque and his colleagues as naïve and misguided idealists.[59] The nationalists of the right, such as François-Albert Angers, were even more harsh. The faculty of social sciences prided itself, according to Angers, that, "in the name of a pretended objectivity, it refused to consider seriously our sociological problems from the vantage point of the French Canadian fact, which is nevertheless an objective reality. [It is] a faculty which can only see objectivity in a centralizing and socializing Canadianism, and which never ceases to bubble over with centralist solutions, especially to our social problems. [It is] a faculty which is currently leading an entire generation of young people towards national apostasy."[60] In sum, for Angers, Lévesque and his colleagues were a "fifth column ..., a gang of traitors and *vendus* ... who do not believe in the cultural ideals" of French Canadians.[61]

The nationalist attack was ferocious, and would create many difficulties within the faculty. It was, ironically enough, these internal disputes that were largely responsible for the decline of the "social passion" and of the dualist approach to the social sciences. The conflicts began in the early 1950s with the arrival of a second generation of social scientists, such as Léon Dion, Guy Rocher, Gérard Bergeron, and Fernand Dumont. Doris Lussier, Lévesque's secretary, precipitated a crisis in the faculty in 1952 when he circulated a Faculty Manifesto signed by all of the first generation of professors. According to Léon Dion, the Manifesto appealed to professors to be faithful to Catholic social doctrine and to Thomist philosophy. Secondly, the Manifesto declared that social-science teaching must be ideologically neutral and must not advance the interests of a Quebec-centred French Canadian nationalism.[62] Father Lévesque acknowledged the existence of the Manifesto but maintained that its chief purpose was to ascertain whether the professors wished to publish a collective response to the article of Angers in *l'Action nationale*, which he and some of his colleagues regarded as defamatory. His impression was that the second generation of professors refused to sign the Manifesto because they thought that such a collective response would constitute a political action on the part of the faculty. They wanted to make it very clear to the public that their dean's public speeches and action did not reflect the official position of the faculty and its staff.[63]

In reality, the professors of the second generation had three reasons for opposing the Manifesto. First, they rejected the dualist approach to social science because it implied teaching "normative" courses on the social doctrine of the church and on the philosophy of Aquinas. This they considered a waste of time. Committed to the objectivity of the social sciences, they disputed the validity of a Catholic sociology. As modern intellectuals they

saw their first task as being to wage war on moralists and theologians who
sought "to put sociology at the service of the establishment of a Christian
society, which would be inspired largely by medieval civilization."[64] These
professors gave first priority to their respective disciplines, at least for the
time being, and if they had a common goal, it was the development of an
entirely secular and liberal university.

Their second reason for rejecting the Manifesto was rooted in their concept
of the role of universities in society. The campaign for liberal social Catholicism and a new social order was not to their taste. Direct political
action, they believed, should be left to those outside the university. The
real responsibilities of a university social scientist lay in research, teaching,
and publication.[65]

The third reason, never openly discussed, was that the second generation
of professors did not accept the pan-Canadian version of French Canadian
nationalism preached by Lévesque and by Maurice Lamontagne. Neither
did they subscribe to the traditional nationalism as represented by Angers.
Rather, these professors would participate very actively during the 1950s
and 1960s in the development of a new québécois nationalism. Stressing
cultural evolution and the socio-economic maturing of the francophone majority in Quebec and of the state, they would come to regard this neo-
nationalism as a new key to the survival and modernization of the secular,
urban, and industrial francophone nationality.

By 1954 the results of this internal crisis were evident. The crusade of
Lévesque and his early colleagues to prompt reform in Quebec society
following the principles of liberal social Catholicism and of "clear-sighted
integration into a new Canadian federalism" had virtually disappeared. The
"normative" courses had disappeared from the faculty's program of studies,
and the new professors were pursuing the "objective" social sciences. The
Department of Political Science was established in 1954, and in 1955 the
faculty received a second grant from the Carnegie Foundation for research
on francophone society in Quebec. The retirement of Father Lévesque in
1955 and the departure of Maurice Lamontagne for Ottawa marked the end
of the era of the reformist "social passion" that from the beginning had
been characteristic of the development of the social sciences at Laval.[66]

CONCLUSION

This study has shown how ideological factors prompted Father Lévesque
and the first generation of social-science professors at Laval to establish and
expand the disciplines and the methodologies of secular social science.
Without the "social passion" that originated in a liberal interpretation of
Catholic social doctrine, and the "jesuitical" concept of the dualistic approach to social science, Lévesque would never have been able to convince

the leading ecclesiastics – at Laval itself, or outside – that the social sciences should have an important role at a modern Catholic university. The struggles that took place did have to do with immediate objectives such as obtaining recognition in society and attaining the institutionalization of the social sciences. Nevertheless, it is the ideological aspirations of Lévesque and his colleagues that largely explains the intensity of the debates and the battles that took place among professors, ecclesiastics, and politicians.

The dean and the first generation of professors believed that the flowering of social science would set in motion among French Canadians a more rational and worldly approach to the discussion of old and new problems that needed to be faced. They believed that the result would be a move towards, in the words of Maurice Lamontagne, "clear-sighted integration into a new Canadian federalism." This view, however, was rejected by the second generation of professors, who could not accept the implication of Lévesque's strategy of renewed "sacralization" of worldly institutions: that the Catholic church would continue to dominate university education. For these younger scholars the purpose of developing the social sciences in Quebec was to offer the *Québécois*, through economic, social, cultural, and political studies, a wider and deeper appreciation of the strengths and weaknesses of Quebec society.[67]

Contrary to the belief entertained by Lévesque and his early colleagues, the development of the social sciences did not lead to convergence of anglophone and francophone nationalisms in Canada. Rather, it contributed to the rediscovery and redefinition of Quebec's collective image, to the preaching of a neo-nationalism that would form the ideological basis for the Quiet Revolution of the 1960s and 1970s.

NOTES

* Translated from the French by John G. Reid.

1 Georges-Henri Lévesque to Radio-Canada, 5 May 1952, in Robert Parisé, *Georges-Henri Lévesque: père de la renaissance québécoise* (Montréal: Alain Stanké 1976), 44. See also G.-H. Lévesque, *Souvenance I* (Montreal: La Presse 1983).

2 Yves Roby, *Les Québécois et les investissements américains* (Québec: Les Presses de l'Université Laval 1976).

3 Marcel Fournier, "L'Institutionnalisation des sciences sociales au Québec," *Sociologie et sociétés* 5, no. 1 (1973): 55.

4 See Kenneth McRoberts and Dale Posgate, *Quebec: Social Change and Political Crisis* (Toronto: McClelland and Stewart 1980), chaps. 3 and 4.

5 Cyrias Ouellet, *La Vie des sciences au Canada français* (Québec: Ministère des affaires culturelles 1964); Pierre Dansereau, "Science in French Canada," *Scientific Monthly* 59 (1944): 261–72.

6 J.-C. Falardeau, "Antécédents, débuts et croissance de la sociologie au Québec," *Recherches sociographiques* (hereafter *RS*) 15 (1974): 142.

7 See Lionel Groulx, *Mes mémoires* (Montréal: Fides 1970), 1:216.

8 École des sciences sociales, politiques et économiques, *Organisation et programme des cours, 1938* (Québec: Université Laval 1938), 3–14.

9 Fournier, "L'Institutionnalisation des sciences sociales au Québec," 31–2; Maurice Tremblay and Albert Faucher, "L'Enseignement des sciences sociales au Canada de langue française," in *Les Arts, lettres et sciences au Canada, 1949–1951; recueil d'études spéciales* (Ottawa: King's Printer 1951), 193–4, 196–7.

10 See Marcel Clément, *Sciences sociales et catholicisme* (Montréal: École sociale populaire, no. 423, 1949), 5–18.

11 Robert Rumilly, *Histoire de la province de Québec* (Montréal: B. Valiquette 1961), 33, 164.

12 G.-H. Lévesque, "La 'Co-opérative Commonwealth Federation,'" in *Pour la restauration sociale au Canada* (Montréal: École sociale populaire, nos. 232–3, 1933), 21.

13 Ibid., 36. For a critical analysis of Lévesque's study, see Gregory Baum, *Catholics and Canadian Socialism* (Toronto: James Lorimer 1980), 97–118. Baum believes that Lévesque and his colleagues misinterpreted the encyclical *Quadragesimo anno* and the program of the CCF, and that the Catholic church should never have condemned the CCF.

14 Interview with Father G.-H. Lévesque, 9 May 1973; Georges-Henri Lévesque, "Itinéraires sociologiques," *RS* 15 (1974): 203–8; Baum, *Catholics and Canadian Socialism*, 100, 118, 128–9.

15 École des sciences sociales, politiques et économiques, *Annuaire de l'Université Laval, 1938–1939* (Québec: Université Laval, nd), 51.

16 Gonzalve Poulin, "L'Enseignement des sciences sociales dans les universités canadiennes," *Culture* 2 (1941): 12.

17 See G.-H. Lévesque, "Action catholique et action sociale," *Cahiers de l'École des sciences sociales de l'Université Laval* 1, no. 4 (1942): 12.

18 Lévesque, "Itinéraires sociologiques," 208. Lévesque's first choice of location for the Faculty of Social Science was Montreal, financial and industrial metropolis of Quebec and Canada, but the presence of Edouard Montpetit and the structure of the University of Montreal – somewhat more autonomous and secular than Laval – forced Lévesque and Cardinal Villeneuve to establish it at Laval.

19 Falardeau, "Antécédents, débuts et croissance," 144.

20 Interviews with Father G.-H. Lévesque, 9 May and 3 September 1976. See also Fournier, "L'Institutionnalisation des sciences sociales au Québec," 37. Professor Everett Hughes was partly responsible for the creation of a true faculty in 1943. Before leaving for Chicago, he had suggested such a course of action in order to stimulate a large-scale program of research. See E.C. Hughes, "Programme de

recherches sociales pour le Québec," *Cahiers de l'École des sciences sociales* 2, no. 4 (1943).

21 J.-C. Falardeau, "Itinéraires sociologiques," *RS* 15 (1974): 221–2, 224. Falardeau describes the difficulties he encountered in finding a course on the history of Canada and of Quebec. His decision to choose sociology was prompted by "the need to understand what was in the process of developing in Quebec society." Ibid., 220.

22 Interview with Father G.-H. Lévesque, 9 May 1973.

23 Léon Dion, "Itinéraires sociologiques," *RS* 15 (1974): 229–31; Gérard Bergeron, ibid., 233–7. Interviews with Léon Dion and Gérard Bergeron, 1 Sept. and 31 Aug. 1976.

24 Guy Rocher, "Itinéraires sociologiques," *RS* 15 (1974): 244–5; Fernand Dumont, ibid., 256–7.

25 See McRoberts and Posgate, *Quebec: Social Change and Political Crisis*, chap. 5.

26 Léon Dion, "Aspects de la condition du professeur d'université dans la société canadienne-française," *Cité libre* 25 (July 1958): 13.

27 See Jean-Charles Falardeau, ed., *Essais sur le Québec contemporain* (Québec: Les Presses de l'Université Laval 1952), for studies of the social repercussions of the industrialization of Quebec that are severely critical of the elites and institutions existing at that time.

28 See Michael D. Behiels, *Prelude to Quebec's Quiet Revolution: Liberalism versus Neo-Nationalism, 1945–1960* (Kingston and Montreal: McGill-Queen's University Press 1985), chap. 4.

29 Interview with Father G.-H. Lévesque, 9 May 1973.

30 Georges-Henri Lévesque, "L'individualisme: source de communisme," lecture given at Laval University in 1934. I thank Father Lévesque for providing a copy of this presentation and other documents from the Lévesque Foundation.

31 Various numbers of *Ensemble*, 1939–44. See also Doris Lussier, "La Faculté des sciences sociales," *Revue de l'Université Laval* 6 (1951): 233–90.

32 Ibid., 278–81.

33 See *Cahiers de l'École des sciences sociales*, 1941–45; *Cahiers du Service extérieur d'éducation sociale*, 1945–49.

34 Interview with Father G.-H. Lévesque, 9 May 1973; Lussier, "La Faculté des sciences sociales," 284–5.

35 G.-H. Lévesque, "Service social et charité," in *Cahiers de la Faculté des sciences sociales* 4 (1944): 3–20; Lévesque, "Integrating the Social Work Curriculum into the Social Sciences," *Social Work Journal* (Apr. 1951): 63–9.

36 G.-H. Lévesque, "L'Université et les relations industrielles," in Congrès des relations industrielles, *Rapport, 1946* (Québec: Les Presses de l'Université Laval 1947); Gérard Dion, "L'Université et les relations industrielles," *Revue de l'Université Laval* 3 (1948): 56–9; Dion, "Notre département des relations industrielles," *Ad Usum Sacerdotum* 5, no. 7 (1950): 73.

37 The two articles written by Lévesque for *Ensemble* can be found in his pamphlet *La Non-confessionalité des coopératives* (Québec: le Conseil supérieur de la co-opération 1946), 26. See also Parisé, *Lévesque*, 82–110.

38 Interview with Father G.-H. Lévesque, 9 May 1973. See also P.-M. Gaudrault, *Neutralité, non-confessionalité et École sociale populaire* (Montreal 1946). Cardinal Villeneuve, in a letter to Lévesque of 17 Aug. 1946, was severely critical of Father Gaudrault for having made his accusation public and of Archbishop Charbonneau of Montreal for having given it his imprimatur. See Groulx, *Mes mémoires*, 4:263.

39 Interviews with Father G.-H. Lévesque, 9 May 1973 and 3 Sept. 1976.

40 G.-H. Lévesque, "Principles and Facts in the Teaching of Social Sciences," *Canadian Journal of Economics and Political Science* (hereafter *CJEPS*) 13 (1947): 501–6. The French-language version was entitled "Sciences sociales et progrès humain," *Revue de l'Université Laval* 3 (1948): 37–41. G.-H. Lévesque, *L'Enseignement de la doctrine sociale de l'Église et la Faculté des Sciences sociales de Laval* (Québec: Université Laval 1947), mimeo, 10 pp, fondation Lévesque, fonds Lévesque. The abbé Gérard Dion reproduced this work in *Ad Usum Sacerdotum* 4, no. 2 (1948): supp. 1–13. This journal was produced for members of the Catholic church in Quebec, but circulated much more widely.

41 Lévesque, "Sciences sociales et progrès humain," 39. Gérard Dion mentioned the same point in "L'Université et les relations industrielles," 57–8.

42 J.-C. Falardeau, "Qu'est-ce que la croissance de la sociologie au Québec?" *Culture* 10 (1949): 250–61; Falardeau, "Antécédents, débuts et croissance," 146.

43 Clément, *Sciences sociales et catholicisme*, 18–31.

44 Lévesque, "Sciences sociales et progrès humain," 40; Falardeau, "Itinéraires sociologiques," 223.

45 Lévesque, *L'Enseignement de la doctrine sociale de l'Église*, 1–6.

46 Ibid., 9.

47 Interview with Father G.-H. Lévesque, 9 May 1973. See also Blair Fraser, "The Fright over Father Lévesque," *Maclean's*, 1 July 1952. This journalist maintains that Bishop Courchesnes of Rimouski, the same who had undertaken to confront Archbishop Charbonneau after the Asbestos strike, was responsible for the two actions brought against Lévesque.

48 J.-C. Falardeau, "Lettre à mes étudiants," *Cité libre* 23 (May 1959): 7.

49 See J.-C. Falardeau, *L'Essor des sciences sociales au Canada français* (Québec: Ministère des affaires culturelles 1964), 47, 50–1; Université Laval, *Faculté des Sciences sociales, Annuaires 1951–52* (Québec: les Presses de l'Université Laval 1951), 40–2, has a description of the work of the Centre for Social Research.

50 J.-C. Falardeau, "Itinéraires sociologiques," 224. He writes: "The Duplessis régime forced all those who were concerned with social progress to repudiate the negative rhetoric and the immobilism which was once again masking the real problems. We of the social sciences at Laval and Montreal, like some of those at Radio-Canada and many others, were engaged in a sort of politics of resistance. It

was necessary to participate in the great leap forward." See also Falardeau, "Antécédents, débuts et croissance," 156.

51 Dion, "Aspects de la condition du professeur d'université," 14.

52 G.-H. Lévesque, "Humanisme et sciences sociales," CJEPS 18 (1952): 268. Jean-Charles Falardeau maintains that Father Lévesque was above all a determined man of action. He never limited himself to the theoretical side of things. Father Lévesque was a social animator seeking to disseminate a liberal social Catholicism, just as Father Joseph-Papin Archambault worked for l'École sociale populaire and the ideology of Christian corporatism. Interview with J.-C. Falardeau, 1 Sept. 1976.

53 Falardeau, L'Essor des sciences sociales au Canada français, 48; Falardeau, "Lettre à mes étudiants," 14.

54 Lévesque, "Humanisme et sciences sociales," 268. Jean-Charles Falardeau, confirming this idealism, recalls that the pervasive atmosphere of the faculty was that of a social crusade: "I had the feeling of being drawn into sociology in the same way as one says one is drawn into religion. This kind of intellectual life was not for me a labour: it was rather a series of passions, highlighted by periodic resurrections." Falardeau, "Itinéraires sociologiques," 223.

55 Interview with Father G.-H. Lévesque, 9 May 1973.

56 Ibid. See also Fraser, "The Fight over Father Lévesque," 52; and Roger Lemelin, "The Silent Struggle at Laval," Maclean's, 1 Aug. 1952, 36. Robert Rumilly mentions the two Jesuit attempts against Father Lévesque and his faculty but makes no mention of an attack by the Duplessis government. Rumilly, Maurice Duplessis et son temps (Montréal: Fides 1973), 2:311, 350–1.

57 Maurice Lamontagne expresses his ideas in his book Le Fédéralisme canadien: évolution et problèmes (Québec: les Presses de l'Université Laval 1954), 295.

58 Behiels, Prelude to Quebec's Quiet Revolution, chap. 9.

59 Gérard Filion, "L'Ingérence du fédéral dans l'enseignement supérieur," Le Devoir, 7 June 1951; Michel Brunet, "Le Rapport Massey: réflexions et observations," L'Action universitaire 18, no. 2 (1952): 39–41.

60 F.-H. Angers, "Deux modèles d'inconscience: le Premier Saint-Laurent et le commissaire Lévesque," L'Action nationale 38, no. 3 (1951): 206.

61 F.-A. Angers, "Les Solutions du Rapport Massey III – À qui la faute?" L'Action nationale 39, no. 4 (1952): 267–72.

62 Interview with Léon Dion, 1 Sept. 1976.

63 Interview with Father G.-H. Lévesque, 3 Sept. 1976.

64 Guy Rocher, "Itinéraires sociologiques," RS 15 (1974): 247.

65 Interview with Léon Dion, 1 Sept. 1976. See also Dion, "Aspects de la condition du professeur d'université," 15–16.

66 Interview with Jean-Charles Falardeau, 1 Sept. 1976.

67 See Fernand Dumont and Yves Martin, Situation de la recherche sur le Canada français (Québec: les Presses de l'Université Laval 1969), 296.

Select Bibliography

The following is a select bibliography of work in the history of universities, including theses, since 1970. It is divided into ten sections: Historiography; Institutional Histories; University, State, and Society; Governance, Finance, and the Economy; Cultural, Intellectual, and Curriculum History; Professionalization; Professors; Students; Women; and Adult Education. For additional listings of published sources see R.S. Harris, "Bibliography," *A History of Higher Education in Canada, 1663–1960* (Toronto: University of Toronto Press 1976), 633–88, and R.S. Harris et al., *A Bibliography of Higher Education in Canada, Supplement 1981* (Toronto: University of Toronto Press 1981).

HISTORIOGRAPHY

Axelrod, Paul, "Higher Education in Canada." *History of Education Quarterly* 19, no. 1 (Summer 1979): 271–6.
– "Historical Writing and Canadian Universities: The State of the Art." *Queen's Quarterly* 89, no. 1 (Spring 1982): 137–44.
Ouellet, Fernand. "La Modernisation de l'historiographie et l'émergence de l'historie sociale." *Recherches Sociographiques* 26, no. 1 (1985): espec. 61–5.
Reid, John G. "Some Recent Histories of Canadian Universities." *American Review of Canadian Studies* 14, no. 3 (Fall 1984): 369–73.
Sheehan, Nancy M. "History of Higher Education in Canada." *Canadian Journal of Higher Education* 15, no. 1 (1985): 25–38.
Smyth, D. McCormack. "The End of Universities in Canada." *Interchange* 13, no. 3 (1982): 29–52.

INSTITUTIONAL HISTORIES

Aytenfisu, Maureen. "The University of Alberta: Objectives, Structure and Role in the Community." MA, University of Alberta 1982.

Baillargeon, H. *Le Séminaire de Québec sous l'espiscopat de Mgr de Laval*. Québec: Les Presses de l'Université Laval 1972.

Bedford, A.G. *The University of Winnipeg: A History of the Founding College*. Toronto: University of Toronto Press 1976.

Bissonette, Leo Adolphe. "Loyola of Montreal: A Sociological Analysis of an Educational Institution in Transition." MA, Concordia University 1977.

Coleman, Brian, "McGill, British Columbia." *McGill Journal of Education* 6, no. 2 (Autumn 1976): 179–89.

Cormier, Clément. *L'Université de Moncton: historique*. Moncton: Centre d'études acadiennes 1975.

De Valk, A. "Independent University or Federated College? The Debate among Roman Catholics during the Years 1918–1921." *Saskatchewan History* 30, no. 1 (Winter 1977): 18–32.

Dumas-Rousseau, M. "L'Université de Montréal de 1852 à 1865: tentatives de foundation." DES, Université Laval 1974.

Duprès, Robert. *L'Université du Québec: la réalisation originale d'un idéal collectif*. Québec: Université du Québec 1978.

Epp, E. "The Rise and Fall of Notre Dame University." *Canadian Association of University Teachers Bulletin* 27, no. 6 (Oct. 1980): 14.

Evans, Mary Godfrey. "Mount Allison Wesleyan Academy and College, 1843–1886." M. Ed, Bishop's University 1979.

Fleming, W.G. *Post-Secondary and Adult Education*. Ontario's Educative Society, vol. 4. Toronto: University of Toronto Press 1971.

Fotheringham, G.H. "A Comparison of Two Small Maritime Universities with Differing Religious Backgrounds: Saint Mary's University and Mount Allison University." MA, St Mary's University 1972.

From Rural Parkland to Urban Centre: One Hundred Years of Growth at the University of Manitoba, 1877–1977. Winnipeg: Hyperion Press and University of Manitoba 1978.

Frost, Stanley B. "The Abbotts of McGill." *McGill Journal of Education* 12, no. 3 (Fall 1973): 253–70.

– *McGill University: For the Advancement of Learning*. Vol. 1 *1801–1895*. Vol. 2, *1895–1971*. Montreal: McGill-Queen's University Press 1980, 1984.

Galarneau, Claude. *Les Collèges classiques au Canada français, 1620–1970*. Montréal: Fides 1978.

Gibson, Frederick G. *"To Serve and Yet Be Free": Queen's University, 1917–1961*. Montreal: McGill-Queen's University Press 1983.

Gibson, William Carleton. *Wesbrook and His University*. Vancouver: Library of the University of British Columbia 1977.

Gorman, J. *Père Murray and the Hounds: The Story of Saskatchewan's Notre Dame College*. Sidney, BC: Gray's Publishing 1977.

Gravel, Jean-Yves, "La Fondation du Collège militaire royal de Saint Jean." *Re-*

vue d'histoire de l'amérique française 27, no. 2 (sept. 1973): 257–80.

Gwynne-Timothy, J.R.W. *Western's First Century.* London, Ont.: University of Western Ontario 1978.

Harris, R. Cole. "Locating the University of British Columbia." *BC Studies* 22, (Winter 1976): 106–25.

Hayden, Michael. *Seeking a Balance: The University of Saskatchewan, 1907– 1982.* Vancouver: University of British Columbia Press 1983.

Healy, D. "University of Halifax, 1875–1881." *Dalhousie Review* 53 (Spring 1973): 39–56.

Holmes, Owen G. *Come Hell or High Water* [a history of the University of Lethbridge]. Lethbridge: Lethbridge Herald 1972.

Jean, Michele. "Le Collège Marie-Anne: fondation et expansion, 1932–1958." MA, Université de Montréal 1975.

Johns, Walter H. *A History of The University of Alberta, 1908–1969.* Edmonton: University of Alberta Press 1981.

Johnston, Charles M. *McMaster University.* Vol. 1, *The Toronto Years.* Vol. 2, *The Early Years in Hamilton, 1930–1957.* Toronto: University of Toronto Press 1976, 1981.

Laberge, Paul André. *L'Université Laval, 1957–1977: vers l'autonomie.* Québec: Presses de l'Université Laval 1978.

Lajeunesse, Marcel, ed. *L'Éducation au Québec au 19ᵉ et 20ᵉ siècles.* Trois-Rivières: Boréal Express 1971.

Lavallée, Andrée. "La Querelle universitaire québécoise 1876–1889." *Revue d'histoire de l'amérique française* 26, no. 1 (juin 1972): 67–84.

– *Québec contre Montréal: la querelle universitaire, 1876–1891.* Montréal: Presses de l'Université de Montréal 1983.

Leefe, John Gordon. "The University of King's College: An Examination of its Relationship with Dalhousie University." MA, Dalhousie University 1971.

Lessard, Claude. "Le Collège-Séminaire de Nicolet (1803–1863)." *Revue d'histoire de l'amérique française* 25, no. 1 (juin 1971): 63–88.

Macdonald, George Edward. "'And Christ Dwelt in the Heart of His House': A History of St. Dunstan's University." PhD, Queen's University, 1984.

McLeod, Norman Leslie. "Calgary College, 1912–1915: A Study of an Attempt to Establish a Privately Financed University in Alberta." PhD, University of Calgary 1970.

MacNutt, W.S. "Universities of the Maritimes: A Glance Backwards." *Dalhousie Review* 53 (Autumn 1973): 431–8.

Masters, D.C. *Bishop's University: The First Hundred Years.* Lennoxville: Bishop's University Bookstore 1983.

Moase, Lorne Robert. "The Development of the University of Prince Edward Island, 1964–1972." M Ed, University of New Brunswick 1972.

Morton, W.L. "The Founding of the University of Manitoba." In Alexander

Gregor and Keith Wilson, eds., *Higher Education in Canada: Historical Perspectives.* Monographs in Education 2. Winnipeg: University of Manitoba 1979, 7–12.

Nearing, P.A. "Rev. John R. MacDonald, St. Joseph's College, and the University of Alberta." *Canadian Catholic Historical Association Study Sessions* 42 (1975): 70–89.

Neatby, Hilda. "Queen's College and the Scottish Fact." *Queen's Quarterly* 80, no. 1 (Spring 1973): 1–11.

– *"And Not to Yield": Queen's University, 1841–1917.* Montreal: McGill-Queen's University Press 1978.

Pilkington, G. "Higher Education in Quebec: A Product of Evolution and Revolution." *Canadian and International Education* 5 (Dec. 1976): 39–70.

Pitsula, James. *An Act of Faith: The Early Years of Regina College.* Regina: Canadian Plains Research Centre 1987.

Power, Michael. *Assumption College: The O'Connor Years, 1870–1890.* Leamington, Ont.: Michael Power 1986.

Rawlyk, George, and Kevin Quinn. *The Redeemed of the Lord Say So: A History of Queen's Theological College, 1912–1972.* Kingston: Queen's Theological College 1980.

Reid, John G. "Mount Allison College: The Reluctant University." *Acadiensis* 10, no. 1 (Autumn 1980): 35–66.

– *Mount Allison University.* Vol. 1, *1843–1914.* Vol. 2, *1914–1963.* Toronto: University of Toronto Press 1984.

Robillard, Jean-Jacques. "Histoire du Collège Sainte-Marie-de-Monnoir, 1853–1912." MA, Université d'Ottawa 1980.

Roe, H. "Reminiscences of the Earliest Lennoxville Days." *Journal of Canadian Church Historical Society* (13 Sept. 1971): 38–43.

Ross, A.M. *The College on the Hill: A History of the Ontario Agricultural College, 1874–1974.* Toronto: Copp Clark 1974.

Ross, Robin. *The Short Road Down: A University Changes.* Toronto: University of Toronto 1984.

Rousseau, Michèle D. "L'Université de Montréal de 1852 à 1865: tentatives de fondation." DES, Université de Laval 1974.

Shook, Laurence K. *Catholic Post-Secondary Education in English-Speaking Canada: A History.* Toronto: University of Toronto Press 1971.

Small, Michael Willoughby. "A Case Study of Educational Policy-making: The Establishment of Atahbaska University." PhD, University of Alberta 1980.

Sylvain, P. "Les Difficiles débuts de l'Université Laval." *Les Cahiers des Dix* (1971): 211–34.

– "Louis-Jacques Cusault, fondateur de l'Université Laval." *Les Cahiers des Dix* (1973): 117–32.

Taft, Michael. *Inside These Greystone Walls: An Anecdotal History of the University of Saskatchewan.* Saskatoon: University of Saskatchewan 1984.

Taylor, William H. "The Evolution of a Policy-making System: A Case in University Governance." PhD, University of Alberta 1980.

Wilmot, Laurence Frank. "The Christian Churches of the Red River Settlement and the Foundation of the University of Manitoba: A Historical Analysis of the Process of Transition from Frontier College to University." MA, University of Manitoba 1979.

UNIVERSITY, STATE, AND SOCIETY

Angrave, J. "John Strachan and Scottish Influence on the Character of King's College, York, 1827." *Journal of Canadian Studies* (11 Aug. 1976): 60–8.

Anisef, Paul, and Norman R. Okihiro. *Losers and Winners: The Pursuit of Equality and Social Justice in Higher Education.* Toronto: Butterworth's 1982.

Axelrod, Paul. "Higher Education, Utilitarianism, and the Acquisitive Society: Canada, 1930–1980." In Michael S. Cross and Gregory S. Kealey, eds., *Modern Canada: 1930–1980s.* Toronto: McClelland and Stewart 1984, 179–205.

Ayre, David J. "Universities and the Legislature: Political Aspects of the Ontario University Question, 1868–1906." PhD thesis, University of Toronto 1981.

Baum, Gregory. "The University and the Christian." *Queen's Quarterly* 81, no. 1 (Spring 1974): 20–7.

Boneau, Louis Philippe. "Université Laval – son rôle au Canada." In Alexander Gregor and Keith Wilson, eds., *Higher Education in Canada: Historical Perspectives.* Monographs in Education 1. Winnipeg: University of Manitoba 1979, 67–82.

Butler, M., and D. Sugarman. "Canadian Nationalism, Americanization, and Scholarly Values." *Journal of Canadian Studies* 5 (Aug. 1970): 12–28.

Cody, Howard Hugh. "Towards a Perspective on the Perpetuation of the Canadian Federal System: Federal-Ontario Relations in University Education, 1945–1970." PhD, McMaster University 1977.

Cole, R.T. "The Universities and Governments under Canadian Federalism." *Journal of Politics* 34 (May 1972): 524–53.

Crowley, R.W. "Towards Free Post-Secondary Education?" *Journal of Canadian Studies* 8 (Aug. 1973): 43–57.

Dandurand, P., and M. Fournier. "Développement de l'enseignement supérieur, classes sociales et luttes nationales au Québec." *Sociologie et sociétés* 12 (1980): 101–31.

Darville, Richard Tulloss. "Political Economy and Higher Education in the Nineteenth Century Maritimes." PhD, University of British Columbia 1977.

Duckworth, H. "Higher Education in Manitoba." In Alexander Gregor and Keith Wilson, eds., *Higher Education in Canada: Historical Perspectives.* Monographs in Education 2. Winnipeg: University of Manitoba 1979, 43–52.

Gill, R.M. *Universities and Development in Quebec.* PhD, Duke University 1976.

Graham, Roger. "Scholar and the State: A Word of Caution." Canadian Histori-
    cal Association, *Historical Papers* 1971, 1–12.
Hamilton, William B. "Education and Reform in Nova Scotia, 1800–1848."
    PhD, University of Western Ontario 1970.
Hurtubise, René, and Donald C. Rowat. *The University, Society and Govern-
    ment: The Report of the Commission on the Relations bet⟋ ·en Universities and
    Government.* Ottawa: University of Ottawa Press 1970.
Jones, David C., and Timothy A. Dunn. "'All of Us Common People' and Edu-
    cation in the Depression." *Canadian Journal of Education* 5, no. 4 (1980): 41–
    56.
Kendle, J.E. "Scholar and the State Revisited: Further Words of Caution." Cana-
    dian Hist   ̇ Association, *Historical Papers* 1982, 1–10.
Killough, Edward Arthur. "Federal Involvement in Canadian Post-Secondary Ed-
    ucation: Certain Social, Economic and Political Considerations with Particular
    Reference to the Years 1950–1967." MA, University of Victoria 1970.
Kodikara, Ananda. "Schooling, Politics and the State: The Pattern of Post-
    Secondary Schooling Changes in Ontario from Post-World War II (1945) up to
    the Bovey Commission (1985)." PhD, University of Toronto 1986.
McKenna, Mary Olga. "Higher Education in Transition." In Vernon Smitheram
    et al., *The Garden Transformed: Prince Edward Island, 1945–1980.* Charlotte-
    town: Ragweed Press 1982.
Moody, Barry M. "Joseph Howe, the Baptists and the 'College Question.'" In
    Wayne A. Hunt, ed., *Proceedings of the Joseph Howe Symposium.* Halifax:
    Nimbus 1984, 53–70.
Pike, R.M. *Who Doesn't Get to University and Why? – A Study on Accessibility
    to Higher Education.* Ottawa: Association of Universities and Colleges 1970.
Pilkington, G. "Higher Education in Quebec: A Product of Evolution and Revo-
    lution." *Canadian and International Education* 5 (Dec. 1976): 39–70.
Pilkington, Gwendoline. *Speaking with One Voice: Universities in Dialogue with
    Government.* Montrea. McGill University 1983.
Porter, John. "The Democ. .tisation of the Canadian Universities and the Need for
    a National System." *Minerva* 8, no. 3 (July 1970): 325–56.
Porter, M.R., J. Porter, B. Blishen. *Does Money Matter? Prospects for Higher
    Education.* Toronto: Institute for Behavioral Research, York University, 1973.
Ross, Murray G. *The University: The Anatomy of Academe.* Toronto: McGraw-
    Hill 1976.
Sheffield, E.F. "The Post-War Surge in Post-Secondary Education." In J.D. Wil-
    son, et al., eds., *Canadian Education: A History.* Toronto: Prentice-Hall 1970.
Symons, T.H.B. *To Know Ourselves.* Report of the Commission on Canadian
    Studies, vols. 1, 2. Ottawa: Association of Universities and Colleges 1975.
– and James E. Page. *Some Questions of Balance: Human Resources, Higher
    Education, and Canadian Studies.* Report of the Commission on Canadian

Studies, vol. 3. Ottawa: Association of Universities and Colleges 1984.

Waite, Peter. "Playing at Universities: Dalhousie and the Sectarian Struggle in Nova Scotia." In Alexander Gregor and Keith Wilson, eds., *Higher Education in Canada: Historical Perspectives*. Monographs in Education 2. Winnipeg: University of Manitoba 1979, 67–82.

Winchester, Ian. ed. *The Independence of the University and the Funding of the State: Essays on Academic Freedom in Canada*. Toronto: OISE Press 1984.

GOVERNANCE, FINANCE, AND THE ECONOMY

Arvay, Stephen. "The Role of Intra-Capitalist Class Conflict in the Development of Education in Ontario, 1955–1962." PhD, York University 1984.

Axelrod, Paul. "Business Aid to Canadian Universities, 1957–1965." *Interchange* 11, no. 1 (1980–81): 25–38.

– "Businessmen and the Building of Canadian Universities: A Case Study." *Canadian Historical Review* 68, no. 2 (June 1982): 202–22.

– *Scholars and Dollars: Politics, Economics and the Universities of Ontario, 1945–1980*. Toronto: University of Toronto Press 1982.

– "Service or Captivity? Business-University Relations in the Twentieth Century." In W. Neilson and C. Gaffield, eds., *University in Crisis: A Medieval Institution in the Twenty-first Century*. Montreal: Institute for Policy Analysis 1986.

Buchbinder, Howard, and Janice Newson. *The University Means Business: Universities, Corporations and Academic Work*. Toronto: Garamond Press 1988.

Clarke, Claude Reginald. "Coordination of Higher Education in Atlantic Canada." PhD, University of Alberta 1975.

Dodge, David. *Returns to Investment in University Training: The Case of Accountants, Engineers and Scientists*. Kingston: Queen's University 1972.

– and D.A.A. Stager. "Economic Returns to Graduate Study in Science, Engineering and Business." *Canadian Journal of Economics* 5 (May 1972): 182–98.

Frederick, N.O. "Autonomy in Universities and Colleges: A Comparative Study of the Degrees of Autonomy from Government in the Academic Activities of the Universities and Colleges of Applied Arts and Technology of Ontario, Canada." PhD, University of Toronto 1978.

Halliday, Terence C. "The Politics of 'Universal Participatory Democracy': A Canadian Case Study." *Minerva* 13, no. 3 (Autumn 1975): 404–27.

Harvey, Edward. *Educational Systems and the Labour Market*. Don Mills, Ont.: Harcourt, Brace, Jovanovich 1974.

Howing, J.F., and L.F. Michaud. *Changes in the Composition of Governing Bodies of Canadian Universities and Colleges, 1965–1970*. Ottawa: Association of Universities and Colleges of Canada 1972.

Hyman, Charles. "An Analysis of Factors Associated with Variations in Canadian
University Expenditures in the Decade 1960/61 to 1969/70." PhD, University
of Alberta 1972.

Ikeda, Jane Yoshiko. "The Struggle over Decision-making Power at Simon Fraser
University, 1965–1968." M. Ed, University of Calgary 1971.

Kefentse, Netto Akono. "Universities and Labour Education in Ontario: A Study
into the Politics of Cooperation between Unions and Universities." MA, University of Toronto 1976.

Leslie, Peter M. *Canadian Universities: 1980 and Beyond, Enrollment, Structural
Change and Finance.* Ottawa: Association of Universities and Colleges of Canada 1980.

Mathis, M.S. "A History of the Financial Administration of the University of
Manitoba, 1877–1936." MA, University of Manitoba 1975.

Mehmet, O. "Economic Returns on Undergraduate Fields of Study in Canadian
Universities: 1961–1972." *Relations Industrielles* 32, no. 3 (1977): 321–39.

Myers, Doug. "Social Responsibility of the University as an Institutional Inves-
tor." *Queen's Quarterly* 89 (Spring 1982): 100–11.

Novek, Joel. "University Graduates, Jobs, and University-Industry Linkages."
Canadian Public Policy 11, no. 2 (1985): 180–95.

Ostry, Sylvia, ed. *Canadian Higher Education in the Seventies.* Ottawa: Information Canada, 1972.

Prakash, Brahm. "The Demand for and Financing of Higher Education in Canada." PhD, University of Toronto 1976.

Reid, John G. "Health, Education, Economy: Philanthropic Foundations in the
Atlantic Region in the 1920s and 1930s." *Acadiensis* 14, no. 1 (Autumn 1984):
64–83.

Sadighian, Masoud. "A Comparative Analysis of University Goals and Governance in North America and Iran." PhD, University of Alberta 1975.

Shrimpton, Gordon. "The Crisis in Canadian Universities." In Terry Wother-
spoon, ed., *The Political Economy of Canadian Schooling.* Toronto: Methuen
1987, 185–210.

Smyth, D.M. "Structures for University Government to the Beginning of the
Twentieth Century with Particular Reference to the American, British and Canadian Institutions." PhD, University of Toronto 1972.

Stager, David. "The Evolution of Federal Government Financing of Canadian
Universities." STOA: Canadian Society for the Study of Higher Education 2,
no. 1 (1972): 23–9.

– "Federal Government Grants to Canadian Universities, 1951–66." *Canadian
Historical Review* 54, no. 2 (Spring 1973): 287–97.

– and Noah Meltz. "Manpower Planning in the Professions." *Canadian Journal
of Higher Education* 7, no. 3 (1977): 73–85.

Statistics Canada. *From the Sixties to the Eighties: A Statistical Portrait of Canadian Higher Education.* Ottawa 1979.

Vanderkamp, J. "University Enrolment in Canada, 1951–83 and Beyond." *The Canadian Journal of Higher Education* 14, no. 2 (1984): 49–62.

Wizman, Maurice. "Le Financement des collèges classiques et sa place dans l'évolution du système scolaire du Québec: étude historique de 1950 à loi de l'enseignement privé." MA, Université de Montréal 1976.

Young, Brian. *In Its Corporate Capacity: The Seminary of Montreal as a Business Institution, 1816–1876* Montreal: McGill-Queen's University Press 1986.

CULTURAL, INTELLECTUAL, AND CURRICULUM HISTORY

Allin, E.J. "Physics at the University of Toronto, 1907–1977." *Physics in Canada* 33, no. 2 (1977): 26–31.

Armour, Leslie, and Elizabeth Trott. *The Faces of Reason: An Essay on Philosophy and Culture in English Canada, 1850–1950.* Waterloo, Ont.: Wilfrid Laurier University Press 1981.

Barker, John. "T.F. McIlwraith and Anthropology at the University of Toronto, 1925–63." *Canadian Review of Sociology and Anthropology* 24, no. 2 (May 1987): 252–68.

Behiels, Michael. "Le Père Georges-Henri Lévesque et l'établissement des sciences sociales à Laval, 1938–1955." *Revue de l'Université d'Ottawa* 52, no. 3 (juillet–sept. 1982): 355–76.

Berger, Carl. *Science, God, and Nature in Victorian Canada.* Toronto: University of Toronto Press 1983.

– *The Writing of Canadian History: Aspects of English-Canadian Historical Writing since 1900.* 2nd edn. Toronto: University of Toronto Press 1986.

Bissell, Claude T. *Halfway Up Parnassus: A Personal Account of the University of Toronto.* Toronto: University of Toronto Press 1974.

Bladen, Vincent. *Bladen on Bladen: Memoirs of a Political Economist.* Toronto: Scarborough College, University of Toronto 1978.

Bowker, Alan. "Truly Useful Men: Maurice Hutton, George Wrong, James Mavor and the University of Toronto, 1880–1927." PhD, University of Toronto 1975.

Cameron, James M. *On the Idea of a University.* Toronto: University of Toronto Press 1978.

Campbell, Terrence Maxwell. "The Social and Political Thought of F.R. Scott." MA, Queen's University 1977.

Charland, Jean-Pierre. *La Science et le pouvoir au Québec, 1920–1965.* Québec: Éditeur officiel 1978.

– *Histoire de l'enseignement technique et professionnel.* Québec: IQRC 1982.

Clark, S.D. "American Takeover of Canadian Sociology: Myth or Reality?" *Dalhousie Review* 53 (Summer 1973): 205–18.

– "Sociology in Canada: An Historical Overview." *Canadian Journal of Sociology* 1 (Summer 1975): 225–34.

352   Bibliography

Clarke, S.C.T. *The Development of Educational Psychology: The University of Alberta, 1950–51 to 1980–81*. Edmonton: Faculty of Education, University of Alberta 1982.

Classen, Hans George. "Religious Studies in Canada." *Queen's Quarterly* 85, no. 3 (Autumn 1974): 389–402.

Conacher, J.B. "Graduate Studies in History in Canada: The Growth of Doctoral Programmes." Canadian Historical Association, *Historical Papers* 1975, 1–15.

Cook, Ramsay. *The Regenerators: Social Criticism in Late Victorian English Canada*. Toronto: University of Toronto Press 1985.

Corry, J.A. *My Life and Work: A Happy Partnership*. Kingston: Queen's University 1981.

Creet, Mario. "H.M. Tory and the Secularization of Canadian Universities." *Queen's Quarterly* 88, no. 4 (Winter 1981): 718–36.

Darche, Jacqueline. "Étude comparative des programmes en sciences familiales dans l'enseignement supérieur au Canada." MA, Université de Montréal 1973.

De Pencier, Marni. "Ideas of the English-Speaking Universities in Canada to 1920." PhD, University of Toronto 1978.

Desroches, Jean-Marie, and Robert Gagnon. "Georges Welter et l'émergence de la recherche à l'École Polytechnique de Montréal, 1939–1970." *Recherches sociographiques* 24 (jan.–avr. 1983): 33–54.

De Vecchi, Vittirio. "The Dawning of National Scientific Community in Canada, 1878–1896." *Scientia Canadensis* 8, no. 1 (June 1984): 32–58.

– "Science and Scientists in Government, 1878–1896 – Part I." *Scientia Canadensis* 8, no. 2 (Dec. 1984): 112–42.

– "Science and Scientists in Government, 1878–1896 – Part II." *Scientia Canadensis* 9, no. 2 (Dec. 1985): 97–113.

Donald, Janet J. "Teaching and Learning in Higher Education over the Last Decade." *Canadian Journal of Higher Education* 15, no. 3 (1986): 77–84.

Drummond, Ian. *Political Economy at Toronto: A History of the Department, 1888–1982*. Toronto: University of Toronto Governing Council 1983.

Duchesne, Raymond. "D'intérêt public et d'intérêt privé: l'institutionalisation de l'enseignement et de la recherche au Québec, 1920–1940." In Yvan Lamonde et Esther Trépanier, eds., *L'Avènement de la modernité culturelle au Québec*. Québec: IQRC, 1986, 189–230.

Eggleston, W. *National Research Council in Canada: The N.R.C., 1916–1966*. Toronto: Clark Irwin 1978.

Enros, Phillip. "The Bureau of Scientific Research and School of Specific Industries: The Royal Canadian Institute Attempt at Organizing Research in Toronto, 1914–1918." *HSTC Bulletin* 7, no. 1 (Jan. 1983): 14–26.

– "The University of Toronto and Industrial Research in the Early Twentieth Century." In Richard A. Jarrell and Arnold E. Ross, eds., *Critical Issues in the History of Canadian Science, Technology and Medicine*. Thornhill, Ont.: HSTC Publications 1983, 155–66.

Feeley, J. "A Library in Crisis: The University of Toronto Library, 1890–1892." *Ontario History* 62, no. 4 (Dec. 1970): 220–34.

Ferguson, Barry. "The New Political Economy and Canadian Liberal Democratic Thought: Queen's University 1900–1925. PhD, York University 1982.

– "Political Economy and Queen's Quarterly, 1893–1939." *Queen's Quarterly* 90, no. 3 (Autumn 1983): 623–43.

– and Doug Owram. "Social Scientists and Public Policy from the 1920s through World War II." *Journal of Canadian Studies* 15, no. 4 (Winter 1980–81): 3–17.

Ferns, H.S. *Reading from Left to Right: One Man's Political History.* Toronto: University of Toronto Press 1983.

Forward, D. *A History of Botany in the University of Toronto.* Toronto: Department of Botany, University of Toronto 1977.

Fournier, Marcel. "L'Institutionnalisation des sciences sociales au Québec." *Sociologie et sociétés* 5, no. 1 (1973): 27–57.

– *Entre l'école et l'usine.* Montréal: Éditions Albert Saint-Martin et CEQ 1980.

– "Édouard Montpetit et l'université moderne, ou l'échec d'une génération." *Revue d'histoire de l'Amérique française* 36, no. 1 (juin 1982): 3–29.

– "Un intellectual à la rencontre de deux mondes: Jean-Charles Falardeau et le développement de la sociologie universitaire au Québec." *Recherches sociographiques* 23, no. 3 (sept.-déc. 1982): 361–85.

– *L'Entrée dans la modernité: sciences, culture et société.* Montréal: Éditions Albert Saint-Martin 1986.

Francis, R.D. "Frank H. Underhill at the University of Saskatchewan: Formative Years in the Intellectual Development." *Saskatchewan History* 34, no. 2 (Spring 1981): 41–56.

– *Frank H. Underhill: Intellectual Provocateur.* Toronto: University of Toronto Press 1986.

Frankena, M., and K. Bhatia. "Canadian Contributions to Economics Journals, 1968–1972." With reply by Clément Lemelin. *Canadian Journal of Economics* 6 (Nov. 1973): 121–4, 598–602.

Gagnon, Serge. *Le Québec et ses historiens de 1840 à 1920: la Nouvelle France de Garneau à Groulx.* Québec: Les Presses de l'Université Laval 1978.

– *Quebec and Its Historians: The Twentieth Century.* Montreal: Harvest House 1985.

Galarneau, G. "L'Enseignement des sciences au Québec et Jérôme Demers (1765–1835)." *Revue de l'Université d'Ottawa* 47 (1977): 84–94.

Gauvreau, Michael. "Philosophy, Psychology, and History: George Sidney Brett and the Beginnings of Social Science at the University of Toronto, 1910–1940." Paper presented to the Canadian Historical Association, Windsor, Ont., 1988.

Gingras, Yves. "La Physique à McGill entre 1920 et 1940: la réception de la mécanique quantique par une communauté 'scientifique périphérique.'" HSTC *Bulletin* 5 (1981): 15–39.

- "Le Développement du marché de la physique au Canada: 1879–1928." In Richard A. Jarrell and Arnold E. Roos, *Critical Issues in the History of Canadian Science, Technology and Medicine.* Thornhill, Ont.: HSTC Publications 1983, 16–30.
- "Croissance de la recherche scientifique et transformation de la Section III de la Société royale du Canada." *Scientia Canadensis* 10, no. 1 (Spring 1986): 53–71.
- "De l'enseignement à la recherche: l'émergence d'une nouvelle pratique de la physique dans les universités canadiennes." *Histoire Sociale / Social History* 19, no. 37 (mai 1986): 73–91.
- "The Institutionalization of Scientific Research in Canadian Universities: The Case of Physics." *Canadian Historical Review* 67, no. 2 (June 1986): 181–94.
Granatstein, J.L. "Culture and Scholarship: The First Ten Years of the Canada Council." In *Canada, 1957–1967: The Years of Uncertainty and Innovation.* Toronto: McClelland and Stewart 1986.
Greenlee, James G. "The Highroads of Intellectual Commerce: Sir Robert Falconer and the British Universities." *Ontario History* 74, no. 3 (Sept. 1982): 185–205.
- *Sir Robert Falconer: A Biography.* Toronto: University of Toronto Press 1988.
Guinsburg, T.N., and G.L. Reuber, eds. *Perspectives on the Social Sciences in Canada.* Toronto: University of Toronto Press 1974.
"Harold Innis." *Journal of Canadian Studies*, special edition, 12, no. 4 (Winter 1977).
Harris, Robin. *A History of Higher Education in Canada, 1663–1960.* Toronto: University of Toronto Press 1976.
- *English Studies at the University of Toronto: A History.* Toronto: University of Toronto Governing Council 1988.
"L'Historiographie." *Recherches sociographiques*, édition spéciale, 15, no. 1 (jan.–avr. 1974).
Helmes-Hayes, Richard. "Images of Inequality in Early Canadian Sociology, 1922–1965." PhD, University of Toronto 1985.
Hiller, Harry H. "Paradigmatic Shifts, Indigenization, and the Development of Sociology in Canada." *Journal of the History of the Behavioural Sciences* 16 (July 1980): 263–74.
- *Society and Change: S.D. Clark and the Development of Canadian Sociology.* Toronto: University of Toronto Press 1982.
Hudon, François. "Le Thème de l'éducation dans la pensée d'Édouard Montpetit." MA, Université de Montréal 1986.
Hull, James P. "From the FPL to Paprican: Science and the Pulp and Paper Industry." *HSTC Bulletin* 7, no. 1 (Jan. 1983): 3–13.
Irving, Allan. "Leonard Marsh and the McGill Social Science Research Project." *Journal of Canadian Studies* 21, no. 2 (Summer 1986): 6–25.

Jarrell, Richard. "Science Education at the University of New Brunswick in the Nineteenth Century." *Acadiensis* 2, no. 2 (Spring 1973): 55–79.

– "The Rise and Decline of Science in Quebec." *Histoire Sociale / Social History* (May 1977): 77–91.

– "The Reception of Einstein's Theory of Relativity in Canada." *Royal Astronomical Society of Canada Journal* 73 (Dec. 1979): 358–69.

– "The Influence of Irish Institutions upon the Organization and Diffusion of Science in Victorian Canada." *Scientia Canadensis* 9, no. 2 (Dec. 1985): 150–64.

– "Differential National Development and Science in the Nineteenth Century: The Problems of Quebec and Ireland." In Nathan Reingold and Marc Rothenberg, eds., *Scientific Colonialism: A Cross Cultural Comparison*. Washington: Smithsonian Institution Press 1987, 323–50.

Jasen, Patricia. "The English Canadian Liberal Arts Curriculum: An Intellectual History, 1800–1950." PhD, University of Manitoba 1987.

Johnson, Micheline. "Le Concept de temps dans l'enseignement de l'histoire." *Revue d'histoire de l'Amérique française* 28, no. 4 (mars 1975): 483–516.

Johnston, Charles M. "Aspects of Science and Technology at McMaster University with Special Reference to Chemistry and Physics, 1939–1959." In Richard A. Jarrell and Arnold E. Roos, eds., *Critical Issues in the History of Canadian Science, Technology and Medicine*. Thornhill, Ont.: HSTC Publications 1983, 3–15.

Klinck, Carl, ed. *Literary History of Canada*. Toronto: University of Toronto Press 1976.

Kutcher, S.P. "Toronto Metaphysicians: The Social Gospel and Medical Professionalization in Victorian Toronto." *HSTC Bulletin* 5, no. 1 (Jan. 1981): 41–51.

Lajeunesse, M. *Les Sulpiciens et la ville culturelle de Montréal au XIXᵉ siècle*. Montreal: Fides 1982.

Lambert, J.H. "Le Haut Enseignement de la religion: Mgr Bourget and the Founding of Laval University." *Revue de l'Université d'Ottawa* 45, no. 3 (juillet-sept. 1975): 278–94.

Lamonde, Yvan. "L'Enseignement de la philosophie au collège de Montréal, 1790–1876." *Culture* (1970): 109–23, 213–24, 312–26.

– *La Philosophie et son enseignement au Québec, 1665–1920*. Québec: Éditions Hurtubise 1980.

Lamontagne, Maurice. "La Faculté des Sciences sociales de Laval: prélude de la révolution tranquille." *Histoire Sociale* 9, no. 19 (mai 1977): 146–51.

Lang, Daniel W. "Claude Bissell's Idea of the University." *Canadian Journal of Higher Education* 4, no. 2 (1974): 21–44.

Lawr, D.A. "Agricultural Education in Nineteenth Century Ontario: An Idea in Search of an Institution." *History of Education Quarterly* 12 (Fall 1972): 334–57. Repr. in M. Katz and P. Mattingly, eds., *Education and Social Change: Themes from Ontario's Past*. New York: New York University Press 1975.

The Learning Society: Report of the Commission on Post-Secondary Education in Ontario. Toronto: Queen's Printer 1973.

Levere, Trevor H., and Richard A. Jarrell, eds. *A Curious Field Book: Science and Society in Canadian History*. Toronto: Oxford University Press 1974.

Lévesque, Georges-Henri. "Prélude à la révolution tranquille au Québec: notes nouvelles sur d'anciens instruments." *Histoire sociale* 9, no. 19 (mai 1977): 134–46.

– et al., eds. *Continuité et rupture. Les sciences sociales au Québec*. 2 vols. Montréal: Les presses de l'Université de Montréal 1984.

Lower, Arthur M. *My First Seventy-Five Years*. Toronto: MacMillan 1967.

McKillop, A.B. *A Disciplined Intelligence: Critical Inquiry and Canadian Thought in the Victorian Era*. Montreal: McGill-Queen's University Press 1979.

– *Contours of Canadian Thought*. Toronto: University of Toronto Press 1987.

McRae, Sandra Francis. "The 'Scientific Spirit' in Medicine of the University of Toronto, 1880–1910." PhD, University of Toronto 1987.

Marett, Clara M. "The Ontario Agricultural College, 1874–1974: Some Developments in Scientific Agriculture." MA, University of Guelph 1975.

Meikle, W.D. "And Gladly Teach: G.M. Wrong and the Department of History at the University of Toronto." PhD, Michigan State University 1977.

Murray, David R., and Robert A. Murray. *The Prairie Builder: Walter Murray of Saskatchewan*. Edmonton: NeWest 1984.

Neatby, Hilda. "Gospel of Research: The Transformation of English-Canadian Universities." *Transactions of the Royal Society of Canada*, ser. 4, vol. 20 (1982): 275–84.

– *So Much to Do, So Little Time: The Writings of Hilda Neatby*. Ed. Michael Hayden. Vancouver: University of British Columbia Press 1983.

Owram, Doug. "Economic Thought in the 1930s: The Prelude to Keynesianism." *Canadian Historical Review* 66, no. 3 (Sept. 1985): 344–77.

– *The Government Generation: Canadian Intellectuals and the State, 1900–1945*. Toronto: University of Toronto Press 1986.

Pouliot, L. Monseigneur Bourget et son temps. Vol. 5. Montréal: Bellarmin 1977.

Priestley, F.E.L., and H.I. Kerpneck. *Report of the Commission on Undergraduate Studies in English in Canadian Universities*. Toronto: Association of Canadian University Teachers of English 1976.

Rabkin, Yakov M. "Spécificités nationales de la science et de la technologie: une étude de deux universités montréalaises." *Recherches sociographiques* 20, no. 1 (jan.–avr. 1979): 87–101.

Rawlyk, G.A., ed. *Canadian Baptists and Christian Higher Education*. Montreal: McGill-Queen's University Press 1988.

Robinson, G. de B. *The Mathematics Department in the University of Toronto, 1827–1978*. Toronto: Department of Mathematics, University of Toronto 1979.

Ross, P.N. "The Establishment of the Ph.D. at Toronto: A Case of American Influence." *History of Education Quarterly* 12, no. 3 (Fall 1972): 358–80.

Repr. in P. Mattingly and M. Katz, eds., *Education and Social Change: Themes from Ontario's Past*. New York: New York University Press 1975.

Rowe, F.W. *Education and Culture in Newfoundland*. Toronto: McGraw-Hill 1976.

Shore, Marlene. "'Overtures of an Era Being Born.' F.R. Scott: Cultural Nationalism and Social Criticism, 1925–1939." *Journal of Canadian Studies* 15, no. 4 (Winter 1980–81): 31–42.

– "Carl Dawson and the Research Ideal: The Evolution of a Canadian Sociologist." Canadian Historical Association, *Historical Papers* 1985, 45–73.

– *The Science of Social Redemption: McGill, the Chicago School, and the Origins of Social Research in Canada*. Toronto: University of Toronto Press 1987.

Shortt, S.E.D. *The Search for an Ideal: Six Canadian Intellectuals and Their Convictions in an Age of Transition, 1880–1930*. Toronto: University of Toronto Press 1976.

Smith, A.H. *The Production of Scientific Knowledge in Ontario Universities*. Toronto: Queen's Printer 1972.

Spinks, J.W.T. *Two Blades of Grass: An Autobiography of John Spinks*. Saskatoon: Western Producer 1980.

Tomovic, V.A. "Sociology in Canada: An Analysis of its Growth in English Language Universities, 1908–1972." PhD, University of Waterloo 1975.

Trofimenkoff, S.M. *Action Française: French Canadian Nationalism in the Twenties*. Toronto: University of Toronto Press 1975.

Trudel, Marcel. "Les Débuts de l'Institut d'histoire à l'Université Laval." *Revue d'histoire de l'amérique française* 27, no. 3 (déc. 1973): 397–403.

Vaillancourt, John Pierre. "John William Dawson: Educational Missionary in Nova Scotia, 1850–1853." MA, Dalhousie University 1974.

Weir, Ruth. "Religious Thought and Evolutionary Ideas: Darwin, Religious Belief and Education in Ontario, 1860–1890." D Ed, University of Toronto 1984.

Wright, Mary J., and Roger C. Myers, eds. *History of Academic Psychology in Canada*. Toronto: C.J. Hogrefe Inc. 1982.

Young, E.G. *The Development of Biochemistry in Canada*. Toronto: University of Toronto Press 1976.

Young, W.R. "Academics and Social Scientists versus the Press: The Policies of the Bureau of Public Information and the Wartime Information Board, 1939–1945." Canadian Historical Association, *Historical Papers* 1978, 217–40.

PROFESSIONALIZATION

Alderson, H.J. *Twenty-five Years of Growing: The History of the School of Nursing*. Hamilton: McMaster University 1976.

Arthurs, H.W. "Paradoxes of Canadian Legal Education." *Dalhousie Law Journal* 3 (Jan. 1977): 639–62.

Barker, C.A.V. "The Ontario Veterinary College: Temperance Street Era." *Canadian Veterinary Journal* 16 (Nov. 1975): 319–28.

Barr, M.C. "James Bertram Collip (1892–1965): A Canadian Pioneer in Endocrinology." *Hannah Institute Publications for the History of Medicine* 1 (1977): 6–15.

Barr, Murray L. *A Century of Medicine at Western: A Centennial History of the Faculty of Medicine, University of Western Ontario.* London: University of Western Ontario 1977.

Bassam, Bertha. *The Faculty of Library Science, University of Toronto, and Its Predecessors, 1911–1972.* Toronto: Library Science Alumni Association 1978.

Bensley, E.H. "The Beginning of Teaching at McGill." *McGill Journal of Education* 6, no. 1 (Spring 1971): 23–4.

Bernier, Jacques. "La Standardisation des études médicales et la consolation de la profession dans la deuxième moitié du xixe siècle." *Revue d'histoire de l'Amérique française* 37, no. 1 (juin 1983): 51–65.

Buckler, G. "The Little College That Could: Journalism at King's." *Atlantic Advocate* 69 (Feb. 1979): 36–9.

Cole, Curtis. "'A Hand To Shake the Tree of Knowledge': Legal Education in Ontario, 1871–1889." *Interchange* 17, no. 3 (1986): 15–27.

– A Learned and Honourable Body: The Professionalization of the Ontario Bar, 1867–1929." PhD, University of Western Ontario 1987.

Collin, Johanne. "Évolution des profils de comportements des clientèles féminine et masculine face aux études universitaires: le cas des facultés professionnelles de l'Université de Montréal, 1940–1980." MA, Université de Montréal 1986.

– "La Dynamique des rapports de sexes à l'université, 1940–1980: une étude de cas." *Histoire Sociale / Social History* 19, no. 38 (Nov. 1986): 365–85.

Collins, P. "Three Hundred Years of Engineering at McGill." *Engineering Journal* 55 (Sept. 1972): 13–21.

Gaucher, Dominique. "La Formation des hygiénistes à l'Université de Montréal, 1910–1975: de la santé publique à la médecine préventive." *Recherches sociographiques* 20, no. 1 (jan.–avr. 1979): 59–85.

Gibson, R.D. "Legal Education – Past and Future." *Manitoba Law Journal* 6 (1976–77): 21–38.

Given, J. "A Study of Anticipatory Socialization on Prospective Nursing Students." MA, University of Toronto 1971.

Godfrey, Charles Morris. "The Evolution of Medical Education in Ontario." MA, University of Toronto 1974.

Harris, Robin S. *Cold Iron and Lady Godiva: Engineering Education at Toronto, 1920–1972.* Toronto: University of Toronto Press 1973.

Helleiner, F.M., and C.J. Sparrow. "Careers for Geographers: the Case of Ontario, 1953–1972." *Canadian Geographer* 21 (Summer 1971): 182–9.

Howell, Colin D. "Reform and the Monopolistic Impulse: The Professionalization of Medicine in the Maritimes." *Acadiensis* 11, no. 1 (Autumn 1981): 3–22.

Jones, D.C. "'We Cannot Allow It To Be Run by Those Who Do not Understand Education': Agricultural Schools in the Twenties." *BC Studies* 39 (Autumn 19??): 30–60.

Kyer, Ian C., and Jerome B. Bickenbach. *The Fiercest Debate: Caeser Wright, The Benchers, and Legal Education in Ontario.* Toronto: University of Toronto Press 1987.

Langston, Glen Graeme. "Teacher Training at Dalhousie University, 1924–1970." MA, Dalhousie University 1972.

Lapp, P.A., et al. *Ring of Iron: A Study of Engineering Education in Ontario.* Toronto: Committee of Presidents of the Universities of Ontario 1970.

Lapp, P.A., and O.W. Thompson. *Careers of Engineering Graduates, 1920–1970, University of Toronto.* Toronto: Engineering Alumni Association and Faculty of Applied Science and Engineering, University of Toronto 1973.

Lederman, W.R. "Canadian Legal Education in the Second Half of the Twentieth Century." *University of Toronto Law Journal* 21 (1971): 141–61.

Leland, D.E., and E. Nelson-Wernick. "Practices in the Recruitment of Faculty for Psychology Departments in Canadian Universities." *Canadian Psychology* 24 (Apr. 1983): 105–18.

Lortie, L. "The Early Teaching of Law in French Canada." *Dalhousie Law Journal* 2 (Sept. 1976): 521–32.

Lucien, P. "La Théologie et l'université: les vrais enjeux du début sur les prêtres laïcisés et l'enseignement de la théologie." *Relations* 35 (Nov. 1975): 298–307.

Macdonald, R.H. *Thorough: An Illustrated History of the College of Engineering [University of Saskatchewan], 1912–1982.* Saskatoon: University of Saskatchewan 1982.

Maheu, Claude. "L'Émergence d'une profession: l'administration." *Recherches sociographiques* 19, no. 2 (mai-août 1978): 189–219.

Marett, C.M. "The Ontario Agricultural College (1874–1974): Some Developments in Scientific Agriculture." MA, University of Guelph 1975.

Moogk, Peter. "Réexamen de l'école des arts et métiers de Saint Joachim." *Revue d'histoire de l'Amérique française* 29, no. 1 (juin 1975): 3–29.

Munroe, D. "Teacher Education at McGill." *McGill Journal of Education* 6, no. 1 (Spring 1971): 29–40.

Murray, H.G. *Nursing in Ontario: A Study for the Committee on the Healing Arts.* Toronto: Queen's Printer 1970.

Navran, L., and R. Walter. "Longitudinal Changes in Vocational Interests of Canadian Military College Graduates." *Canadian Counsellor* 13 (Apr. 1979): 136–9.

Nicholson, Norman L. "The Evolution of Graduate Studies in the Universities of Ontario, 1841–1971." Ed D, University of Toronto 1975.

Overduin, H. *People and Ideas: Nursing at Western, 1920–1970.* London: Faculty of Nursing, University of Western Ontario 1970.

Peake, F.A. "Anglican Theological Education in Saskatchewan." *Saskatchewan History* 35, no. 1 (Winter 1982): 25–33; no. 2 (Spring 1982): 57–78.

Phillips, Charles S. *College of Education, Toronto: Memories of OCE.* Toronto: Guidance Centre, Faculty of Education, University of Toronto 1977.

Pierre-Deschenes, Claudine. "Santé publique et organisation de la profession médicale au Québec, 1870–1918." *Revue d'histoire de l'Amérique française* 35, no. 3 (déc. 1981): 355–75.

Rogue, S.S. "The Organization, Control and Administration of the Teacher Training System of the Province of Ontario, 1900–1920." PhD, University of Ottawa 1973.

Roos, N.P., and D.G. Fish. "Career and Training Patterns of Students Entering Canadian Medical Schools in 1965." *Canadian Medical Association Journal* 70 (Jan. 1975): 65–7, 70.

Rousseau, Jacques. "L'Implantation de la profession de travailleur social." *Recherches sociographiques* 19, no. 2 (mai–août 1978): 171–87.

Roy, Y. *L'École normale Laval, 1857–1870.* Québec: École normale Laval 1971.

St J. Macdonald, R. "An Historical Introduction to the Teaching of International Law in Canada." *Canadian Yearbook of International Law* (1974): 67–110.

Savage, D.C. "Historical Overview of Academic Status for Librarians." *Canadian Library Journal* 39 (Oct. 1982): 287–91.

Schneck, R. *University Business Education in Canada during the Sixties and Seventies.* Ottawa: Statistics Canada 1977.

Shemlit, L.W. *Research Report on Engineering Education in the Maritimes.* Fredericton: Maritime Provinces Higher Education Commission 1976.

Shortt, S.E.D. "Medical Professionalization: Pitfalls and Promise in the Historiography." *HSTC Bulletin* 5, no. 3 (Sept. 1981): 210–19.

Struthers, James. "'Lord Give Us Men': Women and Social Work in English Canada, 1918–1953." Canadian Historical Association, *Historical Papers* 1983, 96–112.

Stryckman, Paul. "Les défis occupationnels du clergé." *Recherches sociographiques* 19, no. 2 (mai–août 1978): 223–50.

Von Zur-Muehlen, M. *University Business Education in Canada during the Sixties and Seventies.* Ottawa: Statistics Canada 1977.

Willis, John. *A History of Dalhousie Law School.* Toronto: University of Toronto Press 1979.

PROFESSORS

Abbott, Frank. "Academic Freedom and Social Criticism in the 1930s." *Interchange* 14, no. 4 (1983–84): 107–23.

– "Founding the Canadian Association of University Teachers, 1945–1951." *Queen's Quarterly* 93, no. 3 (Autumn 1986): 508–24.

Carrigan, D. Owen. "Unionization in Canadian Universities." *International Journal of Institutional Management in Higher Education* 1 (May 1977): 17–31.

Cook R. "The Professor and the Prophet of Unrest." *Transactions of the Royal Society of Canada* (1974): 227–50.

Dixon, Marlene. *Things which Are Done in Secret*. Montreal: Black Rose 1976.

Francis, Douglas. "The Threatened Dismissal of F.H. Underhill from the University of Toronto, 1939–1941." *CAUT Bulletin* 14, no. 3 (Dec. 1975): 17–21. Repr. *CAUT Bulletin* (Oct. 1983).

Garry, Carl. "From Faculty Association to Faculty Union." *Canadian Personnel and Industrial Relations Journal* 23, no. 6 (1976): 11–13, 15–16.

Horn, Michiel. "The History of Academic Freedom in Canada." *CAUT Bulletin* 14, no. 3 (Dec. 1975): 14–15.

– "Academics and Canadian Social and Economic Policy in the Depression and War Years." *Journal of Canadian Studies* 13 (Winter 1978–79): 3–10.

– "'Free Speech within the Law': The Letter of the Sixty-Eight Toronto Professors, 1931." *Ontario History* 72, no. 1 (Mar. 1980): 27–48.

– "Professors in the Public Eye: Academic Freedom and the League for Social Reconstruction." *History of Education Quarterly* 20, no. 4 (Winter 1980): 425–48.

– "The Good Old Days: A 'Golden Age' of Academic Freedom?" *CAUT Bulletin* 30, no. 6 (Oct. 1983): 3–4.

– "Government Funding and the Independence of Teaching and Scholarship." *Interchange* 14, no. 4 (1983–84): 5–12.

– ed. *Academic Freedom: Harry Crowe Memorial Lectures, 1986*. Toronto: York University 1987.

Lawless, David J. "The Canadian University under the Impact of Academic Trade Unions." *Minerva* 14, no. 3 (Autumn 1981): 464–79.

Leland, D.E., and Eleanor Nelson-Wernick. "Practices in the Recruitment and Hiring of Faculty of Psychology Departments in Canadian Universities." *Canadian Psychology* 24, no. 2 (Apr. 1983): 105–18.

McClymont, Ian. "Saint Francis Xavier: Love It or Leave It." *Mysterious East* (July 1971): 19–25.

Mair, Deborah. "Unionization and the Middle Class: the Case of University Faculty." MA, Carleton University 1977.

Moffat, L.K. *Room at the Bottom: Job Mobility Opportunities for Ontario Academics in the Mid-Seventies*. Toronto: Ministry of Colleges and Universities 1980.

Roper, Henry. "The Lifelong Pilgrimage of George E. Wilson: Teacher and Historian." Nova Scotia Historical Society, *Collections* 42 (1986): 139–51.

Ross, Murray G. "The Dilution of Academic Power in Canada: The University of Toronto Act." *Minerva* 10, no. 2 (Apr. 1972): 242–58.

Savage, D.C., and C. Holmes. "The CAUT, the Crowe Case, and the Development of the Idea of Academic Freedom in Canada." *CAUT Bulletin* 14, no. 3 (Dec. 1975): 22–37. Repr. *CAUT Bulletin* (Oct. 1983).

Scarfe, Janet. "Letters and Affection: The Recruitment and Responsibilities of Academics in English-speaking Universities in the Mid-Nineteenth Century." PhD, University of Toronto 1981.

Sheffield, Edward, ed. *Teaching in the Universities: No One Way*. Montreal: McGill-Queen's University Press 1974.

Shrum, Gordon, with Clive Cocking. *Gordon Shrum: An Autobiography*. Vancouver: University of British Columbia Press 1986.

Stokes, L.D. "Canada and an Academic Refugee from Nazi Germany: The Case of Gerhard Herzberg." *Canadian Historical Review* 57, no. 2 (June 1976): 150–70.

Tousignant, Pierre. "La Carrière universitaire du professeur Michel Brunet." *Cahiers d'histoire* 6, no. 1 (automne 1985): 7–13.

Trotter, Bernard, and David L. McQueen. *"The Ten O'Clock Scholar": What a Professor Does for His Play*. Toronto: Council of Ontario Universities 1972.

Von Zur-Muehlen, M., and J.A. Belliveau. *Three Decades of Full-Time Canadian University Teachers: A Statistical Portrait*. Ottawa 1980.

Waite, Peter. *Out of Nova Scotia: U.B.C. Larry Mackenzie*. Vancouver: University of British Columbia Press 1987.

Winchester, Ian. "Government Power and University Principles: An Analysis of the Battle for Academic Freedom in Alberta." *Interchange* 14, no. 4 (1983–84): 41–59.

STUDENTS

Allen, Richard. "Children of Prophecy: Wesley College Students in an Age of Reform [1890–1918]." *Red River Valley Historian* (Summer 1974): 15–20.

Axelrod, Paul. "Patterns of Student Politics." *University Affairs* (Oct. 1973).

– "Moulding the Middle Class: Student Life at Dalhousie University in the 1930s." *Acadiensis* 15, no. 1 (Autumn 1985): 84–122.

Barnard, Élaine. "A University at War: Japanese Canadians at UBC during World War II." *BC Studies* 35 (Autumn 1977): 36–55.

Bourdeleau, Y. "Les Motivations au travail, la conception des objectifs des entreprises et la relation entre ces deux variables chez un groupe d'étudiants canadiens-français en commerce." PhD, Université de Montréal 1974.

Burke, Gary John. "An Historical Study of Intercollegiate Athletics at the University of Western Ontario, 1908–1945." MA, University of Western Ontario 1979.

Chouinard, Denis. "Des contestataires pragmatiques: les Jeune-Canada, 1932–1938." *Revue d'histoire de l'Amérique française* 40, no. 1 (été 1986): 5–28.

Clifton, R.A. "The Socialization of Graduate Students in the Social and Natural Sciences." PhD, University of Toronto 1976.

Ellis, D. "A study of a Cohort of Ontario Engineering Students from 1956 to 1976." *Canadian Journal of Education* 2, no. 4 (1977): 11–22.

Forsythe, D. *Let the Niggers Burn! The Sir George Williams University Affair and Its Caribbean Aftermath.* Montreal: Our Generation Press 1971.

Friesen Gerald. "Principal J.H. Riddell: The Sane and Safe Leader of Wesley College." In Dennis L. Butcher, et al., eds., *Prairie Spirit: Perspectives on the Heritage of the United Church of Canada in the West.* Winnipeg: University of Manitoba Press 1985, 250–64.

Frost, S.B., and S. Rosenberg. "The McGill Student Body: Past and Future Enrolment." *McGill Journal of Education* 15, no. 1 (Winter 1980): 35–54.

Gagnon, J.A. "An Analysis of Student Life Developments in Quebec: Implications for Other Canadian Universities." *Journal of the Council of Student Services* 5 (Autumn–Winter 1970): 7–21.

Gingras, J.B. "La Révolution étudiante: le conflit des générations." *Action Nationale* 56 (mai 1975): 734–57.

Grand-Maison, Georgette. "Les Élèves du collège séminaire de Rimouski, 1863–1903." MA, Université d'Ottawa 1972.

"Idéologies et politiques étudiantes." *Recherches sociographiques*, édition spéciale, 13, no. 3 (sept.–déc. 1972).

Johnston, C.M., and J.C. Weaver, et al. *Student Days: An Illustrated History of Student Life at McMaster University from the 1890s to the 1980s.* Hamilton: McMaster University Alumni Association 1986.

Keane, David Ross. "Rediscovering Ontario University Students in the Mid-Nineteenth Century." PhD, University of Toronto 1981.

Kirkey, D.L. "'Building the City of God': The Founding of the Student Christian Movement of Canada." MA, McMaster 1982.

– "The Decline of Radical Liberal Protestantism: The Case of the Student Christian Movement of Canada." Paper presented to the Canadian Historical Association, Windsor, Ont., 1988.

Kostash, Myrna. *Long Way from Home: The Story of the Sixties Generation in Canada.* Toronto: James Lorimer 1980.

Larochelle, Charles. "Idéologie et pratique du mouvement étudiant à l'Université de Montréal de 1969 à 1982." M Sc, Université de Montréal 1982.

Lessard, C. "Les Élèves du collège de Nicolet: leur origine sociale, leur persévérance, 1803–1969." *Revue d'ethnologie du Québec* (1976): 27–50.

Levitt, Cyril. *Children of Privilege: Student Revolt in the Sixties.* Toronto: University of Toronto Press 1984.

MacLeod, Malcolm. "Students Abroad: Preconfederation Educational Links between Newfoundland and the Mainland of Canada." Canadian Historical Association, *Historical Papers* 1985, 172–92.

Mah, D. *Student Participation at the University of Calgary: Past and Present.* Calgary: University of Calgary Students Union 1976.

Massot, Alain. "Destins scolaires des étudiants de secondaire v: une analyse comparative des secteurs français et anglais." *Recherches sociographiques* 20, no. 3 (sept.–déc. 1979): 383–401.

Nixon, Lucia. "Rituals and Power: The Anthropology of Homecoming at Queen's." *Queen's Quarterly* 94 (Summer 1987): 312–31.

O'Flynn-Brittan, Brian D.J. *The Past as Prologue: A Century of Western Students.* London: University of Western Ontario 1978.

Ouellet, G. "Relations entre les valeurs de travail et de loisir d'étudiants de niveaux collégial et universitaires." PhD, Université de Montréal 1974.

Quarter, Jack. *The Student Movement of the 1960s.* Toronto: Ontario Institute for Studies in Education 1973.

Rodenhizer, John. "The Student Campaign of 1922 to 'Build the University' of British Columbia." *BC Studies* 4 (Spring 1970): 21–37.

Simpson, John H., and Walter Phillips. "Understanding Student Protest in Canada: The University of Toronto Strike Vote." *Canadian Journal of Higher Education* 6, no. 1 (1976): 59–67.

Sutherland, S.L. *Patterns of Belief and Action: Measurement of Student Political Activism.* Toronto: University of Toronto Press 1981.

Sylvain, Philippe. "La Vie quotidienne de l'étudiant universitaire Québécois au XIXe siècle." *Société Canadienne d'histoire de l'Église Catholique* 39 (sept. 1972): 41–54.

Trenton, Thomas N. "Left-wing Radicalism at a Canadian University: The Inapplicability of an American Model." *Interchange* 14, no. 2 (1983): 54–65.

Von Zur-Muehlen, M. *The Educational Background of Parents of Post-secondary Students in Canada: A Comparison between 1968–69 and 1974–75 and Related to the Educational Level of the Population.* Ottawa: Statistics Canada 1978.

Walden, Keith. "Respectable Hooligans: Male Toronto College Students Celebrate Hallowe'en, 1884–1910." *Canadian Historical Review* 68, no. 1 (Mar. 1987): 1–34.

Weisz, George. "The Geographical Origins and Destinations of Medical Graduates in Quebec, 1834–1939." *Histoire Sociale / Social History* 19, no. 37 (May 1986): 93–119.

Westhues, Kenneth. "Intergenerational Conflict in the Sixties." In S.D. Clark, et al., *Prophecy and Protest: Social Movements in Twentieth Century Canada.* Toronto: Gage 1975, 387–408.

Yingst, Larry Ronald. "The Academic and Social Images of the University of Calgary as Perceived by Freshmen Students." PhD, University of Calgary 1973.

WOMEN

Baker, M. "Academic Bees." *Atlantis* 1, no. 2 (Spring 1976): 84–93.

Buckley, Marjorie White. *As It Happened: The University Women's Club of Ed-*

monton: The First 60 Years. Edmonton: University Women's Club of Edmonton 1973.

Danylewycz, Marta. *Taking the Veil: An Alternative to Marriage, Motherhood, and Spinsterhood in Quebec, 1840–1920.* Toronto: McClelland and Stewart 1987.

De la Cour, Lykke, and Rose Sheinin. "The Ontario Medical College for Women 1883 to 1906: Lessons from Gender-Separatism in Medical Education." *Canadian Woman Studies / Les Cahiers de la femme* 7, no. 3 (Fall 1986): 73–7.

Dembski, Peter E. Paul. "Jenny Kidd Trout and the Founding of the Women's Medical Colleges at Kingston and Toronto." *Ontario History* 72, no. 3 (Sept. 1985): 183–206.

Dompierre, Julie. "L'Enseignement professional des filles au Québec: le couvent de la Présentation de Marie, 1873–1982 (Farnham)." MA, Sherbrooke 1987.

Dumont, Micheline, et Nadia Fahmy-Eid, eds. *Les couventines. L'éducation des filles au Québec dans les congrégations religieuses enseignantes, 1840–1960.* Montreal: Boréal 1986.

Fingard, Judith. "Gender and Inequality at Dalhousie: Faculty Women before 1850." *Dalhousie Review* 64 (1984–85): 687–703.

– "They Had a Tough Row to Hoe." *Dalhousie Alumni Magazine* (Winter 1985): 27–30.

Ford, Ann Rochon. *A Path not Strewn with Roses: One Hundred Years of Women at the University of Toronto, 1884–1984.* Toronto: University of Toronto Press 1985.

Gillett, Margaret. "Sexism and Higher Education." *Atlantis* 1, no. 1 (Fall 1975): 68–81.

– *We Walked Very Warily: A History of Women at McGill.* Montreal: Eden Press Women's Publication 1981.

– and Kay E. Sibbald, eds. *A Fair Shake: Autobiographical Essays of Women at McGill.* Montreal: Eden Press 1984.

Groulx, L., and C. Poirier. "La Place des femmes dans l'enseignement supérieur en service social au Québec." *Atlantis* 9, no. 1 (Fall 1983): 25–35.

Jean, Michele. "L'Enseignement supérieur des filles et son ambiguité: le collège Marie-Anne, 1932–1958." In Nadia Fahmy-Eid and Micheline Dumont, eds., *Maîtresses de maison, maîtresses d'école: femmes, famille et éducation dans l'histoire du Québec.* Montréal: Boréal 1983, 143–70.

Katz, Wendy R. *Her and His: Language of Equal Value, A Report of the Status of Women Committee of the Nova Scotia Confederation of University Faculty Associations in Sexist Language and the University, with Guidelines.* Ottawa: Canadian Association of University Teachers 1981.

Kiefer, Nancy. "The Impact of the Second World War on Female Students at the University of Toronto, 1939–1945." MA, University of Toronto 1984.

LaPierre, J.S. "The Debate over Co-education at McGill University." MA, McGill 1985.

Leduc, C. "Les Orientations des femmes à l'Université de Montréal en 1945–50 et en 1974–75." *Canadian and International Education* 7 (June 1978): 51–8.

Lee, D.J. "Les Religieuses du Québec: leur influence sur vie professionnelle des femmes, 1908–1954." *Atlantis* 5, no. 1 (Spring 1980): 22–33.

Marks, Lynne, and Chad Gaffield. "Women at Queen's University, 1895–1900: A Little Sphere All their Own?" *Ontario History* 77, no. 4 (Dec. 1986): 331–49.

Montgomery, L.M. "A Girl's Place at Dalhousie College, 1898." *Atlantis* 5, no. 1 (Fall 1979): 146–53.

Neatby, Nicole. "Women at Queen's in the 1920s: A Separate Sphere." MA, Queen's University 1987.

Nevitte, N., R. Gibbins, and P.W. Codding. "The Career Goals of Female Science Students in Canada." *Canadian Journal of Higher Education* 18, no. 1 (1988): 31–48.

Parr, Joy, ed. *Still Running …: Personal Stories by Queen's Women Celebrating the Fiftieth Anniversary of the Marty Scholarship.* Kingston: Queen's University Alumnae Association 1987.

Reid, John G. "The Education of Women at Mount Allison, 1854–1914." *Acadiensis* 12, no. 2 (Spring 1983): 3–33.

Robinson, Jo. *Faculty Women's Club: Sixty Years of Friendship and Service, 1917–1967: A Brief History.* Vancouver: Faculty Women's Club, University of British Columbia 1977.

Ronash, Donna Ann. "The Development of Higher Education for Women at McGill University from 1857 to 1899, with Special Reference to the Role of Sir John William Dawson." MA, McGill University 1972.

Stewart, Lee J. "Women on Campus in British Columbia: Strategies for Survival, Years of War and Peace, 1906–1920." In Barbara Latham and Roberta Pazdro, eds., *Not Just Pin Money: Selected Essays on the History of Women's Work in British Columbia.* Victoria: Camousun College 1984, 185–93.

– "The Experience of Women at the University of British Columbia, 1906–1956." MA, University of British Columbia 1987.

Strong-Boag, Veronica. "Feminism Constrained: The Graduates of Canada's Medical Schools for Women." In Linda Kealey, ed., *A Not Unreasonable Claim: Women and Reform in Canada, 1880–1920s.* Toronto: Women's Educational Press 1979, 109–29.

– "Mapping Women's Studies in Canada: Some Signposts." *Journal of Educational Thought* 17, no. 2 (Aug. 1983): 94–111.

Swain, Susan Joan. "An Historical Study of Women's Intercollegiate Athletic Conferences in Ontario and Québec, 1965–1971: Alternatives to Women's Intercollegiate Athletic Union Standards and Policies." MA, University of Western Ontario 1978.

Temple, Anna. "The Development of Higher Education for Women in Ontario, 1867–1914." PhD, Wayne State University 1981.

Théberge, Lise. "L'Éducation des filles au collège du Bon-Pasteur de Chicoutimi, 1937–1967." MA, Université du Québec à Chicoutimi 1981.

Thompson, Nancy Ramsay. "The Controversy over the Admission of Women to University College, University of Toronto." MA, University of Toronto 1974.

Travill, A.A. "Early Medical Co-education and Women's Medical College, Kingston, Ontario, 1880–1894." *Historic Kingston* 30 (Jan. 1982): 68–89.

University Women's Club of Toronto, *75 Years in Retrospect: University Women's Club of Toronto, 1903–1978.* Toronto: University Women's Club of Toronto 1978.

Vickers, Jill, and June Adam. *But Can You Type? Canadian Universities and the Status of Women.* Richmond Hill, Ont.: Irwin 1977.

ADULT EDUCATION

The Antigonish Movement, Yesterday and Today (Antigonish Extension Department, St Francis Xavier University 1976.

Blenkinsop, Padraig John. "A History of Adult Education on the Prairies: Learning to Live in Agrarian Saskatchewan, 1870–1944." PhD, University of Toronto 1979.

Blyth, John A. *A Foundling at Varsity: A History of the Division of University Extension, University of Toronto.* Toronto: University of Toronto, School of Continuing Studies 1976.

Campbell, Duncan D. *The New Majority: Adult Learners in the University.* Edmonton: University of Alberta Press 1984.

Clark, Ralph Joseph. "A History of the Department of Extension at the University of Alberta, 1912–1956." PhD, University of Toronto 1986.

Devlin, Lawrence E. "University Extension in British Columbia: 1955–1975." *Canadian Journal of University Continuing Education* 10, no. 1 (Jan. 1984): 17–39.

Dunlop, Edward A. "The Development of Extension Education at Queen's University, 1889–1945." PhD, University of Toronto 1981.

Faris, R. *The Passionate Educators: Voluntary Associations and the Struggle for Control of Adult Educational Broadcasting in Canada, 1919–1952.* Toronto: Peter Martin 1975.

Gagnon, Nicole. "L'Éducation des adultes: dix ans de travaux." *Recherches sociographiques* 13, no. 2 (mai-août 1972): 173–229.

Heap, R. "Un chapitre dans l'histoire de l'éducation des adultes au Québec: les écoles du soir." *Revue d'histoire de l'amérique française* 34, (1981): 577–626.

"Historical Table of Adult Education in Canada." *Continuous Learning* 9 (1970): 233–8.

Keane, P. "A Study of Early Problems and Policies in Adult Education: The Halifax Mechanics Institute." *Histoire Sociale / Social History* 8 (Nov. 1975): 255–74.

- "Dalhousie University and the Nontraditional Student: The First Century."
  Dalhousie Review 63 (Summer 1983): 277–97.
McInnes, Daniel W. "Clerics, Fishermen, Farmers and Workers: The Antigonish
  Movement and Identity in Eastern Nova Scotia, 1928–1939." PhD, McMaster
  University 1978.
Radforth, Ian, and Joan Sangster. "A Link between Labour and Learning: The
  Workers' Educational Association in Ontario, 1917–1951." *Labour / Le Tra-*
  vailleur 8, 9 (Autumn, Spring 1981–82): 41–78.
Selman, Gordon. "Adult Education in Barkerville, 1863–1875." *BC Studies* 9
  (Spring 1971): 38–54.
- "Origins of Public Locally Sponsored Evening Classes in British Columbia."
  Continuous Learning 10 (July 1971): 199–207.
- "Concerning The History of Adult Education in Canada." *Journal of University*
  Continuing Education 1 (Dec. 1974): 24–35.
Stabler, Ernest. "James Tompkins and Moses Coady: The Antigonish Movement
  in Nova Scotia." In *Innovators in Education 1830–1980*. Edmonton: University
  of Alberta Press 1987, 141–82.
Welton, Michael R., ed. *Knowledge for the People: The Struggle for Adult*
  Learning in English-Speaking Canada, 1828–1973. Toronto: OISE Press 1987.
- "'On the Eve of a Great Mass Movement': Reflections on the Origins of the
  CAAE." In Frank Cassidy and Ron Faris, eds., *Choosing Our Future: Adult Ed-*
  ucation and Public Policy in Canada. Toronto: OISE Press 1987, 12–35.

Index